Nikon D5100

Simon Stafford

MAGIC LANTERN GUIDES®

Nikon D5100

Simon Stafford

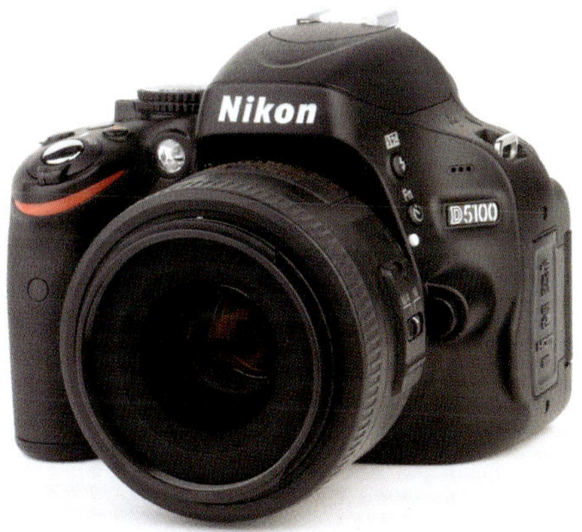

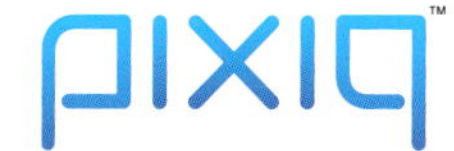

An Imprint of Sterling Publishing Co., Inc.
New York

For more information,
visit our website at www.pixiq.com

Book Design: Michael Robertson
Cover Design: Thom Gaines, Electron Graphics

Library of Congress Cataloging-in-Publication Data

Stafford, Simon.
Nikon D5100 / Simon Stafford. -- 1st ed.
p. cm. -- (Magic lantern guides)
Summary: "Complete guide to operating the Nikon D5100 camera, including features and buttons overview, menus, accessories and compatibility, and full-color sample photos"-- Provided by publisher.
Includes bibliographical references and index.
ISBN 978-1-4547-0365-5 (pbk.)
1. Nikon digital cameras--Handbooks, manuals, etc. 2. Single-lens reflex cameras--Handbooks, manuals, etc. 3. Photography--Digital techniques--Handbooks, manuals, etc. I. Title.
TR263.N5S737 2011
771.3'1--dc23
2011025923

10 9 8 7 6 5 4 3 2 1

First Edition

Published by Pixiq, An Imprint of
Sterling Publishing Co., Inc.
387 Park Avenue South, New York, N.Y. 10016

Distributed in Canada by Sterling Publishing,
c/o Canadian Manda Group, 165 Dufferin Street
Toronto, Ontario, Canada M6K 3H6

Distributed in the United Kingdom by GMC Distribution Services,
Castle Place, 166 High Street, Lewes, East Sussex, England BN7 1XU

Distributed in Australia by Capricorn Link (Australia) Pty Ltd.,
P.O. Box 704, Windsor, NSW 2756 Australia

If you have questions or comments about this book, please contact:
Lark Books
67 Broadway
Asheville, NC 28801
(828) 253-0467

Manufactured in Canada

ISBN 13: 978-1-4547-0365-5

For information about custom editions, special sales, premium and corporate purchases, please contact Sterling Special Sales Department at 800-805-5489 or specialsales@sterlingpub.com.

For information about desk and examination copies available to college and university professors, requests must be submitted to academic@larkbooks.com. Our complete policy can be found at www.larkbooks.com.

To learn more about digital photography, go to www.pixiq.com.

Contents

The Nikon D5100 12

Introduction . . . 13
Production of the Nikon D5100 . . . 16
About This Book . . . 17
Conventions Used in This Book . . . 18
Acknowledgements . . . 18

Introducing the Nikon D5100 20

Design . . . 22
The Sensor . . . 24
Self-Cleaning Optical Low-Pass Filter . . . 27
DX Format . . . 28
The Viewfinder . . . 30
Adjusting Viewfinder Focus . . . 31
Viewfinder and Focus Screen Displays . . . 31
The Multi Selector Button . . . 32
Information Display . . . 33
Preparing the D5100 for Shooting . . . 34
Quick Start Guide . . . 34
Powering the D5100 . . . 36
Using the EN-EL14 Battery . . . 37
External Power Supply . . . 39
Effects of Electrostatic Charge . . . 40
Internal Clock/Calendar Battery . . . 40
Battery Performance . . . 41
Battery Storage . . . 42

The Exposure and Focusing System 44

ISO Sensitivity . . . 45
High ISO Performance . . . 46
ISO Sensitivity Auto Control . . . 48

TTL Metering 49
Matrix Metering 49
Center-Weighted Metering 51
Spot Metering 52
Auto, Scene, and Effects Modes 53
Auto and Scene Mode Options 54
Effects Modes 62
P, S, A, and M Exposure Modes 65
Programmed Auto (P) 65
Aperture-Priority Auto (A) 66
Shutter-Priority Auto (S) 66
Manual (M) 67
Long Exposures 68
Autoexposure (AE) Lock 69
Exposure Compensation 70
Exposure Considerations 72
Digital Infrared and UV Photography 72
The Autofocus System 73
The Autofocus Sensor 74
Scene Recognition System 76
Focus Modes 78
Single-Servo vs. Continuous-Servo 80
Predictive Focus Tracking 82
Using Trap Focus 82
Autofocus Area Modes 83
Selecting an Autofocus Point 85
Focus Mode and AF-Area Mode Overview 86
Focus Lock 87
AF-Assist Illuminator 88
Limitations of the AF System 90

Shoot and Review 92

The Shutter 93
Shutter Release 93
Release Modes 95
Single Frame 95
Continuous 96
Self-Timer 96
Delayed Remote / Quick-Response Remote 98
Quiet Shutter 99
The LCD Monitor 99

Image Review Options 100
Full-Frame Playback 101
Information Pages 101
Viewing Multiple Images 110
Calendar Playback 110
Playback Zoom 111
Protecting Images 112
Deleting Images 112
Assessing the Histogram 113
Image Storage with SD Cards 116
SDHC & SDXC Cards 117
Approved Memory Cards 118
Memory Card Capacity 119
Inserting and Removing Memory Cards 121
Formatting a Memory Card 122
Image Quality and File Formats 124
Expeed 2 Image Processing 124
JPEG 126
NEF (RAW) 128
Which Format? 130
Setting Image Quality and Size 131
Live View 133
Using Live View 134
D-Movie Mode 139
Rolling Shutter Effect 142
Built-in Limitations 143
Using Movie Mode 144
Recording Movies 145
Viewing Movies 147

In-Camera Processing 148

White Balance 149
What is Color Temperature? 150
White Balance Options 151
Preset Manual White Balance 155
Copying a White Balance Value 158
Fine-Tuning White Balance 158
Creative White Balance 161
The Picture Control System 161
Selecting a Nikon Picture Control 162
Modifying Picture Control Attributes 164

Creating a Custom Picture Control 170
Sharing Custom Picture Controls 171
Managing Custom Picture Controls 172
Color Space 172
Active D-Lighting 173

The Menu System 176

Accessing Menus 178
Playback Menu 180
Delete Images 180
Playback Folder 182
Playback Display Options 182
Image Review 183
Rotate Tall 184
Slide Show 184
DPOF Print Order 185
Shooting Menu. 186
Reset Shooting Options 186
Storage Folder 187
Image Quality 189
Image Size 189
White Balance 189
Set Picture Control 189
Manage Picture Control 189
Auto Distortion Control 189
Color Space 189
Active D-Lighting 190
HDR (High Dynamic Range) 191
Long Exposure Noise Reduction 192
High ISO Noise Reduction 193
ISO Sensitivity Settings 194
Release mode 195
Multiple Exposure 195
Movie Settings 196
Interval Timer Shooting 197
Custom Settings Menu 198
Selecting Custom Settings Options 200
Reset Custom Settings 201
Autofocus (a) 202
Metering / Exposure (b) 203
Timers / AE Lock (c) 204

Shooting / Display (d) 206
Bracketing / Flash (e) 208
Controls (f) 209
Setup Menu 212
Format Memory Card 212
Monitor Brightness 213
Info Display Format 213
Auto Information Display 214
Clean Image Sensor 214
Mirror Lock-Up for Cleaning 214
Video Mode 214
HDMI 214
Flicker Reduction 215
Time Zone / Date 215
Language 216
Image Comment 217
Auto Image Rotation 218
Image Dust Off Reference Photo 218
GPS 220
Eye-Fi Upload 221
Firmware Version 221
Retouch Menu 222
Selecting Images 222
Image Quality and Size 223
D-Lighting 224
Red-Eye Reduction 224
Trim 225
Monochrome 225
Filter Effects 226
Color Balance 227
Image Overlay 228
NEF (RAW) Processing 229
Resize 230
Quick Retouch 231
Straighten 231
Distortion Control 232
Fisheye 232
Color Outline 232
Color Sketch 233
Perspective Control 233
Miniature Effect 234

Selective Color 234
Side-by-Side Comparison. 235
Edit Movie 236
Recent Settings / My Menu 238
Using My Menu 239
Reorder Menu Items 239

Nikon Flash Photography 240

The Creative Lighting System. 243
TTL Flash Modes 244
i-TTL Balanced Fill-Flash 244
Standard i-TTL Flash 246
i-TTL Flash Exposure Control 246
Flash Output Assessment 248
Focus Information 249
The Built-In Speedlight 251
Range, Aperture, and ISO Sensitivity 253
Limitations 253
Lens Compatibility 254
Flash Synchronization 256
Shutter Speed Restrictions 258
Using External Speedlights 259
Automatic Flash with the SB-800 and SB-900 263
Manual Flash Exposure Control. 264
Slow Synchronization Flash 265
Rear-Curtain Synchronization 266
Flash Output Compensation 267
Flash Color Information 268
Wide-Area AF-Assist Illuminator 268
Off-Camera Flash 269
Wireless Flash Control 270
Flash Commander Unit Effective Ranges 271

Nikon Lenses and Accessories 274

Mounting / Removing a Lens 276
Demystifying Nikkor Lenses 277
Lens Compatibility 279
Using Nikon AF-S/AF-I Teleconverters 280
Using Non-CPU Lenses. 281
Incompatible Lenses and Accessories 282
Depth-of-Field Considerations 283

Diffraction 284
Shutter Speed Considerations 285
Nikon Software 286
Nikon Transfer 287
Nikon View NX2 287
Nikon Capture NX2 288
Nikon Camera Control Pro2 290
General Nikon Accessories 291
Resources 293
Web Support 294

Digital Workflow 296

Image Information 277
Camera Connections 300
Audio / Video (A/V) 300
Connecting via HDMI 300
Connecting to a Computer 301
Direct Printing 303
Printing a Single Picture 303
Printing Multiple Pictures 304
Caring for Your D5100 309
Cleaning the Low-Pass Filter 310

Index 316

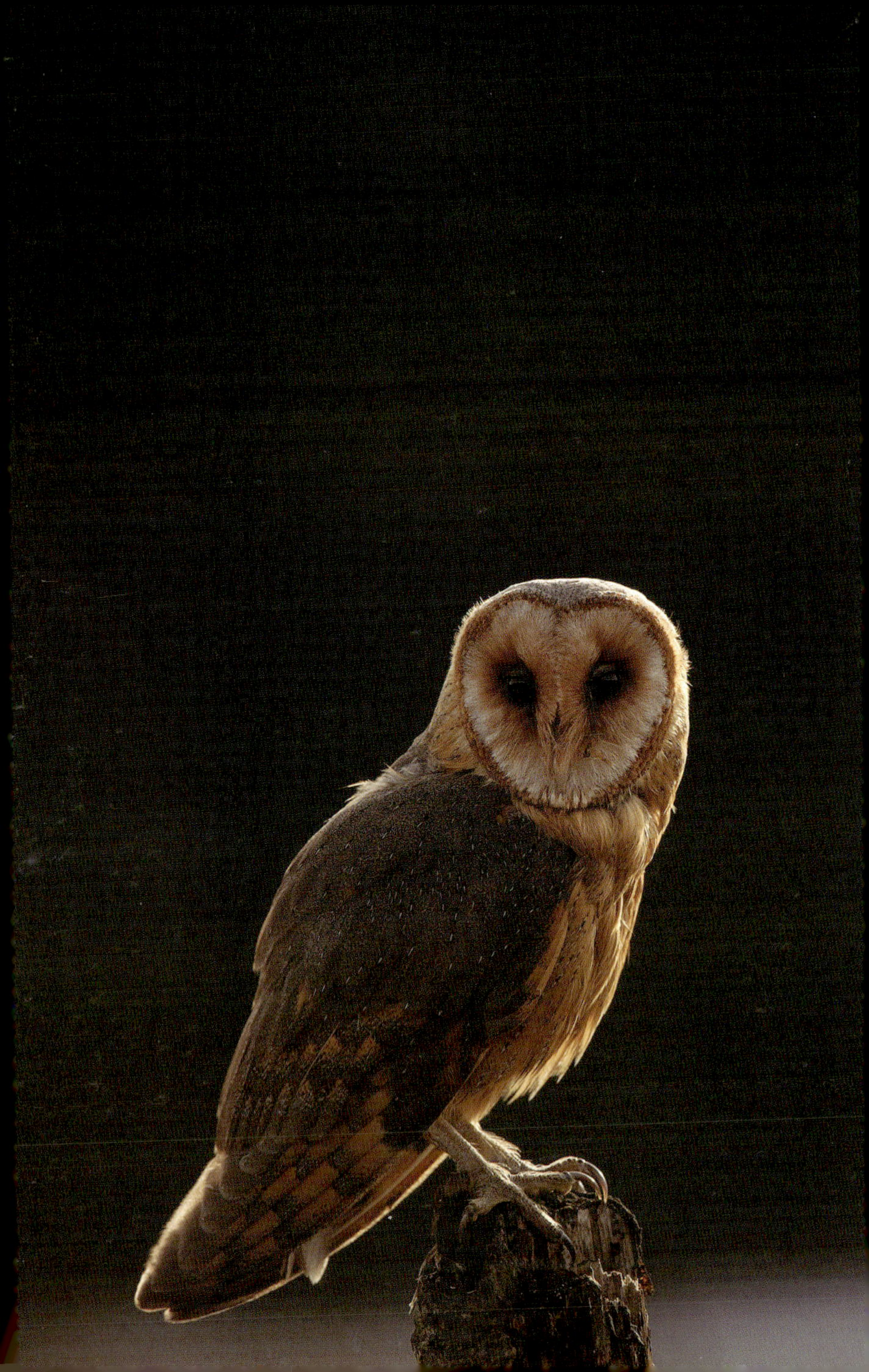

The Nikon D5100

INTRODUCTION

The Nikon Corporation has accrued many years of experience building digital cameras, beginning with a variety of hybrid cameras produced in collaboration with Kodak and Fuji respectively, but their breakthrough came in 1999 with the launch of the Nikon D1. This model represented their first fully independent digital SLR (DSLR) camera design, which not only broke new ground technically, but also made high quality digital photography financially viable for many photographers.

The long and distinguished heritage of the Nikon Corporation is rooted in its origins as an optical engineering company, which can be traced back to the early part of the twentieth century. As such, its predisposition to precision and quality has meant that it has refrained from introducing new camera models at the frequency of some of its well-known competitors. Consequently, the development of Nikon DSLR cameras during recent years can best be described as a process of steady evolution. Nikon has unveiled a variety of models aimed at different sectors of the market, from the popular D100, launched during 2002, to the phenomenally successful D70 that arrived during 2004, and later to the mid-range D200 and D80, together with the professionally specified D2Xs. More recently, the Lilliputian D40 provided the perfect entry point to the extensive Nikon camera system: Small, well specified, and highly affordable, it held great appeal to the first time DSLR user. The groundbreaking D3 and D300 models arrived simultaneously toward the end of 2007, while the following year saw the introduction of the D60, D700, and D3x models together with the D90, the first DSLR camera to incorporate a video capability. During early 2009, the innovative D5000, with its variable-angle monitor screen, was launched, followed closely by the D3000 that replaced the D60 to become the entry level camera to the Nikon DSLR range and D300s, which took over as the flagship of the Nikon DX-format DSLR camera models. Finally, during what had already been an extremely busy year for the Nikon Corporation, it announced the D3s, which was introduced to build on the huge success of the original D3, a camera that not only reversed the fortunes of the company in the professional sector of the market but also redefined the expectations of photographers everywhere in respect of image quality at high ISO sensitivity settings. The following year, 2010, saw the introduction of the D3100, as a replacement for the D3000, and the entirely new D7000. Both models feature new higher-resolution sensors, full (1080p) HD video recording, and a range of other innovations and refinements.

The D5100 has been launched to build on the success of the D5000, which it has replaced. The combination of the prestigious Nikon brand name, compact size, competitive pricing, and intuitive operation enabled the D5000 to become a highly popular camera. Now, the D5100 offers a range of improvements and innovations over its predecessor, in an even smaller and lighter body.

Bristling with new features and functions for its price point, such as the same 16.2 megapixel CMOS sensor as the D7000, a full 1080p HD video capability with variable frame rates, newly designed high resolution variable-angle LCD screen, Live View with a continuous autofocus mode, an HDR function, and a real-time special-effects mode, the D5100 raises the bar in respect of the design and specification of a camera model in this class. Yet it has been designed with everyone from newcomers to DSLR photography to knowledgeable enthusiasts very much in mind, since it possesses a broad range of automated settings to do the heavy lifting to free any user concerned about complicated functionality, while still providing full manual control for those who prefer to shoot in this style.

Thus, the D5100 offers a comprehensive specification that makes it fully commensurate with its role as a camera for photographers with a wide range of experience and skill. Its key highlights include:

- DX-format (15.6 x 23.6 mm) CMOS sensor with 16.2 million pixels that provides a resolution of 4928 x 3264 pixels
- An ISO range of 100 to 6400, with the ability to be extended to an ISO equivalent of ISO 25,600
- D-Movie mode with full 1080p (1920 x 1080) HD video recording at 24, 25, and 30 frames per second (fps)
- A new special-effects mode that offers seven effects that can be applied in real time when shooting both pictures and full (1080p) HD video
- A new two-frame high-dynamic-range (HDR) function for shooting scenes with very high contrast
- Live View with Scene Auto Selector, which selects the best mode to match the shooting situation and AF-F (Full-Time Servo) autofocus mode for continuous focusing on a moving subject in Live View and D-Movie mode
- Nikon's exclusive Expeed 2 processing regime for enhanced performance when recording video, and shooting at high ISO sensitivities, plus improved image quality
- 3-inch (7.5 cm), 921,000-dot, Vari-angle LCD monitor screen, hinged at the side for greater maneuverability, even when using a tripod
- An 11-point autofocus system with a 3D focus-tracking feature
- A shutter unit with the ability to cycle up to 4 fps, and tested to 100,000 cycles
- Self-cleaning mechanism integrates vibration of the optical low-pass filter with the Nikon Airflow Control system that helps draw dust away from the filter
- Nikon's proprietary Scene Recognition System that enhances performance of the autofocus, metering, and Automatic White Balance functions
- Active D-Lighting
- The Picture Control System, which provides a very high degree of control over the way the camera records an image
- 16 Scene Modes for improved point-and-shoot photography
- A remote accessory terminal providing support for the Nikon MC-DC2 remote shutter release and Nikon GP-1 GPS unit
- Front and rear infrared receivers for the Nikon ML-L3 remote control
- A 3.5-mm jack connector for an external stereo microphone, such as the Nikon ME-1
- An enhanced range of options in the Retouch menu, including lens Distortion Control, Miniature Effect, Selective Color, and Perspective Control items

The D5100 is a sophisticated photographic tool with the flexibility to be used for point-and-shoot style photography with complete automation, or with all its settings under the direct control of the user, to enable anyone from the beginner to the more experienced enthusiast photographer to cope with a wide range of subjects and shooting situations.

PRODUCTION OF THE NIKON D5100

The D5100 is assembled at Nikon's wholly owned production facility, Nikon Thailand, near Ayuthaya, the old historical capital of Siam, about 50 miles (80 Km) north of Bangkok, Thailand's present day capital. I say assembled, as a number of core parts of the camera are manufactured elsewhere, such as the camera's main printed circuit board and lens mount, which are produced at the Nikon factory in Sendai, Japan.

The Nikon Thailand plant, which produced its first Nikkor lens back in 1992, currently comprises four separate factories engaged in a wide range of activities from manufacture of specialized lens elements and camera components, to the fabrication of DSLR cameras. Camera and lens production includes the D300s, D7000, D3100, together with a number of consumer grade Nikkor lenses, alongside manufacture of the D5100.

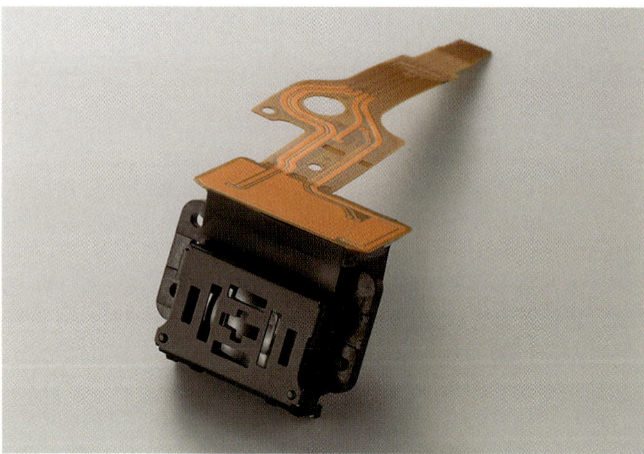

The AF sensor unit of the D5100

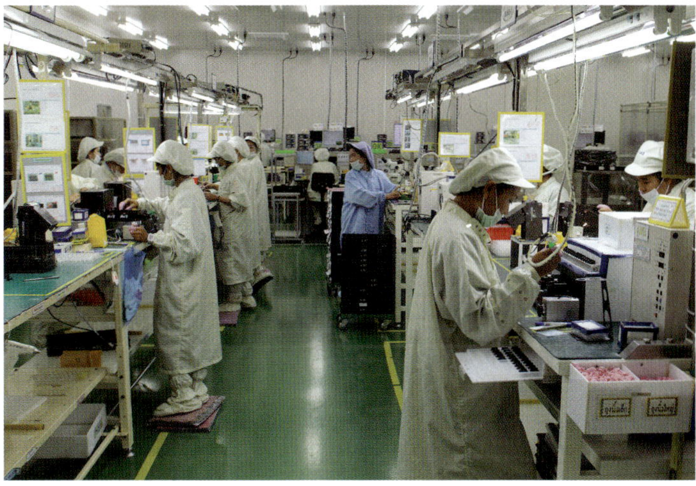

Autofocus sensor units are fitted into the cameras in "clean-room" conditions at the Nikon Thailand factory.

ABOUT THIS BOOK

To get the most from your D5100, it is important that you understand its features so that you can make informed choices about how to use them in conjunction with your style of photography. Besides explaining how all the basic functions work, this book also provides useful tips on operating the D5100 and maximizing its performance. The book does not have to be read from cover to cover. You can move from section to section as required, study a complete chapter, or just broaden your knowledge of the features or functions you want to use.

The key to success, regardless of your level of experience, is to practice with your camera. You do not waste money on film and processing costs with a digital camera; once you have invested in a memory card, it can be used over and over again. Therefore, you can shoot as many pictures as you like, review your results along with a detailed record of camera settings almost immediately, delete your near misses, and save your successes. This trial and error method is a very effective way to learn!

CONVENTIONS USED IN THIS BOOK

Unless otherwise stated, when the terms "left" and "right" are used to describe the location of a camera control, it is assumed the camera is being held to the photographer's eye in the shooting position.

In describing the operation of lenses and external flash units, it is assumed that you are using appropriate D- or G-type Nikkor AF-S and AF-I lenses that have a built-in autofocus motor, and Nikon Speedlight units compatible with the Creative Lighting System to ensure full functionality. Note that lenses and flash units made by independent manufacturers may have different functionality. If you use such products, refer to the manufacturer's instruction manual to check compatibility and operation with the D5100.

When referring to software, either Nikon or third-party, it is assumed that the most recent iterations of each application are used. At the time of writing these are:

- Nikon View NX2 incorporating Nikon Transfer 2 (Mac version 2.1.1 / Windows version 2.1.2)
- Nikon Capture NX2 (version 2.2.7)
- Nikon Camera Control Pro 2 (version 2.9.0)

ACKNOWLEDGEMENTS

I would like to thank the following people for their assistance and support during the writing of this book. At the Nikon Japan, Mr. Tetsuro Goto, Director of Laboratory Research and Development and Mr. Hideki Matsui, Manager of the Speedlight Design Section, and their staffs. At Nikon Europe, Mr. Toru Iwaoka, Managing Director. At Nikon UK, Mr. Michio Miwa, Managing Director, and his staff, in particular Mr. Jeremy Gilbert, Group Marketing Director (Imaging Division), Mr. Simon Iddon, Enthusiast Product Manager, Mr. Mark Fury, Professional Channel Manager, Ms. Jenny Grace and Ms. Lily Bungay, Press & PR, and Mr. James Banfield, Nikon Professional Support.

Simon Stafford
Wiltshire, England

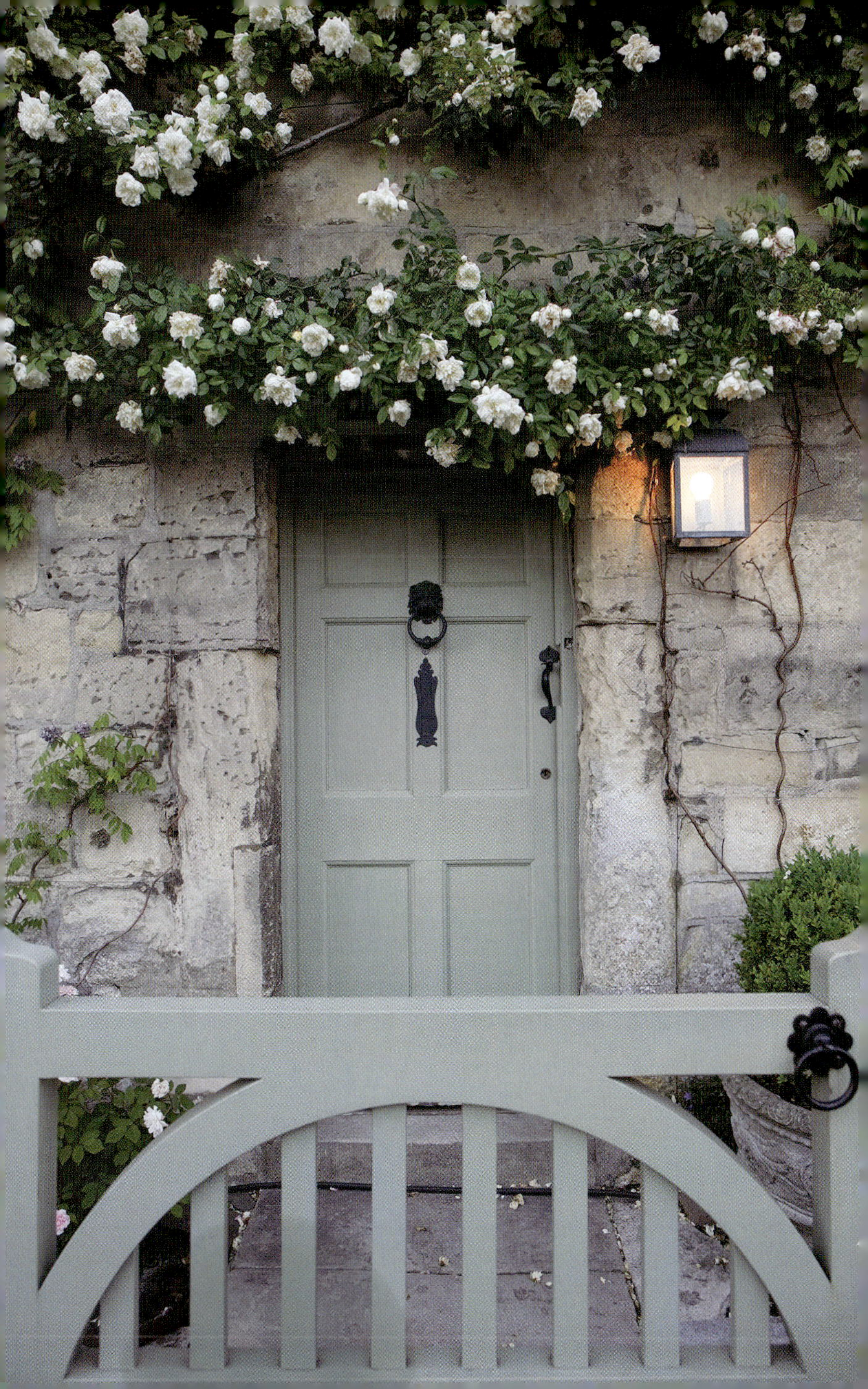

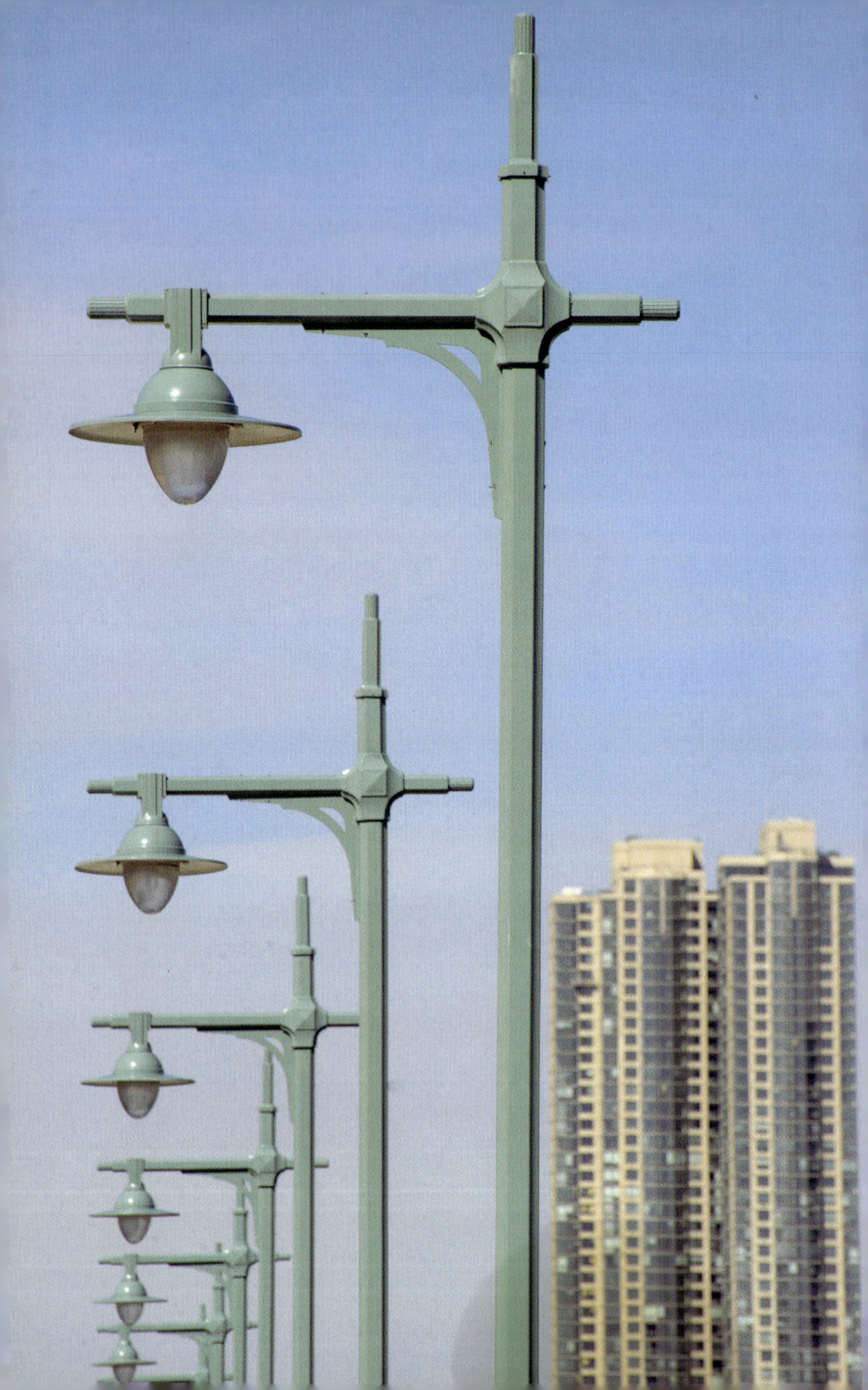

Introducing The Nikon D5100

The D5100 has been designed to build upon the qualities of its predecessor, the D5000, and expand its capabilities by drawing on the rapidly developing technologies of digital imaging. In producing the D5100, Nikon had aimed to deliver high-end features and functions in a compact, easy-to-use, robust camera intended to provide a broad appeal to photographers ranging from the first-time or less experienced DSLR user to the dedicated enthusiast. It is the company's first digital SLR to capture video at 30 frames per second (fps) at a resolution of 1080p (previous models are limited to 24 fps), offer an in-camera High Dynamic Range (HDR) feature, and allow special effects processing to be applied in real time when recording either stills or video. The greater flexibility in video capture combined with the 16.2MP sensor, as used by the more sophisticated D7000 model, promises much in terms of the image quality that can be attained by the D5100.

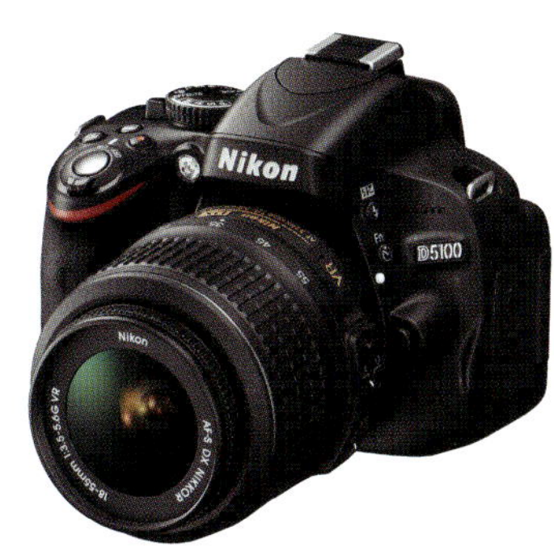

› The D5100 is pictured here with the Nikkor AF-S DX 35mm f/1.8G lens. D- or G-type Nikkor lenses offer the highest level of compatibility with the D5100, although it is possible to use a wide variety of other Nikkor lenses, albeit with the more limited compatibility.

DESIGN

At first glance, the D5100 is remarkably similar in appearance to the D5000, since the two models share a near-identical profile. The most obvious external change is the displacement of switches and buttons as a result of the swiveling rear LCD monitor screen being hinged on the left side of the camera rather than at the bottom, to provide greater maneuverability even when the camera is mounted on a tripod. Internally, there have been some other changes, with a new Nikon DX-format (APS-C size) 16.2MP CMOS sensor that has been lifted straight out of the D7000 model. Also new to the D5100 is its Effects feature (which integrates options from the Retouch menu and applies them on the fly, as still images and videos are captured), the Expeed 2 image-processing engine, an extended ISO range (100 – 6400), and an increase in the size and resolution of the LCD monitor screen (3 inches or 7.5 cm, 920,000-dot resolution). The D5100 does still share many key components and features found in the D5000, such as the same 420-segment RGB sensor for TTL metering, the built-in sensor-cleaning mechanism with the Nikon Airflow Control system, 3D-tracking autofocus, the Picture Control System, and the Multi-CAM1000 autofocus module with 11-point AF system. The TTL metering and autofocus systems work hand-in-hand with the White Balance feature to form the Scene Recognition System, which was first introduced in the D300. Furthermore, the D5000 and D5100 share the same design of built-in Speedlight flash.

It might be said that the D5100 represents a meld of the best qualities of its highly popular predecessor, which have been enhanced and expanded to meet the requirements of an ever more demanding and competitive digital SLR camera market. This has been achieved through uncompromising design criteria harnessed to cutting edge technology, and the many years of experience accrued by Nikon in the manufacture of digital SLR cameras.

For a very compact camera, the D5100 has a pleasant feel in the hand. It has dimensions of: 5.0W x 3.8H x 3.1D inches (128 x 97 x 79 mm) and weighs approximately 20 oz (560 g) with a battery and memory card installed. The variable-angle 3-inch (7.5 cm) LCD monitor on the rear of the D5100 is probably its most notable external feature, among the array of buttons, dials, and switches—the functions of which will be familiar to users of previous Nikon DSLR cameras. However, due to the

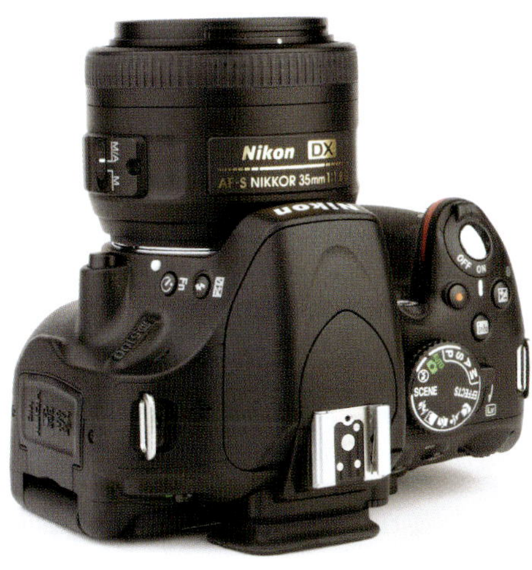

change in their location, the buttons and dials may confuse experienced Nikon shooters, especially if they are switching between the D5100 and any previous Nikon DSLR. The camera chassis and outer panels are made from a sturdy polycarbonate material that imparts a solid, rugged feel to the body, and the seals to prevent the ingress of moisture and dust appear to be commensurate with a camera in this class.

Nikon has long been trumpeting that image quality in the digital world rests on three pillars: optical quality of the lens, sensor technology, and internal camera processing. The D5100 epitomizes this in respect of the latter two aspects, as the sensor of the D5100 and a single ASIC (application-specific integrated circuit) that handles the image-processing system form the core of what Nikon calls their "Expeed 2" image-processing system. It is at the heart of the camera's ability to record, process, and output high-quality images and video at a rapid rate. This fast data processing is combined with a mechanical shutter that enables the D5100 to cycle at a maximum of 4 fps. Furthermore, as part of the uncompromising design, the shutter unit is tested to perform at least 100,000 actuations.

The D5100 has a Nikon F lens mount with an autofocus (AF) coupling and electrical contacts, the design of which can be traced back to the Nikon F film camera, introduced in 1959. The greatest level of compatibility is achieved with either AF-D or AF-G type Nikkor lenses. Other lenses can be used, but they provide a variable level of compatibility: AF and Ai-P type Nikkor lenses offer a somewhat reduced functionality, as autofocus is not supported, plus the camera's TTL metering system defaults from 3D Color Matrix metering to standard Color Matrix metering. Even manual focus Ai, Ai-s, Ai converted, and E-series Nikkor lenses can be used with the D5100, although you are restricted to Manual exposure mode only and must adjust the lens aperture manually, plus the TTL metering and autofocus system, electronic exposure display, and i-TTL flash control are not available.

THE SENSOR

The Complimentary Metal Oxide Semi-conductor (CMOS) sensor used in the D5100 is an entirely new design, developed initially for the D7000 model launched in 2010. There are total of 16.9 million photo sites (pixels), of which 16.2 million are effective for the purpose of recording an image. Each photo site is just 4.78 microns (1 micron = 1/1000 mm) square and is comprised of the photodiode (photo-detector) and an amplifier circuit. This gives the camera a maximum resolution of 4928 x 3264 pixels, sufficient to produce a 20 x 13.5-inch (50 x 34-cm) print at 240ppi without interpolation (resizing). The imaging area is approximately 0.9 x 0.6 inch (23.6 x 15.6 mm), producing a 3:2 aspect ratio. Nikon calls this their DX-format, which is often referred to generically as the APS-C format.

The same "DX" designation is used to identify those lenses that have been optimized for use with their DSLR cameras that have DX-format sensors. Due to the smaller size of the DX-format, the angle of view offered by any focal length is reduced compared with a lens of the same focal length used with the FX-format of the Nikon D700 and D3-series camera models or 35mm film cameras. If it helps you to estimate the angle of view for a particular focal length in comparison with the coverage offered by the same focal length on the FX-format, multiply the focal length by 1.5x (see pages 28-29 for a full explanation).

The CMOS sensor of the D5100 is actually a sandwich of several layers, each with a specific purpose; and it is known as an active-pixel sensor, as each pixel is comprised of a photo-detector (photodiode) and an active amplifier. CMOS sensors offer several advantages over the Charged Coupled Device (CCD) type sensor—a type of passive-pixel sensor, used in some earlier Nikon DSLR cameras such as the D3000—including lower power consumption, faster operation, and lower manufacturing costs. The first layer of the CMOS sensor is the wiring layer, containing the photodiodes and supporting electrical circuitry, which not only carries the electrical signal away from each photodiode, but also amplifies it before it is passed on to the analog-to-digital converter (ADC).

The Bayer pattern filter is a color filter layer found above the light-sensitive layer of capacitors. The photodiodes on the CMOS sensor do not record color—they can only detect a level of brightness. To impart color to the image formed by the light that falls on the sensor, a series of tiny red, green, and blue filters are arranged over the capacitors in a Bayer pattern (which takes its name from the Kodak engineer who invented the system).

These tiny filters are arranged in an alternating pattern of red and green on the odd-numbered rows, and green and blue on the even-numbered rows. The Bayer pattern comprises 50% green, 25% red, and 25% blue filters; the intensity of light detected by each capacitor located beneath its single, dedicated color filter according to the Bayer pattern is converted into an electrical signal before then being converted to a digital value by the ADC, as described above. If the camera is set to record an NEF RAW file, the value for each sampling point on the sensor is simply saved. When you open this file in an appropriate RAW file converter, the software will interpret the digital value derived from each capacitor to produce a red-green-blue (RGB) value, which, in turn, is converted into an image that can be viewed. However, if the camera is set to record JPEG files, then the value from each capacitor is processed in the camera by comparing it with the values from a block of surrounding capacitors, using a process called interpolation. The interpolation process produces a "best guess" for the RGB value for each sampling point (capacitor) on the sensor.

Immediately above the Bayer pattern filter, there is a layer of micro-lenses. Since the photodiodes on the sensor are most efficient when the light falling on them is perpendicular, each one has a miniature lens located above it to channel the light into its well to help maximize its light-gathering ability. Each micro-lens occupies an area larger than the capacitor well below it, and there is virtually no gap between neighboring micro-lenses. This effective ability to gather light, coupled with the relatively large, 4.78-micron pixel pitch of the camera's sensor allows it to scoop up photons very efficiently and contributes to the extremely high image quality that can be attained, especially at high ISO settings, compared with typical point-and-shoot, compact style digital camera models.

Positioned in front of the CMOS sensor, but not connected to it, is an optical low-pass filter (OLPF), sometimes called an anti-aliasing filter. When the frequency of detail in an image, particularly a small, regular, repeating pattern, such as the weave pattern in a fabric, alters at or close to the pitch of the photodiodes on the sensor, there is often a side effect that produces unwanted data (often referred to as artifacts) due to the way in which the in-camera processing converts the electrical signal from the sensor to a digital value via the analog-to-digital (ADC) converter. This additional data is manifest in the final image as a color pattern known as moiré. Furthermore, the same in-camera processing can also result in a color fringing effect, known as color aliasing, which causes a halo of one or more separate color(s) to appear along the edge of fine detail in the image.

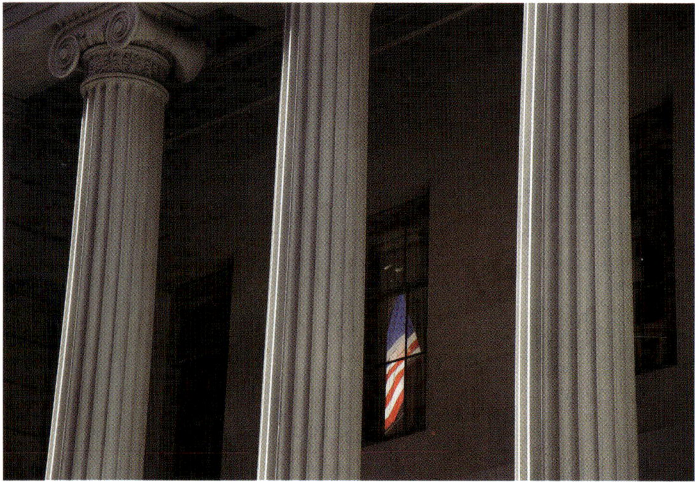

^ The D5100 is capable of recording a very broad dynamic range; at its base ISO of 100, it is typically around 9.0 EV.

The OLPF is used to reduce the unwanted effects of color aliasing and moiré. However, the OLPF reduces the resolution of detail, so the camera designers must strike a balance between its beneficial effect and the loss of acuity in fine detail, which is lost as the strength of the filter is increased. In the D5100, Nikon appears to have done well in this respect, as the JPEG files taken at the camera's default settings show plenty of crisp detail. The OLPF also incorporates a number of important coating layers to help improve image quality:

- To help prevent dust and other foreign material from adhering to the surface of the OLPF, it has an anti-static coating made from Indium Tin Oxide.
- To reduce the risk of light being reflected from the front surface of the OLPF onto the rear element of the lens, which could then result in flare effects or ghost images, the filter has an anti-reflective coating.
- The CMOS sensor is sensitive to wavelengths of light outside the spectrum visible by the human eye. This light, which can be either in the infrared (IR) or ultraviolet (UV) part of the spectrum, will pollute image files and cause unwanted color shifts and a loss of image sharpness; so the OLPF has both an IR-blocking and a UV-blocking coat. These IR and UV blocking coats are very efficient; consequently, the D5100 cannot be recommended for any form of IR or UV light photography, which was possible with some earlier Nikon DSLR cameras, such as the D1 and the D100.

SELF-CLEANING OPTICAL LOW-PASS FILTER

The D5100 has inherited the same self-cleaning feature for the OLPF as used in the D5000. It vibrates the OLPF to help reduce the presence of dust and other unwanted particles on its front surface, which is the surface closest to the rear of the lens. Dust on the OLPF is the bane of all digital photographers, because it causes dark shadow spots to appear in the final image; therefore, keeping the OLPF clean is fundamental to maintaining image quality and avoiding the necessity for time-consuming touchups in post-processing. To supplement this system, the D5100 also has Nikon's Airflow Control system, which uses small changes of air pressure inside the camera caused by the movement of the reflex mirror to draw dust and other similar unwanted particles away from the OLPF to a trap located at the bottom of the reflex mirror box (see pages 310-315 for more details on OLPF cleaning options).

DX-FORMAT

Nikon has used DX-format (APS-C) sensors in most of their digital SLR camera models, beginning with the Nikon D1, which was introduced during 1999. The only exceptions are the D700 and D3-series cameras, which have FX-format sensors that are approximately the same size as a frame of 35mm film. At 15.6 x 23.6 mm, the DX format of the D5100 is considerably smaller than the FX format (23.9 x 36 mm); as a consequence, regardless of the focal length of the lens mounted on the camera, the field of view covered by its sensor is narrower than the field of view produced by a lens of the same focal length on an FX-format sensor.

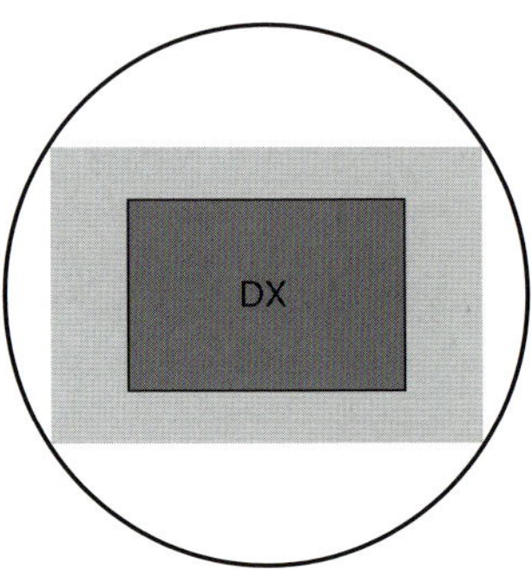

The circle represents the total area covered by the image circle projected from a lens designed to cover the FX / 35mm format. The pale grey rectangle is the image area for the FX-format sensor, while the dark grey rectangle represents the area covered by the DX format.

Through their shooting experience with DX-format Nikon cameras, many photographers have become familiar with the reduced angle of view caused by the smaller format sensor, while others still find the issue confusing. Furthermore, misconceptions persist as to what causes the altered field of view. Use of phrases such as, "it's like getting a free 1.5x teleconverter," or "the focal length is magnified by 1.5x" suggest, as if by some wizardry, that the focal length of a lens increases by 1.5x when mounted on a camera that records pictures in the DX format. This is completely false; the focal length of any lens will remain constant, and regardless of the size of the sensor or part of the sensor it projects an image onto, it is the angle of view that is altered.

To clarify this concept, consider that a lens with a focal length of 200mm will produce a specific angle of view on the FX-format sensor. However, when the same focal length is used with the DX format, the angle of view is reduced, rendering a view equivalent to that produced on the FX-format frame when a lens with a focal length of 300mm is used. In other words, if you are accustomed to choosing a focal length based on the angle of view it produces on the FX / 35mm film frame, you will want to multiply that focal length by 1.5x (the actual factor is closer to 1.52x) in order to estimate the coverage it will provide with the DX format. Using the example of the 200mm focal length discussed above, 200mm x 1.5 = 300mm. The following table provides an approximate effective focal length you can use to estimate the field of view with the DX format.

FOCAL LENGTH EQUIVALENTS

Actual	12	14	17	18	20	24	28	35	50	60
Effective	18	21	25.5	27	30	36	42	52.5	75	90
Actual	70	85	105	135	180	200	300	400	500	600
Effective	105	127.5	157.5	202.5	270	300	450	600	750	900

DX Format Pros and Cons: While this narrower field of view may be an advantage in some shooting situations because of the magnified view it offers, it has the reverse effect when you want to achieve a very wide angle of view; consequently, it is necessary to use a much shorter focal length. However, there is another beneficial side effect to the reduced angle of view of the DX format. Since the D5100 only uses the central portion of the image circle projected by the many Nikkor lenses designed for the FX format or 35mm film SLRs, the effects of optical aberrations and defects are kept to a minimum, as these are generally more prevalent toward the edges of the image circle. Using such as lens will often significantly reduce or eliminate some or all of the following:

- Light fall-off (vignetting) toward the edges and corners of the image area, which can be particularly troublesome at large lens apertures, or when using accessory filters
- Appearance of chromatic aberration (i.e., the inability of the lens to bring light of different wavelengths to the same point of focus)

- Linear distortion—both barrel and pin-cushion (i.e., straight lines are rendered by the lens as curved)
- Effects of field curvature (i.e., center and corners of frame are not in the same plane of focus)

Nikon also produces a range of Nikkor lenses designed specifically for use on their DX-format DSLR camera, known as DX lenses. These lenses need to project an image circle that covers only the DX-format sensor, enabling them to be made smaller and lighter than their counterparts designed for FX-format or 35mm film cameras (see pages 279-282 for further information on Nikkor lens compatibility).

THE VIEWFINDER

The D5100 has a fixed, optical pentamirror, eye-level viewfinder that shows approximately 95% (vertical and horizontal) of the full-frame coverage. It is important to understand the consequence of this: Reducing the viewfinder frame coverage to 95% in both linear directions actually results in a viewfinder that only displays about 90% of the image area recorded by the camera (0.95 x 0.95 = 0.90). As a result, it is not possible to frame an image in the viewfinder with complete accuracy, as there is a small but significant border area outside each edge of the viewfinder that will be included in the recorded picture. However, the LCD monitor displays 100% of the recorded image, so the prudent user will make use of the Image Review and Playback options of the camera to ensure their careful compositions have not been compromised!

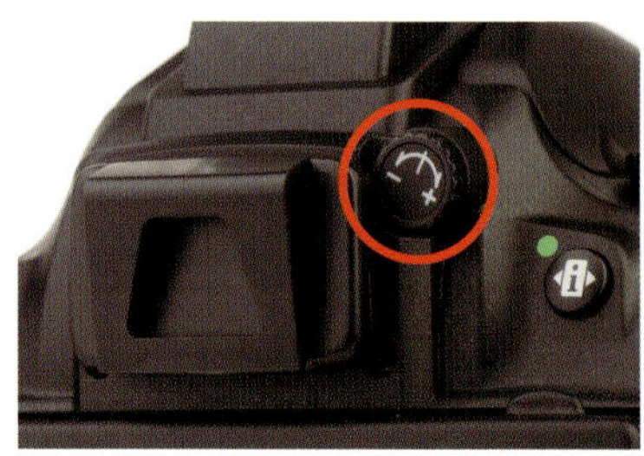

› **The viewfinder eyepiece is shown here covered by the DK-5; note that to fit the DK-5, the DK-20 rubber eyecup must first be removed. The diopter control dial for the viewfinder eyepiece can be seen located to the right.**

Another very important aspect of the viewfinder is to prevent light from entering the viewfinder eyepiece when the D5100 is used remotely (i.e., your eye is not to the viewfinder eyepiece), as it will influence the accuracy of the metering system adversely; so make sure the viewfinder eyepiece is covered with the supplied DK-5 cap when shooting this way.

ADJUSTING VIEWFINDER FOCUS

The viewfinder has an eyepoint of 0.7 inch (18 mm). Users who wear eyeglasses may find the view of the focusing screen and viewfinder information a little restricted. However, there is a built-in diopter adjustment of -1.7 to +0.7 m-1 to adjust the focus of the eyepiece to an individual user's eyesight. To do this, mount a lens on the camera and leave it set to its infinity focus mark. Switch the camera on and point it at a plain surface that fills the frame. Rotate the diopter adjustment dial to the right of the viewfinder eyepiece until the AF point and focus screen markings appear sharp. It is essential to do this to ensure you see the sharpest view of the focusing screen. If the built-in diopter correction is not sufficient, optional eyepiece correction lenses, with the product code DK-20C, are available from -5 to +3 m-1; these are attached by sliding them on to the eye piece frame (the standard DK-20 viewfinder eyecup must be removed first). The strength of these lenses may not match that of your prescription eyeglasses, so make sure you try them before making a purchase.

VIEWFINDER & FOCUS SCREEN DISPLAY

The viewfinder, which provides a magnification of approximately 0.78x (with a 50mm f/1.4 lens at infinity; -1.0m-1), displays all the essential information about exposure and focus. The camera is supplied with the Nikon B-type Mark VII, clear matte focusing screen, which is marked with seven pairs of square brackets that encompass the 11 autofocus points. Nikon does not offer an alternative interchangeable focusing screen for the D5100.

The focusing screen of the D5100 employs simple etched markings, so even with the battery removed from the camera they remain visible. The AF point markings and their surrounding square bracket markings are considerably fainter than the comparable marking of the D5000, and the new model does not offer the viewfinder grid-line display or reference arcs for Center-Weighted metering of its predecessor. Also gone are the screen overlays for warning that no memory card is inserted and the battery charge status, although the latter is shown below the focusing screen in the general viewfinder information. A single, red LED illuminates each of the 11 AF points when they are active, so it is always possible to determine which AF points are in use.

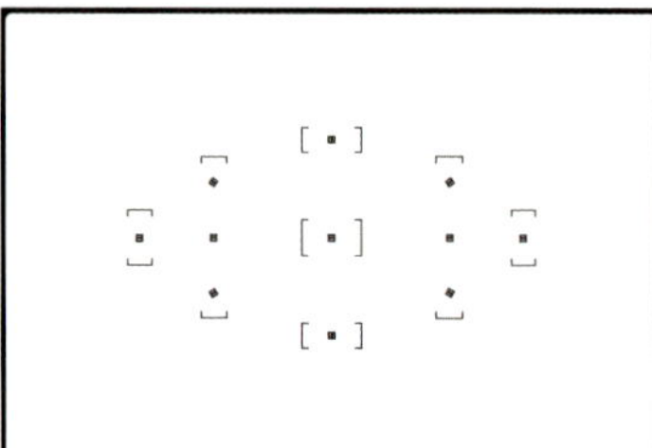

› The focus screen display of the D5100 is marked by 11 small squares to indicate the position of each AF point.

THE MULTI SELECTOR BUTTON

The Multi Selector button, located on the rear of the camera, is used to navigate the Information Display and the menu system of the D5100, plus select the AF point. Note that there is no locking switch available for this principal control, as there is on other Nikon camera models, and I have found that due to its relatively high profile that it is all too easy for the heel of my right thumb to depress the Multi Selector button inadvertently when holding the camera; in particular, I often find this causes the selection of the AF point to shift to the right side of the frame area, so be warned! Always check to see which AF point is highlighted before you shoot. The function of the Multi Selector is as shown below:

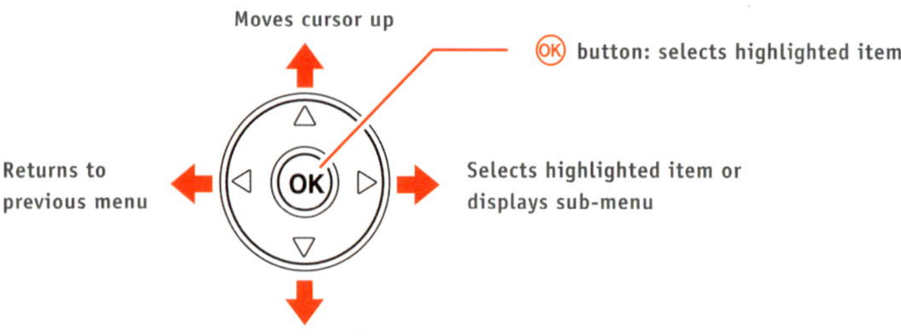

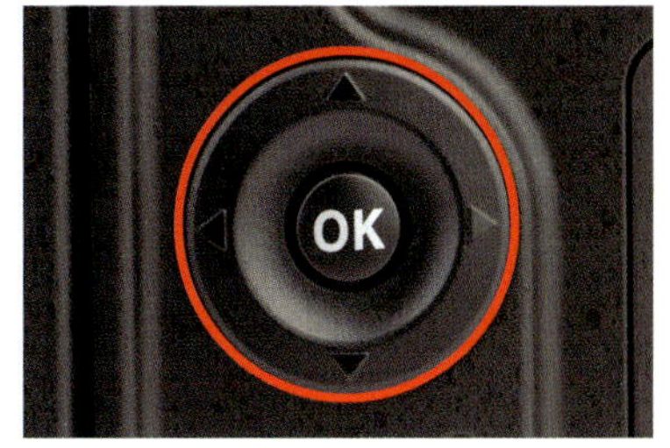

› The Multi-Selector button is used to navigate camera menus, controls, and select the AF point.

INFORMATION DISPLAY

The Information Display (ID) shows all the essential information about camera settings and controls on the camera's LCD monitor. Due to the size of the screen, the display is large and clear. The format of the display can be altered using the **[Info display format]** item in the Setup menu (see page 213).

To open the ID, press the info button once. To change a setting for an item shown in the display, press the i button, which highlights the item selected most recently in yellow. To shift the yellow cursor, use the Multi Selector button. Once the required item is highlighted, press the OK button to show the options available for that item.

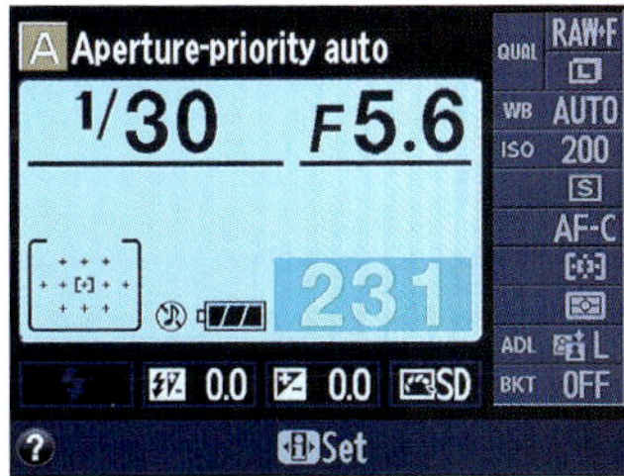

^ The Information Display provides a comprehensive view of current camera settings.

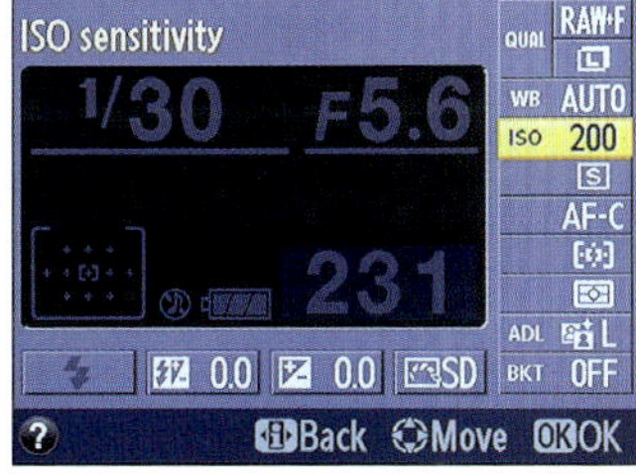

^ Pressing the i button displays the most recently selected item; here the ISO value is shown highlighted.

To clear the ID from the monitor, press the Info button or press the shutter release button down halfway. The length of time the ID is shown is selected via the CS-c2 **[Auto off timers]** item in the Custom Settings menu; the default duration is 8 seconds. The **[Auto info display]** and **[Info display format]** items in the Setup menu can be used to further customize how and when the ID operates.

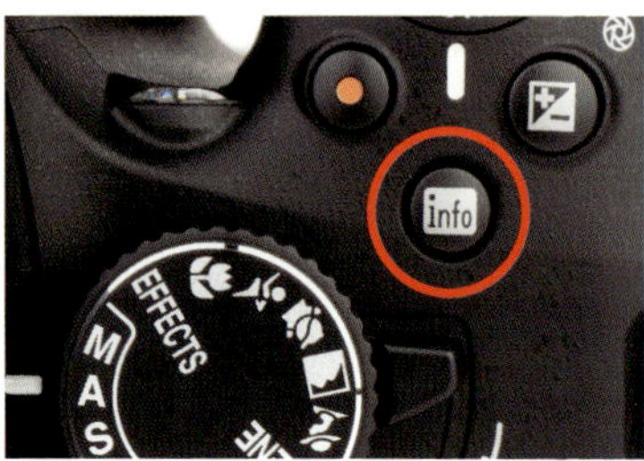

› The Info button is used to open and close the Information Display.

PREPARING THE D5100 FOR SHOOTING

In order to appeal to a broad range of users with various skill levels, the D5100 includes the simple point-and-shoot AUTO mode, the Auto Flash Off mode, a further 16 fully automated subject- or scene-oriented, point-and-shoot Scene modes, plus four dedicated exposure modes for the more experienced photographer. Additionally, the D5100 offers seven Effects modes (see pages 61-64).

The section below is intended to assist those less experienced users eager to take some pictures with their new D5100, but either unable or reluctant to spend the time, at this point, to learn how to take control of the camera.

QUICK START GUIDE

- Charge the EN-EL14 battery in the MH-24 charger until the charge lamp stops blinking. Switch off the charger, remove the battery, and open the battery chamber door on the base of the D5100. Insert the battery as per the diagram on the inside of the chamber door, and then close it.
- When the camera is switched on for the first time, it will display a language-selection menu. Use ▲ and ▼ on the multi selector switch to select the required language and then press OK.

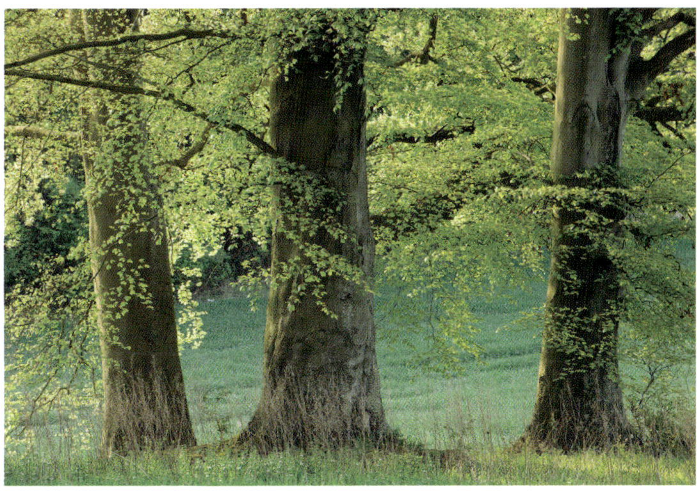

^ **The D5100's TTL metering system has no difficulty producing consistently accurate exposures in scenes with a broad range of tones.**

- Next, a time zone display will be shown. Use ◀ and ▶ to select your time zone, and then press ⓄⓀ. Use ▲ and ▼ to select the required date format, then press ⓄⓀ. A Daylight Saving time option will be displayed; if Daylight Savings is in effect in the current time zone, press ▲ to select **[On]**, then press ⓄⓀ. Now set the date and time. Use ◀ and ▶ to select an item, and use ▲ and ▼ to change it. Finally, press ⓄⓀ to set the camera clock.
- Attach a lens to the D5100. If the lens has a focus mode switch with options for either A-M, or M/A-M, set the focus mode to either A (autofocus), or M/A (autofocus with manual override).
- Adjust the viewfinder focus by turning the diopter control dial (located beside the viewfinder eyepiece) until the viewfinder display and AF points appear sharp.
- Open the memory card port on the right side of the camera and insert a memory card, ensuring that the main label of the card is facing toward the back of the camera.
- Format the memory card by pressing the MENU button and selecting the **[Format memory card]** item from the Setup menu. Next press ▶, then highlight the **[Yes]** option, and finally press the ⓄⓀ button to complete the formatting process.

- To set the camera to its AUTO mode—a fully automated point-and-shoot mode that controls virtually all camera settings automatically—select AUTO using the Mode dial on the top of the camera. The built-in flash will fire automatically if the camera determines the light level is low. If you don't want the flash to fire, select ⊕ Auto Flash Off mode.
- Compose a picture, ensuring that an AF point covers an area of the subject required to be in focus. Press lightly on the shutter release button to activate the focusing system. If the camera can acquire focus, the focus indicator ● will appear in the viewfinder; if ● is shown blinking, the camera has not been able to acquire focus. Recompose the picture, place the selected AF point over an alternative part of the subject, and press lightly on the shutter release button again.
- The shutter button has a two-stage release mechanism: Pressing it down halfway activates the AF and TTL metering systems, while pressing it down all the way fires the shutter. Avoid stabbing you index finger down on the shutter release button, as this will increase the risk of camera shake. Simply roll the tip of your index finger smoothly over the edge of the shutter release button to take the picture. The green access lamp on the back of the camera will illuminate as soon as an exposure has been made, indicating that the camera is saving the image.
- To review a picture, press the ▶ button. Use ◀ and ▶ to review other pictures stored on the memory card. To view additional shooting information about the displayed picture, press either ▲ or ▼. To return to the Shooting mode, press the shutter release button lightly.
- To delete a picture, press the ▶ button to display it on the monitor, then press the 🗑 button. A confirmation dialog will be displayed. Press the 🗑 button again to complete the process.

POWERING THE D5100

The D5100 can be powered either by a dedicated battery or an AC supply. The battery supplied with the camera is the rechargeable lithium-ion EN-EL14 (7.4V, 1030mAh) that weighs approximately 1.7 oz (48 g).

The profile of the EN-EL14 battery ensures that it can only be inserted the correct way into the camera. It is charged with the dedicated MH-24 Quick Charger, also supplied with the camera. A fully discharged EN-EL14 can be completely recharged in approximately 90 minutes. The EN-EL14 supplied with the D5100 is supplied partially charged.

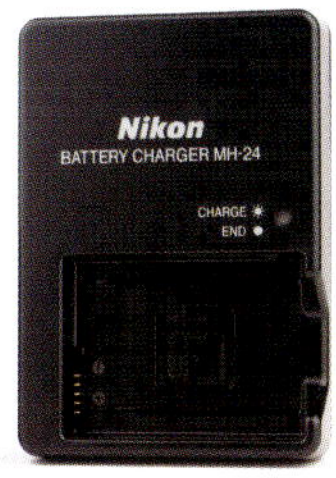

‹ The MH-24 Quick Charger requires approximately 90 minutes to fully recharge the EN-EL14 battery.

However, it is advisable to charge a new battery until the battery cools down in the charger before removing it. Do not be tempted to remove it as soon as the charging / charged indicator lamp on the MH-24 stops flashing to indicate charging is complete, as the battery is unlikely to have reached a full 100% charge.

USING THE EN-EL14 BATTERY

Whenever you insert or remove an EN-EL14, it is essential that you set the power switch of the D5100 to the Off position.

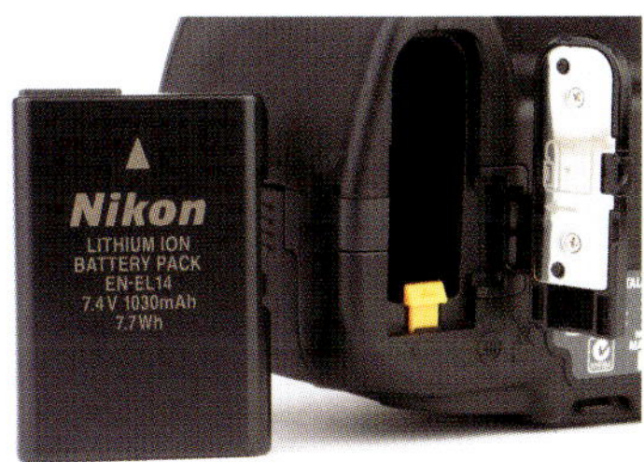

‹ The EN-EL14 battery shown next to the empty battery chamber of the D5100; note the diagram on the inside of the chamber cover and the yellow safety-catch that prevents the battery dropping out when the chamber door is open.

To insert an EN-EL14 battery into the D5100:

1. Turn the camera upside down and push the small button on the battery chamber lid toward the tripod socket. Turn the camera over and the battery chamber lid should swing open.
2. Open the lid fully and slide the battery into the camera observing the diagram on the inside of the chamber lid.
3. Press the lid down (you will feel a slight resistance) until it locks. You will hear a click as the latch closes.

To remove an EN-EL14 from the D5100:

1. Repeat step 1 (above).
2. Hold the lid open, turn the camera upright, slide the small yellow retaining catch toward the back of the camera and allow the battery to slide out taking care that it does not drop.
3. Close the battery chamber lid.

NOTE: If you are in the process of making any changes to the camera settings and the battery is removed while the power switch is still set to the on position, or the power supply from the EH-5a AC adapter is interrupted, the camera may not retain the new settings. Likewise, if the camera is still in the process of transferring data from the buffer memory to the storage media when the battery is removed, image files are likely to be corrupted or data lost.

To charge an EN-EL14:

1. Connect the MH-24 to an AC power supply.

NOTE: The MH-24 can be used worldwide, connected to any AC supply, at any voltage from 100V to 250V, via an appropriate power adapter.

2. Align the battery so its contacts are facing down and the small arrowhead printed on the opposite side of the battery casing from the contacts is pointing toward the contacts inside the MH-24. Slot the battery into the MH-24, and then push it down gently so that it seats properly in the battery aperture of the charger. Switch on the AC power supply and the charge lamp should begin to flash immediately, indicating that charging has commenced.

Lithium-ion batteries do not exhibit the same charge memory effects associated with certain types of rechargeable batteries, therefore a partially discharged EN-EL14 can take a top-up charge without any adverse consequences to battery life or performance. However, I do recommend that you avoid giving a battery a top-up charge when its charge level is at 90% or more, and likewise, do not repeatedly run a battery down to a charge level of 10% or less before recharging it. In the former case, there is a risk of reducing overall battery capacity; and in the latter, successive charging of a battery from near exhaustion to full charge will likely reduce its life expectancy. The battery charge status is shown in the Information Display, while a warning to indicate either a low battery charge or exhausted battery is displayed in the viewfinder. See the table below.

MONITOR	VIEWFINDER	BATTERY STATUS
[battery icon: full]	—	Fully charged
[battery icon: partial]	—	Partially discharged
[battery icon: low]	—	Low – charge battery
[battery icon: empty]	—	Discharged – charge battery; shutter disabled

EXTERNAL POWER SUPPLY

The Nikon EH-5b AC adapter, which is an optional accessory, can also power the D5100 via the EP-5A DC power connector (the earlier EH-5 and EH-5a AC adapters are also compatible with the D5100 and EP-5A DC power connector). The AC adapter is rated for an input of 100–240v, AC 50–60Hz and is particularly useful for extended periods of shooting, image Playback, or data transfer directly from the camera to a computer.

The EH-5b cannot be connected directly to the D5100; it requires the EP-5A DC power connector to be inserted in the camera's main battery chamber, substituting for the EN-EL14 battery (ensure the + and – terminals of the EP-5A are in the correct orientation). The cord from the EP-5A should be laid in the small notch in the edge of the battery chamber (this requires the rubber grommet set in to the edge of the battery chamber to be swung outward) before closing the chamber cover. Connect the DC plug of the EH-5b to the DC terminal of the EP-5A. Finally, connect the EH-5b AC plug of the AC cord to the EH-5A AC terminal, and connect the other end to the AC supply. When powered from an AC supply, the AC indicator of the D5100 will show in the Information Display.

NOTE: Always ensure that the power switch on the D5100 is set to OFF before connecting / disconnecting the EH-5b and EP-5A. There is a risk that the camera's circuitry could be damaged if you plug / unplug the EH-5b and EP-5A while the power switch is set to ON.

EFFECTS OF ELECTROSTATIC CHARGE

Operation of the D5100 is totally dependent on electrical power. Occasionally, the camera may stop functioning properly, or display unusual characters or unexpected messages in the viewfinder and monitor displays. Such behavior is generally due to the effects of a strong external electrostatic charge. If this occurs, try switching the camera off, disconnecting it from its power supply (remove the installed EN-EL14 or unplug the EH-5b AC adapter / EP-5A power connector), then reconnecting the power, and switching the camera back on. If the symptoms persist, the camera will require inspection by a technician at a Nikon authorized service center.

INTERNAL CLOCK / CALENDAR BATTERY

The D5100 has an internal clock / calendar that is powered by a fixed, internal, rechargeable battery; fully charged, it will power the clock / calendar for approximately one month. This battery requires charging for approximately 72 hours by the camera's power supply: This can be either an EN-EL14 inserted into the camera body or an EH-5b adapter and the EP-5A power connector. Should the clock battery become exhausted, a message that the clock is not set will be displayed on the monitor when the camera is turned on. The clock will display a date and time of 2011.01.01 00:00:00. If this occurs, the clock / calendar will need to be reset to the correct time via the **[Time Zone and Date]** item in the Setup menu.

NOTE: Should the internal clock / calendar battery fail and not retain a charge, the camera must be returned to a Nikon-approved service center for a replacement battery to be fitted.

BATTERY PERFORMANCE

Operation of the D5100 is totally dependent on an adequate electrical power supply. Obviously, the more functions the camera has to perform, the greater the demand on its battery, so reducing the number of functions and the duration for which they are active is fundamental to reducing power consumption. This can be an important consideration, especially if you are traveling. I have set out below some of the principal causes of battery power drain, together with a few suggestions as to how you can conserve battery power.

Using the camera's LCD monitor increases power consumption, so turn it off unless you need it. Consider setting the **[Image review]** item in the Playback menu to **[Off]** (the default setting is **[On]**). If **[On]** is selected and you want to leave it that way, you may instead simply press the shutter release button lightly as soon as you have finished assessing the picture, since this returns the camera to its Shooting mode, switching the monitor off immediately. To help reduce time spent scrolling through the camera's menu system for any items you use frequently, consider consulting the Recent Settings menu, which lists the 20 most recently used menu items, or alternatively, use the My Menu option to create a custom list, so you only need to consult a single menu. When using the Live View and / or the D-Movie (video) mode functions, the battery drain will be significant compared with just shooting still pictures, so I recommend very strongly that if you intend to make regular use of either, that you carry at least one spare EN-EL14 battery.

Recording NEF RAW files draws far more power compared with recording JPEG, although the power management of the D5100 appears to have been enhanced in this respect compared with previous camera models. While driving the autofocus mechanism of lenses draws relatively little power, the Vibration Reduction (VR) feature available with some Nikkor lenses is another matter. The VR function of all Nikkor lenses draws power from the camera battery and it tends to be active for far longer periods compared with AF operation. Consequently, VR can reduce battery life by approximately 10–15% when active.

Using the built-in Speedlight flash unit will place a significant demand on the battery and shorten the duration of any shooting session considerably, so turn it off if you don't absolutely need it. If you do need flash, consider using an accessory Speedlight.

If the optional Nikon GP-1 GPS device is connected to the D5100, it draws its power from the camera battery, so it will also reduce the battery charge level. In order to reduce this power drain, you can set the camera to shut off the GPS unit when the camera's meter shuts off after the amount of time specified using CS-c2 **[Auto off timers]** in the Custom Settings menu (pages 204-205) via the **[GPS]** item in the Setup menu. See pages 220-221 for information on how to set the GPS to turn off with the camera's meter.

Lithium-ion batteries are fairly resilient to cold conditions. However, to ensure you can keep shooting, particularly in freezing conditions (i.e., below 0°C/32°F), keep at least one spare battery in a warm place such as an inside pocket, and as the performance of the battery in the camera dwindles, exchange it with the warm one. Allow the used battery time to warm up again and keep rotating between the batteries to maximize the shooting capacity.

Despite my warnings above, in my experience, shooting in an average ambient temperature range of 60° to 75°F (16° to 24°C) using autofocus with Vibration Reduction (VR) switched on, moderate use of the monitor for picture assessment, I have found that a single EN-EL14 battery will still deliver sufficient power for approximately 500 exposures.

BATTERY STORAGE

A fully charged Nikon Lithium-ion EN-EL14 battery in good condition will retain its full capacity over a short period of non-use. However, if the battery is left dormant for a month or more, regardless of whether it is installed in a camera or not, expect it to suffer a perceptible loss of charge, so ensure it is recharged fully before use (see comments concerning top-up charging on pages 38-39). If you expect to store a camera battery for a protracted period, avoid leaving it fully charged or heavily discharged. Storing a fully charged battery can have a long-term effect on its overall capacity, while storing a heavily discharged battery can risk it shifting to a deeply discharged state, which can damage it. The optimum charge level for a battery that will be stored for four weeks or more is 20–80%. Always store your camera and batteries in a well-ventilated, cool, dry place, and ensure the protective terminal cover is in place.

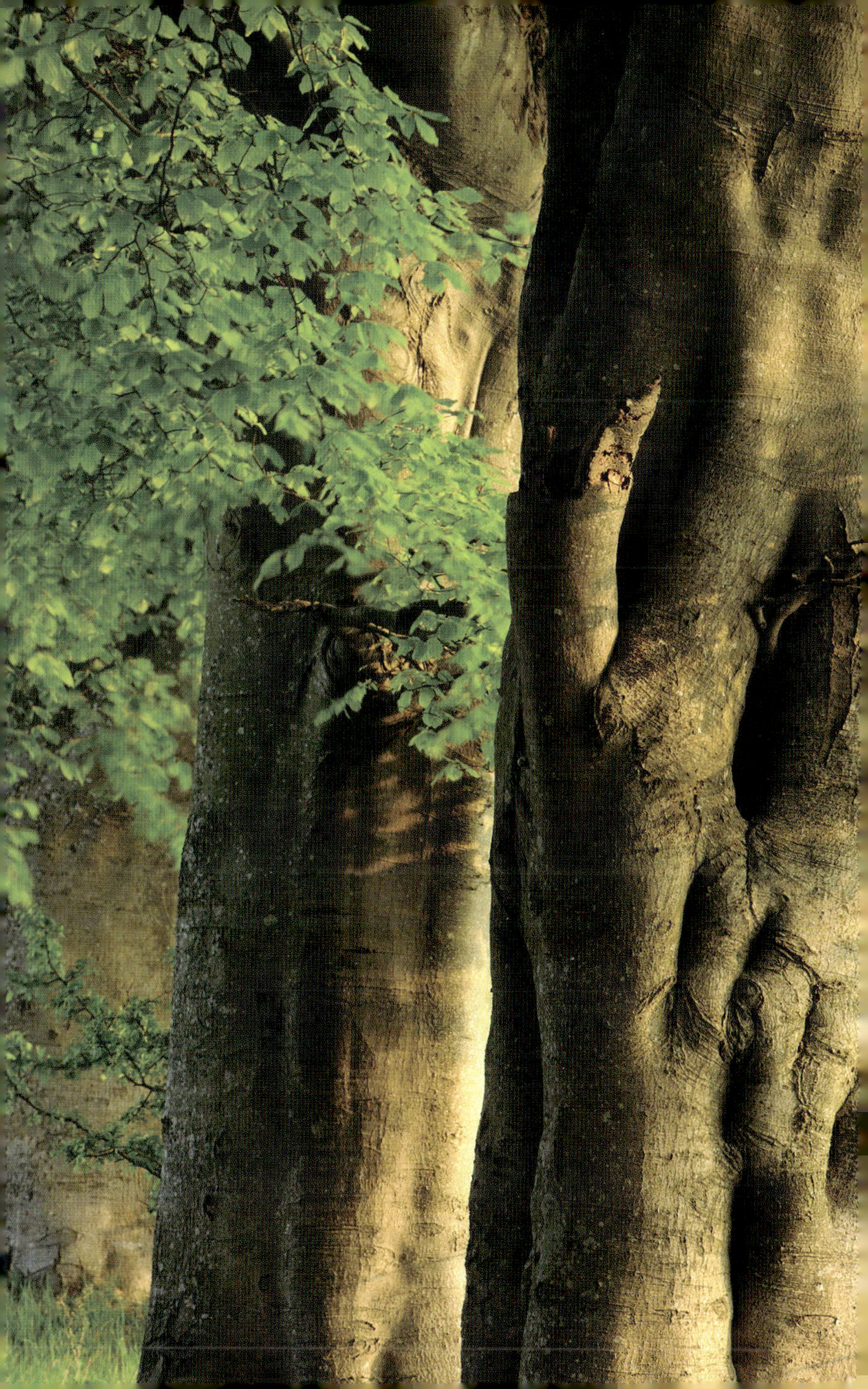

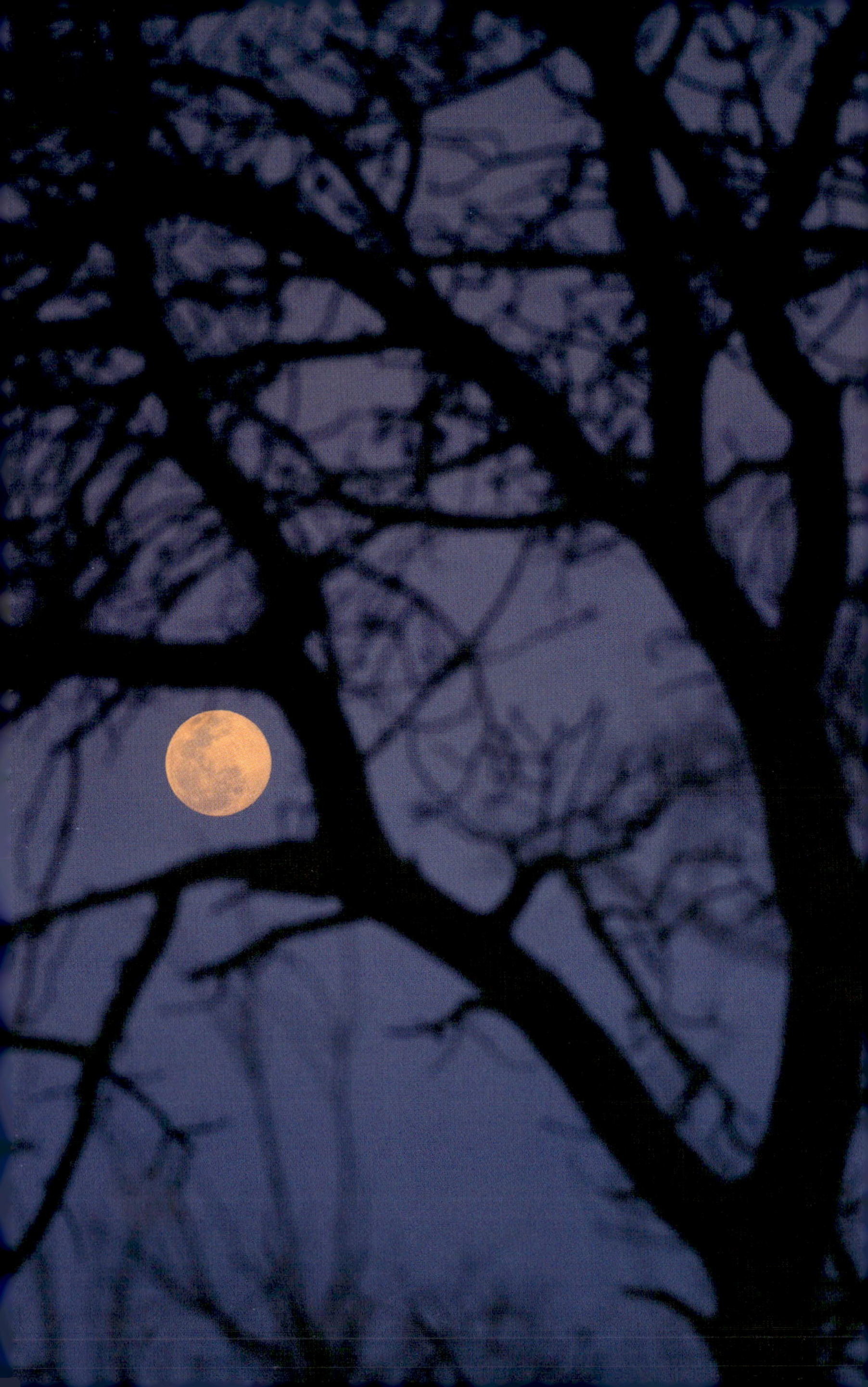

The Exposure and Focusing Systems

Regardless of whether you are content to let the D5100 make decisions about exposure settings or you prefer to take control of the camera and make them for yourself, it is essential to understand how the camera reads, evaluates, and records light.

ISO SENSITIVITY

Shooting with film requires you to make a decision about which ISO (sensitivity) rating to choose in order to cope with the prevailing or expected lighting conditions, and the entire roll must be exposed at the same ISO value. One of the great advantages of digital photography is that digital cameras allow you to adjust the ISO sensitivity from picture to picture. The ISO sensitivity rating used by Nikon DSLR cameras follows the guidelines laid down by the International Organization for Standardization for rating film speed (sensitivity) using the ISO scale; therefore, where the sensitivity setting on a camera complies with these guidelines, it is referred to as being ISO equivalent.

The D5100 offers ISO equivalent sensitivity settings from 100 to 6400 that can be adjusted in steps of 0.3 EV, plus the option to increase it by up to 2 EV above ISO 6400 in single steps of 0.3, 0.7, 1.0, or 2.0 EV (offering an extended ISO range equivalent to 100 – 25,600). The option to shift the sensitivity outside the normal range is referred to as Hi 0.3 (ISO 8000), Hi 0.7 (ISO 10,000), Hi 1 (ISO 12,800) and Hi 2 (ISO 25,600).

The base level ISO sensitivity of ISO 100 is where the sensor of the D5100 delivers its optimal performance, with the broadest dynamic range and lowest signal-to-noise ratio, so use this to derive the maximum potential image quality. To adjust the ISO sensitivity, press the info button to open the Information Display, and then press the i button, place the highlighted cursor on the current ISO value and press OK. Use ▼ and ▲ to select the required value and then press OK. The Hi options are at the bottom of the list of sensitivity values. Alternatively, the ISO sensitivity can be adjusted via the **[ISO sensitivity settings]** item in the Shooting menu. The camera also has the ability to adjust the ISO sensitivity automatically according to the light conditions; this feature is also set via the same item in the menu.

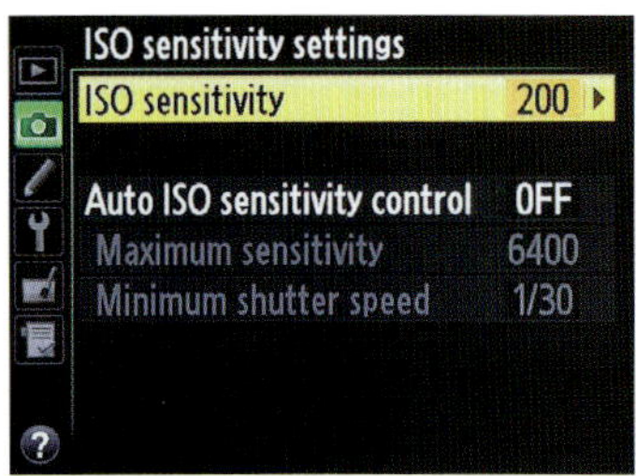

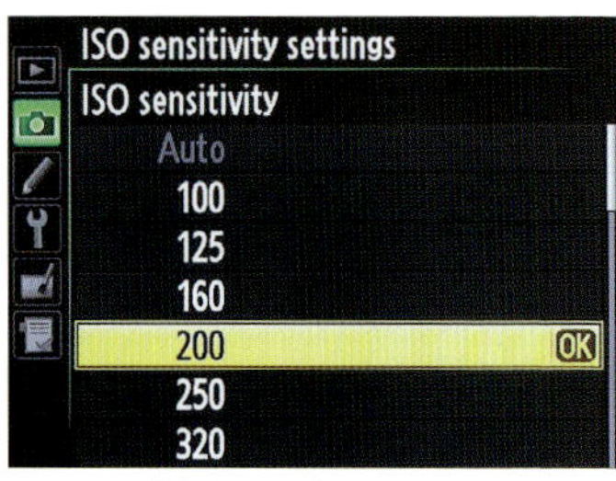

These two screen shots above show the main [ISO sensitivity settings] menu and a partial list of the ISO values within the menu item

HIGH ISO PERFORMANCE

The analogy with film ISO continues insomuch as, at higher ISO sensitivity settings, a digital image will show an increasing amount of electronic noise. Generally, as the ISO sensitivity value is hiked higher and higher, other unwanted effects appear increasingly too: Dynamic range is reduced (by about one stop of dynamic range for each full stop increase in ISO), plus the saturation of color and the tonal separation are reduced, leading to a flatter and duller appearance to the image.

When exposure settings are accurate, the high ISO performance of the D5100 is remarkably good. For the absolute optimum image quality, keep ISO sensitivity set to 100, where the D5100 is easily capable of producing a dynamic range of no less than nine stops. That said, unless you really ramp up the level of contrast and sharpening in-camera or photograph a scene with excessively high contrast, separating shots taken at an ISO 100, 200, or 400 is an exercise in splitting hairs. The ISO performance of the D5100 is still very good up to ISO 800, making it possible to shoot at just about any combination of camera settings (e.g., Compression, Contrast, Saturation, Sharpening) with virtually no detrimental effect on image quality. That said, you can still expect to see noise in any image if you take a long exposure (i.e., 1 second or longer) and forget to use the Long Exposure Noise Reduction **[Long exposure NR]** feature in the Shooting menu.

Dynamic range, color saturation, resolution of detail, and noise levels, remain remarkably good at ISO 1600 and 3200, offering practical solutions in low light conditions, provided that Contrast and Saturation are set appropriately (i.e., do not set these too high, as it is far better to adjust them at a later stage in post processing). Furthermore, the noise at ISO 1600 to 3200 can be used for creative purposes, and is particularly effective with the black-and-white options available on the D5100, emulating the qualities of high-speed, grainy black-and-white film. Push the ISO to the top end of its normal range, ISO 6400, and the effects seen at ISO 1600 appear stronger with an increase in blurring of detail and noise grain pattern, but the latter is still tight and the results are very acceptable. Move beyond the normal ISO range to the Hi 1 (ISO 12,800) setting, and there is a noticeable change in ISO performance, where there is a perceptible loss in dynamic range, a further increase in noise and contrast, noticeably stronger blurring of detail and some yellow / purple blotchiness in dark-tone areas of the image, while at Hi 2 (ISO 25,600), all of these adverse effects are even more noticeable.

I would consider the highest ISOs as last resort options, particularly the Hi 2 setting. To help reduce the effects of noise at higher ISO sensitivity settings, select the High ISO Noise Reduction **[High ISO NR]** feature available via the menu. While this can be quite effective, it will result in some loss of definition in very fine detail. Unless you have good reason to try and deal with ISO noise in-camera, it is preferable to use either the noise reduction feature of an NEF (RAW) file converter, or a dedicated noise reduction application, such as Dfine (www.niksoftware.com), Noise Ninja (www.picturecode.com), or Neat Image (www.neatimage.com).

ISO SENSITIVITY AUTO CONTROL

It is important to understand how this feature works, as it may not be quite what you expect. In the Programmed-Auto (P) and Aperture-Priority (A) autoexposure modes, the ISO sensitivity will not be altered unless underexposure would occur at the value specified for **[Minimum shutter speed]** option under the **[Auto ISO sensitivity control]** item, which is a sub-heading item under the **[ISO sensitivity settings]** item in the camera menu. The range of shutter speeds for **[Minimum shutter speed]** extends from 1 second to 1/2000. However, if the camera cannot achieve a proper exposure at the ISO sensitivity specified as the **[Maximum sensitivity]** value, which covers the range from ISO 200 to Hi 2 (ISO 25,600), the D5100 will then begin to select slower shutter speeds.

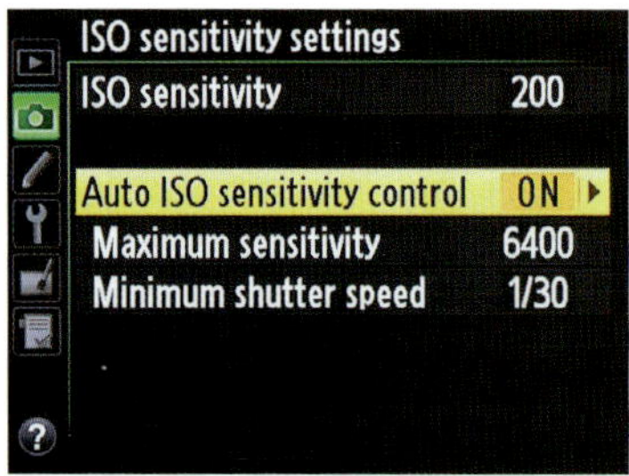

› The screen shot shows the Auto ISO sensitivity control option has be activated, and values for the **[Maximum sensitivity]** (ISO 6400) and **[Minimum shutter speed]** (1/30 s) have been selected.

In Shutter-Priority (S) autoexposure mode, the ISO sensitivity is shifted when the exposure reaches the maximum aperture available on the lens. The automated control of ISO is probably most useful with this exposure mode because it will raise the sensitivity setting, and thus maintain the pre-selected shutter speed, which is usually critical to the success of the picture when shooting fast-paced action. Again, the **[Maximum sensitivity]** option for the ISO sensitivity can be specified under the **[Auto ISO sensitivity control]** item. In Manual exposure mode, the sensitivity is shifted if the selected shutter speed and aperture cannot attain a correct exposure (as indicated by the analog exposure scale displayed in the viewfinder). When the **[Auto ISO sensitivity control]** feature is active, ISO-AUTO is displayed in the viewfinder and ISO-A is shown in the Information Display; these warnings will blink if the ISO sensitivity is altered from the value set by the user.

TTL METERING

The D5100 has three options for its through-the-lens (TTL) metering pattern that will be familiar if you have used a Nikon AF camera before: Matrix, Center-Weighted, and Spot, which are available in P, A, S, and M shooting modes only. In all other exposure modes, the camera selects the Matrix metering pattern automatically. To select a metering pattern, press the info button to open the Information Display, and then press the i button, place the highlighted cursor on the current metering option and press OK. Use ▼ and ▲ to select the required option and then press OK. The appropriate icon will be displayed in the Information Display.

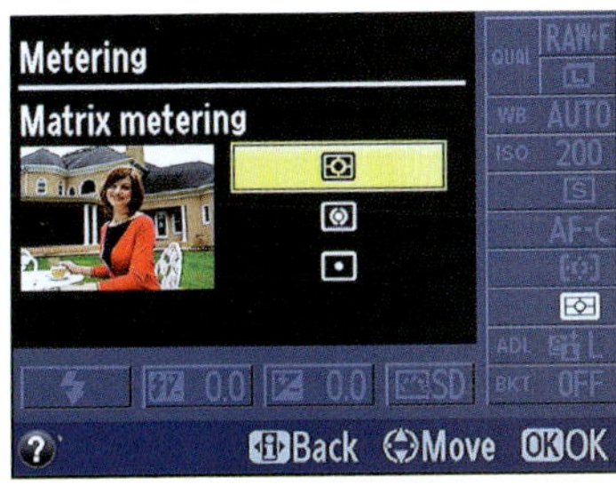

MATRIX METERING

The metering pattern for this mode covers virtually the entire frame area with each of its 420 segments. The 420-segment (pixel) RGB metering sensor is located in the viewfinder head of the camera just above the eyepiece and acts as a sampling point.

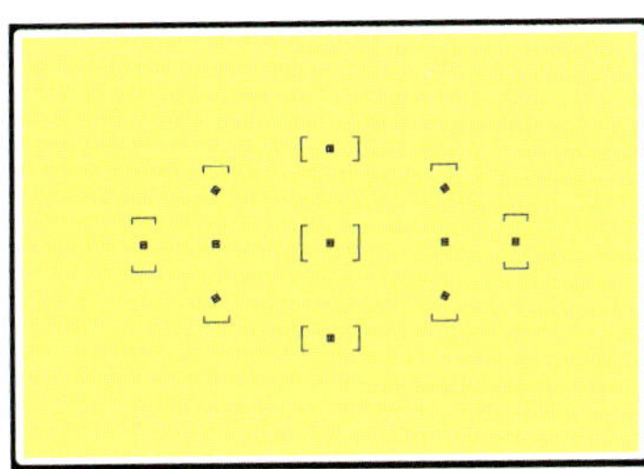

› The coverage of the Matrix metering pattern extends virtually to the edge of the full frame area (as indicated by the yellow shading, which is shown for illustrative purposes only).

There is a small diffraction grating located immediately in front of this sensor, and together, the two elements form the core of Nikon's innovative Scene Recognition System. The purpose of the diffraction grating is to separate the light falling on the sensor into its component colors and thus improve the efficiency and accuracy with which the camera assesses both the color and contrast of the light from the scene being photographed. The D5100 uses this enhanced information to improve metering accuracy, especially for skin tones.

To derive the most from the Matrix metering capabilities, you must use a D- or G-type Nikkor lens, since these provide additional focus distance information, which assists the camera in estimating how far away the subject is. The metering system also knows which AF point is selected and uses this information to estimate the subject's position. Nikon calls the system 3D Color Matrix Metering II. If you use an AF Nikkor lens that does not communicate distance information to the camera, the system defaults to standard Color Matrix Metering II (i.e., the distance information is not integrated in the exposure computations).

In Matrix metering (and i-TTL flash control) the D5100 benefits from the enhanced analysis of highlights within the frame achieved by the Scene Recognition System feature, which is combined with its assessment of color, as well as brightness and contrast, and then compared against a database containing a total of over 30,000 brightness distribution patterns derived from actual sample images that cover an enormous range of lighting conditions. Matrix metering uses four main factors when calculating exposure:

- The overall brightness level in a scene
- The ratio of brightness between the 420 segments
- The focused distance, provided by the lens (D- or G-type only)
- The location of the active AF point

When shooting an evenly illuminated scene with moderate contrast, where the active AF point covers a mid-tone value, the D5100 produces consistently good exposures via its Matrix metering. Furthermore, when shooting a scene filled with very light tones, for example snow or white sand, the Matrix metering system of the D5100 will usually cope very well and not require anywhere near as much Exposure Compensation to be applied, compared with previous Nikon camera models in this class.

However, the Matrix metering does appear to produce greater variability in results when using Single-Point AF Area mode and the active AF point covers a very light or very dark tone (i.e., the camera's metering seems to pay more attention to the tone under the active AF point compared with some Nikon camera models). In these situations, it is advisable to check the histogram display to monitor both highlight and shadow levels.

CENTER-WEIGHTED METERING

Available in P, A, S, and M exposure modes only, the Center-Weighted metering pattern harkens back to the TTL metering systems used by early Nikon SLR film cameras. In these cameras, the frame area was usually divided in a 60:40 ratio, with the bias placed on the central portion of the frame. The D5100 uses a higher ratio of 75:25, with 75% of the exposure reading based on the central area of the frame and the remaining 25% based on the outer area. For an unknown reason, Nikon has decided to dispense with marking the focusing screen that indicates the area covered by the 8-mm-diameter circle at the center of the viewfinder image, so use the position of the inner nine AF points as an approximate guide instead. Unlike Matrix metering, no color information is assessed when the Center-Weighted pattern is selected, so metering is performed using a grayscale.

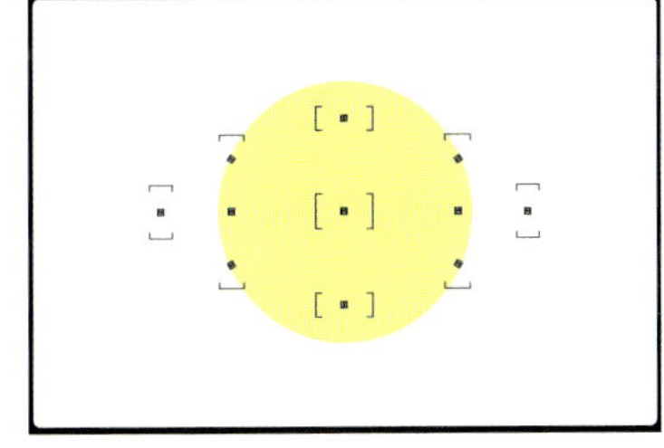

› The coverage of the Center-Weighted metering pattern places its emphasis within an 8-mm-diameter circle at the center of the frame area, although this area is not marked specifically on the D5100's focusing screen.

HINT: Center-weighted metering offers nowhere near the level of sophistication of Matrix metering, but for some subjects, its simplicity can be an advantage for photographers who like to control exposure and understand how it works.

SPOT METERING

Available in P, A, S, and M exposure modes only, Spot metering is extremely useful for metering from a highly specific area of a scene. For example, when faced with a subject against a virtually black background, the Matrix metering system may overexpose the subject. The Spot meter, on the other hand, allows a reading to be taken from the subject only, without it being influenced by the background. The sensing area for the Spot metering pattern is a circle approximately 0.14 inch (3.5 mm) in diameter, which represents about 2.5% of the total frame area. This circle is centered on the active AF point, unless Auto-Area AF is selected for AF-Area mode when shooting still pictures, in which case the central AF point is the only area to perform metering. Again, as with the Center-Weighted pattern, no color information is assessed when the Spot metering pattern is selected, so metering is performed using a grayscale.

HINT: It is essential to remember that in Center-Weighted and Spot metering, the TTL metering system measures reflected light, and is calibrated to give a correct exposure for a mid-tone (middle gray). When using either of these two metering patterns, you must make sure that the part of the scene you meter from represents such a mid-tone. Otherwise, you may need to compensate the exposure value. It is the tone (degree of reflectivity) that is important, not the color.

HINT: In Dynamic Area AF, the D5100 will attempt to follow a moving subject by shifting focus control between different AF points. If this occurs, the Spot metering also shifts, following the active AF point.

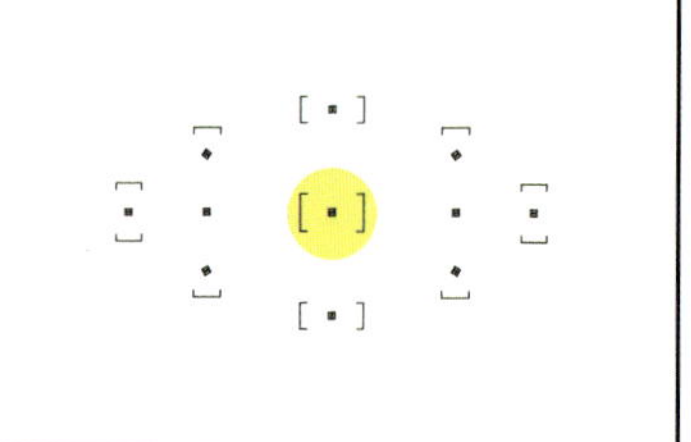

‹ The coverage of the Spot metering pattern covers a circle centered on the active AF point that represents about 2.5% of the total frame area.

AUTO AND SCENE MODES

The Auto mode, Auto Flash Off mode, sixteen dedicated scene modes, and seven Effects modes represent the most automated level of control available on the D5100. The camera manages many key controls and features in an attempt to select a combination of shutter speed and aperture that will be appropriate for the current scene. It does this by using information from the through-the-lens (TTL) metering system, which assesses the overall level of illumination, contrast, and color quality of the prevailing light, together with information from the autofocus system—used to estimate the location of the subject in the frame area and its distance from the camera, plus additional information from the camera's sensor to control Automated White Balance. This leaves you with limited ability to intervene and override settings—for example, the metering pattern, Exposure Compensation, White Balance, and Picture Controls cannot be adjusted from their default settings. This is unlikely to be of any concern to the novice who is content to let the D5100 make decisions on their behalf, or for the user who is content to use the special effects created by the in-camera image processing when shooting in the Effects modes. But for more seasoned users, I would recommend avoiding these Shooting modes and suggest working in Aperture-Priority (A), Shutter-Priority (S), or Manual (M) exposure mode.

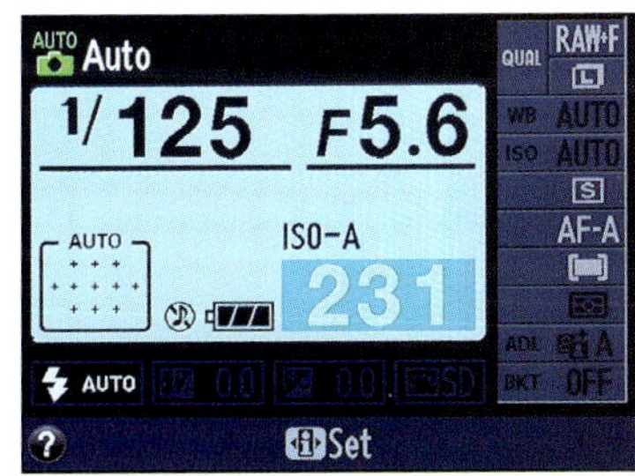

› Shown at right is the Information Display for the AUTO mode. Notice that a number of items are grayed out, because those settings cannot be altered from their defaults in the AUTO, Scene, and Effects modes.

If the **[Graphic]** option is selected under the **[Info display format]** item in the Setup menu, the relationship between the shutter speed and aperture is shown by way of a diagram in the Information Display, which shows how the aperture changes to a large value (low f/number) as the duration of the shutter speed decreases, and conversely, how the aperture changes to a small value (high f/number) as the duration of the shutter speed increases.

AUTO, AUTO (FLASH OFF), AND THE SCENE MODE OPTIONS

When using the AUTO and Scene modes, the level of user control is restricted, but the following controls can be adjusted from their default settings in most cases: Image Quality, Image Size (JPEG only), release mode, AF mode, AF-Area mode, and Flash mode. If you alter any default setting, it is only retained while the camera remains in the current shooting mode. If you turn the Mode dial to another shooting mode, the default setting is restored.

- The following controls cannot be adjusted from their default settings: White Balance, metering, ISO sensitivity, Active D-Lighting, and the Picture Controls (Contrast and Sharpening are applied automatically).
- The following functions are not available: Exposure Bracketing, Exposure Compensation, and Flash Compensation.

AUTO Auto: The AUTO mode is designed as a universal point-and-shoot mode and is most effective for general-purpose snapshot photography, such as family events or vacations.

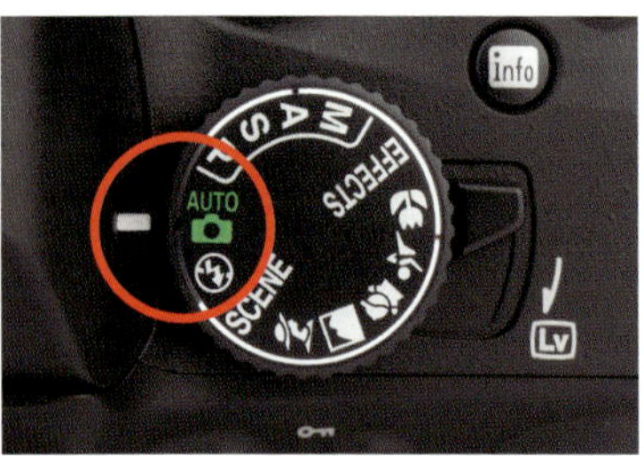

Auto (Flash Off): This mode is essentially the same as the AUTO mode, with the exception that the built-in flash is turned off and will not operate, regardless of the ambient illumination (even if it is very dark). It is useful in situations when the use of flash is undesirable—for example, when shooting in a museum where flash is prohibited, or in natural low-light conditions where you do not want to spoil the atmosphere by using flash. Although the operation of the built-in flash is cancelled, the AF-Assist illuminator lamp will still function to assist autofocus operation in poor lighting conditions.

HINT: Since the camera can set slow shutter speeds in this mode, always check the viewfinder information to ensure that the selected shutter speed will allow the camera to be held without risk of camera shake affecting the picture. At slow shutter speeds, consider using a camera support, such as a tripod.

The following Scene modes are selected directly from the Mode dial:

Portrait: The mode is designed to select a wide aperture (low f/number) in order to produce a picture with a shallow depth of field. Generally, this renders the background out-of-focus so it does not detract from the subject, although the effect is also dependent on the distance between the subject and the background, and the focal length of the lens used, both of which influence subject magnification. This mode is most effective with focal lengths of 100mm or more and when the subject is relatively far away from the background.

Landscape: The mode is designed to select a small aperture in order to produce a picture with an extended depth of field. Generally, this renders everything from the foreground to the horizon in focus, although this will depend to some degree how close the lens is to the nearest subject. This mode is most effective with wide-angle or wide-angle zoom lenses, and when the scene is well lit.

HINT: When using a short focal length lens (i.e., less than 35mm), try to include an element of interest in the foreground of the scene, as well as in the middle distance, to help produce a balanced composition and a way of leading the viewer's eye into the picture.

Child: The parameters are similar to the mode, except the Picture Control is Standard to give a more vibrant rendition of color.

HINT: One of the simplest ways to improve pictures of children is to lower the camera to your subject's eye level.

Sports: The mode is designed to select a wide aperture in order to maintain the highest possible shutter speed to "freeze" motion in fast–paced action. It also has a beneficial side effect: This combination produces a picture with a very shallow depth of field that helps to isolate the subject from the background. This mode is most effective with telephoto or telephoto-zoom lenses, and when there are no obstructions between the camera and the subject that may cause the autofocus function to focus on something other than the subject.

HINT: There is always a slight delay between pressing the shutter release button and the shutter opening; therefore, it is important to anticipate the peak moment of the action and press the shutter just before it occurs. The decisive moment will be missed if you wait to see it in the viewfinder before pressing the shutter release.

Close-Up: The mode is for taking pictures at short shooting distances of subjects such as flowers, insects, and other small objects. It is designed to select a small aperture (high f/number) in order to produce a picture with an extended depth-of-field. Generally, depth of field is limited when working at very short focus distances, even when using small apertures, so this program tries to render as much of the subject in focus as possible. The final effect will also be dependent on how close the camera is to the subject and the focal length of the lens used.

The following Scene modes are selected by turning the Mode dial to SCENE. Then rotate the Command dial until the required Scene mode is displayed on the monitor screen:

Night Portrait: The mode is designed to capture properly exposed pictures of people against a background that is dimly lit. It is useful when the photographer wants to include background detail, such as a cityscape or sunset, in the photo and is most effective when the background is in low light, as opposed to near dark, or totally dark conditions. The built-in Speedlight will activate automatically in low light; alternatively, an external Speedlight such as the SB-400 or SB-700 can be used to supplement the ambient light.

Night Landscape: The parameters are similar to the mode, except the Picture Control is Standard to give a more vibrant colors, while the built-in flash and AF-Assist illuminator are disabled; it is optimized for shooting cityscapes by improving the rendition of artificial lighting and reducing image noise.

HINT: Do not wait for the sky to turn a featureless inky black, but try to shoot in the twilight period when there is still color in the sky.

Party/Indoor: It is optimized for shooting pictures of people using flash, as the red-eye reduction feature is activated. Auto ISO is set in an effort to capture as much ambient light as possible.

Beach/Snow: The parameters are similar to the mode, except the exposure is optimized to account for the very light tones of sand and snow, and prevent them from causing underexposure.

Sunset: Designed to ensure the rich red/orange hues of a sunset are retained the White Balance is set to Direct Sunlight. Exposure is biased toward using larger aperture values to compensate for the relatively low light condition that is likely to be encountered.

Dusk/Dawn: The parameters are similar to the mode, except the White Balance is set to a color temperature of 4550K to help preserve the colors of a pre-dawn, or post-sunset sky. Exposure is biased toward using larger aperture values to compensate for the relatively low light condition that is likely to be encountered.

Pet Portrait: The parameters are similar to the mode, except the built-in flash can be used, although the AF-Assist illuminator is turned off. Exposure is biased toward using fast shutter speeds to capture a moving subject with crisp definition.

Candlelight: The White Balance is set to 4350K to help achieve accurate rendition of color in conditions where the only light source is candlelight. Exposure is biased toward using larger aperture values to compensate for the relatively low light condition that is likely to be encountered. Use of a tripod is recommend as shutter speeds are likely to be very slow. Flash is set to Off to preserve the atmosphere of the scene.

Blossom: Color rendition is optimized for the bright colors of flowers but without causing them to become over-saturated.

Autumn Colors: Similar to except the Picture Control is set to Vivid to boost the color saturation and contrast levels to produce a very vibrant rendition of typical autumn leaves.

Food: Similar to except the flash mode is set to Fill-flash, so the built-in flash will not pop-up automatically in conditions of low light.

The following Effects modes are selected by turning the Mode dial to EFFECTS. Then, rotate the Command dial until the required mode is displayed on the monitor screen:

Night Vision: Intended for use in very low light conditions this option sets a high ISO value and produces a black-and-white image. Expect the image to exhibit a noticeable level of electronic noise due to the high ISO sensitivity setting, but this is intentional as it adds ambiance to the picture. Autofocus is only available when using this mode from

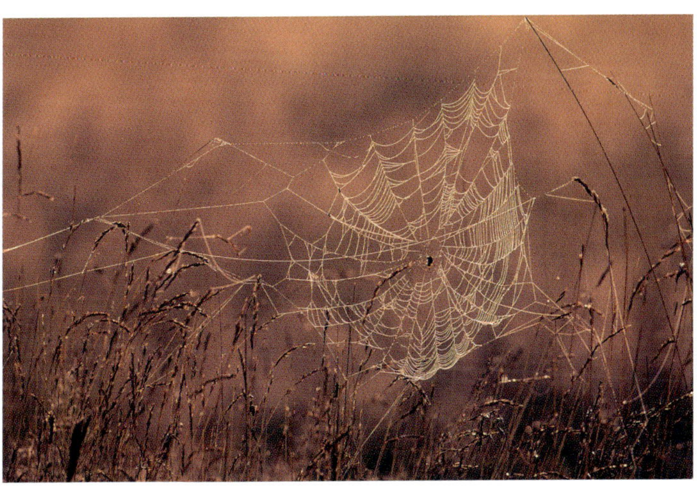

^ Here, the Dusk/Dawn Scene mode has helped to retain the natural warmth of the early morning light.

Live View; otherwise it is necessary to focus manually if shooting via the optical viewfinder. Use of a tripod is recommended, as shutter speeds are likely to be very slow. Flash and the AF-Assist lamp are set to Off to preserve the atmosphere of the scene.

Color Sketch: The camera analyzes the detail in the scene, detecting edges between distinct colors or tones, before enhancing those edges to make them more prominent while also adjusting the color rendition to create the appearance of a hand-drawn color sketch. The definition of the edges and intensity of the color rendition can be adjusted within a limited range from within Live View, but the effects are applied in both viewfinder and Live View shooting. The high level of in-camera processing results in a significant reduction when shooting in Continuous release mode, while the refresh rate of the monitor screen in Live View is noticeably slower compared with normal Live View operation. If you record video in this mode with the D-Movie function it will playback as with stop-motion effect, as the video comprises a series of stills pictures. Autofocus does not operate during video recording.

Miniature Effect: Simulating the effect of using tilt movements on a tilt/shift lens, this option alters the focus characteristics so that only a very narrow portion of the image appears to be in focus, which creates the appearance of looking at a model (miniature) of the scene. It works best when shooting from a high camera position to give an elevated view of the scene. Settings for the orientation and size of the focus zone are set from within Live View, but the effects are applied in both viewfinder and Live View shooting. The high level of in-camera processing results in a significant reduction in frame rate when shooting in Continuous release mode, while the refresh rate of the monitor in Live View is noticeably slower compared with normal Live View operation. When using D-Movie mode, recordings are played back at high-speed, sound is not recorded, and autofocus does not operate. Use of a tripod is recommended to ensure the plane of focus remains fixed at one specific point in the scene. Flash and the AF-Assist lamp are set to off to preserve the atmosphere of the scene.

Selective Color: Up to three separate colors in the scene can be selected, so that only the chosen color(s) appear in the image, while the rest of the picture is rendered in black-and-white. The colors are selected from within Live View, but the effects are applied in both viewfinder and Live View shooting. Flash is set to off.

Silhouette: Very similar to except the Active D-Lighting is switched off to prevent the camera from adjusting the highlight and shadow tones to ensure the maximum silhouette effect between a bright background and dark subject.

High Key: Exposure is biased to provide a very full exposure to make light tones appear very bright; it is best suited to scenes filled with very light tones in good lighting conditions.

Low Key: Exposure is biased to provide a very restrained exposure to make dark tones appear very dense and preserve detail in bright highlights; it best suited to scenes filled with very dark tones lit by high contrast lighting.

AUTO, FLASH OFF, SCENE, AND EFFECTS MODE DEFAULT SETTINGS

MODE / CONTROL	WHITE BALANCE	PICTURE CONTROL	FLASH MODE [1]	ACTIVE D-LIGHTING	AF-AREA MODE
AUTO	Auto	Standard	Auto	Auto	Auto Area
FLASH OFF	Auto	Standard	Flash off	Auto	Auto Area
PORTRAIT	Auto	Portrait	Auto	Auto	Auto Area
LANDSCAPE	Auto	Landscape	Flash off	Auto	Auto Area
CHILD	Auto	Portrait	Auto	Auto	Auto Area
SPORT	Auto	Standard	Flash off	Auto	Dynamic Area
CLOSE-UP	Auto	Standard	Auto	Auto	Single Point
NIGHT PORTRAIT	Auto	Portrait	Auto slow	Auto	Auto Area
NIGHT LANDSCAPE	Auto	Standard	Flash off	Auto	Single Point
PARTY/INDOOR	Auto	Standard	Auto + Redeye	Auto	Auto Area
BEACH/SNOW	Auto	Landscape	Flash off	Auto	Single Point
SUNSET	Dir. Sun	Landscape	Flash off	Auto	Single Point
DAWN/DUSK	4550K	Landscape	Flash off	Auto	Single Point
PET PORTRAIT	Auto	Standard	Auto	Auto	Dynamic Area
CANDLELIGHT	4350K	Standard	Flash off	Auto	Single Point
BLOSSOM	Auto	Landscape	Flash off	Auto	Single Point
AUTUMN COLORS	Auto	Vivid	Flash off	Auto	Single Point
FOOD	Auto	Standard	Fill-flash	Auto	Single Point
NIGHT VISION	Dir. Sun	Monochrome	Flash off	Off	N/A
COLOR SKETCH	Auto	Standard	Auto	Off	Auto Area
MINIATURE EFFECT	Auto	Vivid	Flash off	Off	Single Point
SELECTIVE COLOR	Auto	Standard	Flash off	Off	Auto Area
SILHOUETTE	Auto	Landscape	Flash off	Off	Single Point
HIGH KEY	Auto	Standard	Flash off	Off	Single Point
LOW KEY	Auto	Standard	Flash off	Off	Single Point

[1] The flash mode applies to the built-in Speedlight flash unit of the D510

SELECTING SETTINGS IN EFFECTS MODES

When using the , and Effects modes, it is necessary to make the required settings from within Live View, although the modes can be used in both normal viewfinder and Live View shooting. I have set out below the procedure for adjusting these settings:

Color Sketch: Rotate the Mode dial to EFFECTS, open Live View, and turn the Command dial to display the mode. Press the button to display the **[Vividness]** and **[Outlines]** options. Press and to highlight the required option and press and to adjust its value. Increase **[Vividness]** to boost color saturation, and decrease it to produce less intense colors. Increase **[Outlines]** to make outlines appear broader and decrease it to make outlines narrower. Press the button to confirm settings and return the normal Live View display. Rotate the switch to close Live View.

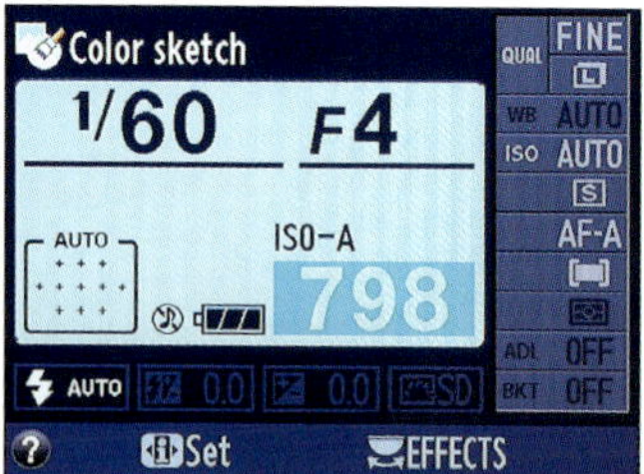

The Color Sketch mode is selected when its icon is shown at the top of the Information Display screen.

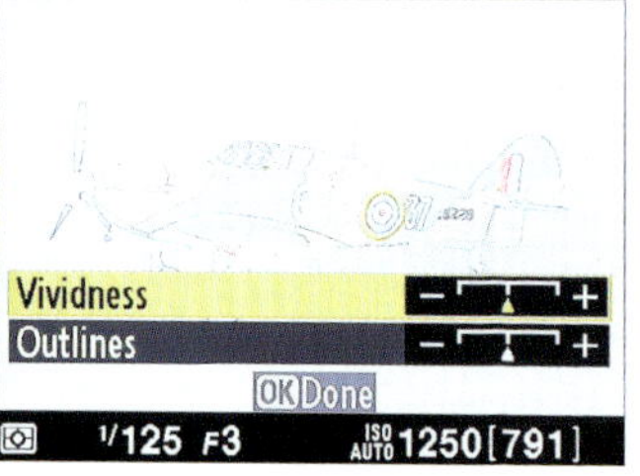

The **[Vividness]** and **[Outlines]** options are only displayed in Live View.

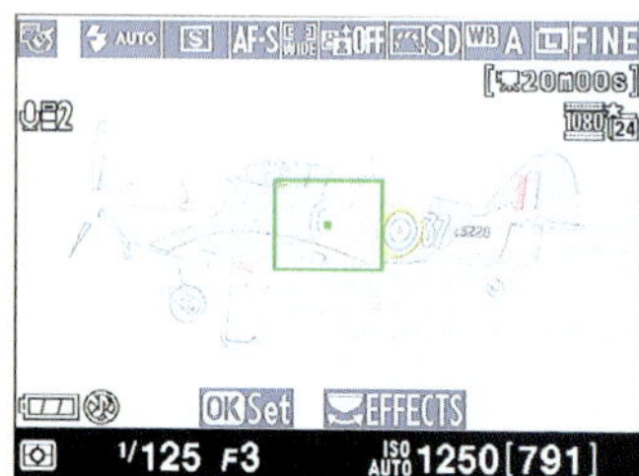

At the minimum setting for **[Vividness]** the image is almost black-and-white.

Miniature Effect: Rotate the Mode dial to EFFECTS, open Live View and turn the Command dial to display the mode. Frame the scene and shift the focus point to the area that you want to be in focus, and then press the shutter release button halfway to acquire focus (confirm the AF point turns green). Use the button to enlarge the subject to check focus and press to return to the normal, full-frame view. Press the button to display the focus zone markers (two pairs of short lines at the edge of the screen). Press ◀ and ▶ to set the orientation of the focus zone and press ▼ and ▲ to adjust its width. Press the OK button to confirm settings and return to the normal Live View display. Rotate the LV switch to close Live View.

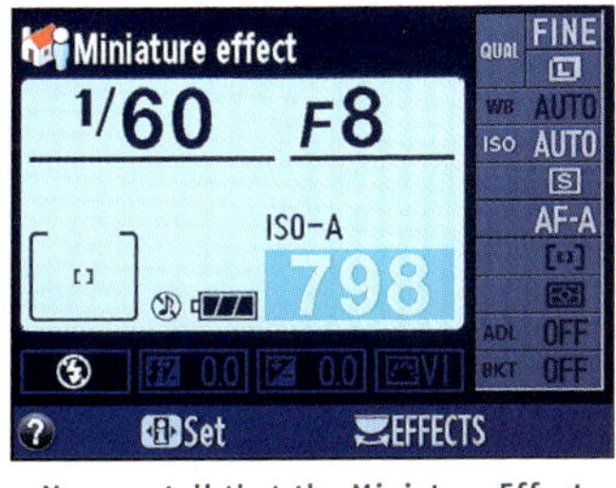

You can tell that the Miniature Effect mode is selected when its icon is shown at the top of the Information Display screen.

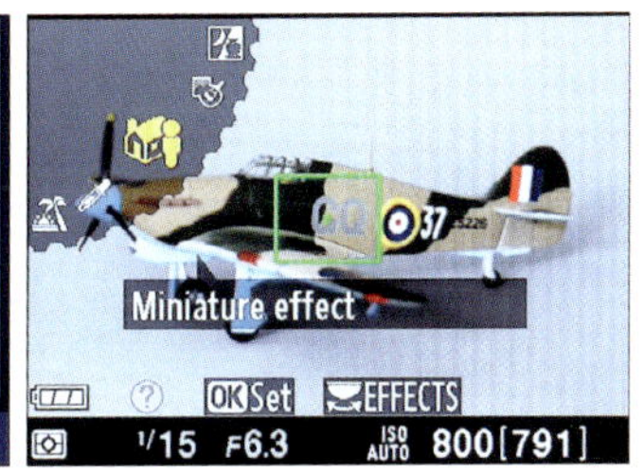

Position the AF point over the area of the subject that you require to be in focus; the focus zone markers will be aligned on this point.

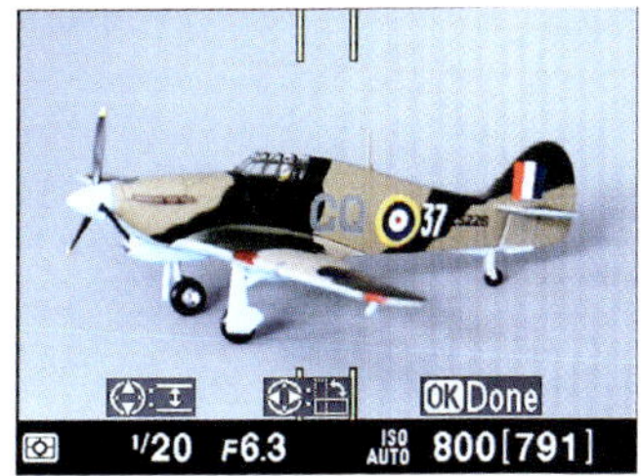

Here, the focus zone markers are set to the narrowest setting and orientated vertically, so the area of the image to the left and right of the focus zone will appear progressively out-of-focus.

Selective Color: Rotate the Mode dial to EFFECTS, open Live View, and turn the Command dial to display the mode. Press the OK button to display the color setting options. Position the small white square at the center of the screen over the first color in the scene that you wish to retain in the image and press ▲ to select it (the camera may not be able to detect weak colors). To aid selection of the color, use the zoom-in button to enlarge the central area of the scene. Press zoom-out to return to the normal, full-frame view. Press ▼ and ▲ to adjust the range of similar hues to the selected color that will be retained in the image; the value is shown next to the color box at the top of the screen (higher values increase the range of hues). Rotate the Command dial to highlight another of the color boxes and repeat the steps to select up to a maximum of three colors. To deselect a color, highlight the appropriate color box and press the delete button. Hold the delete button to delete all the selected colors. Press the OK button to confirm settings and return the normal Live View display. Rotate the LV switch to close Live View.

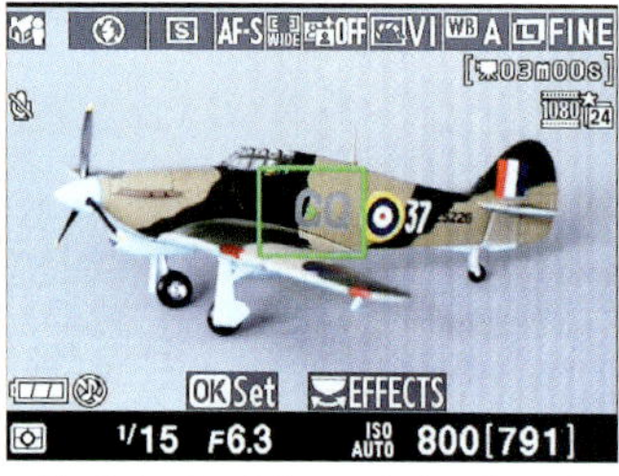

^ The Selective Color mode is selected when its icon is shown at the top of the Information Display screen.

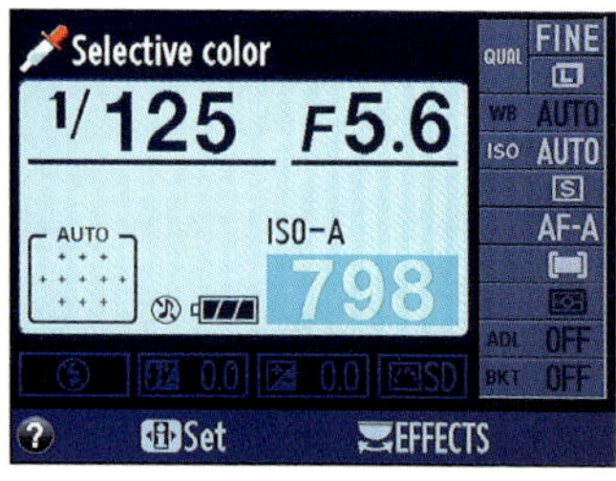

^ Here, red/orange and green colors have been selected in two of the color boxes, while the third box is clear.

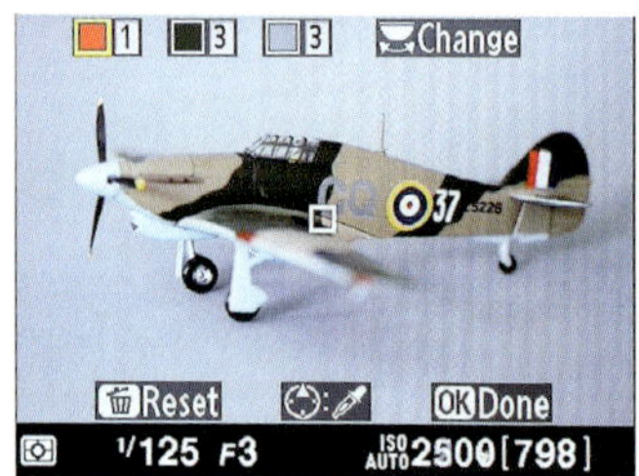

^ Here, red/orange and green colors have been selected in two of the color boxes, while the third box is clear.

P, S, A, AND M EXPOSURE MODES

The D5100 offers four further exposure modes, which are also set via the Mode dial.

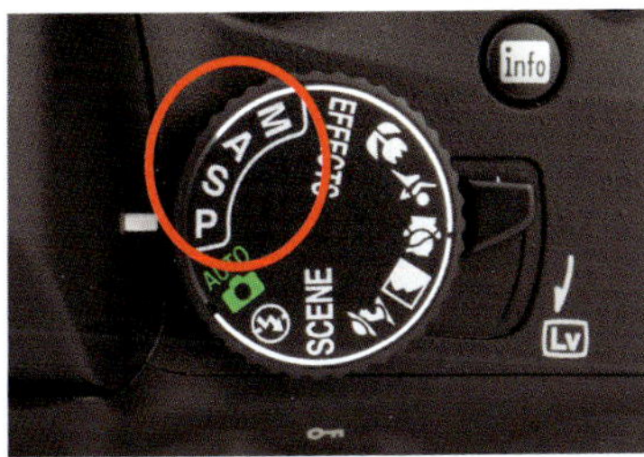

P PROGRAMMED AUTO

Programmed-Auto mode, also referred to as Program mode (P), adjusts both the shutter speed and lens aperture automatically to produce what the camera considers to be a properly exposed image, as determined by the selected metering mode. If you decide that a particular combination of the shutter speed and aperture chosen by the camera is not suitable, you can override the P mode settings by turning the Command dial while the camera's TTL metering is active. This is called Flexible Program mode and P* appears in the Information Display and the viewfinder to indicate that you have overridden the exposure from the shutter speed and aperture values selected initially by the camera. The two values change in tandem, so the overall exposure level remains the same (i.e., setting a longer shutter speed results in the size of the lens aperture being reduced); rotating the Command dial to the right sets a larger aperture (smaller f/number) and a faster shutter speed, while rotating the Command dial to the left sets a smaller aperture (larger f/number) and a slower shutter speed.

NOTE: If you override the Program mode, it will remain locked to its new settings for shutter speed and aperture even if the meter auto-powers off and is then switched on again by pressing the shutter release halfway. To cancel the override, you must do one of the following: rotate the Command dial until the asterisk * next to the P is no longer displayed, change the exposure mode, or turn the power off.

In my opinion, Program mode is little better than the point-and-shoot exposure control options of the AUTO and Scene shooting modes, as you effectively relinquish control of exposure to the camera. If you want to make informed decisions about shutter speed and aperture to achieve the most accurate exposure, regardless of the shooting conditions, or to impart your own creativity to your photography, do not use P mode!

A *APERTURE-PRIORITY AUTO*

In this mode (A), the photographer selects an aperture value (f/number) and the D5100 will choose a shutter speed to produce an appropriate exposure, as determined by the camera using the selected metering mode. The aperture is controlled by the Command dial and is changed in steps of 0.3 EV (assuming CS-b1 is set to 1/3 step). The shutter speed the D5100 selects will also change in steps of 0.3 EV.

S *SHUTTER-PRIORITY AUTO*

In this mode (S), the photographer selects a shutter speed between 30 seconds and 1/4000 second and the D5100 will choose an aperture value to produce an appropriate exposure, as determined by the camera using the selected metering mode. The shutter speed is controlled by the Command dial and is changed in steps of 0.3 EV (assuming CS-b1 is set to 1/3 step). The aperture value the D5100 selects will also change in steps of 0.3 EV.

NOTE: In P, A, and S modes, the D5100 will display ? as a warning in the viewfinder if the subject or scene is too dark; and conversely, the camera will display the ? warning if the subject or scene is too bright

---

HINT: If you use the D5100 remotely when you make an exposure (i.e., your eye is not to the viewfinder eyepiece) you must ensure the viewfinder eyepiece is covered (the DK-5 cap is supplied for this purpose). The 420-segment RGB metering sensor of the D5100 is located within the viewfinder-head; therefore, light entering via the viewfinder eyepiece will influence exposure calculations made in P, A, and S exposure modes.

M MANUAL

Manual mode (M) offers total control over exposure, and is probably the most useful if you want to learn more about the relationship between shutter speed and aperture and how they affect the final appearance of your pictures. You control both the shutter speed, via the Command dial, and lens aperture, via the Command dial plus the [+/-] button.

An analog exposure scale displayed in the Information Display and viewfinder indicates the level of exposure your settings would produce. If the camera determines the exposure values are set for a proper exposure, a single indent mark appears below the central 0 point of the scale. If the camera determines that the settings would produce an underexposed result, the degree of underexposure is indicated by the number of indent marks that appear to the right (minus) side of the central 0. Conversely, if the chosen settings would create an overexposed result, the degree of overexposure is indicated by the number of indent marks to the left (plus) side of the central 0. The more indent marks that appear, the greater the degree of deviance from the "correct" exposure, as calculated by the camera (see the illustration below).

Suggested Optimal Exposure	Underexposed by 0.3EV	Overexposed by more than 2EV
+. . 0 . .-	+. . 0 . .-	+ 0 . .-

If the **[Graphic]** option under the **[Info display format]** in the Y menu is selected for P, A, S, and M modes, the relationship between the shutter speed and aperture is shown by way of a diagram in the Information Display, as described previously, under "AUTO and Scene modes," (page 54).

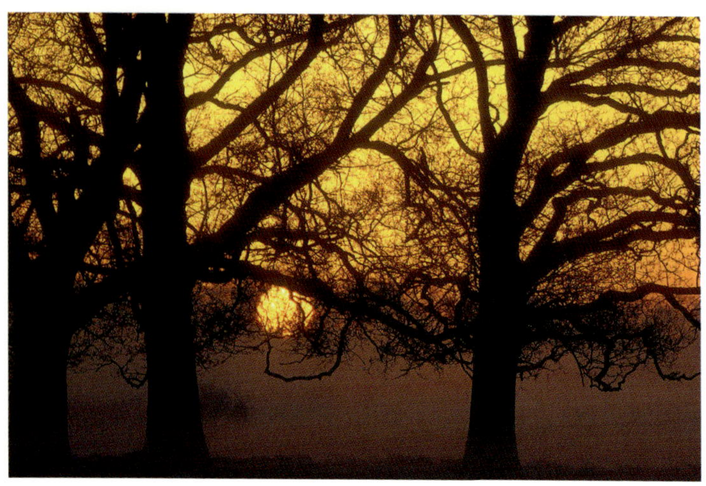

Autoexposure (AE) Lock was used here to prevent the brighter sky from causing the picture to be underexposed. A Spot meter reading was taken from the mist between the trees, and the exposure value was retained by holding down the **AE-L/AF-L** button.

LONG EXPOSURES

To shoot at exposure durations of more than 30 seconds, the D5100 has the **[Bulb]** setting and the **[Time]** option when using one of the remote control shutter release modes. These options are only available in the M exposure mode, but can be useful when shooting in very low-light conditions, or for creating special effects, such as photographing fireworks or light-trails of moving traffic at night. Using a tripod or some other form of stable camera support is essential for this type of shooting if details in the scene being photographed are to be rendered with good definition. You may also want to consider using the **[Long Exposure NR]** feature, which can be found in the Shooting menu, as electronic noise in the image tends to be more prevalent when shooting at long shutter speeds.

Select M on the Mode dial and rotate the Command dial until the shutter speed is displayed as **[Bulb]** in the viewfinder and Information Display (for 'Time,' select a Remote Control release mode after selecting **[Bulb]** as the shutter speed), focus the camera, and then press and hold the shutter release button down all the way (in a Remote Control release mode, press and release the shutter release button of the ML-L3); to end the exposure, let go of the shutter release button (in a Remote Control release mode, press the shutter release button of the ML-L3 again). To prevent jarring the camera while holding down the shutter release button at a shutter speed of Bulb, use of the optional accessory Nikon MC-DC2 remote release cable is recommended, as it is possible to lock its shutter release button. The maximum duration of any single exposure is 30 minutes.

AUTOEXPOSURE (AE) LOCK

If you take a meter reading in any of the three automated exposure modes (P, A, or S) and recompose the picture after taking a reading, it is likely, particularly with Spot metering, that the metered area will now fall on a different part of the scene and probably produce a different exposure value. The D5100 allows you to lock the initial exposure reading in Center-Weighted or Spot metering before you reframe and shoot (note this feature is less effective for Matrix metering, because Matrix metering assesses the entire frame area and the range of contrast within it, as well as the level of overall scene brightness to produce the most balanced exposure).

Start by positioning the part of the scene you want to meter within the appropriate metering area. Next, press the shutter release halfway to acquire focus and an exposure reading, then press and hold the **AE-L/AF-L** button to lock the exposure (and focus, except in Manual focus mode). You can now recompose and take the picture at the metered value. The **AE-L** icon will appear in the viewfinder display while this function is active. If the **[AE Lock hold]** option is assigned to the **AE-L/AF-L** button using CS-f1 in the Custom Settings menu, pressing the **AE-L/AF-L** button locks the exposure level until the button is pressed again.

It is also possible to adjust the shutter speed/aperture, depending on which exposure mode is selected, to set a different combination of settings while retaining the same overall exposure level. For example, if the initial settings were 1/250 second and f/5.6 in A mode, the aperture value could be set to f/8 by rotating the Command dial and the camera will alter the shutter speed, automatically, to 1/125.

HINT: It is also possible to use the shutter release button to lock the exposure level; select **[On]** under CS-c1 **[Shutter-release button AE-L]** in the Custom Settings menu.

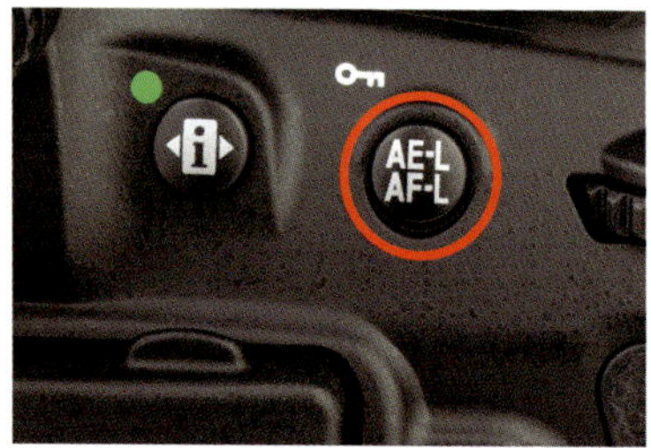

EXPOSURE COMPENSATION

Exposure Compensation can be applied regardless of the TTL metering option in use, but the most consistent results are achieved with either Center-Weighted or Spot metering. As mentioned previously, in these latter two metering options, the D5100 uses simple grayscale metering with no color information or influence of the Scene Recognition System to affect the metered reading. Working on the assumption that the camera is pointed at a scene with a reflectivity that averages out to that of a midtone, it appears Nikon has calibrated the TTL metering of the D5100 against a reference that has a reflectivity value of approximately 15% to 18%. Hence, if you use an 18% gray photographic card to estimate exposure, you should find your results are properly exposed.

Many scenes you encounter will not reflect 15% to 18% of the light falling on them. For example, a landscape under a blanket of fresh snowfall is going to reflect far more light, while an animal with a coat of dark brown or black fur will reflect less than an average midtone. Unless you compensate your exposure accordingly for these extremes, the camera will attempt to render them as midtones, causing a light tone to appear underexposed and a dark tone to be overexposed.

To set an Exposure Compensation factor in P, A, and S exposure modes (it is disabled in AUTO Scene and Effects shooting modes), hold down the button, located to the rear and right of the shutter release button, and turn the Command dial until the required value is shown in the Information Display and viewfinder. Compensation can be set to values between -5 EV and +5 EV in steps of 0.3EV (assuming CS-b1 is set to 1/3 step). The value is also displayed in the viewfinder while the button is held down. Exposure Compensation can also be set via the Information Display, where the level of any compensation applied will be shown. The icon remains visible in the viewfinder, as a reminder that you have an Exposure Compensation value applied. Once you have set a compensation factor, it will remain locked until you hold down the button and reset the compensation value to 0.0.

In M exposure mode, the exposure is set according to the values selected by the user for the shutter speed and aperture; if the analog display shows no deviance to either side of the 0 midpoint, the TTL metering system is suggesting the settings will produce a proper exposure level. This may not be the case, or the "correct" exposure may not be to your liking, so to compensate the exposure level in M mode, adjust either the shutter speed and/or the aperture value, so the display shows one or more indent marks on the analog scale, either to the right (positive compensation), or left (negative compensation) of the 0 midpoint, according to the amount of adjustment that is applied.

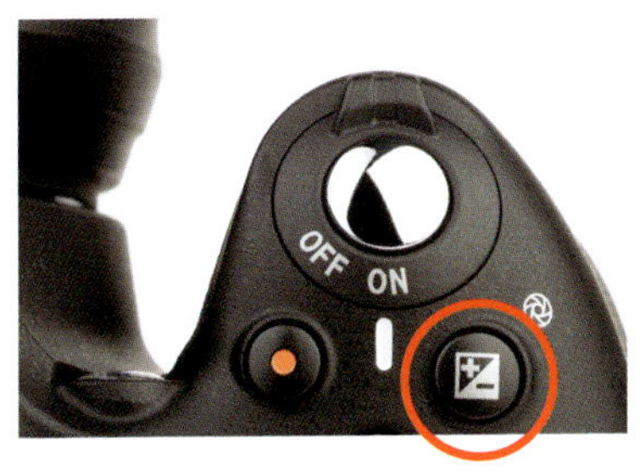

EXPOSURE CONSIDERATIONS

If the D5100 is your first DSLR camera, and your previous photography has been with color negative film, you may find controlling exposure with the camera more demanding. Color negative (print) film is very tolerant to exposure errors, particularly overexposure, and the processing machines used to produce your prints are capable of correcting exposure errors over a range of –2 to +3 EV while adjusting color balance at the same time. Chances are that you will never have noticed your exposure errors when looking at the finished prints!

Controlling exposure with a DSLR is analogous to shooting slide film—there is virtually no margin for error. Even moderate overexposure will "blow out" highlight detail, leaving no usable image data in these areas. Underexposure is no better, since it gives rise to electronic noise, which will degrade image quality, particularly in areas of dark tone, by producing a grainy texture and some blotchiness in colors. To help assess the accuracy of an exposure, make sure you check the histogram and pay attention to all three color channels, not just the luminance histogram, which is displayed in white. There are other aspects to the selection of shutter speed and lens aperture to keep in mind beyond just exposure, such as attaining acceptable image sharpness when shooting with a handheld camera or photographing a moving subject, and the effect of aperture settings on depth of field.

DIGITAL INFRARED AND UV PHOTOGRAPHY

Many digital cameras have the ability to record light beyond the visible spectrum, particularly in the region of near-infrared (IR), around a wavelength of 780nm (one nanometer = one millionth of a millimeter). Designers of digital cameras work hard to exclude IR light from digital cameras because it adversely affects sharpness, reduces contrast in skies, and can reveal unappealing features of skin that would otherwise not be visible. Similar adverse effects occur due to UV light. The low-pass filter array in front of the CMOS sensor in the D5100 includes a layer designed to reduce the transmission of IR and UV light. It is very effective, and therefore, the D5100 cannot be recommended for either IR or UV light photography.

THE AUTOFOCUS SYSTEM

The autofocus (AF) system of the D5100 includes a 3D-Tracking capability made possible by the innovative Scene Recognition System (SRS) that has won wide acclaim in other recent Nikon DSLR camera models. However, the implementation of the 3D-Tracking in the D5100 is a little different from most of those models, with the exception of the Nikon D3100, since the camera has only eleven AF points. Therefore, less of the autofocus area (the total area of the frame covered by the AF points) provides focus information. The D5100 has fewer focus sampling points with its Multi-CAM1000 AF module compared with higher-specified Nikon models that have up to 3.5 times as many. And finally, the processing power of the D5100 is considerably lower compared with these other models. Hence, Nikon promotes the abilities of the 3D-Tracking in the D5100 as being best-suited to rapid changes of composition where the camera to subject distance does not alter significantly between consecutive exposures, rather than trying to keep pace with a subject that is moving rapidly toward or away from the camera, particularly if that movement is erratic in both its speed and direction.

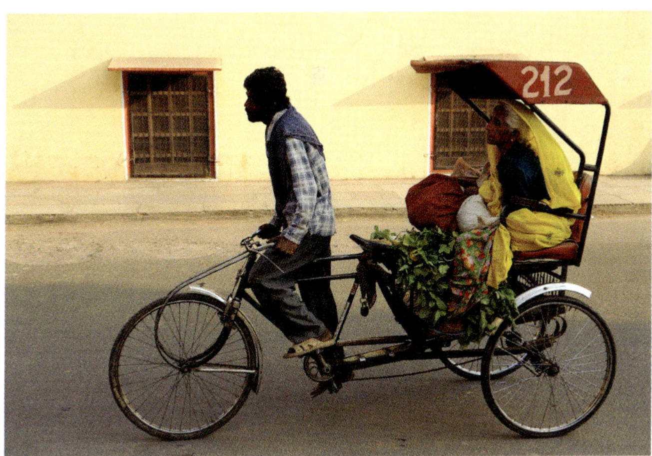

For this photo, a combination of AF-C (Continuous-Servo) AF mode and Dynamic-Area AF-Area mode enabled the camera to maintain focus as the subjects moved through the scene.

THE AUTOFOCUS SENSOR

The Multi-CAM 1000 AF module has—as its name implies—a total of 1000 photodiodes distributed between the 11 AF points. The 11 points are subdivided into one cross-type sensor at the center of the frame and ten line-type sensors; the latter are oriented in a variety of directions (see the diagrams on the next page).

When autofocus operation is initiated, the D5100 uses a phase-detection focusing method; the system uses a beam splitter comprising two optical prisms in a small semi-transparent area of the main-reflex mirror that capture the light rays coming from the opposite sides of the lens. They are coupled with a small secondary mirror located behind the main mirror that directs the light from these prisms to the Multi-Cam 1000 module, which is located in the base of the mirror box at the bottom of the camera. The double image projected onto the AF module is then analyzed for the patterns of light intensity and the phase difference between them and calculated to determine whether the subject is in front of or behind the current plane of focus. This not only informs the AF system which way the focus must be adjusted, but also by how much. The focus point is adjusted immediately and the phase difference checked; provided it is within the tolerances of the AF system, focus will not be altered again.

The central AF point is a cross-type, meaning it is sensitive to detail in both horizontal and vertical orientations; therefore, it is the most reliable AF point. The remaining ten points are line-types; these are generally only sensitive to detail in a direction that is perpendicular to their orientation, for example, with the camera held horizontally, the two AF points farthest to the left and right of the frame generally only detect detail aligned with the long edge of the viewfinder frame. An innovation in the D5100 is the diagonal alignment of some of the AF points; in previous cameras (except the D3100), the line-type sensors are aligned with either the long or short edges of the frame. In some shooting situations, where the line-type sensor aligns with a straight edge in the scene being photographed like a horizon line or the side of a building, the AF system can have difficulty in acquiring focus, whereas a diagonally aligned AF sensor is more likely to detect such an edge. It is also important to understand that the coverage of the AF point extends some way beyond the area covered by the markings for each shown on the focusing screen.

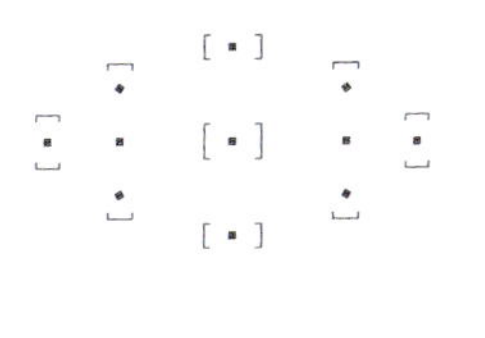

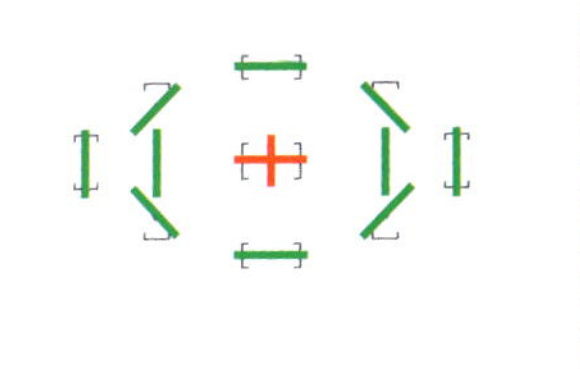

The approximate coverage of the 11 AF points. In each case, the coverage extends farther than the area defined by the small squares and square brackets marked on the focusing screen. The central AF point is a cross-type sensor (red), while the remaining ten (green) are line-type sensors (the colors are purely for illustrative purposes).

HINT: Sometimes when using one of the line-type sensing areas, the autofocus system of the D5100 will "hunt" (i.e., the camera will drive the focus of the lens back and forth, but is unable to attain focus). This indicates that the detail in the subject is aligned in the same orientation as the focus sensing area of the active AF point, and thus there is insufficient contrast in the subject for the AF system to acquire focus. If this occurs, try twisting the camera slightly (10 – 15°). This slight adjustment is often enough to allow the camera to acquire focus, as the focus sensing area can detect more contrast in the detail of the subject. Once focus is confirmed, lock it and recompose the picture before releasing the shutter.

The AF point you select in either Single-Point AF or Dynamic-Area AF can have a profound effect on the camera's ability to achieve autofocus, depending on whether it is a cross- or a line-type. For example, the single cross-type sensor at the center of the frame is far more reliable in low-light or low-contrast conditions compared with the line-type sensors, which can often take longer (or even fail) to acquire focus in such conditions.

HINT: The AF system is designed to work with any Nikkor AF lens that has a maximum aperture of f/5.6, or larger (lower f/number). If an accessory, such as a teleconverter or extension tube is used with the lens and reduces its effective maximum aperture to less than f/5.6, autofocus operation is likely to become slower and less reliable.

SCENE RECOGNITION SYSTEM

The autofocus system of the D5100 also benefits from the capabilities of Nikon's Scene Recognition System (SRS). This has enhanced the abilities of the 420-pixel, RGB-metering sensor, as described in the metering section (see page 50). It enables the 420-pixel sensor to recognize a subject by its shape, size, and color. To employ the benefits of the SRS, it is necessary to use a D- or G-type Nikkor lens. The SRS requires the focus distance information these lenses provide to perform the necessary calculations in order for its two principal features, subject identification and subject tracking, to function. The system brings significant benefits to the performance of the autofocus system, as well as improving the autoexposure and Auto White Balance functions.

The SRS is optimized to recognize skin tones, particularly in any area on the 420-segment RGB sensor that relates to the average size of a human face; this is why the focus data from a D- or G-type lens is essential, as the camera calculates the size of the area on the 420-segment RGB sensor based on the distance information supplied by the lens. To the human eye, the range of skin tones can look noticeably different; however, a metering system that uses a red-green-blue sensor does not "see" in the same way, and skin tones all appear very similar to such a system. An example of how this improves the autofocus can be seen in how this subject identification information is used in the Auto-Area AF mode to assist the D5100 in focusing on people in a scene. The subject identification is also used in the 3D-Tracking (11 points) mode to enhance tracking a subject moving laterally across the frame. In very simple terms, once the camera has acquired focus initially, it monitors the location of the pattern of pixels on the 420-segment RGB sensor created by the shape and color distribution of the subject (i.e., the subject identification information based on subject color and contrast) to determine the position of the subject in the frame. This mapping of the subject by the 420-segment RGB sensor is combined with the focus tracking information from the Multi-CAM 1000 autofocus sensor module, enabling the AF system to predict with speed and precision which AF point(s) to use to maintain focus.

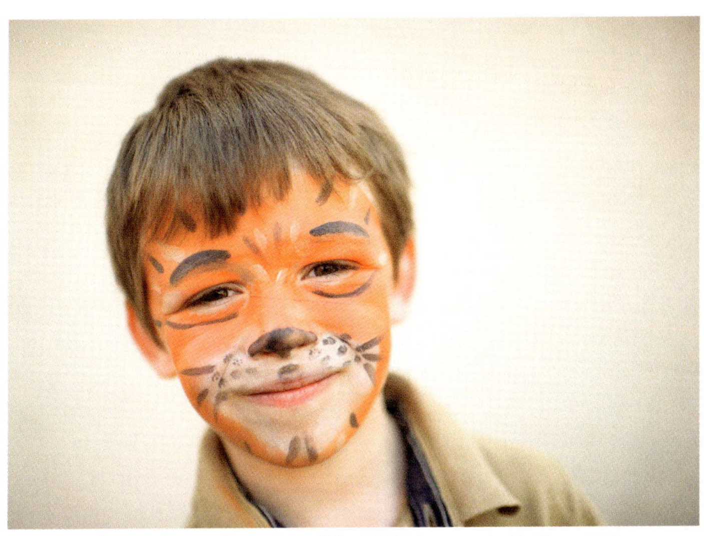

The 3D Color Matrix metering system of the D5100 is supported by D- and G-type Nikkor lenses only. These lenses contain an electronic chip that communicated lens and focus information to the camera.

Remarkably, the 420-segment RGB sensor's subject mapping, which covers virtually the entire frame area, continues to operate if the subject moves momentarily outside the area covered by the 11 AF points; as soon as the subject returns to the area within the AF points, autofocus resumes, even if the subject is at a different location within the area covered by the 11 AF points from the one it occupied immediately before it left the area (note that if the subject moves completely outside the frame area, so it is no longer visible in the viewfinder/monitor, it will be necessary to re-acquire focus). This combined tracking of the subject by the AF sensor and the 420-segment RGB metering sensor is only used in the Auto-Area and 3D-Tracking AF-Area modes. Although far from foolproof (the Auto-Area tends to be more reliable than 3D-Tracking), this system can produce quite amazing results and certainly offer a very advanced form of focus tracking.

The 3D-Tracking (11 points) mode differs from the Dynamic-Area AF mode because the camera automatically selects the active focus point as soon as focus is acquired even if the camera and/or subject move relative to one another. This enables focus to be maintained while rapid and significant changes in composition are made, because it is no longer necessary to maintain tracking by keeping the selected AF-point over the subject, which is necessary except for brief lapses in the Dynamic-Area AF mode.

However, when Dynamic-Area AF is selected, the D5100 only uses its Multi-CAM 1000 AF sensor to perform normal focus tracking (i.e., following a subject as it travels toward or away from the camera). Essentially, the camera reverts to the established AF system used by earlier Nikon DSLR cameras. In some situations, this can be an advantage, since the camera has far fewer computations to perform compared with the 3D-Tracking option; therefore, the AF response is faster. This option will be more reliable when shooting some types of moving subjects under artificial light, where the light source is non-white (e.g., some types of fluorescent and mercury-vapor lighting), as this affects the ability of the 420-segment RGB sensor to detect skin tones, which renders the SRS less effective, which in turn will impinge on the performance of the Auto-Area AF and 3D-Tracking (11-point) AF.

FOCUS MODES

The D5100 has three principal methods of focusing when you shoot still pictures (the focusing options when using Live View or recording video in the D-Movie mode are dealt with on pages 134-137), known as focusing modes: AF-S (Single-Servo AF), AF-C (Continuous-Servo AF), and Manual focus (M). A fourth option AF-A (Auto-Servo AF), which is the default setting, leaves the camera to automatically select either AF-S, if it determines the subject is stationary, or AF-C if the camera detects the subject is moving. To set the AF mode, press the info button to open the Information Display, and then press the i button. Place the highlighted cursor on the current AF mode and press OK. Use ▼ and ▲ to selected the required option and then press OK.

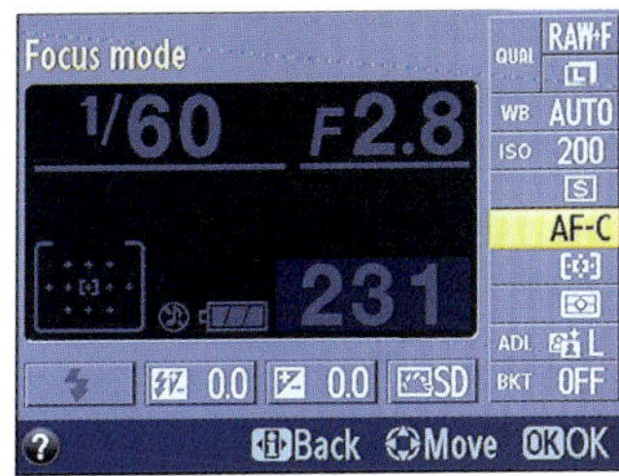

^ The focus mode in use is highlighted in the Information Display. Here, AF-C (Continuous-Servo AF) is selected currently.

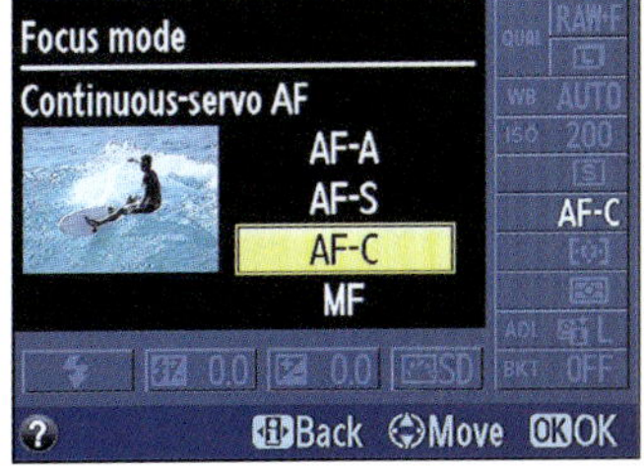

^ Once you press OK, you will see the four focus modes options.

AF-A Auto-Servo (default setting): In an attempt to remove the burden of choosing which of the two principal autofocus modes (AF-S and AF-C) you should use, Nikon developed this option. In AF-A mode, the D5100 assesses the focus information and selects either AF-S or AF-C mode, depending on whether the camera determines that the subject is stationary or moving. More often than not, the AF-A option will select the appropriate AF mode, but if it makes the wrong choice, the result can spell disaster for your photos! In my opinion, the fully automated nature of the AF-A option simply does not provide sufficient reliability for correct autofocus-mode selection. I recommend you select the specific AF mode you require, based on the nature of the subject being photographed.

AF-S Single-Servo AF: As soon as the shutter release button is pressed down halfway, the D5100 focuses the lens. The shutter can only be released once focus has been acquired and the In-Focus indicator ● is displayed in the viewfinder. Focus will remain locked while the shutter release button is depressed halfway. No form of focus tracking is performed when the camera is set to AF-S; therefore, this mode should be used when the camera-to-subject distance will remain constant (i.e., the subject is not moving).

AF-C Continuous-Servo AF: The D5100 focuses the lens continuously while the shutter release button is pressed down halfway. If the camera-to-subject distance changes (i.e., the subject begins to move), the camera will initiate Predictive Focus Tracking in order to shift focus as it follows the subject. This mode monitors focus constantly, so it does not matter whether the subject continues to move or stops and starts periodically; the camera will continue to focus until either the shutter is released or you remove your finger from the shutter release button.

M Manual Focus: You must rotate the focusing ring of the lens to achieve focus. There is no restriction on when the shutter can be released. When using a lens with a maximum aperture of f/5.6 or larger, the electronic rangefinder feature will display the In-Focus confirmation signal ● when focus is achieved. This confirmation can be particularly useful in low-light or low-contrast conditions.

NOTE: If the lens you are using has a switch that allows you to select an M/A (manual/autofocus) mode on the lens, you need only to touch the focusing ring to disengage AF and the lens can then be focused manually. The camera will resume autofocus operation as soon as you release the focusing ring and press the shutter release button halfway.

SINGLE-SERVO VS. CONTINUOUS-SERVO

It is important that you appreciate the fundamental difference between the Single-Servo AF (AF-S) and Continuous-Servo AF (AF-C) modes. In Single-Servo AF (AF-S), the shutter cannot be released until focus has been acquired; Nikon refers to this mode as having "focus priority." Once focus is acquired in this mode, the focus distance is locked as long as the shutter release button is pressed down halfway. In most shooting conditions, particularly in good light, the delay in acquiring focus is so brief that it is not perceptible and it is has no practical consequence. However, under certain conditions, such as low light or low contrast, there can be a discernable lag between pressing the shutter release button and the shutter opening. This is because it generally takes longer for the camera to establish focus in these circumstances, particularly if one of the outer, line-type AF sensing areas is used. Conversely, in Continuous-Servo AF (AF-C), the camera monitors focus constantly even after focus is acquired—as long as the shutter release button is held down halfway or the **AE-L/AF-L** button is pressed when it is set is perform the **[AF-ON]** role (selected via CS-f2 **[Assign AE-L/AF-L button]** item in the Custom Settings menu)—and will shift the point of focus accordingly if the camera-to-subject distance alters. The shutter will operate immediately when you press the shutter release button all the way down, regardless of whether focus has been achieved; Nikon refers to this mode as having "release priority" (it is possible to set AF-C to "focus priority" via CS-a1 **[AF-C priority selection]**)

Some photographers mistakenly assume that if the shutter is released before the camera has attained focus in the AF-C mode, the picture will always be out of focus. In fact, the combination of constant focus monitoring and Predictive Focus Tracking engaged when the camera detects a moving subject in this mode is normally successful in causing the focus point to be shifted within the split-second delay between the reflex mirror lifting and the shutter opening, resulting in a sharp picture. Even if the camera's calculations are slightly off, the depth of field of the image often masks minor focusing errors. That said, to maximize AF performance while using AF-C to photograph a moving subject, it is imperative that the camera is given sufficient time to assimilate information to perform the focusing action. To achieve this, press and hold the shutter release button halfway down as long as possible before releasing the shutter to make the exposure. You may prefer to use the **AE-L/AF-L** button in its **[AF-ON]** role, as you can then use it to activate autofocus and concentrate on timing the exposure by pressing the shutter release when required.

PREDICTIVE FOCUS TRACKING

Whenever the shutter release is pressed all the way down to activate the shutter mechanism, there is a very short delay between the reflex mirror lifting out of the light path to the camera's sensor and the shutter actually opening. If a subject is moving toward or away from the camera, the camera-to-subject distance will change during this delay. In Continuous-Servo AF-C mode, the D5100 uses its Predictive Tracking system to shift the point of focus on the lens to compensate for this change in camera-to-subject distance; regardless of whether the subject is moving at a constant speed, is accelerating or decelerating. Predictive Focus Tracking is always initiated when the camera detects the camera-to-subject distance is changing (i.e., the subject is moving toward or away from the camera) while the shutter release is held down halfway or the **AE-L/AF-L** button is pressed when it is set is perform the **[AF-ON]** role, regardless of whether this occurs while the camera is establishing focus, or if it detects that the subject moves after focus is first acquired.

USING TRAP FOCUS

It is possible to use the functionality of the focus system in the D5100 to perform the "trap focus" technique. Trap focus allows the camera to be pre-focused at a specific point and have the shutter released automatically as soon as a subject passes through the area. If you can accurately predict the path of the subject, this technique can be very effective.

The following steps will enable you to set up the D5100 for trap focusing:

1. Select **[AF ON]** for CS-f2 **[Assign AE-L/AF-L button]** item in the Custom Settings menu, so that focusing is only performed when the **AE-L/AF-L** button is pressed, not when the shutter release button is pressed down halfway.
2. Select AF-S (Single-Servo AF) focus mode.
3. Select Single-Point as the autofocus area mode (see below). If the lens you are using has a focus mode switch on it, set it to A or M/A.

Pre-focus the lens on a point that is the same distance from the camera as the point the subject will pass through by aligning it with the selected autofocus sensing area and pushing the **AE-L/AF-L** button. Once focus is acquired, release the **AE-L/AF-L** button (focus is now locked at that distance). Re-compose the picture so the selected AF point covers the point you expect the subject to pass through. Now, fully depress and hold the shutter release button down (this is necessary to keep the camera activated and enable the shutter to be released as soon as focus is detected—remember the camera is set to AF-S focus mode). Using the locking shutter release button of the optional MC-DC2 remote release cable makes this task much easier than holding down the camera's shutter release button. When the subject enters the space covered by the selected AF point, the camera will detect focus and the shutter will automatically be released.

AUTOFOCUS AREA MODES

The D5100 has four Autofocus-Area modes (not to be confused with the three autofocus modes described above) that determine how the 11 AF points will be used: Single-Point AF, Dynamic-Area AF, Auto-Area AF, and 3D-Tracking (11 points); the 3D-Tracking (11 points) is only available when the AF mode is set to AF-C or AF-A.

To select the AF-Area mode, press the info button to open the Information Display, and then press the i button. Place the highlighted cursor on the current AF-Area mode and press OK. Use ▼ and ▲ to selected the desired option and then press OK.

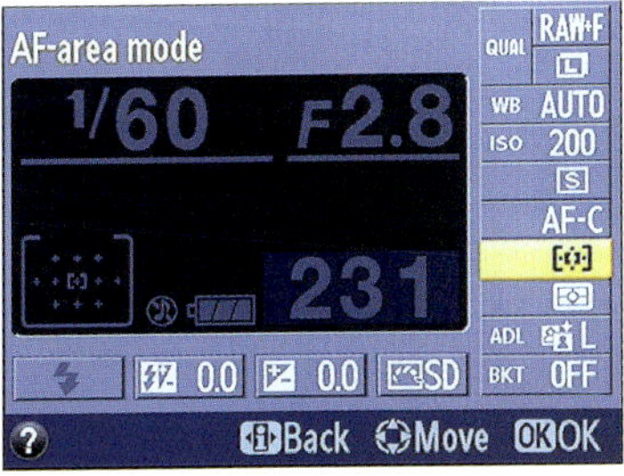

[ ] Single-Point AF: The D5100 uses only the one AF point that you selected with the Multi Selector button. The camera takes no part in choosing which AF point is used. The selected AF point is shown in the Information Display. The selected AF point is highlighted for approximately 1 second.

[·:·] **Dynamic-Area AF:** In AF-A and AF-C, the D5100 uses the user-selected AF point for focusing. However, if the subject leaves the area covered by this AF point briefly, the camera immediately evaluates information from the other surrounding AF points and will attempt to maintain focus using these AF points as needed until the originally selected AF point covers the subject. The area selected initially is highlighted in the viewfinder and Information Display where it remains highlighted, even if another AF point is used to momentarily maintain focus. In AF-S mode, the camera only uses the single AF point that you selected for autofocus; therefore there is no benefit in selecting this AF-Area mode when the camera is set to AF-S autofocus mode. The selected AF point is highlighted for approximately one second.

[■] **Auto-Area AF:** The D5100 selects the AF point(s) automatically, in all three AF focus modes, using information from the Multi-CAM 1000 autofocus module. If a D- or G-type Nikkor lens is used, the subject identification information based on the color and contrast pattern of the subject as established by the Scene Recognition System, will also be used to map the position of the subject within the frame. Generally, the camera will set focus on what it determines to be the subject closest to it. This system is particularly adept at identifying skin tones and is, therefore, very useful when photographing people. The active AF point(s) is/are highlighted for approximately one second.

[3D] **3D-Tracking (11 points):** In AF-A and AF-C, the D5100 uses the user-selected AF point for focusing. Operation is similar to the Auto-Area AF mode insomuch as, when shooting with a D- or G-type Nikkor lens, the subject identification information based on the color and contrast pattern of the subject as determined by the Scene Recognition System, will be used to map and track the position of the subject as its position shifts within the frame. In 3D-Tracking, however, the highlighting of the AF point changes according to which AF point is active as the focusing system follows the subject, even if there is a significant change from the original composition. You will always know which AF point the camera is using because the active AF point blinks. If the subject moves outside of the frame area while the AF system attempts to follow it, the 3D-Tracking will not resume when the subject reappears inside the frame area, so it is necessary to lift your finger off the shutter release button, recompose the picture and use the AF point selected originally.

NOTE: I recommend that the 3D-Tracking (11 points) AF area mode is most appropriate for subjects that remain at or close to a constant distance from the camera.

SELECTING AN AUTOFOCUS POINT

In Single-Point AF, Dynamic-Area AF, or 3D-Tracking (11 points) AF, the AF point that the D5100 will initially use to acquire focus must be selected manually by pressing the Multi Selector button. In the viewfinder and in the Information Display, the selected AF point will be shown highlighted in red for approximately one second. The center AF point can be selected by pressing the ⓞ button at the center of the Multi Selector.

The D5100 lacks a locking mechanism on the Multi Selector to prevent unintentional selection of an alternative AF point; I have found this to be a weak point in its design, as all too often while holding the camera, the heel of my right thumb will press the Multi Selector inadvertently and shift the AF point selection. Make sure you check the position of the selected AF point before you shoot!

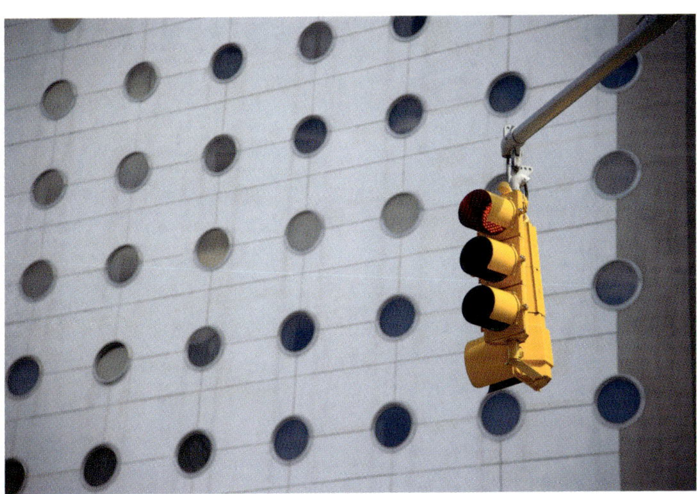

^ Here, I used Single-Point AF because the subject was static; I selected an AF point to the right side of the frame and placed it over the red light.

FOCUS MODE AND AF-AREA MODE OVERVIEW

If you are new to Nikon's AF system, it will probably take a while to get used to the functionality of the Focus Mode and Focus Area Mode options of the D5100. Therefore, you may wish to re-read the sections above and refer to the following table that summarizes the various autofocus operations.

AF MODE	AF-AREA MODE	SELECTION OF FOCUS AREA
Manual	Single-Point AF	User
AF-S (Single-Servo)	Single-Point AF	User
AF-S (Single-Servo)	Dynamic-Area AF	User [1]
AF-S (Single-Servo)	Auto-Area AF	Camera
AF-C (Continuous-Servo)	Single-Point AF	User
AF-C (Continuous-Servo)	Dynamic-Area AF	User [3, 4]
AF-C (Continuous-Servo)	Auto-Area AF	Camera [2, 3]
AF-C (Continuous-Servo)	3D-Tracking (11 point)	User [4]

1 Only the selected AF point is used; camera makes no reference to other AF points

2 Active focus point(s) is not displayed.

3 Camera will use an alternative AF point if the subject momentarily leaves the selected AF point.

4 Camera will shift focus to an alternative AF point if the composition is altered; the subject is tracked automatically, based on color and contrast pattern information.

As you change from Single-Point to Dynamic-Area to Auto-Area to 3D-Tracking (11 points), you relinquish more control to the camera in the selection of the AF point; therefore, consider the most appropriate option based on the nature of the subject you are photographing and whether or not it is moving. For static subjects, use AF-S (Single-Servo) with Single-Point AF-Area mode. For subjects that move in a predictable direction, use AF-C (Continuous-Servo) with Dynamic-Area AF. And, when photographing a subject that moves in an unpredictable manner, or when you need to recompose the picture rapidly while maintaining focus, use AF-C (Continuous-Servo) with 3D-Tracking (11 points). Finally, for point-and-shoot style photography, especially with people in the scene, consider using AF-C (Continuous-Servo) with Auto-Area AF. Remember, a D- or G-type Nikkor lens is necessary to make the most of the 3D-Tracking (11 points) and Auto-Area options.

FOCUS LOCK

Once the D5100 has acquired focus, it is possible to lock the autofocus system so the shot can be recomposed and the original focus distance will be retained, even if an AF point no longer covers the subject.

In Single-Servo AF, pressing the shutter release button halfway will activate autofocus. As soon as focus is acquired, the In-Focus indicator ● is displayed in the viewfinder and focus is locked and will remain locked while the shutter release button is held halfway down. Alternatively, press and hold the **AE-L/AF-L** button to lock focus—it is then no longer necessary to keep the shutter button pressed down halfway (an appropriate AF lock option must be selected under CS-f2)

NOTE: If CS-f2 **[Assign AE-L/AF-L button]** in the Custom Settings menu is set to **[AE/AF lock]**, its default option, pressing the **AE-L/AF-L** button will lock both exposure and focus. You may wish to consider selecting the **[AF lock only]** option, if you want to use the **AE-L/AF-L** button to lock focus only.

In Continuous-Servo AF, the autofocus system remains active while the shutter release button is held down halfway, constantly adjusting focus as necessary; therefore, if you recompose the picture so that the selected AF point no longer covers the subject, the focus will shift to the point now covered by the selected AF point. To lock focus in Continuous-Servo AF, press and hold the **AE-L/AF-L** button (consider the options available at CS-f2 **[Assign AE-L/AF-L button]** in the Custom Settings menu, as described in the note below). Alternatively, in AF-C mode, which is most useful for photographing a moving subject, it is possible to lock focus by assigning activation of the AF system to the **AE-L/AF-L** button instead of the shutter button, using the **[AF-ON]** option at CS-f2. Press and hold the button down until focus is achieved, and then release the button to lock focus. Now the picture can be recomposed and the shutter release button can be pressed to make the exposure without having any effect on the focus.

NOTE: If CS-f2 **[Assign AE-L/AF-L button]** in the Custom Settings menu is set to **[AF-ON]** the Vibration Reduction (VR) feature, available on some Nikkor lenses, will not operate when the **AE-L/AF-L** button is pressed; VR is only activated by pressing the shutter release button. If you use the technique of locking focus by controlling autofocus operation via the **AE-L/AF-L** button, when you decide to take a picture press the shutter release button and pause briefly at the point it is depressed halfway to allow the VR system to activate and settle, before pressing it all the way down to operate the shutter.

Once focus has been locked in either AF-S or AF-C focus mode, ensure the camera-to-subject distance does not alter. If it does, reactivate autofocus and refocus the lens at the new distance before using the Autofocus Lock options.

AF-ASSIST ILLUMINATOR

The D5100 has a small, built-in AF-Assist Illuminator, which is designed to facilitate autofocus in low-light conditions; it is located on the front of the camera between the finger grip and the viewfinder head. Whatever the intentions of the camera's design team were, I consider this feature largely superfluous! Here are a few reasons why I suggest setting the **[AF-assist]** item in the Shooting menu to **[Off]**.

- The lamp only works if you have an autofocus lens attached to the camera, the focus area mode is set to either Single-Point AF or Dynamic-Area AF with the center focus point selected, or if Auto-Area AF is active.
- It is only usable with focal lengths of 18mm – 200mm.
- The operating range is restricted to 1.6 – 9.8 feet (0.5 – 3.0m).
- Due to its location, many lenses obstruct its output, particularly if they have a lens hood attached.
- The lamp overheats quite quickly (6 to 8 exposures in rapid succession is usually sufficient) and will automatically shut down to allow it to cool. Plus, at this level of use, it also drains battery power fairly quickly.

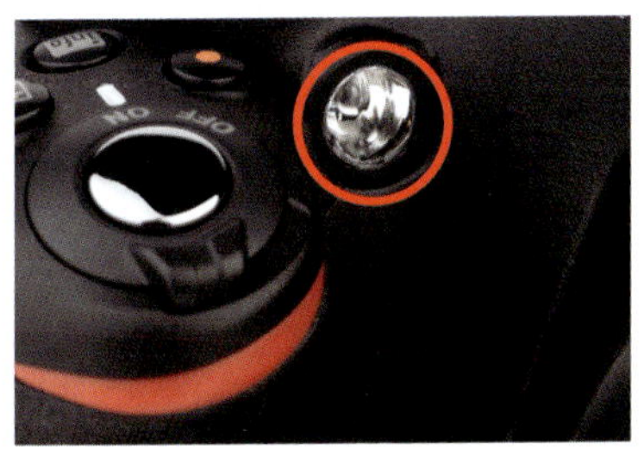

‹ The AF-Assist lamp of the D5100 may help the camera acquire focus in low-light conditions, but its value is questionable.

The D5100 can also use the built-in AF-Assist Illuminator lamp of either the SB-900, SB-800, SB-700, or SB-600 Speedlights, or that of the SU-800 Speedlight Commander unit (operation of the camera's lamp is disabled in these circumstances). The wider coverage provided by the AF-Assist Illuminator of the external units is particularly useful with cameras such as the D5100, with its relatively wide array of 11 AF points, plus the AF-Assist Illuminator is located farther off the lens axis, reducing the risk that its light will be obstructed by the lens. The AF-Assist function can be used in isolation on the SB-900 and SB-800 by canceling flash firing via the Custom Settings menu of the Speedlight.

When used with AF lenses with focal lengths of 17–135mm, the SB-900 provides AF-Assist for autofocus with the following AF points:

17–105 mm		106–135 mm	

When used with AF lenses and focal lengths of 24-105mm, the SB-800, SB-600, and SU-800 provide AF-Assist for autofocus with the following AF points:

24–34 mm		35–105 mm	

If you want to use either the SB-600, SB-800, or SB-900 off-camera, the SC-29 TTL flash lead has a built-in AF-Assist lamp that attaches to the camera's accessory shoe.

LIMITATIONS OF THE AF SYSTEM

Although the autofocus system of the D5100 is quite capable, there are some circumstances or conditions that can impair or limit its performance:

- Low light
- Low contrast
- Highly reflective surfaces
- Subject too small within the autofocus sensing area; this is more likely to occur with wide-angle lenses
- The AF point covers a subject comprising fine detail
- The AF point covers a regular geometric pattern
- The AF point covers a region of high contrast
- The AF point covers objects at different distances from the camera

If any of these conditions prevent the camera from acquiring focus, either switch to Manual focus mode or focus on another object at the same distance from the camera as the subject, then use the AF Lock feature to lock focus before recomposing the picture.

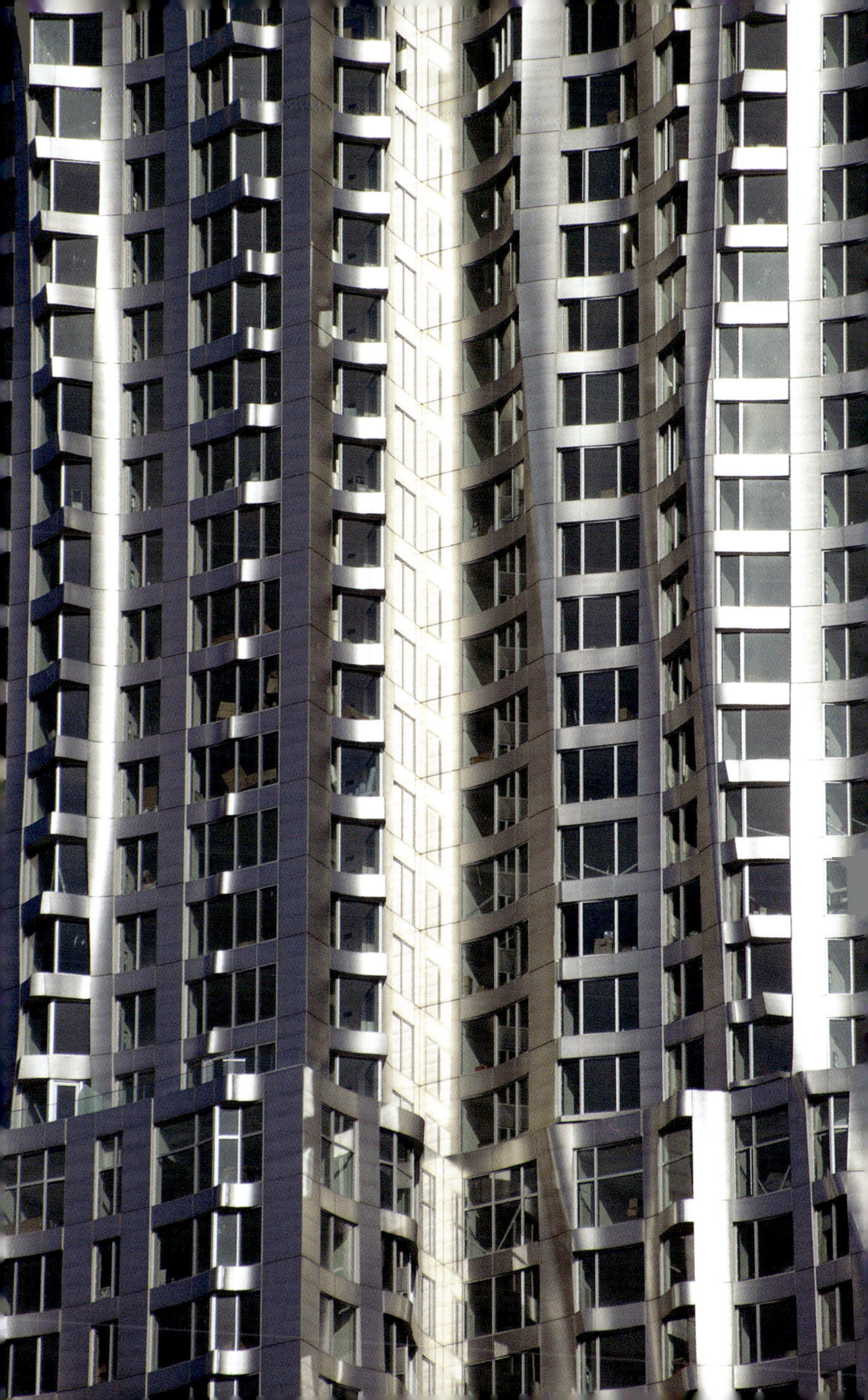

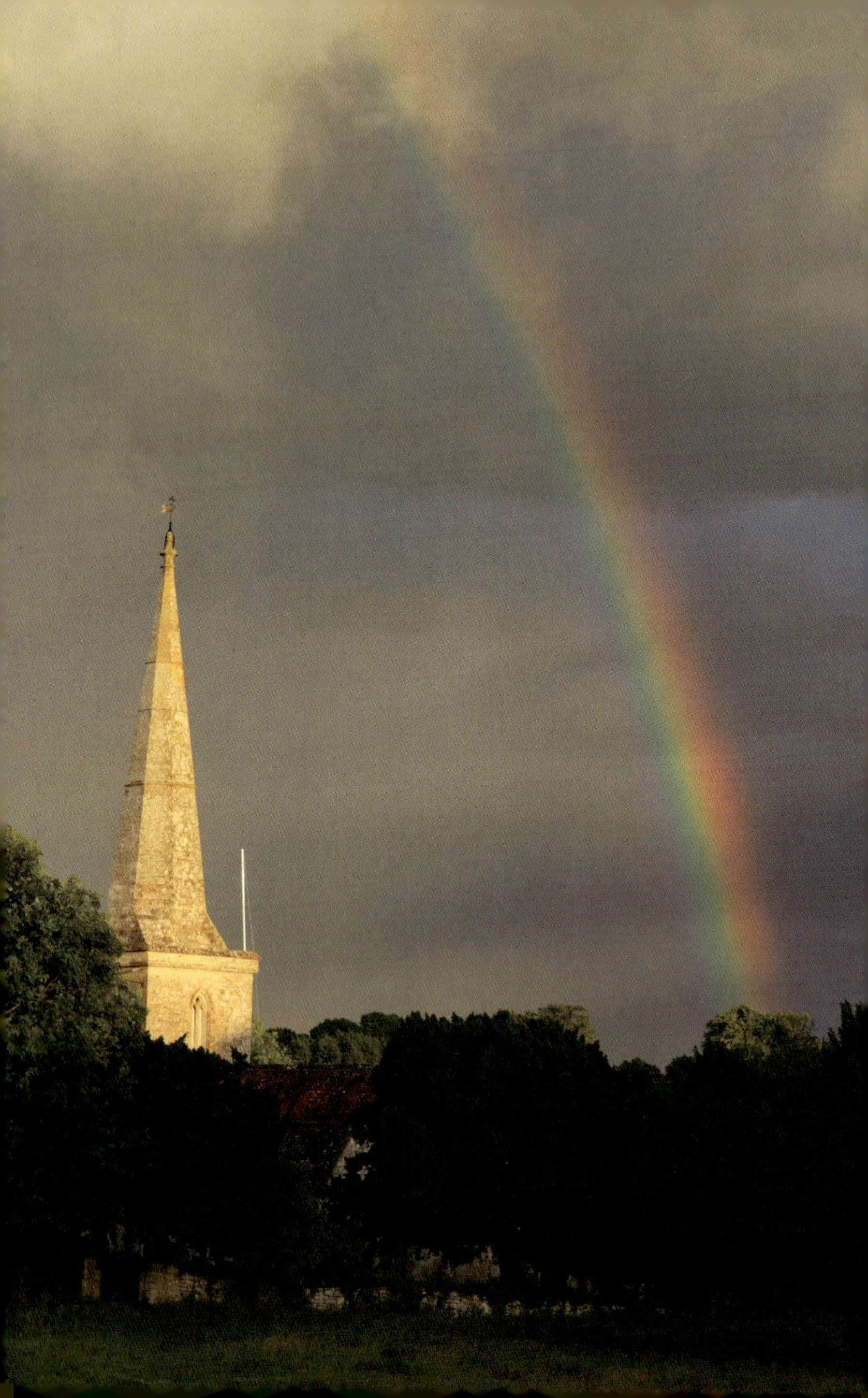

Shoot and Review

THE SHUTTER

The electronically timed, mechanical shutter used in the D5100 is impressive for a camera in its class. The shutter blades are constructed from a durable composite of Kevlar ™ and carbon-fiber material, which provides great strength with low mass to ensure both durability and accuracy; the unit is proven to perform at least 100,000 cycles.

The shutter speed range of the D5100 runs from 30 seconds to 1/4000 second and can be set in steps of 1/3EV or 1/2EV. There is also an option for exposures beyond 30 seconds by using the bulb setting, or a time exposure controlled via the optional ML-L3 remote shutter release with a maximum duration of 30 minutes. The D5100 has a Long Exposure Noise Reduction feature, which should be used in such circumstances (see pages 192-193 for more details). The maximum flash synchronization shutter speed is 1/200 second.

SHUTTER RELEASE

The main shutter release button of the D5100 is located, conventionally, on the right top of the camera, surrounded by the power switch collar. When the camera is switched to **[ON]**, a light pressure on the shutter release button, which depresses it halfway, will activate the metering system and initiate autofocus if it is selected. If pressure is no longer applied to the shutter release button, the camera will remain active for a fixed period of time, the duration of which depends on the selection made under CS-c2 **[Auto-off timers]** item in the Custom Settings menu (CSM); eight seconds is the default setting.

If you fully depress the shutter release button, the shutter mechanism will operate and an exposure will be made. There is a very short delay between pressing the button all the way down and the shutter opening; this delay is known as shutter lag.

The capacity of the buffer memory is probably the most common cause of shutter delay. It does not matter if you shoot in Single Frame or Continuous Release mode (read on for descriptions); once the buffer memory is full, the camera must write data to the memory card before any more exposures can be made. As soon as sufficient space for another image is available in the buffer memory, the shutter can once again be released. For this reason, using memory cards with a fast data write speed is recommended. The D5100 supports a maximum data write speed of approximately 15MB/second, so using any card that can sustain a write speed of 20MB/s (133x) will ensure the maximum performance as far as clearing the buffer memory is concerned (in this respect a card with an even faster write speed will deliver no additional benefit, since the camera imposes the limiting factor). Other factors that may contribute to shutter delay include the following:

- When the camera is set to Single-Servo autofocus mode, the shutter is disabled until the D5100 has acquired focus. In low-light or low-contrast scenes, the autofocus system will often take longer to achieve focus, particularly if one of the outer single-line sensor type AF points is used.
- In low-light conditions, the D5100 can activate its AF-assist lamp, or that of an external Speedlight, or the SC-29 TTL flash control cable, which can introduce a short delay while the lamp illuminates and focus is acquired.
- The Red-Eye Reduction function (one of the flash modes available on the camera) introduces an additional, and significant, one-second delay between pressing the shutter release button and the exposure being made (see page 256 for details on Red-Eye Reduction with the D5100).

RELEASE MODES

The D5100 offers a range of release modes that are set via the Release mode item in the Information Display. Open it by pressing the info button, and then press the i button to illuminate the cursor in the display. Use the Multi Selector to highlight the current release mode setting, and press the OK button to display a list of the additional options. Highlight the required setting by pressing ▲ or ▼, and then press the OK button again. Choose one of the following options:

S SINGLE FRAME

A single image is recorded each time the shutter release button is pressed. To make another exposure, the button must be released and pressed again. You can continue to do so until the buffer memory is full, in which case you must wait for data to be written to the memory card. The shutter release button will also lock if the memory card is full.

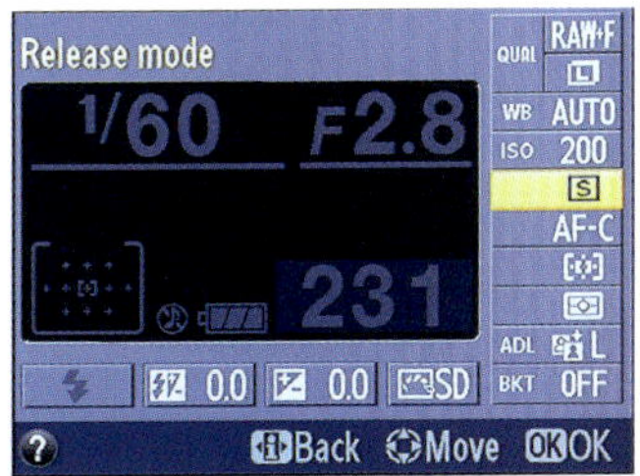

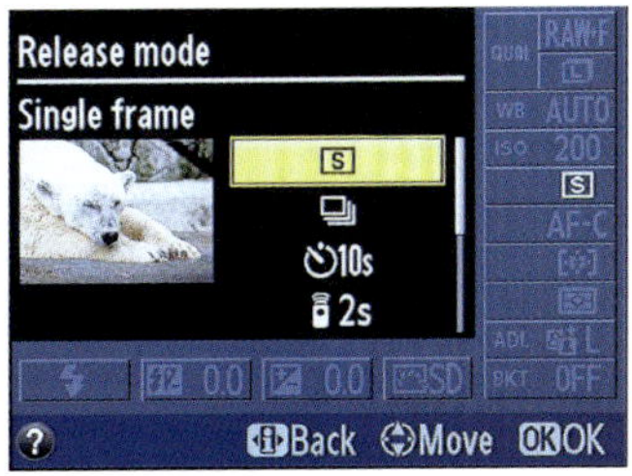

HINT: You do not have to remove your finger from the shutter release button completely between frames; by raising it slightly after each exposure but maintaining a slight downward pressure on the shutter release button, you can keep the camera active and be ready for the next shot. If you want to take a rapid sequence of pictures in Single Frame mode, avoid "stabbing" your finger down on the shutter release button in quick succession. Keep a light pressure on the button and roll your finger over the top of the button in a smooth, repeating action. This will reduce the risk of camera shake spoiling your pictures.

CONTINUOUS

In this mode, if you press and hold down the shutter release button, the D5100 will continue to record images up to a maximum rate of 4 frames per second (fps). The Continuous Release mode can be particularly helpful in situations where your subject is moving quickly, or there is only a fleeting moment in which to capture the image.

NOTE: The quoted frame rates for the D5100 are based on the camera being set to manual exposure (M), or Shutter-Priority autoexposure mode (S), and a minimum shutter speed of 1/250 second. It is important to remember that the selected shutter speed, use of the Vibration Reduction (VR) feature available on some Nikkor lenses, the buffer capacity, other autoexposure modes, and autofocus (particularly in low light) can, and often will, reduce the maximum frame rate significantly.

SELF-TIMER

The Self-Timer releases the shutter after a predetermined delay. The default delay is 10 seconds, but can be changed to 2, 5, 10, or 20 seconds via CS-c3 **[Self-timer]** in the Custom Settings menu. The function also allows for between 1 and 9 pictures to be taken once the Self-Timer operates by setting the required number of frames using the [Numbers of shots] option under CS-c3.

Once the required delay for the Self-Timer has been selected, place the camera on a tripod or other stable support and frame the picture. Select the Self-Timer Release mode from the Information Display and press the shutter release button down halfway to focus the lens (the shutter release will be disabled unless focus is acquired in Single-Servo AF mode). When the shutter release button is fully depressed, the Self-Timer lamp will begin to blink (a beep will accompany the blinking light if CS-d1 **[Beep]** has been activated in the CSM). Approximately 2 seconds before the exposure is made, the lamp will stop blinking and remain on (the beep will become more rapid) until the shutter is released. To cancel the Self-Timer Release mode at any time during the delay, turn the camera off.

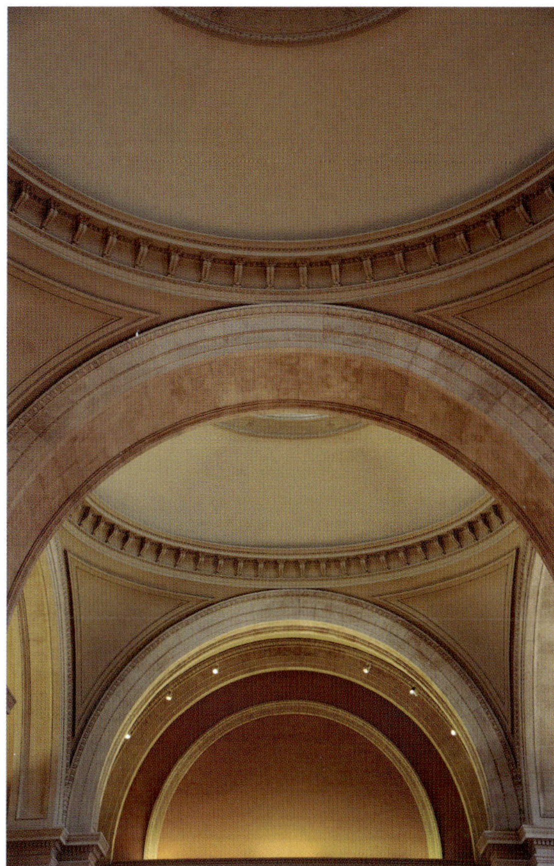

› For this shot, I mounted the camera on a tripod and selected the Delayed Remote release option so that I could fire the shutter using the ML-L3 remote release without having to touch the camera and risk vibration spoiling the shot.

Traditionally, the Self-Timer has been used to enable the photographer to be included in the picture, but there is another very useful function for this feature. The Self-Timer allows the photographer to release the shutter without directly touching the camera, thus reducing the chance of camera shake. This is particularly useful for long exposures when the subject is static and precise timing of the shutter release is less critical.

HINT: Make sure nothing passes in front of the lens when pressing the shutter release button down halfway, as autofocus operation may shift the point of focus. You may find that manual focus mode more convenient and reliable when using the Self-Timer function.

HINT: Since the camera is not held to the photographer's eye while utilizing the Self-Timer or Remote Control Release modes, it is essential to cover the viewfinder eyepiece to prevent extraneous light entering the viewfinder and influencing the camera's TTL metering sensor, which is located in the top of the viewfinder head. Nikon provides the DK-5 eyepiece blind for this purpose. However, fitting the DK-5 requires removal of the DK-20 rubber eyecup; this is a nuisance and increases the risk of losing the eyecup. I find it far more convenient to keep a small square of thick black felt material in my camera bag to drape over the viewfinder eyepiece when using the camera remotely in Aperture-Priority (A), Shutter-Priority (S), and Programmed Auto exposure modes, or any of the fully automated Scene/Effects exposure modes. In Manual (M) exposure mode, there is no requirement to block the viewfinder eyepiece when using the camera remotely, as the camera will only use the exposure settings made by the photographer.

2s DELAYED REMOTE/ QUICK-RESPONSE REMOTE

The Delayed Remote and Quick-response Remote functions both require the use of the optional Nikon ML-L3 infrared (IR) remote control. In the 2s Delayed Remote mode, the shutter is released two seconds after the shutter release button of the ML-L3 is pressed, while in the Quick-Response mode, the shutter is released as soon as the shutter release button on the ML-L3 is pressed. To set the duration of the time period the camera will wait for a signal from the Ml-L3, use CS-c4 **[Remote on duration]**. Start by placing the camera on a tripod or other stable support and frame the picture. Select the required Remote Control mode from the Release mode options via the Information Display, as described above. If no camera operations are performed for approximately 60-seconds after selecting a Remote Control mode, the camera will default back to Single Frame, Continuous, or Quiet Shutter Release modes. Once one of the Remote Control modes is active, confirm focus by pressing the shutter release button down halfway; note that even if the shutter release is pressed down fully, no exposure will be made. Finally, point the transmitter window on the curved edge of the ML-L3 toward either of the IR receivers on the D5100 and press the shutter release button of the ML-L3. In Delayed Remote mode, the Self-Timer lamp will light for approximately two seconds before the shutter is released, while in Quick-response Remote mode, it will flash after the shutter has been released.

NOTE: The ML-L3 has a maximum effective range of approximately 16-feet (5 m), although this is likely to be reduced in very bright sunlight due to the high level of naturally occurring IR light.

NOTE: The camera's timer may not start or the shutter may not be released if focus is not acquired.

Q *QUIET SHUTTER*

In this release mode, the camera exposes a single image just like in Single Frame Release, but the operation of lifting the reflex mirror up out of the light path and the opening/closing of the shutter is separated from the action of recycling the shutter mechanism. This helps to reduce the overall level of noise generated by the D5100 when you press and hold the shutter release button down all the way or lift off the release button of the optional Nikon MC-DC2 remote release cable (in this release mode the camera does not make a beep sound when focus is achieved) because the reflex mirror will remain in the raised position until you lift your finger off the button. This makes the operation of the camera noticeably quieter compared with the Single Frame Release mode. An extra damping mechanism has been added to the D5100 to slow the movement of the reflex mirror on its return. The Q Release mode is ideal for shooting discreetly in any environment where the noise may be intrusive.

THE LCD MONITOR

On the rear of the D5100 is a 3-inch (7.5 cm), 921,000-dot (VGA), color TFT LCD monitor. The LCD monitor screen shows approximately 100% of the image file when used for review. Still pictures can be displayed either as a single image or in multiples, while video recorded using the D-Movie mode can be replayed on the screen. When used to display a single image, the review function has a zoom facility that enables it to be enlarged by up to 31x—this is for [Large] size images only—lower magnifications are available for **[Medium]** (23x) and **[Small]** (15x).

The maximum magnification of a **[Large]** size image is equivalent to a 400% view, so to examine the image at a 100% (i.e., actual pixel level), press the 🔍 button until the maximum magnification is reached, and then press the 🔍 button twice to reduce the image to a 100% view.

Use the Multi Selector to scroll through a range of pages containing shooting information, which are superimposed on any image reviewed in Single-Image Playback (see pages 101-109 for more details). Pictures can be edited in the camera by reviewing them on the LCD monitor, with the options to delete them, protect them from being deleted unintentionally, or make adjustments using the items in the Retouch menu. In addition to the display of images and image information, the LCD monitor is used to display the various camera menus.

IMAGE REVIEW OPTIONS

One of the most useful features of a digital camera is the ability to get nearly instant feedback on photographs as you shoot. Using the Playback functions on the D5100 will allow you to view not only the images you have taken, but also a range of useful information about them. As mentioned above, the monitor screen of the D5100 provides virtually a 100% view of the image file when it is played back. Pictures can be displayed either as a single image or in multiples.

Assuming **[On]** is selected for **[Image review]** in the ▶ Playback menu, the most recently taken image in Single Frame and Self-Timer/Remote Control Release modes will be displayed in the monitor screen almost instantaneously. In the Continuous Release mode, or when the camera records a sequence of pictures quickly, it must write the image data from the buffer memory to the memory card for each image taken before it can be viewed. This causes a short delay that becomes cumulative as more images are recorded; the camera displays each image chronologically as soon as it has been saved. If **[Off]** is selected for **[Image review]** in the ▶ Playback menu, no image is displayed after an exposure is made. In this case, use Single-Image Playback to evaluate images by pressing the ▶ button.

FULL-FRAME PLAYBACK

To view the last image recorded by the camera, press the ▶ button. If you wish to view other images saved on the memory card, press ◀ and ▶ to scroll through them. To display the information pages for a still image, use ▲ and ▼ (see below for full details). To return to the Shooting mode, press the ▶ button again—although the quicker method, if you are in the midst of shooting, is to press the shutter release button down halfway.

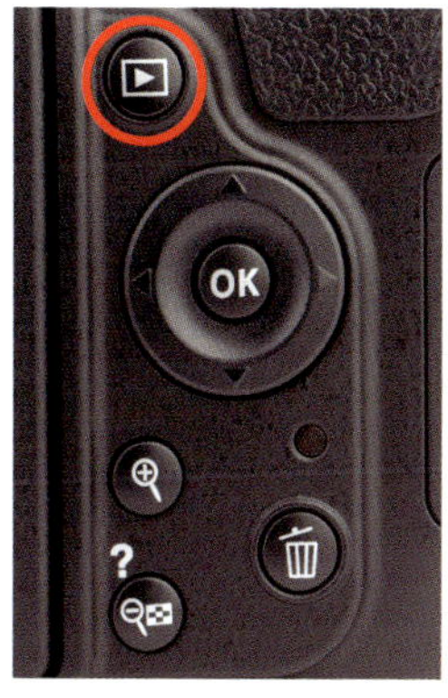

‹ The ▶ Playback button is located on the back of the camera, just above the Multi Selector.

To display images shot in an upright (vertical) format in the correct orientation, select **[On]** for the **[Auto image rotation]** item in the Setup menu, and select **[On]** for the **[Rotate tall]** item in the ▶ Playback menu. Although this may seem a convenient method to display an image, the size of the displayed picture is reduced in order to fit the long edge of the image within the short edge of the monitor screen.

INFORMATION PAGES

A very useful feature of the Playback function on the D5100 is the wealth of information that can be accessed while viewing the image on the monitor screen. This information can help ensure that you have achieved a good exposure, as well as give you detailed information about how, when, and where the exposure was made. Depending on the selections made in the **[Playback display options]** item in the ▶ menu, there are up to eight different pages of information that can be displayed for each image file viewed on the monitor screen.

To access these information displays, press ▼ to scroll through each page in the following order: File Information, Highlights (warning), RGB and Composite Histograms, Shooting Data (1), Shooting Data (2), Shooting Data (3), GPS, Overview data and None (image only). Press ▲ to scroll through in the reverse order.

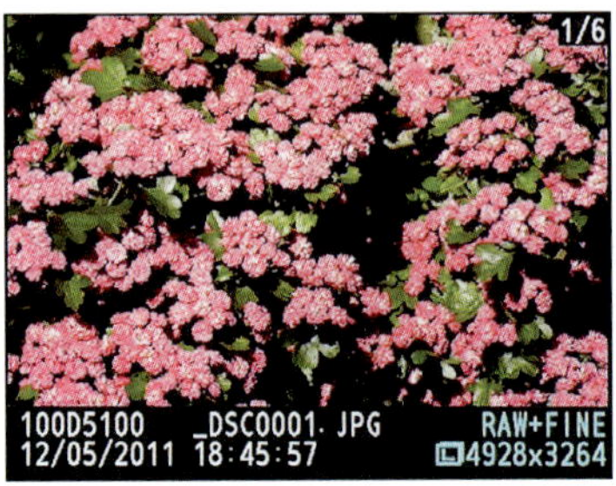

› The File Information page provides the date and time the image was created as well as other useful information, such as the file name.

File Information: This page displays an unobstructed view of the image while providing the following additional information:

- Protect status
- Retouch indicator
- Frame number/total number of frames
- File name
- Image quality
- Image size
- Time of recording
- Date of recording
- Folder name

Highlights: The Highlights page shows an unobstructed view of the entire image. Any area of the image that may be overexposed is shown with a flashing border. This page is only displayed if **[Highlights]** is selected under the **[Display mode]** item in the ▶ menu, and provides the following information:

- Protect status
- Retouch indicator
- Image highlights
- Camera name
- Frame number/total number of frames

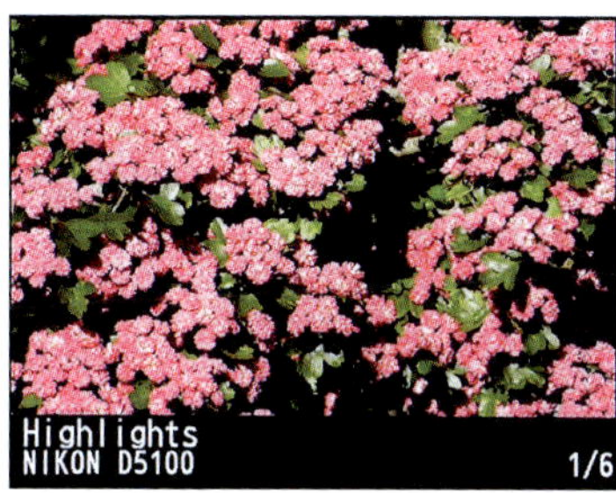

RGB Histogram: The RGB Histogram page provides an individual histogram for each of the red, green, and blue channels, together with an RGB composite (luminance) histogram and a thumbnail of the image file. The horizontal axis indicates the pixel brightness with black at the extreme left end and white at the extreme right end. The vertical axis indicates the number of pixels. To magnify a part of the image, press the 🔍 button and use the Multi Selector to scroll around the full image (a smaller thumbnail image is displayed to assist navigation within the full-frame area). The histogram will represent only the enlarged section of the image displayed on the monitor screen. This page is only displayed if **[RGB histogram]** is selected under the **[Display mode]** item in the ▶ Playback menu. The following information is displayed on this page:

- Protect status
- Retouch indicator
- White Balance/White Balance Fine-tuning/Preset manual
- Camera name
- Histogram—RGB (luminance)
- Histogram—red channel
- Histogram—green channel
- Histogram—blue channel
- Frame number/total number of frames

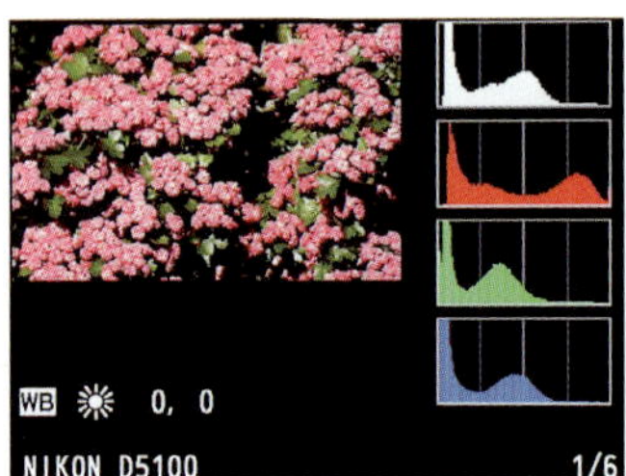

^ The histogram display shows a luminance histogram (white) and the three individual color channel histograms.

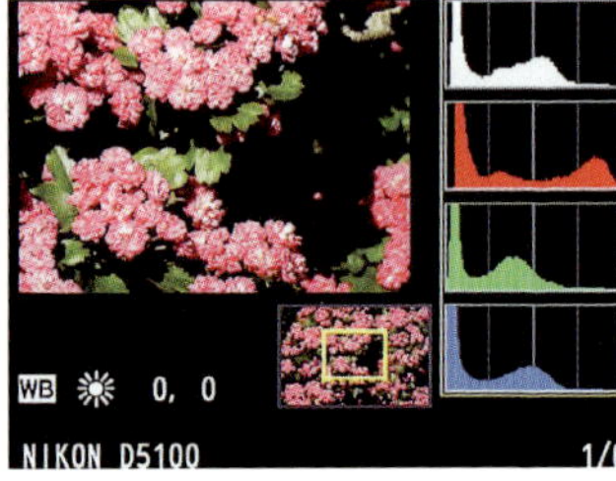

^ To display a histogram for a specific section of an image, press the zoom button to zoom in. Use the Multi Selector to move the yellow frame that indicates the selected section. The histogram applies to only the area within the yellow border.

NOTE: The preview image, including those for NEF files, is derived from a JPEG file to which in-camera processing (White Balance, Contrast, Saturation, etc.) has been applied. The actual NEF file will contain more data and have a wider range of tonal values and colors; therefore, an overexposed highlight in the JPEG preview may not be an overexposed highlight when the NEF file is examined in a RAW file converter such as Nikon Capture NX2. Because they are derived from an 8-bit JPEG preview image, you should treat the highlights warning and histograms that the camera displays with a degree of latitude, and not as an absolute definitive that over- or underexposure has occurred.

Shooting Data Page 1: A block of information will be superimposed over the center portion of the screen, obstructing the view of the image. This page is only displayed if **[Data]** is selected under the **[Display mode]** item in the ▶ menu and displays the following information:

- Protect status
- Retouch indicator
- Metering method
- Shutter speed
- Aperture
- Shooting mode
- ISO sensitivity [1]
- Exposure compensation
- Focal length
- Lens data
- Focus mode
- VR lens [2]
- Flash type/Commander mode [3]
- Flash mode
- Flash control/Flash Compensation
- Camera name
- Frame number/total number of frames

[1] Displayed in red if ISO Auto Control was on
[2] Displayed only if a VR lens is attached
[3] Displayed only if optional flash unit with Commander function was used

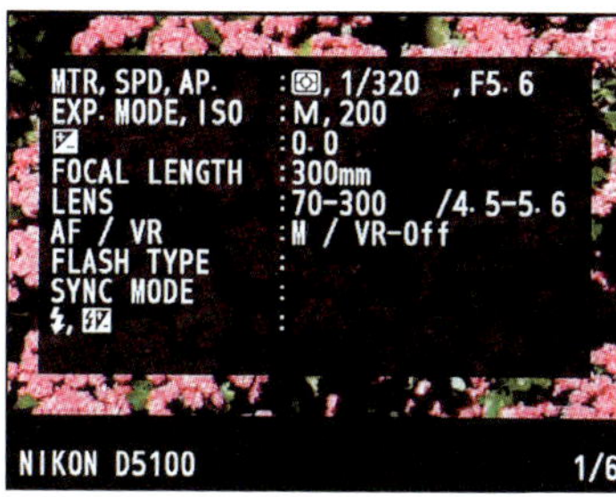

Shooting Data Page 2: A block of information will be superimposed over the center portion of the screen, obstructing the view of the image. This page is only displayed if **[Data]** is selected under the **[Display mode]** item in the ▶ menu and displays the following information:

- Protect status
- Retouch indicator
- White Balance/Color Temperature/WB Fine-tuning/Preset manual
- Color space
- Picture Control
- Quick Adjust[1]
- Original Picture Control[2]
- Sharpening
- Contrast
- Brightness
- Saturation[3]
- Filter effects[4]
- Hue[3]
- Toning[4]
- Camera name
- Frame number/total number of frames

[1] [Standard], [Vivid], [Portrait], and [Landscape] Picture Controls only
[2] [Neutral], [Monochrome], and custom Picture Controls
[3] Not displayed with Monochrome Picture Controls
[4] Monochrome Picture Controls only

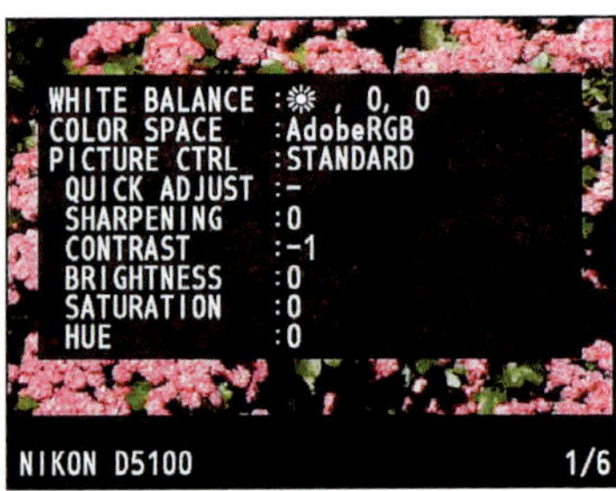

NOTE: This screen can help you understand the effects of image settings and adjustments on the appearance of your picture.

Shooting Data Page 3: A block of information will be superimposed over the center portion of the screen, obstructing the view of the image. This page is only displayed if **[Data]** is selected under the **[Display mode]** item in the ▶ Playback menu and contains the following information:

- Protect status
- Retouch indicator
- High ISO noise reduction
- Long exposure noise reduction
- Active D-Lighting
- HDR exposure differential
- HDR smoothing
- Retouch history
- Image comment
- Camera name
- Frame number/total number of frames

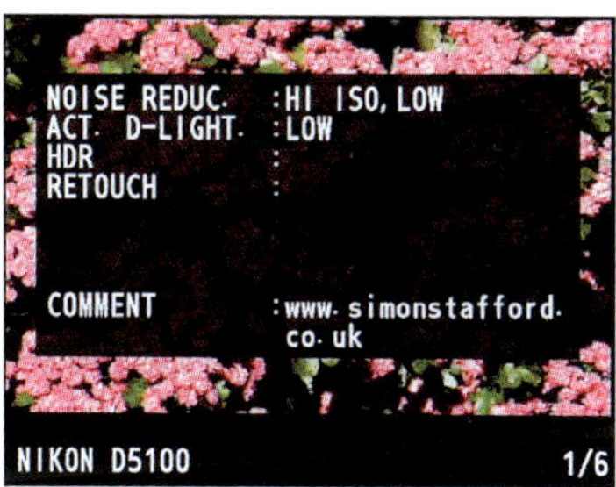

GPS Data: A block of information will be superimposed over the center portion of the screen, obstructing the view of the image. This page is only displayed if the optional Nikon GP-1 GPS device was connected to the D5100 and active when the picture was recorded (when recording in D-Movie mode, the GPS data applies to the position of the camera at the start of recording). This screen displays the following information:

- Protect status
- Retouch indicator
- Latitude
- Longitude
- Altitude
- Coordinated universal time (UTC)
- Camera name
- Frame number/total number of frames

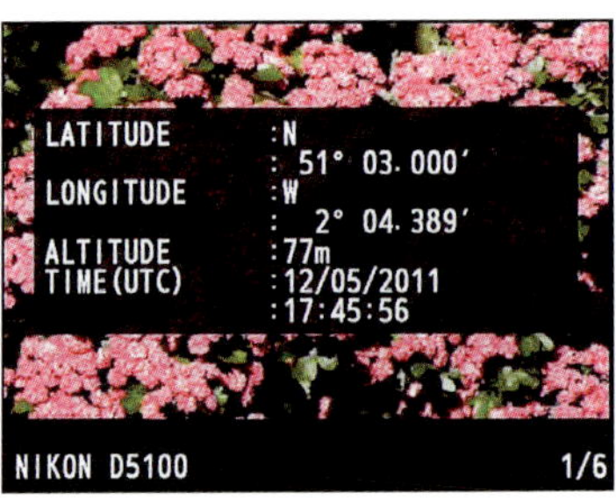

Overview Data: This page provides a thumbnail view of the image file with two panels containing the following information:

- Frame number/total number of frames
- Protect status
- Camera name
- Retouch indicator
- Histogram (composite only)

- ISO sensitivity [1]
- Focal length
- GPS data indicator
- Image comment indicator
- Flash mode
- Flash Compensation/Commander mode [2]
- Exposure Compensation
- Metering method
- Shooting mode
- Shutter speed
- Aperture
- Picture Control
- Active D-Lighting
- File name
- Image Quality
- Image Size
- Time of recording
- Date of recording
- Folder number
- White Balance/Color Temperature/WB Fine-tuning/Preset manual
- Color space

[1] Displayed in red if ISO Auto Control was on during shooting
[2] Displayed only if optional flash unit with Commander function was used

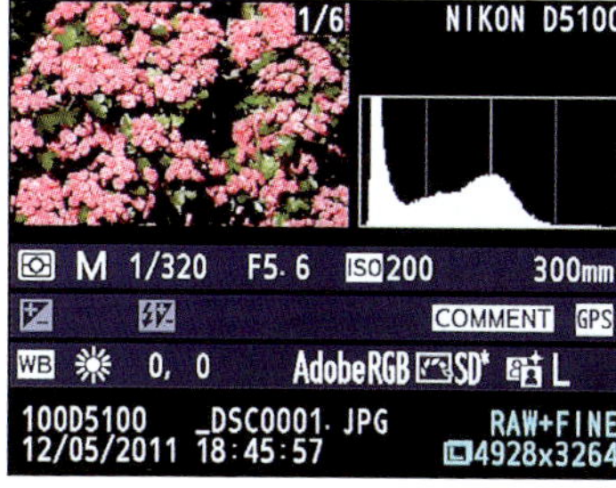

VIEWING MULTIPLE IMAGES

If you wish to view multiple thumbnails of images on the monitor screen, press the button to change from the view of a single image to see four, nine, or seventy-two images, and finally to the Calendar Playback, which displays pictures based on the date they were taken. To return to a single image view from multiple image display, press the button repeatedly until a single image is showing.

In a multiple thumbnail display, a yellow border surrounds the currently highlighted image file. To highlight an alternative thumbnail image, scroll with the Multi Selector. To view the highlighted image in full-frame view, press ; to return to the thumbnail view, press the button. To magnify the selected image press the button repeatedly, a yellow frame indicates the enlarged section of the image; press the button to reduce the degree of magnification until the multiple image display is shown. The highlighted thumbnail image can be protected by pressing the /**AE-L/AF-L** button, and deleted by pressing the button. To return to the Shooting mode at any time, press the button, or press the shutter release button down halfway.

CALENDAR PLAYBACK

To view an image file taken on a specific date, press the button until 72 thumbnail images are displayed, and then press it once more. Once the Calendar Playback display is shown, any date on which one or more images was recorded will be indicated by a thumbnail image on that date; use the button to switch back and forth between the calendar of dates **[Date list]** and the list of thumbnails **[Thumbnail list]** displayed to the right of the calendar. To highlight a specific date or image in the thumbnail image list, use the Multi Selector button.

In the **[Date list]**, use to exit to the 72-thumbnail display, to view the first picture taken on the selected date, to highlight a date, or to delete all the pictures taken on the selected date. In the **[Thumbnail list]**, press and hold to enlarge the highlighted picture, to view the highlighted picture, to highlight a picture, or to delete the highlighted picture; to return to the Shooting mode, press the button, or press the shutter release button down halfway.

PLAYBACK ZOOM

The image displayed on the LCD monitor is usually too small to check its sharpness with any certainty. The Playback Zoom will allow you to enlarge a **[Large]** size image by up to 31x (equivalent to approximately a 400% view on a computer screen), a **[Medium]** size image up to 23x, and a **[Small]** size image up to 15x. To see a 100% view (i.e., an actual pixel view) of a **[Large]** image, enlarge to full magnification and then press the ⊖ button twice. At this magnification, given the relatively high resolution of the monitor screen (921,000 dots), it is possible to make a reliable check of image sharpness and noise level in the image, especially if a relatively high level of sharpening is selected via the Picture Control settings.

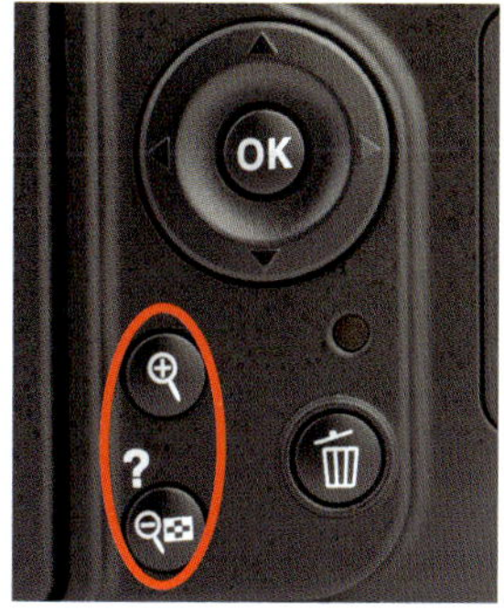

To zoom into the image displayed on the monitor, press the ⊕ button. The enlarged image will be displayed with a yellow frame inside a navigation window. To increase the degree of magnification, keep pressing ⊕ button; the size of the yellow frame will reduce to indicate the area of the image that is being displayed. The selected area, as defined by the frame, is shown in the monitor. To view an alternative part of the image at the same magnification, use the Multi Selector to scroll through the image. The same area of another image at the same magnification can be viewed by rotating the Main Command dial to scroll through the images. This is a useful feature if there are a number of similar images of the same subject on your memory card and you want to check a specific detail, such as a certain person's eyes in a group portrait. To return to the Shooting mode, press the ▶ button, or press the shutter release button down halfway.

PROTECTING IMAGES

To protect an image file against inadvertent deletion, display the image or video file on the monitor in full-frame Single-Image Playback or highlight it in multiple-thumbnail Playback, and then press the ⊶ / (**AE-L/AF-L**) button. A small key icon ⊶ will appear in the upper left corner of the monitor, superimposed over the image. To remove the protection, open or highlight the image or video file and press ⊶ again. Check to make sure the ⊶ is no longer displayed. A protected image will still be "deleted" if the memory card is formatted; however, the protect status is preserved when the file is transferred to another storage device or computer. To remove the protection from all images in a folder or folders currently selected in the **[Playback folder]** menu, press and hold ⊶ and 🗑 simultaneously for approximately 2 seconds.

DELETING IMAGES

Images can be deleted using one of two methods. The quickest and easiest way to delete a single image file is to press the 🗑 button when the image to be deleted is displayed on the LCD monitor. The first press of the button opens a warning dialog box that asks for confirmation of the delete command. To complete the process, simply press the 🗑 button again. To cancel the delete process, press the ▶ button.

Images can also be deleted in multiples via the **[Delete]** item in the ▶ Playback menu. There are three options: **[Selected]**, in which only those image files selected for deletion will be deleted; **[Selected date]** will delete all image files taken on a selected date; or **[All]**, which deletes all image files in the folder currently selected for Playback.

HINT: Never be in too much of a hurry to delete pictures unless they are obvious failures. I always recommend that it is better to leave the editing process to a later stage—your opinions about a particular picture can, and often do, change. Memory cards are remarkably cheap and come in much larger capacities than only a few years ago, so there is no excuse to skimp on image storage!

ASSESSING THE HISTOGRAM

The histogram is a graphical display of the tonal values recorded by the camera. The shape and position of the histogram curve indicates the range of tones that have been captured in the picture. The horizontal axis represents 256 different tonal values from pure black at the extreme left end to pure white at the extreme right end; darker tones will be distributed to the left of the histogram graph and lighter tones to the right. The vertical axis represents the number of pixels that have that specific tonal value.

In a well-exposed picture of a scene containing an average distribution of tones that includes a few very dark shadows, a sizable number of mid-tones, and a few bright highlights, where no clipping of shadow or highlights has occurred, the curve will extend across much of the horizontal axis; in this case all tones in the scene will have been recorded. Obviously, not all scenes contain an even spread of tones; many have a natural predominance of light or dark areas. In these cases the histogram curve will be biased to the right with scenes containing mainly light tones, or to the left when the scene contains mainly dark tones; this is not an indication of over- or underexposure, respectively, but an indication of the limited range of tones in the scene. Hence, there is no single, perfect, or ideal histogram curve for all scenes and subjects; the shape of the histogram curve will vary widely depending on the nature of the scene recorded. Provided the histogram curve stops on the bottom axis before it reaches either end of the graph, the image will contain the fullest range of tones from the darkest to the lightest in the scene being photographed.

However, if the curve begins at a point part way up the left or right vertical axis of the histogram display (i.e., it does not end on the horizontal axis, but the histogram curve looks as though it has been cut off abruptly), the camera will not have recorded some tones. This is often referred to as "clipping." If the curve is stacked up against the left axis, or there is a peak in the histogram against the left axis, some of the darker tones (i.e., shadows areas in the image) will likely be compromised due to underexposure. In contrast, if the curve is stacked up against the right axis, or there is a peak in the histogram against the right axis, some of the lighter tones (i.e., highlight areas in the image) will likely be compromised due to overexposure. The exception would be in a scene with very bright specular highlights, such as the sun reflecting off water, or streetlights in a nighttime cityscape—these small areas will almost invariably be much brighter than most of the other light tones in the scene, and therefore it is of little consequence if they are overexposed. Significant under- or overexposure is to be avoided if possible; but especially overexposure, as it is unlikely that highlight areas that have been overexposed will be able to render any detail, and nothing can be done to rectify this in post-processing. It is often possible to recover shadow detail lost due to slight underexposure; however, there is likely to be a penalty of reduced image quality in these areas due to the effects of an increased level in noise, which will become progressively more apparent as a greater degree of correction is applied to compensate for higher levels of underexposure.

Many photographers adopt a technique known as "expose to the right," in which they adjust the exposure to the point that the histogram curve is as far to the right as possible without clipping, to ensure they capture as wide a tonal range as possible and with as many levels to describe those tones. While this is a valid technique, for best results, do not base your exposure on just the composite RGB histogram; look carefully at the histograms for the three individual channels. It is often possible to encounter a situation where one of the color channel histograms begins to show clipping not apparent in the composite RGB histogram. A common example occurs when photographing a sunrise or sunset, when it is likely the red channel will begin to clip first due to the higher level of red/orange/yellow light in the scene.

As previously mentioned, the clipping of the histogram curve is usually an indication of under- or overexposure, but do remember that the preview image, including those for NEF (RAW) files, is always derived from an 8-bit JPEG file to which the camera settings (White Balance, Contrast, Saturation, etc.) have been applied, and it is the tonal distribution of this JPEG file that the histogram describes. An NEF file will contain more data and have a wider range of tonal values; therefore, an overexposed highlight in the JPEG preview may not be an overexposed highlight when the NEF (RAW) file is examined in a RAW file converter such as Nikon Capture NX2. Even if an NEF file has been incorrectly exposed, it is possible to apply retrospective Exposure Compensation using software such as Nikon View NX2 or Nikon Capture NX2, between about -1 EV to +1.5 EV; no such flexibility is possible with a JPEG file.

Scenes that are low in contrast will have a rather narrow curve that ends before reaching either the left- or right-hand extremities of the bottom axis. You have two choices for how to deal with this situation: (1) Use the Picture Control system to increase the contrast level, or (2) adjust the contrast level at a later stage using an image-processing software application. I would recommend the latter approach, as it offers a far greater degree of control.

HINT: It is always preferable to err on the side of lower image contrast because it is far easier to boost contrast than it is to try and reduce it at any stage subsequent to the original exposure.

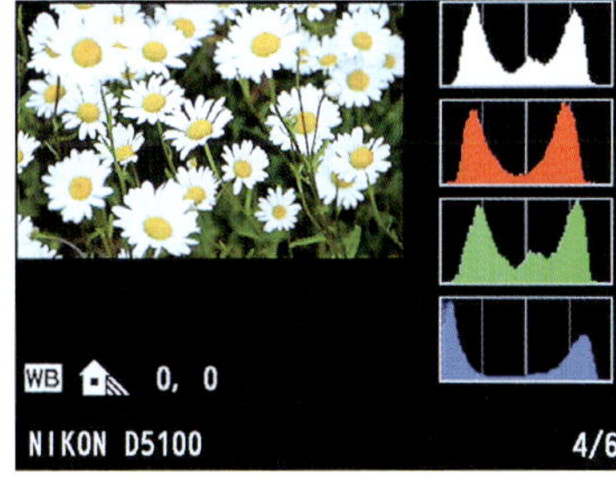

^ The histogram indicates that a full range of tones has been recorded in the image. The curve extends to the right side representing the lighter tones in the subjects without bisecting the right side vertical axis, which would indicate possible overexposure, and equally to the left side where the darker tones are represented, but again with out bisecting the left side vertical axis, which would indicate underexposure.

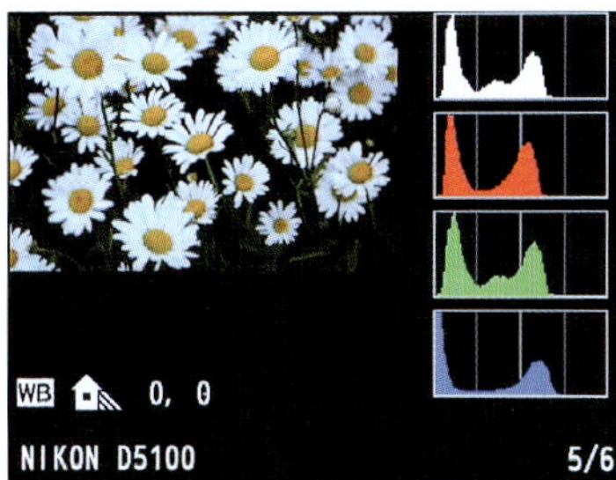

^ Here, the exposure has been reduced by 2 EV; notice how the curve has shifted to the left to represent the range of (denser) darker tones that have been recorded. The reduction in the exposure level has caused the curve of the composite RGB and individual color channel histogram curves to become bunched to the left side, suggesting that shadow detail may well have been compromised in this picture.

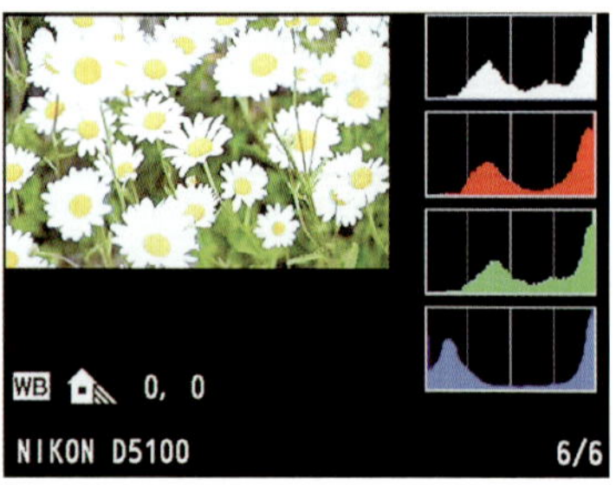

^ Here, the exposure was increased by 2 EV; notice how the histogram curve has been shifted to the right to represent the lighter (brighter) tones that have been recorded. The increase in the exposure level has caused the curve of the composite RGB and individual color channel histograms to become stacked against the right side vertical axis, indicating that highlight detail has been compromised in this picture, and it highly unlikely that that it could be recovered in post-processing.

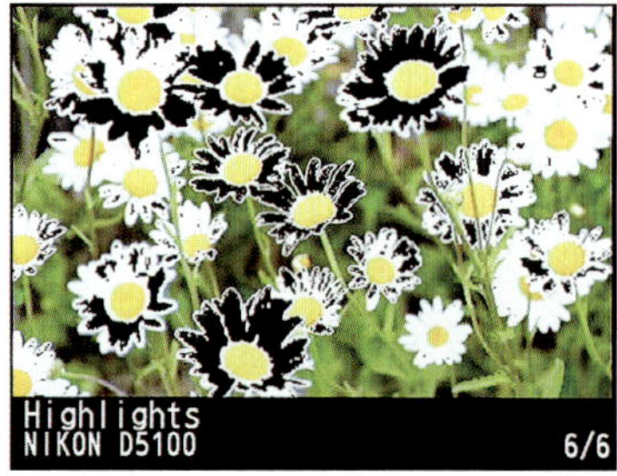

^ Here, by way of comparison is the Highlights warning display for the image exposed at +2 EV; note how any potentially overexposed area is displayed alternatively in black/white.

IMAGE STORAGE WITH SD CARDS

SD (Secure Digital) memory cards are small, solid-state cards that measure 1.3 x 0.9 x 0.08 inches (34 x 22 x 2 mm), have a capacity of up to 2GB, and are structured rather like the hard drive disk of your computer in that they have a file directory, a file allocation table, folders, and individual files. They are capable of retaining data even when they are not powered, and since they have no moving parts they are reasonably robust, so a minor impact from the card being dropped 8 to 10 feet

(2.7 – 3 m) or exposure to the natural elements should not cause any problems. But total immersion in water should be avoided! Obviously, you should treat any memory card with the same care you would all your camera equipment, and it is advisable to keep them in the small plastic case supplied with each card.

Typically, SD cards have a temperature operating-range of -4F° to 167F° (-20°C to 75°C), and no altitude limit. They also have a small, sliding write-protect switch on one edge that, when set to the locked position, prevents any data being written or deleted (if you insert a locked SD card into the D5100, the camera will emit a beep sound as a warning if you try to release the shutter). Finally, unlike photographic film, they are not affected by ionizing radiation from X-ray security equipment that is widely used these days.

SDHC AND SDXC CARDS

As camera development led to larger file sizes, there was soon a requirement for SD cards with a capacity greater than 2GB. Secure Digital High Capacity (SDHC) cards were introduced as a new standard to meet this demand. They have the same physical dimensions and write-protect feature of SD cards, comply with the SD specification version 2.0 (which supports a card capacity of 4GB and over), and come in three speed classes of performance capability and minimum requirements. Full details on the SD 2.0 specification can be viewed at: www.sdcard.org.

The D5100 is fully compatible with memory cards that comply with the SDHC standard and, at the time of writing, most manufacturers already offer card capacities up to 16GB, with some producing 32GB cards. While such capacious storage may sound tempting, I believe it is important to consider the potential risks of placing all your proverbial "eggs in one basket," and suggest it would be prudent to disperse the risk of loss or corruption of image data by using multiple cards with smaller capacities.

More recently, SDXC memory cards, which represent the next generation of flash memory card, have been introduced and in time will be the natural successor to the popular SDHC card format. Based on the latest SD 3.0 specification, capacities of the new SDXC cards are planned to range between 32GB and 2TB, and SanDisk has already released a 64GB SDXC card. The file structure of the SDXC format cards enables long duration HD video recording at a high data transfer rate; widespread adoption of the new format is expected as many cameras, such as the D5100, incorporate an HD video capability.

› The D5100 is compatible with SD, SDHC, and SDXC memory cards.

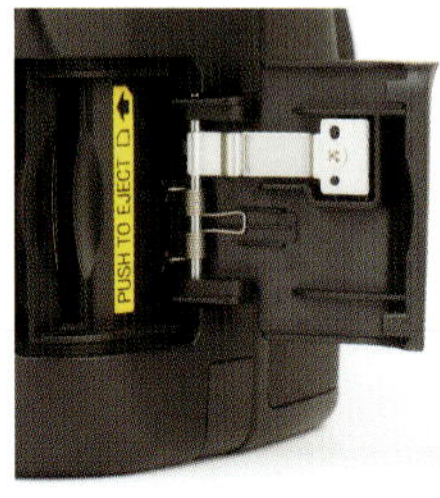

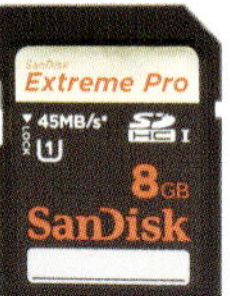

NOTE: Some older devices, including cameras, only support the SD standard and are not compatible with the newer SDHC and SDXC cards. It is important to check that whatever external device you use supports the appropriate SD standard for the memory card(s) you use. For example, an SDHC-compliant card reader supports both SD and SDHC cards, but will not support the SDXC format.

APPROVED MEMORY CARDS

There is a plethora of memory cards on the market, but Nikon has only tested and approved those listed in the table below for use with the D5100. SD, SDHC, and SDXC card technology is well established, so although Nikon will not guarantee operation with other makes of cards, you should not experience any problems or have any concerns if you use an alternative brand. In the chart below are the Nikon approved memory cards for use with the D5100; all cards of the make and capacity listed here can be used regardless of their read/write speed.

CAPACITY / MANUFACTURER	SD	SDHC	SDXC
Lexar Media	1GB, 2GB	4GB, 8GB, 16GB, 32GB	N/A
Panasonic	1GB, 2GB	4GB, 6GB, 8GB, 12GB, 16GB, 24GB, 32GB	48GB, 64GB
SanDisk	1GB, 2GB	4GB, 8GB, 16GB, 32GB	64GB
Toshiba	1GB, 2GB	4GB, 8GB, 16GB, 32GB	64GB

Nikon states that other brands and capacities of cards have not been tested with the D5100; therefore, operation cannot be guaranteed. If you intend to use a memory card not listed in the table above, it is advisable to check with the manufacturer in relation to its compatibility with the D5100. If you purchase a new memory card, always test it a few times before using it for any important photography. Should you experience any problems related to the memory card, use one of the approved cards for the purposes of troubleshooting.

MEMORY CARD CAPACITY

When considering the capacity of the memory cards you will use, bear in mind that the 16.2MP resolution of the D5100 will result in larger file sizes compared with the 12.3MP D5000 camera model or earlier 6MP Nikon camera models such as the D40. So, if you have been in the habit of using 1GB or 2GB memory cards regularly with your 6MP to 8MP DSLR, you may want to think about stepping up to 4GB or 8GB. On average, I find that when shooting NEF (RAW) files, I can expect to record about 500 images, saved in the NEF (Raw) format, on an 8GB card. This provides plenty of scope, especially if you shoot for techniques such as high dynamic range (HDR) or panoramic, requiring multiple shots per final image. I find an 8GB card offers a good compromise between storage capacity and the risks (card failure or loss) inherent with saving all your shots to a single, high-capacity 16GB or 32GB card. However, if you expect to use the HD video capability of the D5100, the higher capacity cards will be more convenient.

The table on the next page provides information on the approximate number of images that can be stored on a typical 8GB SDHC UHS-1 memory card at the various image quality and size settings available on the D5100. All memory cards use a small proportion of their memory capacity to store data required for the card to operate. Therefore, the amount of memory available for storing image files will be slightly less than the quoted maximum capacity of the card. Likewise, capacities may vary slightly if a different brand of memory card is used.

QUALITY	IMAGE SIZE	FILE SIZE[1]	NO. IMAGES[1]	BUFFER CAPACITY[2]
NEF (RAW)	n/a	16.4	343	16
NEF (RAW) + JPEG Fine[3]	L	23.9	244	10
	M	20.8	279	10
	S	18.4	311	11
NEF (RAW) + JPEG Normal[3]	L	20.4	285	10
	M	18.6	307	10
	S	17.4	325	12
NEF (RAW) + JPEG Basic[3]	L	18.3	311	10
	M	17.5	324	10
	S	16.9	333	12
JPEG Fine	L	7.1	844	100
	M	4.4	1,400	100
	S	2.0	3,300	100
JPEG Normal	L	3.9	1,600	100
	M	2.2	2,900	100
	S	1.0	6,200	100
JPEG Basic	L	1.8	3,300	100
	M	1.0	5,700	100
	S	0.5	11,400	100

1 File size will vary according to the scene photographed and the make of memory card used; therefore, all figures are approximate.

2 This is the maximum number of image files that can be stored in the buffer memory. Capacity of the buffer will be reduced by the following: ISO sensitivity set to Hi 1.0, Noise Reduction turned on, Active D-Lighting turned on.

3 File size is the combined total for the NEF (RAW) and JPEG files. The size of an NEF file cannot be altered, so the image size applies to JPEG files only.

INSERTING AND REMOVING MEMORY CARDS

Switch the power off before inserting a memory card into the D5100. Open the memory card slot cover by sliding it toward the back of the camera; the door will spring open to reveal the memory card slot. Insert the card with its contact terminals pointing toward the front of the camera and main (top) label of the card facing toward the back of the camera (i.e., toward yourself with the camera in shooting position). The beveled corner of the card will be to the upper left as it enters the camera. It will slide in a short distance and then you will feel a slight resistance—keep pushing the card until it locks into place (the green memory card access lamp illuminates briefly as confirmation that the card is installed properly).

To remove the card, switch the camera off, open the memory card slot cover, and press the exposed edge of the card toward the camera; then release it. The card will pop partially out of its port; then slide it free from the camera. Memory cards can become warm during use; this is normal and not an indication of a problem.

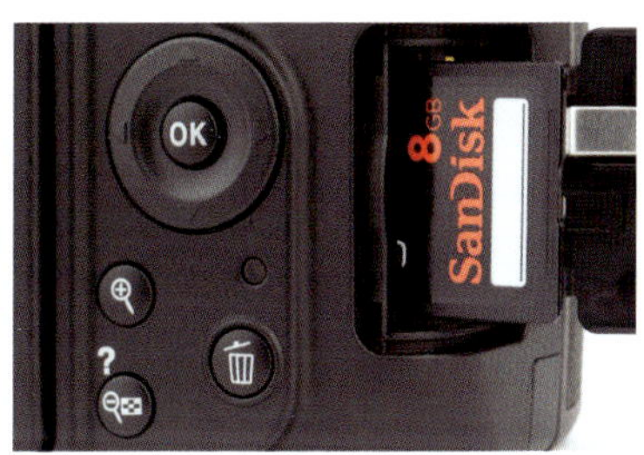

‹ The memory card will only fit into the camera one way, so it is virtually impossible to insert it incorrectly.

If the memory card is removed when a charged battery is installed in the camera, or it is connected to an AC power supply, [-E-] appears within the exposure counter brackets in both the viewfinder (blinking) and shooting Information Display, plus the ? icon blinks in the lower left corner of the viewfinder frame area as a warning.

If **[Release locked]** is selected under the CS-f4 **[Slot empty release lock]** item in the Custom Settings menu, the shutter release is disabled when no memory card is installed in the camera. If the **[Enable release]** option is selected, it is possible to take a picture and it will be displayed on the monitor screen but marked with the warning "Demo," and the image is not recorded.

FORMATTING A MEMORY CARD

As data is written to and deleted from SD, SDHC, and SDXC cards, small areas of its memory can become corrupted and files can become fragmented. This is particularly true if you repeatedly delete individual image files. Formatting the card in the camera will clean up the majority of the worst effects of fragmentation.

In the D5100 instruction book, Nikon states that formatting memory cards "permanently deletes any data they may contain." While this is a salutary warning, it is somewhat misleading. The formatting process actually causes the existing file directory information to be overwritten, so the indicators that direct any reading device, including the camera itself, to the image data held on the card are removed; it does not actually delete/erase all the data, as Nikon states. However, it does make it difficult, although not impossible, to recover previously written data from a card once it is formatted. If you inadvertently format a card, it is often possible to recover the image files by using appropriate recovery software, provided no further data is written to the card. Since prevention is better than a cure, always save your images to a computer or other storage device before formatting a card. Also make sure to create a backup copy of these files.

To format a card using the D5100, insert the memory card and turn the camera on. Press the MENU button to display the menu system and open the Setup menu. Navigate to the **[Format memory card]** item, and then press ▶. Highlight **[Yes]** and press the OK button. The message "Formatting memory card" is displayed during the formatting process. To leave the process without formatting the memory card, highlight **[No]** and press OK.

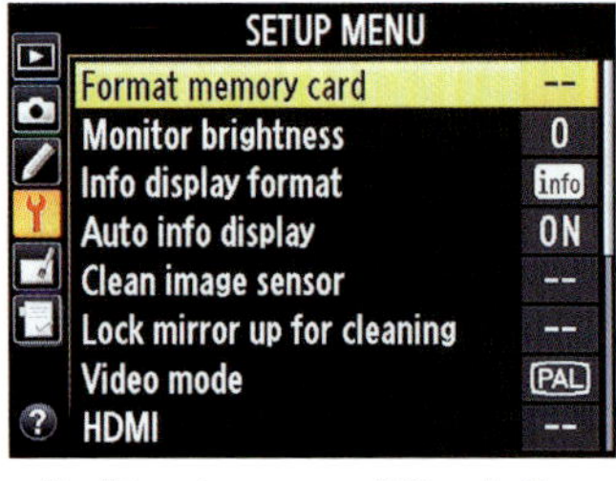

^ The **[Format memory card]** item is the first item in the Setup menu.

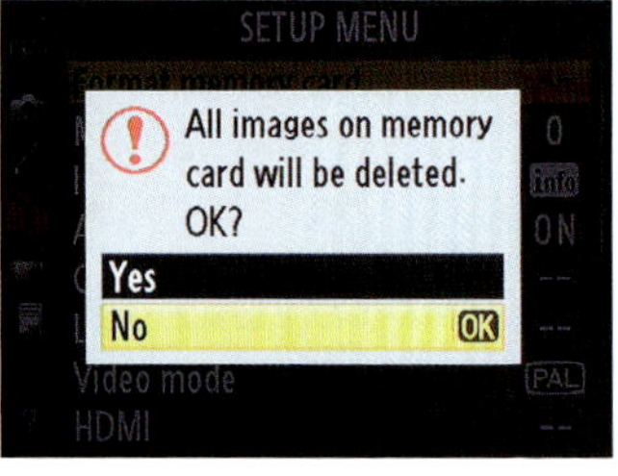

^ A warning is displayed in the Setup menu before the formatting process can be activated.

Once formatting is complete, the Information Display can show the approximate number of photographs that can be recorded on the installed memory card at the current size and quality settings. The displayed figure is only an approximation because file size will vary due to file compression; it is often possible for the camera to record and store more images than the remaining exposure count display initially suggests after formatting.

HINT: After ensuring its contents have been saved and backed up, format the memory card each time you insert it into the camera. This is especially important if it has been used in a different camera model, or formatted by a computer or other device. Failure to follow this procedure may lead to the card not functioning properly in the camera, resulting in image files being rendered as unreadable or becoming corrupted.

NOTE: You should never switch the camera off or otherwise interrupt the power supply to the camera during the formatting process, as this results in the corruption of the memory card.

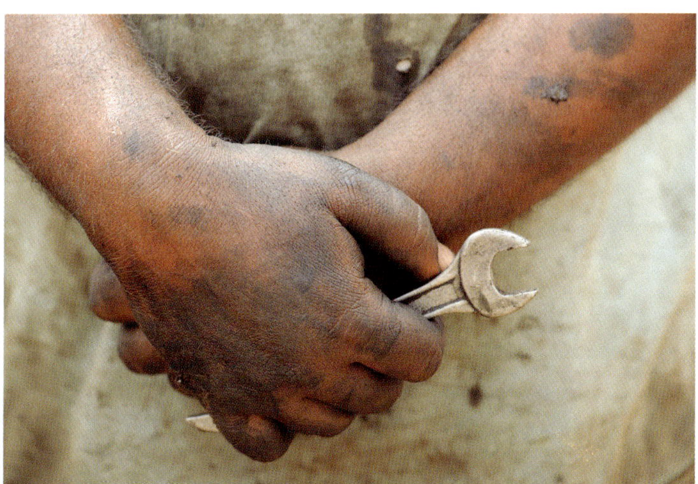

By practicing good "housekeeping" and formatting a memory card every time you insert it into the camera, the risk of the data stored on the card being corrupted will be reduced significantly.

IMAGE QUALITY AND FILE FORMATS

The D5100 saves still images to the memory card in two file formats: Joint Photographic Experts Group (JPEG) and Nikon Electronic File (NEF) RAW format.

EXPEED 2 IMAGE PROCESSING

Expeed 2 is the name given by Nikon to its latest in-camera image-processing engine; in combination with the Picture Control system (see pages 161-174), its purpose is to ensure consistency in the appearance of images in terms of color and contrast, although component parts of the system—both hardware and software—may differ from camera model to camera model. If you have experience shooting film, it might help to understand the concept by thinking about the way a specific film type can be matched with particular developer to produce consistent, repeatable results, regardless of which camera was used.

The Expeed 2 processing concept applied to the D5100 is an enhanced version of the Expeed system used by the D5000, D90, and D300-series models. When the camera is set to record images in the JPEG file format, it uses the integrated ADC (analogue to digital converter) to convert the electrical signals generated by the capacitors (pixels) on the sensor to 14-bit RAW data before the value for each pixel is rendered via a demosaicing (conversion) process to 14-bit RGB data. Remember, the demosaicing process is necessary to render an RGB value for each pixel because each sampling point on the sensor (pixel) only records a value for red, green, or blue.

Next, the 14-bit RGB data is passed to the Expeed 2 processing engine where all further processing, such as color manipulation, contrast control, and sharpening (plus an automated reduction of the effects of lateral chromatic aberration to reduce color fringing at distinct edges in image detail) is performed in a 16-bit depth space to ensure there is no compromise of the data. The final stage of the image processing is the encoding of the data to create the JPEG file; it is only at this point that the 14-bit data is reduced to 8-bit. The result is a noticeable improvement in image quality compared with JPEG files generated by earlier Nikon DSLR camera models that lacked the Expeed system, particularly in the lower shadow tones. This is of considerable benefit when the finished 8-bit JPEG files are to be subjected to post-processing in a computer, which would otherwise compound errors generated during in-camera processing had it been performed on 8-bit data rather than the 14-bit data handled by the D5100.

When the D5100 is set to record an image in the Nikon Electronic File (NEF) format, the data saved is essentially the "raw" data generated by the ADC with no interpolation or other adjustment of the information from the sensor. The settings for the Picture Control System are not applied in-camera but recorded and appended to the RAW file as a set of instructions, to be subsequently read by the RAW converter used to open the NEF (RAW) file. This lack of processing is the reason such a file is referred to as a RAW file, and the ability to modify the instruction set to each RAW file at any subsequent point after the original image is recorded is the key to the tremendous flexibility offered by the RAW format.

However, unlike other higher-specified Nikon camera models, which offer a choice of bit depth, the D5100 can only record NEF (RAW) files at a 14-bit depth, and it always applies compression to the image data. So the ADC performs the conversion of the information from the sensor at 14 bits. The data is maintained in the selected bit depth while it is built and output; this means that at a 14-bit depth each pixel can have one of 16,384 distinct values. Essentially, an NEF file uses the same structure as a TIFF file; it starts with tags that point to the EXIF (camera settings) and White Balance value information, then saves a small thumbnail image as a JPEG file, followed by the raw pixel data. However, since the D5100 can only save NEF files in a compressed form, some of the original information captured by the sensor is discarded in a process that Nikon describes as being "visually lossless."

To summarize, when comparing between the JPEG and NEF formats, the principal differences lie in how the camera deals with the data from the sensor. Using the JPEG format, the camera produces a finished image based on the sensor data and camera settings at the time of the exposure. Although it is possible to use these finished files directly from the camera to produce a print or post to a website, these files can still be post-processed after they have been imported to a computer. However, using the NEF format requires the photographer to process the image after the fact, using a computer with NEF-compatible software.

If you are beginning to form the impression that, to eek out every last ounce of quality the D5100 has to offer, you should shoot in the NEF format, you are not too far off the mark! However, while many photographers prefer the NEF format, I prefer to consider this issue in terms of the flexibility the formats offer and recommend that you use the one that is best suited to your specific requirements.

JPEG

Probably the greatest benefit of the JPEG format it that it can be read by most software and it supported by HTML, the computer language used to build web pages. This enables these files to be shared widely, regardless of the type of computer or software that may be used.

The process of saving a JPEG file involves taking 8 x 8 blocks of pixels and subjecting each block to a series of calculations that determines compression. Essentially, the numeric value of the pixels is converted into an equation that represents an average value of the pixels in that block. The compressed result for each block is then brought together as a single sequence of binary values, which is encoded using a further lossless form of compression. While the compression process varies with the range of pixel values in each block, it will ultimately result in the permanent loss of some data. As a rule of thumb, a JPEG compression ratio of 1:4 or less will produce an image in which the effects of the process are imperceptible.

However, the JPEG format has three properties that can potentially influence image quality in an adverse manner. The in-camera processing reduces the 14-bit data from the sensor to 8-bit values when it creates a JPEG file. The D5100 does have the advantage that it makes all in-camera adjustments to image attributes (i.e., Sharpening, Contrast, and Saturation) at a 14-bit level before the data is reduced to 8-bits. Therefore, if you have no intention of doing any post-processing, the reduction to 8 bits is of no real consequence. However, if you make significant changes to an image using software in post-processing, then the 8-bit data of a JPEG file can limit the manipulation that can be applied. This is particularly true of Color, Sharpening, and Contrast adjustments.

In respect to color and contrast, it appears that Nikon has maintained consistency with their current crop of camera models: The default settings on the D5100 tend to produce images that have slightly over-vivid color and boosted contrast. Consequently, JPEG files straight from the D5100 work well if they are to be used for web publishing or printed through a commercial printing process, without any further adjustment. However, these JPEG files that can be a little more difficult to handle in post-processing, when it is often preferable to start with an image with a slightly flatter contrast and more neutral color, since it is much easier to increase color saturation and contrast levels than it is to reverse their effects.

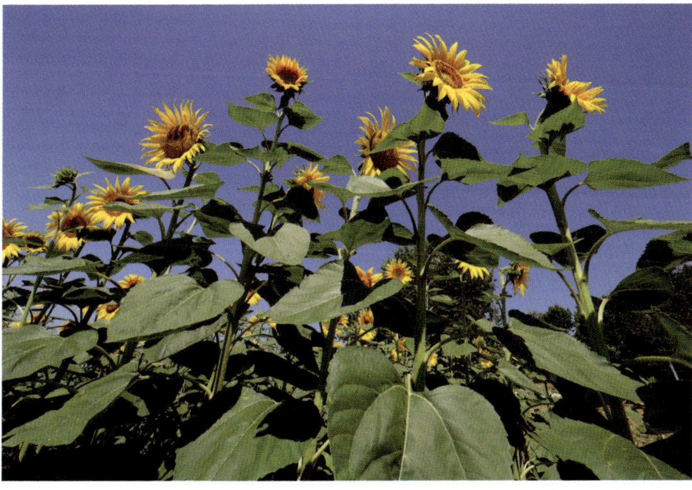

^ The choice between JPEG and NEF (RAW) formats should be based on how the image will be used; the JPEG format offers speed and convenience, while to derive the maximum flexibility and potential image quality, I recommend recording images in the NEF (RAW) format.

So, if you expect to work on your JPEG images after the event using digital imaging software, you may wish to consider turning down the saturation/contrast levels in the Picture Control System. Likewise, you may want to reduce or remove in-camera sharpening. However, if you wish to produce images direct from the camera with no intentions of any post-processing, I suggest you leave the D5100 at its default settings for the Picture Controls.

When the camera saves an image using the JPEG format, it encodes most of the camera settings for attributes such as White Balance, Sharpening, Contrast, Saturation, and Hue into the image data. If you make an error and inadvertently select the wrong setting, you will need to try to fix your mistake in post-processing. Inevitably, this is time consuming and there is no guarantee it will be successful, particularly in respect to trying to reduce the effects of over-sharpening, reducing contrast, or correcting color because the wrong White Balance setting was used for the original image.

The development of digital imaging technology is extremely fast-paced, and the electronics used in any particular camera are only as good as the day the manufacturer decided on the specifications and finalized the design of the camera. Granted, most modern cameras can have their firmware (installed software) upgraded by the user. This helps to offset obsolescence, but it is only effective for so long. By processing images in software on a computer you can often take advantage of the very latest advances in image processing, which are unavailable in the camera.

NEF (RAW)

Using the NEF format has only one serious disadvantage in my mind—the extra time you will need to invest in post-processing each image to produce a finished picture. However, this will be time well spent if you want to achieve the best possible image quality from your D5100, especially for any images you intend to print. The larger file size of the NEF format can also present an issue in terms of the amount of available storage in your memory card or external storage device; but modern data storage devices are relatively cheap, so this shouldn't be too much of a concern. Additionally, there can be limitations and variability with third party software's ability to read and interpret Nikon NEF files. On the other hand, the benefits of the NEF format include:

- More consistent and smoother tonal gradations.
- Color that is more subtle and true to the original subject or scene.
- A slight increase in the level of detail resolved, compared with JPEG.
- The ability (within fairly limited parameters) to adjust exposure in post-processing to correct for slight exposure errors, or to help extend the dynamic range of an image—for example, it is often possible to gain an extra 1 stop (1 EV) in the highlights of an image to reveal more detail and tonal gradation.
- Increased post-processing ability to correct and/or change image color by resetting attributes such as the White Balance value, Saturation, and Hue—plus improved control over image contrast and brightness

I have already alluded to the fact that unlike some of its current stable mates in the Nikon lineup, such as the D300s and D7000, the D5100 does not allow you to choose the bit depth used to record the NEF (RAW) file, nor whether or not compression should be applied to an NEF (RAW) image.

Compressed NEF (RAW): Inevitably, since you have no option but to record compressed NEF files with the D5100, the question is: what, if any, effect does this have on image quality? Nikon describes the compression applied to NEF files as "visually lossless," by which they mean it is almost impossible to differentiate visually between an image produced from an uncompressed file and one produced from a compressed file. The compression process used by Nikon is selective; it only works on certain image data while leaving other data unaffected. Nikon's use of the word "compression" in this context is rather misleading, as the process involves two distinct phases. The first phase sees certain tonal values grouped and then rounded, and the second phase is the point at which a conventional lossless compression is applied. Once the analog signal from the sensor has been converted to digital data, the first phase of the compression process separates the values that represent the very darkest tones from the rest of the data. Then the data with values that represent the remaining lighter tones is divided into groups, but this process is not linear. As the tones become lighter, the size of the group increases; so the group with the lightest tones is larger than a group containing mid-tone values. A lossless compression is then applied to each individual dark tone value and the rounded value of each group in the mid and light tones.

When an application such as Nikon Capture NX2 opens an NEF file recorded by the D5100, it reverses the lossless compression process. The individual dark tone values are unaffected (remember the compression applied here is lossless), but, and here is the twist, each of the grouped values for the mid and light tones must be expanded to fit its original range. Since the rounding error in each group becomes progressively larger as the tonal values it represents become lighter and lighter, the gaps in the data caused by the rounding process also become progressively larger at lighter tonal values.

It is important to put these data "gaps" into perspective. A single compression/decompression cycle performed on an NEF file produces an image that is, for most intents and purposes, indistinguishable from one produced from an original, uncompressed NEF file. The human eye does not respond in a linear way to increased levels of brightness; therefore, it is incapable of resolving the very minor changes that have taken place, even in the lightest tones where the rounding error is greatest and therefore the data gap is largest (remember, Nikon's phrasing is "visually lossless").

Furthermore, our eyes are generally only capable of detecting tonal variations equivalent to those produced by 8-bit data. Since even a compressed NEF file has the equivalent to more than 8-bit data, the data gaps caused by Nikon's compression process are of no consequence. Similarly, many photographers will ultimately reduce their 14-bit NEF (RAW) file to an 8-bit RGB-TIFF or JPEG file prior to printing, which can mask any loss of tonal gradation caused by compressing the original NEF file.

In spite of our eyes' inability to recognize these changes, it is important to understand that the data loss caused by compression of NEF files can affect final image quality. Thankfully, this unwanted effect is rare and likely to manifest itself only in the highlight area(s) of an image subjected to a significant level of color and/or contrast adjustment during post-processing, or where excessive sharpening is applied; the result is posterization, which creates coarse shifts in color and tone where there should be gentle, smooth transitions.

WHICH FORMAT?

In considering the attributes of the JPEG and NEF formats, many photographers make an analogy with film photography; they consider the NEF file as though they have the original film negative to work from, and the JPEG file as being akin to a machine-processed print. I do not disagree, but this is where my point about the flexibility of the two formats comes back: not every photographer has the desire, ability, or time to post-process NEF files. The good news is that we have a choice, so consider the points made in this section and make your decision based on which format is best suited to your purposes. If you have sufficient storage capacity on your memory card(s), you could always select the NEF + JPEG combination from the **[Image Quality]** options, as the D5100 can record a picture in both formats simultaneously.

JPEG Image Quality: The D5100 allows you to save JPEG files at one of three different levels of quality:

- FINE: uses a low compression ratio of approximately 1:4
- NORMAL (default): uses a moderate compression ratio of approximately 1:8
- BASIC: uses a high compression ratio of approximately 1:16

As the processing involved in the creation of a JPEG file uses compression that discards data, you should select the lowest level of compression to maintain the highest image quality. A file saved at the FINE setting will be visually superior to a file saved at the BASIC setting.

JPEG Image Size: Each JPEG can be saved by the D5100 at one of three different sizes:

- L: Large (4,928 x 3,264 pixels)
- M: Medium (3,696 x 2,448 pixels)
- S: Small (2,464 x 1,632 pixels)

NOTE: Image size/quality settings do not apply with NEF (Raw) files, which are always recorded at the dimensions of the Large option (4,928 x 3,264 pixels), and always with the NEF (Raw) compression process described previously.

SETTING IMAGE QUALITY AND SIZE

To set Image Quality on the D5100, open the Information Display by pressing the info button, and then press the Information Display i button to highlight the cursor. Highlight the **[Image quality]** item and press the OK button to open the list of options. Use the multi selector to highlight the required setting; there are seven options available: RAW+F (NEF + JPEG Fine), RAW+N (NEF + JPEG Normal), RAW+B (NEF + JPEG Basic), RAW (NEF Raw), Fine (JPEG Fine), Norm (JPEG Normal), and Basic (JPEG Basic). Finally, press the OK button to confirm the selection.

To set Image Size for the JPEG format on the D5100, open the Information Display by pressing the info button, and then press the i button to highlight the cursor. Highlight the **[Image size]** item and press the OK button to open the list of options. Use the multi selector to highlight the required setting. There are three options available: L (Large), M (Medium), or S (Small).

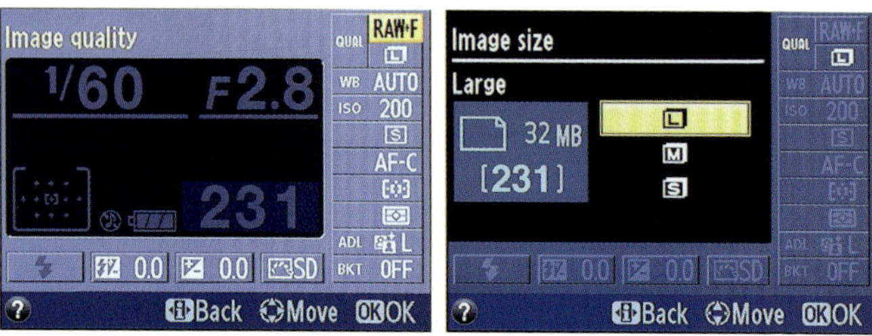

Alternatively, the **[Image quality]** and **[Image size]** items in the Shooting menu can be used to assign selection of Image Quality and Image Size, although it takes somewhat longer compared with using the method described for the i and multi selector buttons, because it is necessary to scroll through the menu system.

NOTE: The file size displayed in the Information Display for the various file format options represents the full, uncompressed file size, while the files saved in-camera will be in a compressed form. Consequently they will have a smaller size, for example, selecting RAW+F (NEF + JPEG Fine) with Large selected for **[Image size]** the file size displayed in the Information Display is 32MB but the actual size of the combined files once compressed will be approximately 23.9MB.

NOTE: When using the RAW + JPEG options, two image files are saved, one NEF (Raw) file and a JPEG file; however, when reviewing images on the camera, it is only the JPEG file that is displayed on the LCD monitor. If you delete a picture recorded using one of the dual file format options, both files are deleted. Likewise, if you set the D5100 to record RAW files only, the image displayed by the camera is a small preview JPEG file created when the NEF (Raw) file is saved. This preview JPEG file will have the image attributes selected at the current Picture Control applied to it when it is displayed.

LIVE VIEW

Live View provides a real-time video signal from the camera's sensor to the LCD monitor to show the view of the scene (it is the same view as the optical viewfinder). This enables pictures to be composed in situations when using the optical viewfinder is difficult or not desirable—for example, when shooting from a very low camera position, which can be facilitated further by adjusting the angle of the camera's monitor (which folds out and rotates), or when the enlarged view offered by the monitor is helpful in composition or for checking focus.

One fundamental difference between the optical viewfinder and Live View on the D5100 is the method of autofocus. In Live View, the camera uses contrast detection autofocus, which employs information from the CMOS sensor to assess contrast at the selected focus point and adjust focus based on the highest level of contrast. The advantage of this system is that the focus point can be positioned anywhere within the area of the frame and is not restricted to the 11 AF points used by the phase detection AF system in normal shooting via the optical viewfinder. However, contrast detection AF has the distinct disadvantage of being considerably slower. Plus, to acquire focus, it must shift focus through the plane of the intended point of focus, so that the system can sense a lower contrast level before readjusting focus to where maximum contrast is achieved at the point of focus. In a nutshell, autofocus for Live View is very good for static subjects, especially when the most accurate focus is required, as in close-up photography, but it is of little use for moving subjects because it simply is not quick enough.

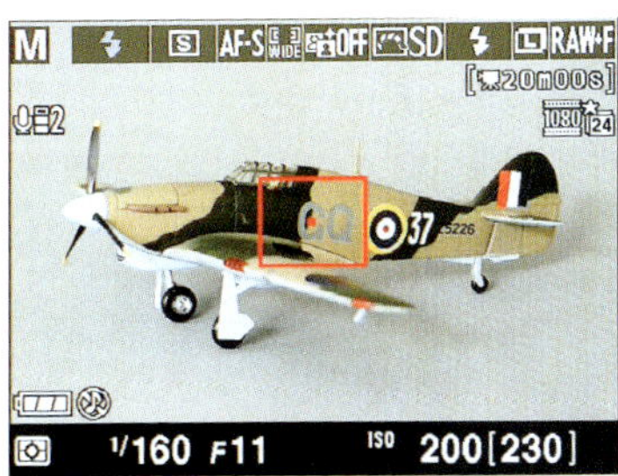

‹ The Live View display is shown here with the Live View Information Display turned on; note the camera settings displayed across the top edge of the screen and the AF point shown in red to indicate that focus has not yet been acquired.

One welcome refinement to the handling of the D5100 is the single "flick" type switch used to open Live View; located on a collar around the Mode dial on the top of the camera, where it can be reached very conveniently with the right index finger, it is quick and efficient compared with several previous Nikon cameras where a separate button had to be pushed, or dial positioned, before pressing the shutter release button down. It may be stating the obvious, but for Live View to operate, the reflex mirror of the D5100 must be raised out of the light path from the lens to the camera's sensor; therefore, the optical viewfinder is always blacked out when Live View and D-Movie mode are active, plus the normal Information Display is not available. In Live View, the Show Indicators display shows much of the information you would see in the optical viewfinder display and the Information Display shown on the LCD monitor, without impinging too much on the Live View image area. The information displayed in Show Indicators includes: exposure mode, AF mode, AF-Area mode, Active D-Lighting, Image Size, Image Quality, White Balance, metering mode, shutter speed, aperture, ISO, Exposure Compensation, battery status, number of shots remaining, and time remaining (displayed if Live View will end automatically in 30-seconds, or less). Also shown is the recording time (minutes and seconds) remaining in D-Movie mode at the current resolution and quality settings, plus an indicator for the status of the built-in microphone. There are two further Live View display options: Hide Indicators removes most of the camera setting information and only shows the exposure settings at the bottom of the screen, while the other—Framing Grid—overlays the screen with a grid pattern to facilitate framing and composition. Both Hide Indicators and Framing Grid also include small framing marks on the left and right side of the screen to indicate the 16:9 aspect ration of the video frame used in the D-Movie mode. However, there is no support on the D5100 for a real-time live histogram in Live View to assess exposure prior to releasing the shutter or recording a video clip.

USING LIVE VIEW

To open Live View, pull the Lv switch toward the back of the camera; the reflex mirror will lift and the view through the lens will be displayed on the LCD monitor together with the Live View display option last used and the AF point, which will vary in appearance according to the option selected for Live View AF-Area mode. To scroll through the Live View display options, press the Info button to show or hide the Indicators display, or display the framing gridline pattern.

Next, choose the focus mode by pressing the i button. The Live View display will close and be replaced by the Information Display. Highlight the focus mode item and press OK to display the following options:

- AF-S (Single-Servo AF): Ideal for stationary subjects, the focus will be adjusted and lock when the shutter release button is pressed down halfway. The shutter can only be released if focus is acquired.
- AF-F (Full-Time Servo AF): Intended for moving subjects, the camera focuses continuously during Live View and D-Movie mode. The shutter can only be released if focus is acquired.
- MF (Manual focus): The lens must be focused manually. The shutter can be released at any time, regardless of the focus status.

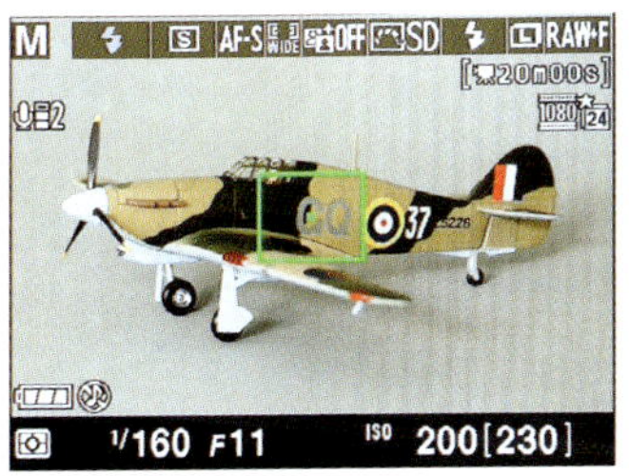

Here, the camera is in Live View with AF mode set to AF-S and AF-Area mode to Wide-Area. The AF point is green, indicating that focus has been acquired.

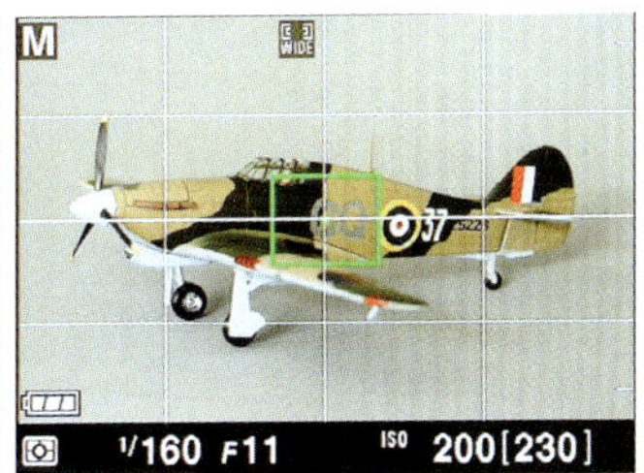

Here, the Live View display option has been changed to the Framing Grid by pressing the Info button.

Highlight the required focus mode and press OK to select it. Assuming that either AF-S or AF-F mode is selected, it is also necessary to set the AF-Area mode. AF-Area mode can be selected in all Shooting modes except AUTO and (flash off); if Live View is selected in the AUTO and (flash off) Shooting modes, the D5100 will activate its Automatic Scene Selection mode to analyze the subject/scene and select what it considers to be the most appropriate Shooting mode when autofocus is enabled (see Note below). From Live View press the i button to open the Information Display, highlight the AF-Area mode item, and then press OK to display the following options:

- Face-Priority AF: The D5100 detects the face of a person facing the camera and focuses on it automatically. The subject's face usually needs to be square to the camera lens for positive detection. The camera can detect up to a maximum of 35 faces and will focus in the face it determines to be closest. To select an alternative subject, shift the AF point using the Multi Selector button.
- Wide-Area AF: The AF point covers a large area of the frame, making it ideal for handheld picture-taking of large subjects or scenes. Use the Multi Selector button to shift the AF point to the required spot in the frame area.
- Normal-Area AF: Use this option for precision focus on a very specific area in the frame. It is best suited to shooting from a tripod and is particularly useful in close-up photography. Use the Multi Selector button to shift the AF point to the required spot in the frame area.
- Subject-Tracking AF: In this mode, the D5100 will attempt to track a selected subject as it moves within the frame area. It is most effective and reliable when the camera-to-subject distance remains constant (i.e., the subject moves laterally across the frame).

Highlight the required AF-Area mode and press OK to select it. Press the i button to return to the Live View display. The nature of the AF point will depend on the AF-Area mode selected and focus status as follows:

- Face-priority AF: A double yellow border will be displayed when the camera detects a person's face pointing toward it (if there are multiple faces, the camera, will focus on the one it considers to be closest; to focus on an alternative face, shift the AF point using the Multi Selector). Press the shutter release halfway to focus. If the subject looks away from the lens so their face is no longer visible to the camera, the AF point borders will no longer be displayed.
- Wide-Area AF & Normal-Area AF: Initially, this will be displayed as a red square. Use the Multi Selector to shift the AF point to the required spot in the frame area, or press the OK button to position the AF point at the center of the frame (when centered in the screen, the AF point will be displayed with a point at its center). Press the shutter release halfway to focus and the AF point will turn green if the D5100 can acquire focus on the subject, or it will blink red if it cannot acquire focus.
- Subject-Tracking AF: Initially, this will be displayed as a white square with four additional corner markings; position the AF point over the subject and press the OK button. The focus point will change color to yellow and track the subject as it changes position within the frame

area. Press the shutter release down halfway to focus and the AF point will turn green if the D5100 can acquire focus on the subject, or blink red if it cannot acquire focus. The AF point will continue to track the subject. To end AF tracking, press the OK button.

NOTE: Except in AUTO and ⊛ shooting modes, pressing the **AE-L/AF-L** button will lock the exposure level.

NOTE: In P, S, A and Night Vision modes, the exposure level can be adjusted by ±5 EV in steps of 0.3 EV, although the effects of values beyond ±3 EV will not be shown in the monitor.

NOTE: When Live View is selected in the AUTO and ⊛ Shooting modes, the D5100 will activate its Automatic Scene Selection mode; the camera selects what it considers to be the most appropriate Shooting mode when autofocus is enabled. The Shooting mode is displayed in the monitor screen as follows:

	Portrait	Human portrait subjects
	Landscape	Landscape & cityscapes
	Close up	Subjects close to the camera
	Night Portrait	Human portrait subject set against a dark background
AUTO	Auto	Subjects appropriate for AUTO and ⊛ modes, or those that do not match the 4 categories above
⊛	Auto (flash off)	

To take a picture from Live View, press the shutter release button down all the way; the LCD monitor will turn off. If the **[Image review]** item in the ▶ menu is set to **[On]**, the picture will be displayed on the monitor for approximately four seconds, or until the shutter release button is pressed down halfway; if the **[Image review]** item is set to **[Off]**, the monitor will remain blank. The D5100 will then return to its Live View mode. Finally, to exit Live View, rotate the Lv switch, pulling it toward the back of the camera again. There are a few general points to consider when shooting in Live View:

- Since the sensor is exposed continuously during Live View, never point the camera directly at the sun or any other high-intensity light source; this may damage the sensor.
- The LCD monitor display will adjust its brightness automatically, so the final exposure may differ from the image seen on the screen.
- It is possible to magnify the image in Live View to assist in precise focusing; press the ⊕ button to magnify the image, and press the ⊖ button to reduce magnification. In Wide-Area and Normal-Area AF, you can use the Multi Selector to scroll to other areas of the image. However, since the camera only uses a small proportion of its pixels in Live View, the resolution of an image enlarged in this way is lowered.
- It is essential to block light from entering the viewfinder eyepiece in all Shooting modes when using Live View, as it will influence the TTL metering and therefore the exposure level, so always fit the DK-5 viewfinder eyepiece blind (one is supplied with the camera).
- A countdown of 30 seconds will be displayed before Live View ends automatically; the timer display turns red at 5 seconds remaining. This feature is designed to prevent the sensor from overheating and protect the other electrical circuitry of the camera from thermal damage.
- Live View may end automatically in advance of the normal countdown timer in conditions of high ambient temperature if the camera has already been used for protracted periods in Live View or D-Movie mode or has been shooting in Continuous Release mode for extended periods.
- You may observe banding or flickering in the Live View image displayed on the monitor under certain types of artificial lighting, such as fluorescent lighting. Use the **[Flicker reduction]** item in the Y menu.

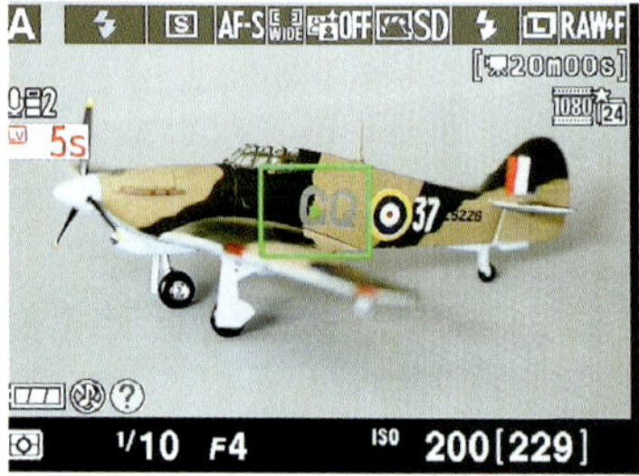

› **In the Live View display, the countdown timer—in the upper left of the screen—will turn red when five seconds or less remain before Live View is switched off automatically. Live View duration is set from CS-c2 [Auto off timers] > [Custom] > [Live view].**

D-MOVIE MODE

The D5100 follows in the footsteps of the D3100 and D7000 as the third Nikon DSLR to offer a full HD 1080p resolution (its predecessor the D5000 had a maximum resolution of HD 720p), plus it is has a full-time AF capability during video recording; although this employs a contrast-detect method, as described in the Live View section above, so it is inherently slower than the phase-detection AF used for normal autofocus shooting. The D5100 also employs a different compression regime for video compared with the D5000, replacing Motion JPEG with H.264/MPEG-4 AVC compression and stores video recordings in a .MOV container file (H.264/MPEG-4 AVC compression is far more efficient in terms of file size than Motion JPEG).

The D5100 records video with a wider variety of resolutions and frame rates compared with any previous video-enabled Nikon D-SLR, and has maximum clip duration of 20-minutes, making it the most flexible iteration of this function seen to date. A frame rate of 30/25/24 fps is available at resolutions of both 1080p and 720p, while there are also frame rates for 30 and 25 fps at the lower resolution of 640 x 424 pixels. The frame rate will depend on the video standard set under **[Video mode]** in the Y Setup menu: at a resolution of either 1080p or 720p with **[NTSC]** selected, the frame rate can be set to 30/24 fps, while with **[PAL]** selected, the frame rate can be set to 25/24 fps. At the lowest resolution of 640 x 424, a frame rate of 30 fps is set with **[NTSC]** and 25 fps with **[PAL]**. The monaural microphone records in 16-bit PCM audio with an apparent sampling rate of 24 kHz (Nikon has not disclosed the precise figure), regardless of the video resolution and frame rate. There is also the option to use an external stereo microphone with the D5100, such as the Nikon PG-1.

However, once you begin to peel away at exactly what the D5100 can deliver in its Movie mode, it soon becomes apparent that there are a number of significant restrictions imposed by the system. The D5100 is without doubt an extremely fine, state-of-the-art, entry-level digital SLR camera, but it is not a fully-fledged video camera by any stretch of the imagination! Once the camera is in D-Movie mode, you relinquish any control over shutter speed, aperture, and ISO level. In effect, the camera shifts into a fully automated point-and-shoot mode. The reason behind this is the way that Nikon has implemented the recording of video in the D5100; in essence, the camera takes the video feed that provides the real-time image displayed on the monitor in Live View and uses this for its D-Movie mode. In D-Movie mode, the exposure settings for shutter speed and ISO used for shooting still pictures are irrelevant since you cannot change them. The only parameters you can control are Manual focus, manual lens zooming, Exposure Compensation, and AE lock.

The lens aperture, which can be set to any value between the maximum aperture and f/16 (when using a Nikkor lens with an electronic aperture control), must be selected prior to opening Live View; it is not possible to adjust the aperture value once in Live View or D-Movie mode. Likewise, any of the parameters that can be set within the Picture Control system must be set beforehand. It is important to avoid setting the level of contrast and sharpening too high when recording video, as the former will cause a reduction in dynamic range, and the latter can result in a "ghost" image, in which a black edge appears to follow any moving elements; equally, you will probably not want to reduce color saturation and contrast levels too far, so it is worth spending some time experimenting with the Picture Control settings to achieve a result that meets your requirements. Similarly, the White Balance setting should also be selected prior to entering Live View (it is possible to adjust the White Balance setting once in Live View, but this requires the Information Display to be opened by pressing the ‹i› button, selecting the required option, and then returning to Live View by pressing the ‹i› button again).

Unless you intervene, the D5100 will exercise fully automatic control of the exposure. Matrix metering is used during video recording, regardless of the metering pattern selected on the camera. This raises a series of issues. First, if the level of illumination in the scene changes—for example, the camera is panned from an area that is lit brightly to an area of deep shadow—the camera will adjust shutter speed and ISO accordingly in order to maintain what the camera thinks is an appropriate exposure. As a consequence, the noise level in the image can increase perceptibly as the ISO level is increased. Furthermore, as with any automated exposure system, it is highly likely that if the scene is predominantly filled with particularly dark tones, it will be overexposed; while it may well be underexposed if the tones in the scene are primarily light. Allied to this problem is the way the camera adjusts exposure changes in a distinctly stepped manner, causing a noticeable shift in the level of illumination in the recorded image.

So, how can you tame the D5100 in its D-Movie mode and exercise some degree of control over the exposure to obtain both greater consistency and accuracy? Well, there are two options: it is possible to use the Exposure Compensation feature, or you can use the **[AE Lock (hold)]** option for the **AE-L/AF-L** button available under CS-f2 **[Assign AE-L/AF-L button]** item in the Custom Settings menu. Both of these controls must be used after the camera has entered its Live View mode if they are to be effective during video recording. So the following is my suggested sequence for setting up the D5100 to achieve a consistent exposure level when recording video:

1. Before activating Live View, set the camera to either the A or M Shooting mode and select the required lens aperture value in the camera's normal still-picture Shooting mode (remember, the minimum aperture value available in Movie mode using a Nikkor lens with electronic aperture control is f/16). Also, confirm that the **[AE Lock (hold)]** option is selected for operation of the **AE-L/AF-L** button.
2. Activate Live View by rotating the Lv switch. Next, set the AF mode and AF-Area mode as described previously in the Live View section.
3. Point the camera at the subject and focus using Live View autofocus; if the subject comprises tones that are significantly lighter or darker than average, middle-value tones, use the Exposure Compensation to set a positive or negative value, respectively, and then press the **AE-L/AF-L** button.
4. As an alternative to Step 3, use a middle-tone reference, such as a photographic 18% gray card. Ensure it is placed in the same light as the light falling on the subject, and then point the camera at the reference, and press the **AE-L/AF-L** button. This approach ensures that the camera will set an exposure level to record average tones accurately, which will result in lighter and darker tones also being rendered accurately, provided they are within the dynamic range of the sensor. Plus, the lens can be zoomed without risk that the camera will shift the exposure level if the tonal range in the scene changes significantly.
5. By pressing the **AE-L/AF-L** button as described in either step 3 or step 4 above, the exposure level calculated by the camera will be locked until the **AE-L/AF-L** button is pressed again—the **[AE Lock (hold)]** option can be switched on and off as required during a video recording by pressing the **AE-L/AF-L** button; when it is active "AE-L" is displayed in the lower left corner of the LCD next to the Matrix metering icon ().

NOTE: It appears that the application of an Exposure Compensation value also influences the shutter speed the D5100 will use during the video recording. Although no definitive values are available, setting any negative Exposure Compensation seems to result in use of a faster shutter speed, while positive Exposure Compensation values cause a slower shutter speed to be selected by the camera.

NOTE: When using a zoom lens, adjusting the focal length during movie recording can cause the exposure level to alter, due to groups of lens elements being shifted within the lens, which results in a change in the level of illumination at the sensor. Consequently, there can be a noticeably stepped change in the density of the recorded image as the camera takes a short while to adjust the exposure level automatically to compensate. My advice is to avoid altering the focal length with such lenses during movie recording if you want to maintain a consistent exposure level in the video clip.

NOTE: It is important to understand that most zoom lens do not hold the point of focus when their focal length is changed; therefore, when using AF-S (Single-Servo) AF or manual focus mode in Live View or D-Movie mode, the subject may not remain critically sharp if the focal length of the lens is altered after focus has been acquired.

ROLLING SHUTTER EFFECT

There is one other surprise that awaits the uninitiated user of the D5100 in D-Movie mode; it concerns the way in which the readout from the sensor is handled. The CMOS sensor does not capture each frame of video simultaneously, but records in a scanning process of horizontal lines that starts from the top edge of the sensor and works toward the bottom. The consequence of this is exhibited when the camera and/or the subject moves rapidly during recording; the subject can appear at different parts of the frame leading to vertical lines in static subjects that are skewed in a diagonal direction, or moving subjects that appear to have a cartoon-like, exaggerated lean.

A more pernicious version of this skewing effect occurs with a handheld camera that, due to a lack of stability, moves laterally left and right during recording with the result that vertical static lines in the frame, such as the edge of a building, take on a wavy appearance and look as though they are wobbling. If the lens in use offers Nikon's

Vibration Reduction (VR) feature, I very strongly recommend that you switch it on for handheld video recording.

In my opinion, the results produced by the D5100 in terms of the rolling shutter effect are reasonably well suppressed compared with some other recent Nikon DSLR cameras, such as the D3100. Therefore, it is a matter of anticipating them in certain situations and attempting to mitigate the worst effects by shooting appropriately—for example, panning the camera slowly, or following a moving subject accurately and accepting the inevitable distortion in the foreground and background. The single most effective step you can take to avoid this problem is to use a tripod to support the D5100 when recording in D-Movie mode.

BUILT-IN LIMITATIONS

There are several limitations built into the D-Movie mode of the D5100:

- Due to the high data rates at Full HD resolution, Nikon recommends the use of at least a Class 6 SD memory card for recording video clips.
- The maximum recording duration for a single video clip is twenty-minutes.
- It is important to keep the autofocus capabilities during video recording in perspective. The contrast-detect system used for Live View and D-Movie mode is slower than the phase-detection system used in normal shooting. Do not expect too much of the system and you will not be disappointed. For example, it will not keep pace with a subject involved in fast paced action or sports, but will do better with far more modest levels of subject movement, especially if the subject is not too close to the camera and/or moving laterally across the frame, so the camera-to-subject distance remains fairly constant.
- The camera controls the maximum duration for the use of the Live View and the D-Movie mode automatically to prevent the camera from overheating and its circuitry being damaged. In high ambient temperatures, or after protracted use of Live View and/or D-Movie mode, the camera may end Live View/D-Movie mode unexpectedly before the end of the normal 20-minute maximum clip duration in D-Movie mode.
- The audio recording of the D5100 uses its built-in 16-bit mono channel microphone, which has a relatively low sampling rate of just 11 kHz (most dedicated video cameras provide stereo channel sound recording with a sampling rate of 48 kHz). This leaves something to be desired in sound quality—the sounds generated by camera operations,

such as rotating the Command dial, adjusting the zoom position of a lens, or the AF and manual focus actions are recorded with distressing clarity! The built-in microphone may be acceptable for casual recording, but if you want to include ambient sounds with video clips, I would recommend use of an external microphone connected to the D5100 via its 3.5 mm jack socket (located under the rubber cover on the left side of the camera). Better still, use of a separate audio recorder and combine the video and audio tracks together in appropriate video-editing software.

- As well as data being continuously written to the memory card and the running of Live View, it is likely the VR function of appropriate Nikkor lenses will also be active when recording movies. Such camera functions demand significant power, so pack plenty of spare batteries if you anticipate extended use of the Live View and/or D-Movie mode.
- The D-Movie mode is simply an extension of the Live View function, so make sure you never point the camera at the sun or any other very intense light source when Live View or D-Movie mode are active. Doing so risks damage to the sensor and/or other associated electrical circuitry.

USING D-MOVIE MODE

To use the D-Movie mode, the first step is to set the options under the **[Movie settings]** item in the Shooting menu, so highlight **[Movie settings]** and press ▶.

Movie Quality: Select **[Movie quality]** and press ▶ to choose a resolution and frame rate as outlined the chart below, and then press (OK). The available frame rate will depend on the video standard selected under the **[Video mode]** item in the menu, as follows: 30 fps for NTSC devices; 25 fps for PAL devices; and 24 fps to match the frame rate of cinematic motion pictures and thus emulate their 'look'.

	NSTC		PAL	
Frame size (pixels)	Frame rate	Maximum clip duration	Frame rate	Maximum clip duration
1920 x 1080	Choose 30, or 24 fps		Choose 25, or 24 fps	
1280 x 720	Choose 30, or 24 fps	20 minutes	Choose 25, or 25 fps	20 minutes
640 x 424	30 fps		25 fps	

NOTE: The actual frame rate when 24 fps is set is 23.976 fps, and 29.97 fps when 30 fps is selected.

Microphone: To set the options for the built-in or optional external microphone, highlight **[Microphone]** and press ▶. The microphone sensitivity should be set according to the prevailing conditions; it is best to avoid the **[Auto sensitivity (A)]** setting, because auto gain will often produce variable recording levels that make achieving consistent sound impossible, especially if the sound(s) to be recorded may change in volume very rapidly. For example, if you attempt to record a person talking against some low-level background noise, as soon as the person stops talking the auto gain will boost the background noise and then suppress it as soon as the person begins speaking again. To prevent any audio recording select the **[Microphone off]** option. As with most aspects of recording video, you should exercise as much manual control over the camera as possible. Therefore use of the three other options is recommend as follows:

- In a noisy environment, set microphone sensitivity to **[Low sensitivity (1)]**.
- In a normal environment, for example conversation between two people with no strong background noise, microphone sensitivity can be set to **[Medium sensitivity (2)]**.
- In very quiet environments, it can be set to **[High sensitivity (3)]** .

Highlight the required option and press ⓞ.

RECORDING MOVIES

If you are content to let the D5100 do all the work for you, follow these steps to record video in the camera's D-Movie mode:

1. Select the required Shooting mode (in A and M modes set the lens aperture value) and set **AE-L/AF-L** button to the **[AE Lock (hold)]** option.
2. Rotate the [Lv] switch to activate Live View and select the required AF mode and AF-Area mode as described in the Live View section.

3. Compose the opening frame of your video and acquire focus, as described in the Live View section. If required, adjust the exposure level in P, S, A, and Night Vision modes using the Exposure Compensation feature, and/or lock the exposure level by pressing the **AE-L/AF-L** button (the exposure level will be held until the button is pressed again). Exposure lock is not available in the AUTO and shooting modes.
4. To start recording, press the record button. A recording indicator and the time remaining for recording will be displayed on the monitor screen.
5. If you use the built-in microphone, which is located on the front of the camera just above the D5100 badge, take care not to obstruct it. Also remember, the built-in microphone is prone to record the operation of camera controls and any noise generated by handling the camera/lens.
6. To stop recording, press the record button again. Recording will stop automatically after 20 minutes or when the memory card is full. A countdown display will be shown for 30 seconds before recording in the D-Movie mode ends automatically; depending on the shooting conditions this may appear considerably sooner than the full 20-minute clip duration has elapsed if the camera's electronics have become too warm. If this occurs, allow the camera to cool before resuming D-Movie mode recording.

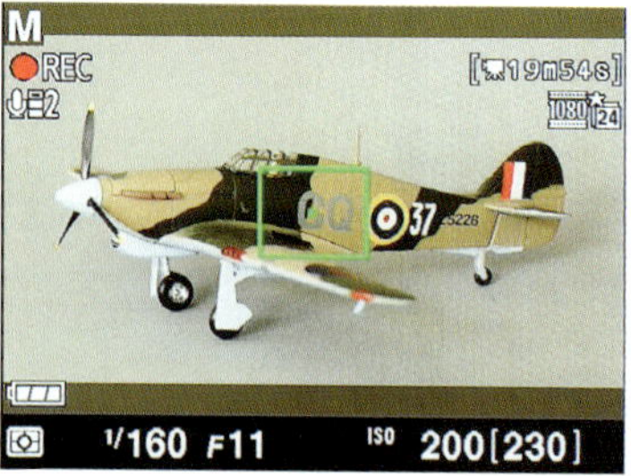

› The camera displays a recording indicator when the D-Movie mode is active; it can be seen in the top left of the monitor. Also, notice the shaded strips along the top and bottom edges of the frame, which mask the image area to the 16:9 aspect ratio of the video recording frame area.

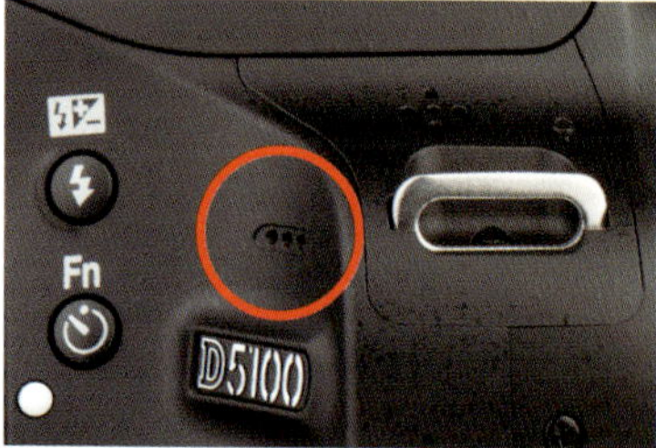

› The D5100's built-in microphone is located just above the camera's badge; it is prone to pick up any noise generated by handling the camera or camera operations, such autofocus or shifting of the Command dial. For better audio results, use a separate, external microphone connected to the camera's 3.5-mm jack.

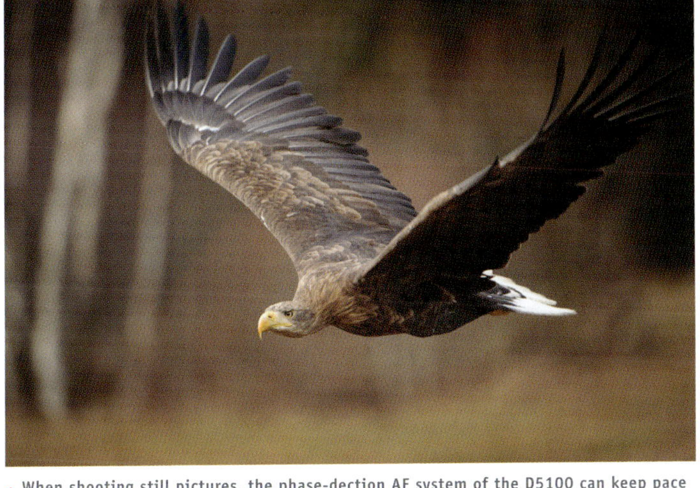

When shooting still pictures, the phase-dection AF system of the D5100 can keep pace with a fast-moving subject. However, the inherently slower contrast-detect AF system used in Live View and D-Movie mode is far less effective for this purpose.

VIEWING MOVIES

A video file is indicated by a movie icon in full-frame Playback; press the OK button to begin viewing it. The following operations can be performed:

- To pause, press ▼.
- To resume Playback, press the OK button.
- To rewind/advance press ◀ or ▶, respectively.
- To increase the volume, press the zoom in button; to decrease the volume, press the zoom out button.
- To edit the video clip, press the **AE-L/AF-L** button, while the movie clip is paused.
- To resume shooting, press the shutter release halfway.
- To display menus, press the **MENU** button.
- To exit to full-frame Playback, press ▲ or ▶.

NOTE: To edit D-Movie clips in the D5100, or to capture a single frame from a video clip, use the **[Edit movie]** item in the Retouch menu. (See pages 236-237.)

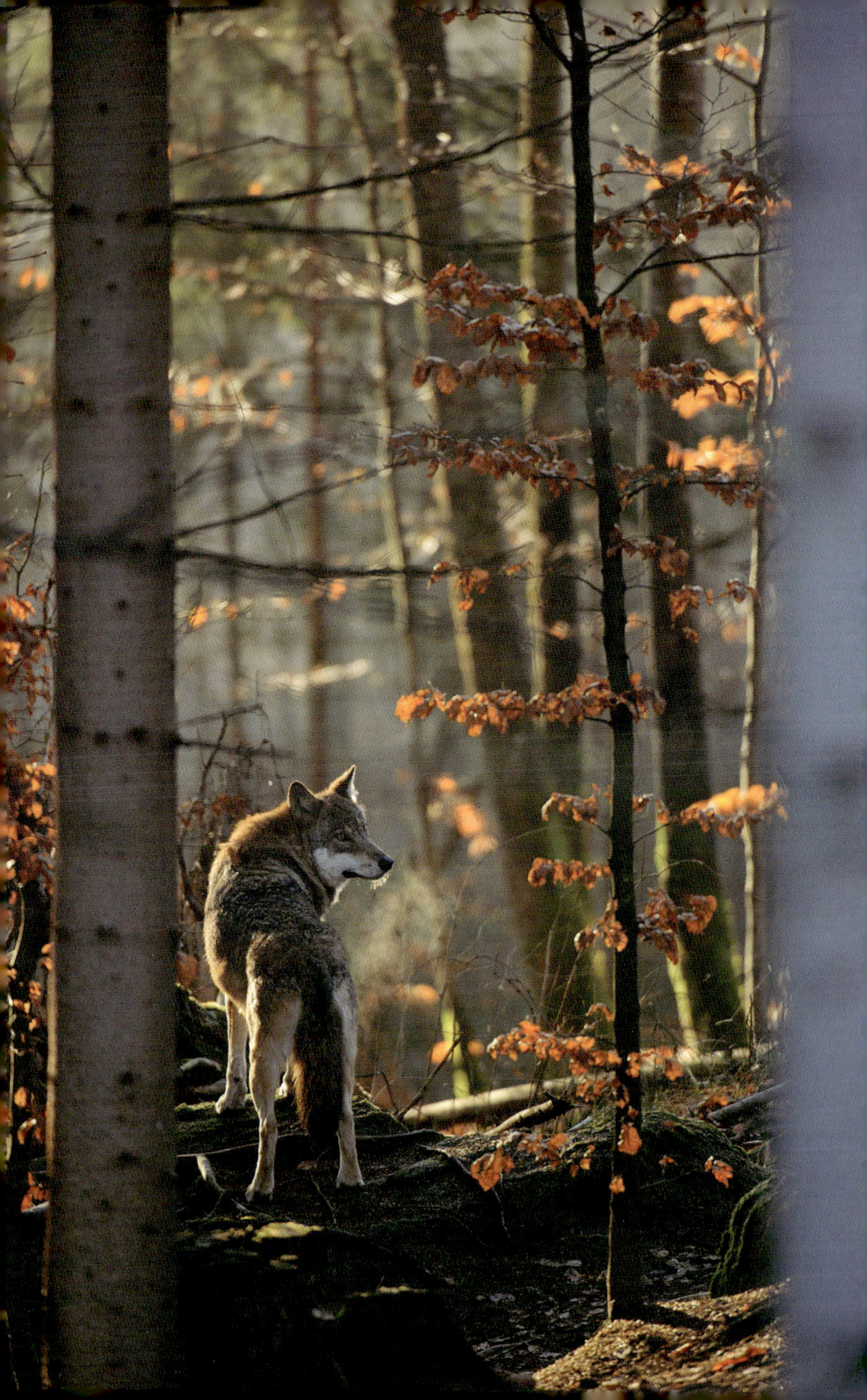

In-Camera Processing

WHITE BALANCE

We are all familiar with the way the color of sunlight changes during the course of a day from the warm orange / yellow colors immediately after sunrise, to the cooler (blue) color of light around midday, returning to the orange / yellow colors as the sun sets. These changes are significant, and our eyes can see them quite clearly. However, the color of light changes in subtle ways at other times of the day and in different climatic conditions. Furthermore, artificial light sources, such as a household light bulb or camera flash unit, emit light with a wide range of different colors. In many instances, our eyes and brain are remarkably good at adapting to the changes in the color of the light, so they are not visibly apparent to us. Think about what you see when you stand outside a building during later daylight hours when the interior lamps have been switched on. The lamplight often appears very yellow. But, if you look into the same building after dark, the light from the lamps will appear to be more neutral or white. This is an example of the adaptive process that our eyes and brain apply to light, one which cameras, regardless of whether they use film or a digital sensor, do not perform!

Film has a response limited to a specific color (for daylight-balanced film that is equivalent to direct sunlight at midday under a clear sky). Digital cameras, such as the D5100, arc far more flexible; they can process the picture data to equate to a variety of specific light colors, either automatically or by selecting settings manually. This function is known as the White Balance control.

WHAT IS COLOR TEMPERATURE?

The color of light is often referred to by its color temperature, which is expressed in units called degrees Kelvin (K). It sounds counterintuitive, but warm light (red / orange colors) has a low color temperature and cool light (blue tones) has a high color temperature. Why is this? Well, the color temperature of a light source equates to the color of something called a black body radiator—a concept used by scientists that involves a theoretical object that can re-emit 100% of the energy it absorbs. As heat is applied to this black body radiator, it becomes hotter and its color changes from black to red, orange, yellow, through to blue. The color temperature of a particular light source is said to approximate the color of a black body radiator at the same temperature. Thus, at a low temperature the color of the light emitted would contain a high proportion of red wavelengths, and at a high temperature the light would contain a high proportion of blue wavelengths.

Generally, film is balanced to either direct sunlight under a clear sky at midday (~5500K), or the light emitted by a tungsten photoflood lamp (~3400K). If the temperature of the ambient light in which you are shooting differs from these values, your photographs will take on a colorcast (unnatural tint), and you will need to use color-correction filters to counter the effects.

NOTE: The color temperature of daylight will vary according to a number of factors, including time of day, latitude, altitude, and the prevailing atmospheric and climatic conditions. The color temperature of 5500K, to which daylight film is balanced, is a somewhat arbitrary value and should only be used as a rough guide.

Digital cameras are far more versatile and can either automatically adjust their response to light within a range of different color temperatures or allow you to set a specific color temperature. This feature is known as the White Balance control. Assuming the color temperature value of the chosen White Balance corresponds to the color temperature of the prevailing light in the scene, it will be rendered without any noticeable color cast (unnatural tint). You can also use the White Balance feature creatively by setting an alternative value that does not correspond to the prevailing light to induce a deliberate color shift.

WHITE BALANCE OPTIONS

When shooting in the P, A, S, or M exposure modes, the D5100 camera offers two different methods for setting White Balance: via the Shooting menu or the Information Display. (In all other exposure modes, White Balance is automatically set by the camera.)

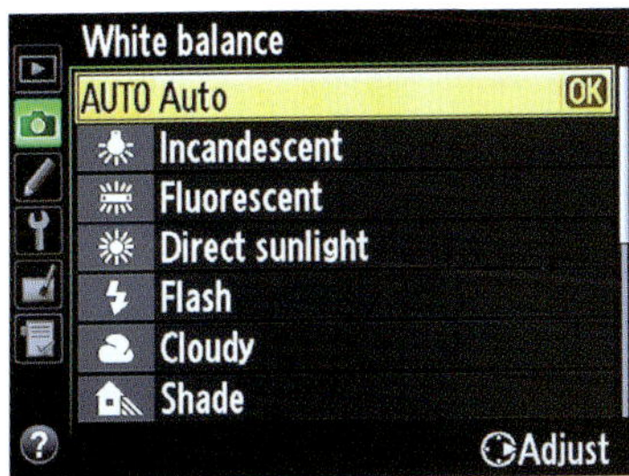

Open the Shooting menu and navigate to the **[White balance]** option, press ▶ on the Multi Selector, and highlight the required option from the displayed list by pressing either ▲ or ▼ (you must take this route if you want to alter the color temperature value for the **[Fluorescent]** option or access the White Balance Fine-Tuning feature). Then press ▶ to open the Fine-Tuning control and set any desired adjustment. Finally, press OK to confirm the selection.

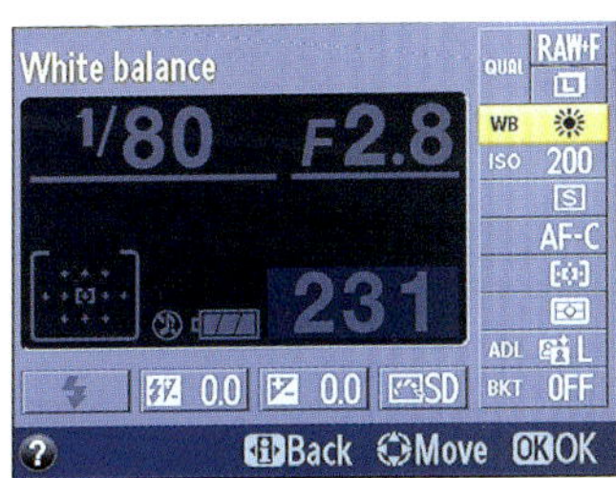

^ The Information Display (ID) is a quick way to access commonly used settings like White Balance. The above screen grab shows the ID with the White Balance option highlighted. It is currently set to ☀ Direct Sunlight.

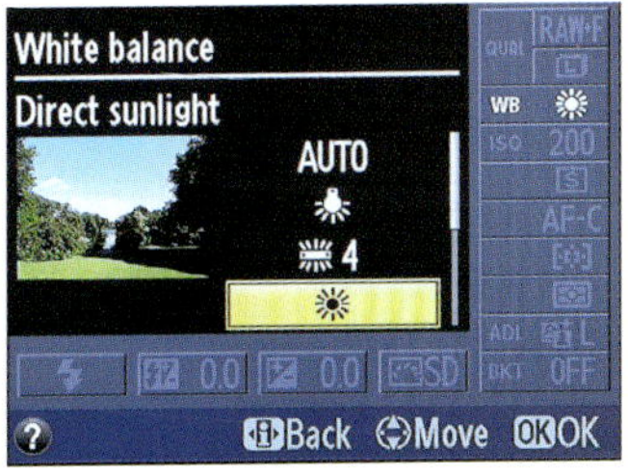

^ Once you highlight the White Balance item in the Information Display, you'll see the above list of options.

The alternative, and in my opinion the quicker method, is to use the Information Display. Open it by pressing the info button, and then press the i button to illuminate the cursor in the display. Use the Multi Selector to highlight the current White Balance setting, and press the OK button. Select the setting you want and press the ⓞ button again. It is not possible, however, to access the White Balance Fine-Tuning feature from the Information Display. The White Balance control of the D5100 offers eight White Balance options:

AUTO Automatic (3500 – 8000K): The D5100 uses its Scene Recognition System (SRS), which enhances the abilities of its 420-pixel, RGB-metering sensor. For example, the system helps the D5100 to distinguish between the greens of foliage and the green wavelengths of light produced by a florescent light tube.

The effective color temperature range of the Automatic White Balance option on the D5100 is approximately 3500K to 8000K. While I have found this option to be very effective and very reliable when shooting in the middle of that range (i.e., typical daylight conditions), I would suggest that the color temperature range is closer to 4000K to 6500K. For example, in lighting conditions with low color temperature values, such as typical domestic incandescent lighting, I find the D5100 consistently sets a color temperature that is too high, resulting in an overly "warm" amber color cast. As with all automatic features, you will need to be aware of the limitations of the **AUTO** White Balance option. This is especially true in situations such as the following: under normal household lighting when the color temperature of light sources is likely to be lower than 4000K, outdoors in bright overcast conditions, or at high altitudes where the color temperature of daylight is likely to exceed 6500K.

Incandescent (3000K): Use this option when shooting under typical household incandescent lighting, as it usually provides a better color temperature match. However, you may find that results still have a color cast and look too warm (i.e., the red content is too high), in which case you should use either the Fine-Tuning feature or a Preset manual measurement.

Fluorescent (2700K – 7200K): The light emitted from fluorescent tubes is notorious for causing unwanted color casts. This is primarily due to the variability in the color temperature of the light they produce and the way light is emitted in a rapid series of peak and decay cycles. In an effort to increase the accuracy of color rendition under the wide variety of fluorescent bulbs, the D5100 has seven sub-options available under the [Fluorescent] White Balance option in the Shooting menu. To access these options, open the Shooting menu and navigate to the [White balance] option, press ▶ on the Multi Selector and highlight [Fluorescent], then press ▶ again to display the seven bulb types. Highlight the required bulb type and press ⓞ to confirm. The bulb type will be displayed in the Shooting menu as next to a number from 1 to 7.

BULB TYPE	COLOR TEMPERATURE	SHOOTING MENU DISPLAY
Sodium-vapor lamps	2700	1
Warm-white fluorescent	3000	2
White fluorescent	3700	3
Cool-white fluorescent	4200	4
Day white fluorescent	5000	5
Daylight fluorescent	6500	6
Mercury-vapor	7200	7

Selecting [Fluorescent] from the Information Display will select the bulb type set via the [White balance] option in the Shooting menu, but only is displayed. It is not possible to select the bulb type when setting the White Balance via the Information Display route.

Direct Sunlight (5200K): This option is intended for subjects or scenes photographed in direct sunlight during the middle part of the day (i.e., from around two hours after sunrise to two hours before sunset). At other times, when the sun is low in the sky and the light tends to be warmer, using this setting will produce pictures with a higher red content, retaining the natural coloration of the light.

HINT: White balance is a very subjective issue, but in my opinion, Nikon's color temperature value for the [Direct sunlight] option is too low. When shooting in these conditions, I often prefer to use either the [Flash], or [Cloudy] options. I recommend you experiment to find a setting that meets your requirements.

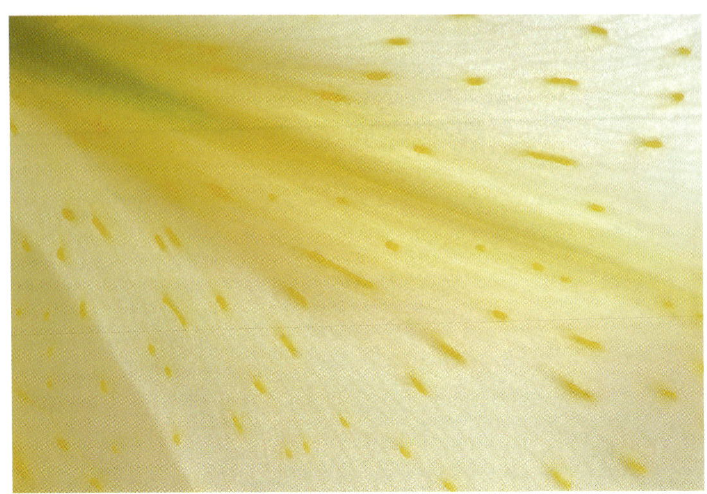

By careful control of the White Balance setting, it is possible to either achieve a neutral color balance, or induce a deliberate color cast for creative purposes.

Flash (5400K): As its name implies, this option is intended for use whenever a flash (Nikon refers to its own flash units as Speedlights) is the main lighting source.

HINT: Similar to the **[Direct sunlight]** option, I consider the color temperature of the **[Flash]** option to be slightly too low. The color temperature of light emitted by Nikon Speedlights is generally in the range of 5500 – 6000K, so I often select the **[Cloudy]** option when working with Nikon flash units as the main lighting source.

Cloudy (6000K): This White Balance option is intended for shooting under overcast skies, when daylight has a high color temperature. It ensures the camera renders colors properly without the typical cool (blue) tone, which can impart a "cold" look to colors. This is particularly noticeable in pale skin tones, which makes them rather unappealing!

Shade (8000K): This option applies a greater degree of correction than the Cloudy option and is intended for those situations when your subject or scene is in open shade beneath a clear, or nearly clear, blue sky. Under these conditions, the light will have a very high blue content, as it is principally comprised of light reflected from the blue sky above.

PRE Preset Manual: This option allows you to manually obtain a measurement of the exact color temperature of the light illuminating the subject or scene by making a test exposure of a white or neutral gray test target. Alternatively, the color temperature value from an existing image stored on the memory card can also be used as the source for obtaining a preset reading.

PRESET MANUAL WHITE BALANCE

The **[Preset manual]** option allows you to manually set a White Balance value measured from the lighting falling on the subject or scene being photographed. This generally provides the most accurate way of setting a White Balance value in conditions with mixed lighting sources or any type of lighting that has a strong color bias, such as artificial light sources.

HINT: The Nikon instruction manual suggests that you can use either a white or gray object, for example a piece of poster board, as a reference target for the Preset Manual White Balance option. I strongly recommend that you use only a gray card for two reasons: First, white cards often contain pigments used to whiten them; these can cause the camera to render colors inaccurately. Second, it is more difficult to expose correctly for a pure white subject. To try to compensate for this, the D5100 will automatically increase exposure by 1 EV when measuring for the Preset Manual White Balance in P, A, or S exposure modes; but errors in exposure from a white test target can occur nonetheless and will affect the White Balance reading you obtain from the test target. To correct these exposure errors, use M mode and adjust the exposure to ±0.0 (the exposure reading is automatically offset by +1 EV when performing the Preset White Balance measurement in this exposure mode).

HINT: In place of a test target, such as a piece of gray card, there are a number of products that can be attached directly to the lens and allow the camera to not only obtain a White Balance measurement but also take an incident reading for the ambient light, using its TTL metering system. Probably the best device I have used for this purpose is the ExpoDisc (www.expodisc.com).

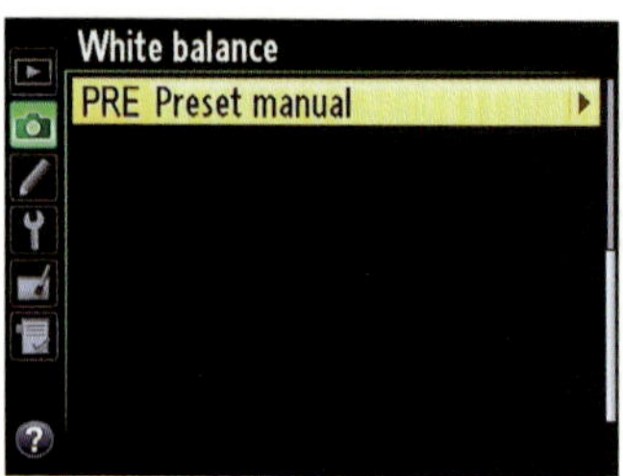

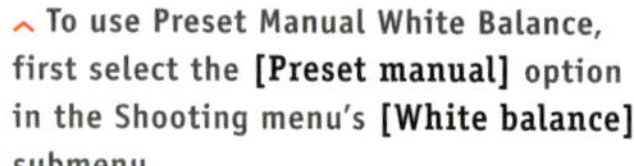
To use Preset Manual White Balance, first select the **[Preset manual]** option in the Shooting menu's **[White balance]** submenu.

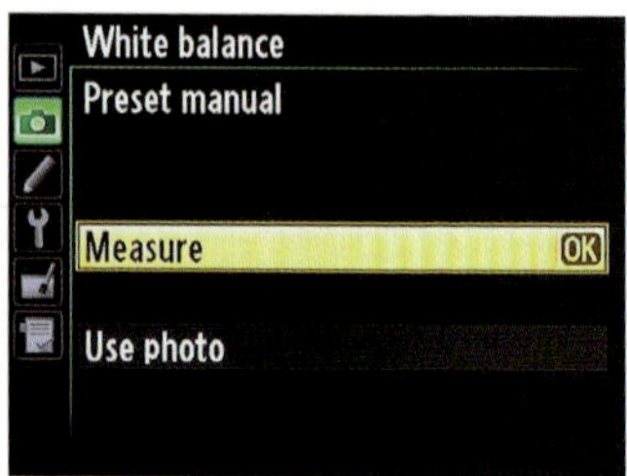

Next, highlight the **[Measure]** option to use a reference test target.

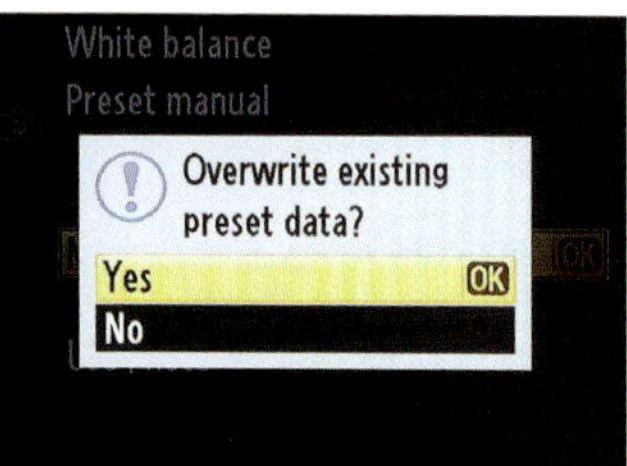

The following page shows this warning because the camera can only store one Preset White Balance value at a time.

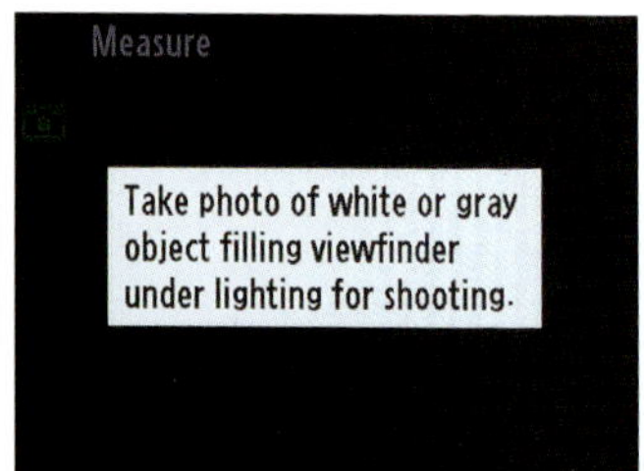

The final page in the sequence provides instructions for taking the Preset White Balance reference exposure.

There are two methods available with the D5100 for obtaining a value for a Preset Manual White Balance: direct measurement from a reference target or copying the White Balance value from a photograph stored on the memory card installed in the camera. The camera can store only one value at a time for the Preset Manual White Balance option.

To measure a Preset Manual White Balance value, start by placing your gray card test target in the same light that is illuminating the subject to be photographed. The exposure mode you use is not critical, but I suggest using Aperture Priority (A). If you use the Manual exposure mode, it is important to ensure the reference test target is not under- or overexposed (see hint above and set exposure to ±0.0). Next, select the **[Preset manual]** option via the **[White balance]** item in the Shooting menu, as described above, and press ▶. Highlight **[Measure]** and press ▶, then highlight **[Yes]** and press the OK button (the screen shots above show the sequence of menu pages). The following message will be displayed on the LCD screen: "Take a photo of a white or gray object filling the viewfinder under lighting for shooting."

You can also access the measurement phase of the Preset Manual White Balance option directly from the Information Display by first selecting the PRE option via the Information Display, and then pressing and holding the OK button for a few seconds. Alternatively, selection of the White Balance option can be assigned to the Fn button via CS-f1 **[Assign ⏲/Fn Button]** in the Custom Settings menu. Press and hold the Fn button, while rotating the Command dial to select the PRE option. If the Preset option is selected using this route, pressing and holding the Fn button for a few seconds will also access the preset measurement phase directly and PRE will begin to flash in the Information Display.

Whichever of these three routes you follow, as soon as the camera is ready to measure the ambient light, it will display PRE in the Information Display and PrE in the viewfinder, both icons flashing. While they continue to flash, frame the reference test target so it completely fills the viewfinder (make sure you do not cast a shadow over the test target card), and then press the shutter release down all the way (it is not necessary for the camera to focus on the reference test target). The shutter will cycle, but no image will be recorded.

If the camera is able to obtain an adequate measurement and set a White Balance value, Gd will appear, blinking, for approximately eight seconds in the viewfinder before the camera is restored to its Shooting mode. Pressing the shutter release button down halfway will return it to this mode immediately. If the camera is unable to set a White Balance value, it probably means that the light level is either too low or too high. In this case, no Gd will blink in the viewfinder; press the shutter release button down halfway and PrE will be displayed, blinking, in the viewfinder. Repeat the process of taking a measurement from the test target, adjusting either the lens aperture value or the illumination level of the test target until a measurement is achieved.

NOTE: The D5100 can only store one value at a time for the Preset Manual White Balance. If no White Balance value is measured for the **[Preset manual]** option, the color temperature will be set to 5200K (the same as the **[Direct sunlight]** option).

The White Balance is now set for the prevailing light falling on your subject. This value will automatically be stored and retained, replacing any previous value stored there until you take another Preset White Balance measurement. To use the new White Balance value immediately, ensure that **PRE** is selected as the White Balance option.

COPYING A WHITE BALANCE VALUE

If you want to use the White Balance value of a photograph previously recorded by the D5100, open the **[White Balance]** option in the Shooting menu, highlight the **[Preset manual]** option, and then press ▶. Highlight **[Use photo]** and press ▶.

The next page offers two options. **[This image]** selects the last image to be used for Preset White Balance. Press ⓞ to complete the process. To use a different image, highlight **[Select image]** and press ▶ to display a list of all the picture folders. Select the folder containing the source picture and press ▶; a thumbnail view of the images stored in the folder will be displayed. Highlight the desired photograph using the Multi Selector; a narrow yellow border will surround the currently selected picture. To magnify this image on the LCD screen, press and hold the 🔍 button. To copy the White Balance value from this picture, press ⓞ.

FINE-TUNING WHITE BALANCE

This feature enables the White Balance to be fine-tuned to compensate for variations in the color temperature of a particular light source or to create a deliberate color cast in a picture. The system effects change in equally spaced MIRED values (see "What is MIRED?" on page 160). You may find this system easier to use than the somewhat counterintuitive Kelvin scale, where positive and negative values create cooler and warmer results, respectively.

The Fine-Tuning of White Balance provides control over adjustment of both color temperature and color rendition in all White Balance options, except the Preset Manual. Open the Shooting menu, and navigate to the **[White Balance]** option, and press ▶ to display the list of options. Highlight the desired White Balance option, then press ▶ to display a color graph; its horizontal axis is used to fine-tune for the level of amber (A) to blue (B), while the vertical axis is used to adjust the level of magenta (M) to green (G). If **[Fluorescent]** is selected, you must select a bulb type and press ▶ before the color graph is displayed.

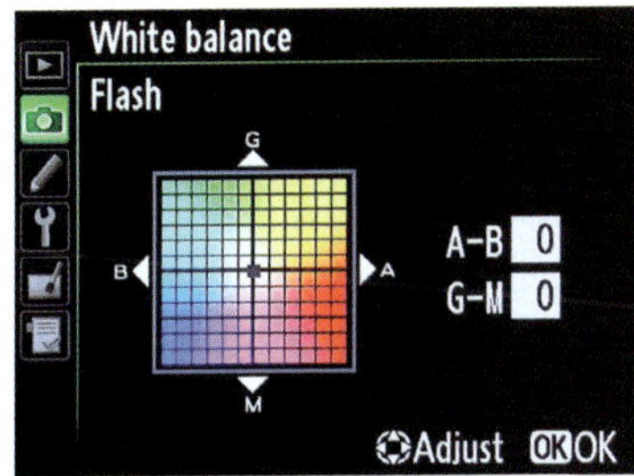

^ In the screen grab above, I have set White Balance to Flash, and then accessed the Fine Tuning graph. Use the Multi Selector as shown in the diagram to make small adjustments to the D5100's rendering of color in the Flash White Balance mode.

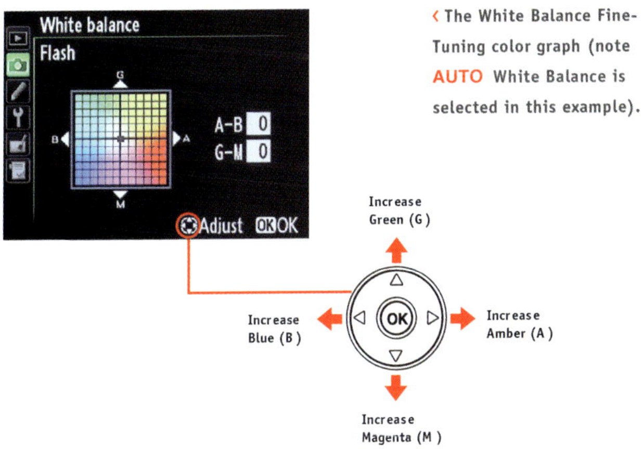

‹ The White Balance Fine-Tuning color graph (note AUTO White Balance is selected in this example).

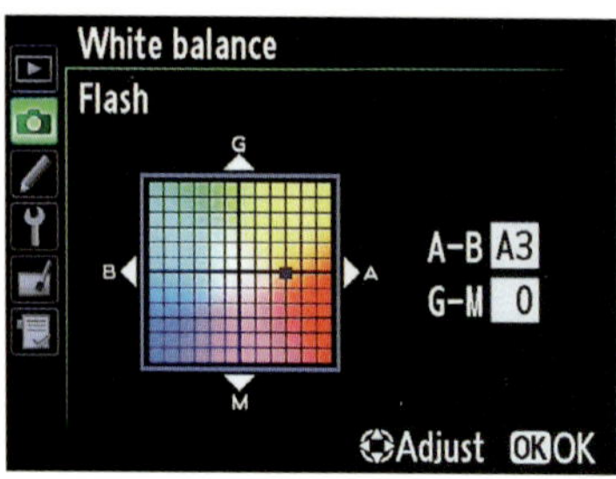

‹ Here, the White balance has been fine-tuned toward Amber (A3), so the picture will appear with slightly "warmer" colors.

Using the Multi Selector, select an adjustment value between 1 and 6 along each axis of the color graph, working from the central point (see graphics). Shifting along the amber (A) / blue (B) axis is similar to adjusting the color temperature; by increasing the B value colors become "cooler," while increasing the A value makes colors appear "warmer." Each step on the A / B axis is equivalent to about 5 MIRED; the higher the number, the greater the color shift. Shifting along the green (G) / magenta (M) axis is analogous to using color compensating filtration, as you may have done when shooting on film. A combined color temperature and color balance shift is possible by moving the cursor of the graph display into one of the four quadrants of the graph. Once you have set the Fine-Tuning adjustment, press OK button to save the setting and return to the Shooting menu.

It is important to appreciate that the colors on the axes of the color graph are relative and not absolute. This means shifting the cursor toward A (amber) when a White Balance option with a high color temperature value, such as Cloudy, is selected will only make the picture slightly "warmer"; it will not result in a strong amber color cast.

What is MIRED? MIRED (Micro Reciprocity Degree) is a method of defining a shift in color in such a way that each shift in MIRED value is equivalent to the difference in color we perceive. The disadvantage of degrees Kelvin (K) is that a relatively small shift in Kelvin value at low color temperatures (e.g. less than 4000K) creates a much larger perceived shift in visible color than the same small shift in Kelvin value at high color temperatures (e.g. more than 6000K). The MIRED value is calculated by multiplying the reciprocal of the color temperature by ten to the power six (10^6). For example, the difference of 1000K between a color temperature of 3000K and 4000K is equal to 83 MIRED, whereas the difference between 6000K and 7000K is only 24 MIRED.

CREATIVE WHITE BALANCE

Feel like getting creative? It is easy with the White Balance control on the D5100. You do not have to set the White Balance to match the color temperature of the prevailing light—try mismatching it instead! For example, rather than shooting a subject or scene lit by daylight using one of the daylight White Balance values, set the White Balance to Incandescent—now your picture will have a strong blue color cast. The great appeal of digital photography is the ability to experiment!

Remember, if the color temperature of the prevailing light is lower than the color temperature of the White Balance value set on the camera, the subject or scene will be rendered with a warmer appearance. Conversely, if the color temperature of the prevailing light is higher than the color temperature of the White Balance value set on the camera, the subject or scene will be rendered with a cooler appearance.

THE PICTURE CONTROL SYSTEM

The Picture Control System (PCS) replaces the Color Mode options and Optimize Image features that were used in previous Nikon DSLR cameras, such as the D80 and D200, to influence the appearance of pictures in terms of sharpening, contrast, brightness (gamma), color saturation, and hue. In the P, S, A, and M exposure modes, the six Picture Controls of the D5100 can be selected at will to suit the shooting conditions or create a particular effect; in all other exposure modes, the camera selects the Picture Control automatically.

The purpose of the PCS is to provide a single, all-encompassing solution for obtaining consistent results with different Nikon cameras, while also integrating Nikon software, particularly Nikon Capture NX2. Once you have adjusted settings to achieve your desired result on one camera, the result can be replicated by using the same settings on another D5100 camera. Furthermore, within Nikon View NX2 and Capture NX2 software, it is possible to apply the same settings to an NEF (RAW) file recorded by a Nikon DSLR camera that has the PCS.

It is important to mention that full integration of the PCS with Nikon Capture NX2 means that the settings made within the PCS on the D5100 are only really relevant if you shoot in the JPEG format. The values for the various parameters are embedded in those file types and cannot be altered at a later stage; at least not without a lot of trial-and-error testing, and even then, there is no guarantee the process will be successful. Since the full range of the PCS settings is also available in Nikon View NX2 and Nikon Capture NX2, it is possible to adjust all PCS settings at will subsequently if pictures are recorded in the NEF (RAW) format.

The Picture Control System offers six preset Picture Controls: Standard, Neutral, Vivid, Monochrome, Portrait, and Landscape. Depending on which item is selected, a range of attributes can be adjusted, including sharpening, contrast, brightness, saturation, and hue. The Monochrome item offers controls to simulate traditional contrast control filters used for black-and-white photography, and toning effects. The Standard, Vivid, Portrait, and Landscape items also have a Quick Adjust feature that allows sharpening, contrast, and saturation to be adjusted simultaneously. Plus, there is also an automated option to adjust sharpening, contrast, and saturation. Finally, a graphical display available on the camera's LCD screen maps contrast against saturation to assist you in your understanding of how one group of settings relates to another. The PCS of the D5100 provides the ability to modify each of the six preset Picture Control items to customize them.

SELECTING A NIKON PICTURE CONTROL

In AUTO, ⊕, and all Scene and Effects modes, the D5100 selects one of the preset Nikon Picture Controls automatically, and there is no option to alter this selection. In the P, S, A, and M exposure modes, it is possible to select one of the preset Nikon Picture Controls to suit the type of subject or scene being photographed. To select the Picture Control, open the Shooting menu and navigate to the **[Set Picture Control]** item, then press ▶ to display the six preset Nikon Picture Control options. Highlight the required option and press OK.

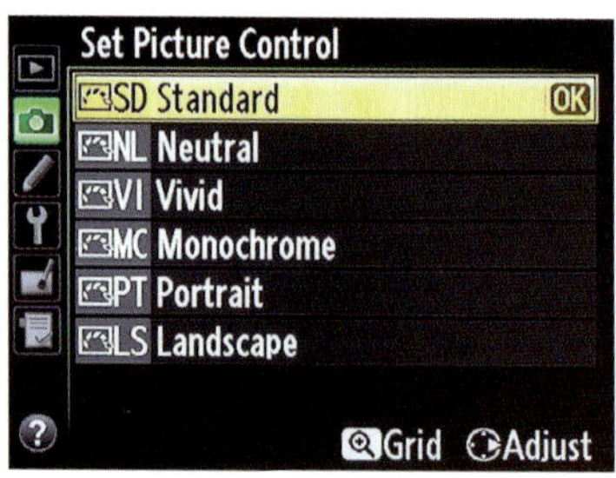

ITEM	SHARPENING	EFFECT
SD Standard	3	Probably the most useful option for most shooting situations; modest levels applied to image attributes such as color saturation and contrast.
NL Neutral	2	Provides a good starting point for any image that will be subjected to extensive post-processing, as processing applied in camera is very restrained.
VI Vivid	4	Useful for images that will be printed directly from the camera. Saturation and contrast are relatively high.
MC Monochrome	3	Use for producing black-and-white images directly from the camera.
PT Portrait	2	Color rendition is optimized for skin tones, while sharpening is reduced.
LS Landscape	4	Saturation of blues and greens tends to be boosted, plus sharpening level is raised.

HINT: There is no indication in the viewfinder as to which Picture Control is selected, but if you press the info button, the information will be shown in the Information Display.

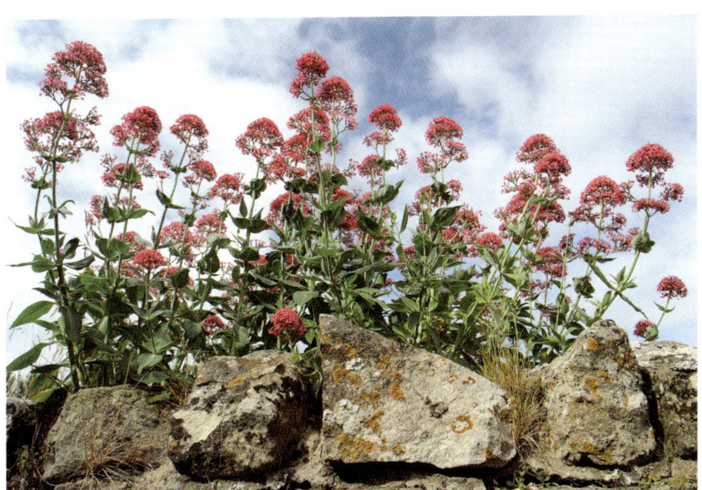

^ The Nikon Picture Controls are only relevant if the image is recorded in the JPEG format, since the settings will be embedded in the image file. Images saved in the NEF (RAW) format enable Picture Control settings to be adjusted at any time after the original exposure using appropriate Nikon software.

MODIFYING PICTURE CONTROL ATTRIBUTES

The PCS enables you to modify any one of the six basic Nikon Picture Controls so that settings match a particular shooting situation more appropriately, or so you can use the settings for a specific creative purpose (note this option is only available in the P, S, A, and M exposure modes). However, it is not possible to create an entirely custom Picture Control; you can only modify an existing set of parameters.

Start by navigating to the **[Set Picture Control]** item in the Shooting menu, then press ▶ to display the six preset Picture Control items. Highlight the required Picture Control and press ▶ to display the settings for the various attributes. Use ▲ and ▼ to select the required attribute, and use ◀ and ▶ to adjust its value.

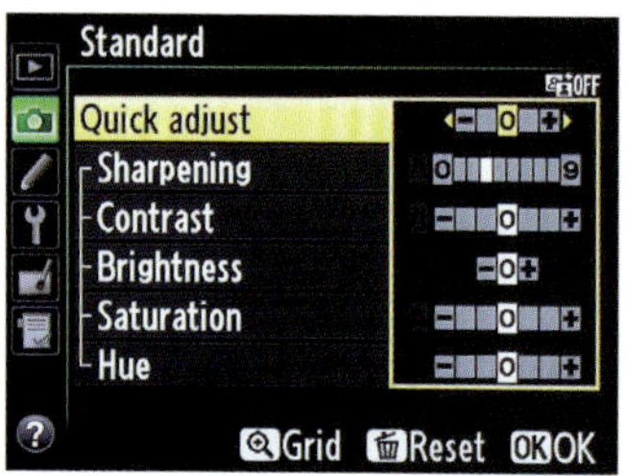

By default, the Quick Adjust option, where available, will be highlighted when entering the Picture Control adjustments.

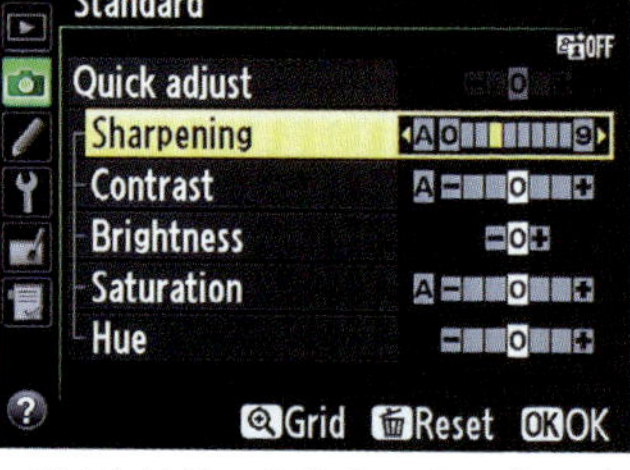

Highlight the attribute to be adjusted and use ◀ and ▶ to change the value.

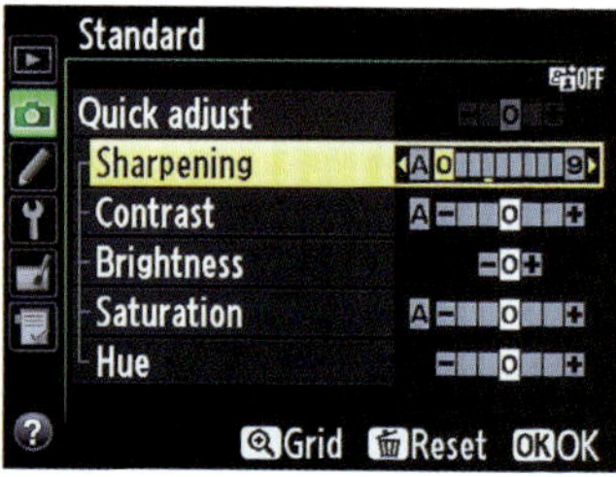

Here, Sharpening has been set to zero for the Standard Picture Control.

Alternatively, with Picture Control settings that offer the **[Quick adjust]** option, you can intensify or tone down all of the attribute settings for that specific Picture Control (i.e., if you select +1 in **[Quick adjust]** for Portrait, it will increase sharpening, contrast and saturation). When you adjust the level of a Picture Control setting, a yellow underscore line is displayed beneath the previous level for your reference. To save the settings you have selected, press the ⓞ button. If a Picture Control is modified from its default settings, it will be marked with an asterisk. If at any time you want to restore a Picture Control to its original settings, press the 🗑 button, highlight **[Yes]**, and press ⓞ.

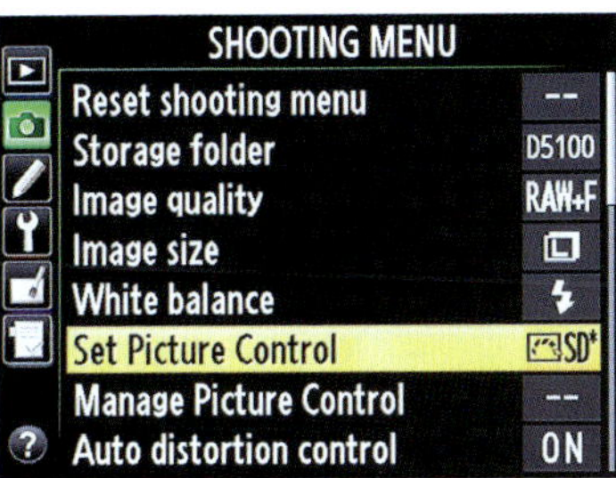

‹ An asterisk beside the Picture Control icon indicates that the Standard Picture Control has been modified from its default settings.

NOTE: To access the graphical display of contrast and saturation, in order to compare the current settings of those attributes with those of other Picture Controls, press the 🔍 button (if the Monochrome option is selected, only the value for contrast is shown). You can use ▲ and ▼ to scroll through the list of available Picture Controls, which is shown to the right of the graph. Press the 🔍 button to return to the Picture Control menu.

NOTE: I would not recommend using the LCD monitor screen of the D5100 to make any critical assessment of color, saturation, or contrast due to its restricted gamut (which is close to the sRGB color space). However, the screen has sufficient resolution to check focus accuracy, especially if the level of sharpening is high. If you record pictures in NEF (RAW), the level of sharpening can always be adjusted afterwards in post-processing, but with JPEGs it will be embedded in the image file.

The settings available for each of the Picture Control options are outlined in the following table:

OPTION	SETTINGS
Quick adjust	Choose values between ±2 to reduce (negative value) or enhance (positive value) the effect of the selected Picture Control. This option resets any manually adjusted settings; it is not available with the Neutral and Monochrome Picture Controls.
Sharpening	A (Auto), or a manually set value between 0 (no sharpening) and 9 (maximum sharpening); available with all Picture Controls
Contrast	A (Auto), or a manually set value between ±3; negative values reduce contrast, while positive values increase contrast; available with all Picture Controls
Saturation	A (Auto), or a manually set value between ±3; negative values reduce saturation, while positive values increase saturation; available with all Picture Controls except Monochrome
Hue	Manually set value between ±3; available with all Picture Controls except Monochrome
Filter effects	Use to emulate the effect of contrast control filters used with traditional black-and-white photography; only available with Monochrome Picture Controls
Toning	Use to emulate the effect of chemical toners used in traditional black-and-white photography; only available with Monochrome Picture Controls

[Sharpening]: Sharpening is a process applied to digital data that can increase the apparent sharpness (acuity) of a picture. It is applied to correct the side effects of converting light into digital data, which often causes distinct edges between colors, tones, and objects in a digital picture to look ill defined (fuzzy). The process identifies an edge by analyzing the differences between neighboring pixel values. It then lightens the pixels immediately adjacent to the brighter side of the edge and darkens the pixels adjacent to the dark side of the edge. This causes a local increase of contrast around the edge, increasing the perceived level of sharpness; the higher the level of sharpening applied, the greater the contrast at the edge. Sharpening is not a method for rescuing an out-of-focus picture—remember once out of focus always out of focus!

If you select the automatic setting for this option, you surrender all control to the camera and have no way of ensuring consistency in the degree of sharpening it applies; the camera will vary the amount of sharpening according to the nature of the scene being photographed. Scenes with a high degree of fine detail will receive a greater degree of sharpening compared with scenes that contain large areas of continuous tone.

There is no single level of sharpening that is appropriate for all shooting conditions. Remember that with JPEG files, sharpening is fixed by in-camera processing. Any sharpening applied in post-processing will be cumulative. With an NEF (RAW) file, the original level of in-camera sharpening can be altered or removed altogether within Nikon View NX2 or Nikon Capture NX 2. The level of sharpening should be based on your ultimate intentions for the image (i.e., display on a webpage, publication in a book or magazine, or producing a print for framing). Therefore, it is often preferable to only apply sharpening during the final stages of post-processing, particularly if you want to work on images for a range of different output purposes. I would make the following suggestions with regard to in-camera sharpening when shooting with the D5100:

- For general photography, when shooting JPEGs that you intend to work on in post-processing, set sharpening to zero or a low value.
- For general photography, when shooting JPEGs that you intend to print directly from the camera without any further post-processing, set sharpening to a mid-range value.
- On occasions when you need to expedite the output of pictures for publishing on a webpage or in newsprint, shoot JPEGs and set the sharpening level in the mid to high range. In this specific case, a slightly stronger degree of sharpening is probably more appropriate, as images will be viewed on computer monitors or at low reproduction resolutions. It is probably also more prudent because it will save valuable time in post-processing.
- If you shoot in NEF (RAW), you can adopt one of two methods regarding sharpening: You can set it to zero to prevent any risk of in-camera sharpening, that, when applied by a RAW file converter, would create a cumulative effect with any further sharpening you apply. Or, you can set sharpening relatively high, so that you can assess focus accuracy when reviewing images on the LCD monitor. The preview image is a JPEG file created when the NEF (RAW) file is saved, so it will have the selected level of sharpening applied to it. If you opt for the latter approach, just remember to control sharpening in your chosen RAW file converter or during post-processing.

[Contrast]: The contrast control allows you to adjust the distribution of tones in an image and works by applying a curve control similar to those used in software for digital image post-processing. I feel the D5100 tends to err toward too much contrast when left at the default level in the Nikon Picture Controls, except in the Neutral option; therefore, I recommend that this control be used judiciously. This is especially important if you intend to subject the image to further contrast adjustments in post-processing. If so, it will be far easier to increase contrast in post-processing that it will be to reduce it.

[Saturation]: Adjusting the saturation of an image changes the overall vividness (chroma) of color without affecting the brightness (luminance) of an image. A positive value increases saturation and a negative value decreases it. As with contrast, I have found the D5100 sets saturation a little too strongly for my liking in both the automatic option and at the default settings in the Standard, Vivid, and Landscape Picture Controls. I suggest you exercise restraint with the saturation control—overdoing it will make returning an image to a more natural-looking color a difficult task.

HINT: There will always be a degree of subjective opinion when assessing color, but I find the D5100 tends to produce slightly oversaturated color. A combination of the Neutral Picture Control and Adobe RGB color space renders the most natural and neutral colors, so it probably represents a good reference point when adjusting other Picture Controls; in very high contrast situations try setting the contrast level to -1 / -2.

NOTE: If achieving consistent results is important to you, I recommend very strongly that you avoid using the A (Auto) option for **[Contrast]** and **[Sharpening]**, since the levels applied by the D5100 for these settings will vary according to a number of different parameters, including the exposure level and scene contrast.

[Hue]: The RGB color model (sRGB or Adobe RGB), used by the D5100 to produce images, is based on combinations of red, green, and blue light. By mixing two of these colors, a variety of different colors can be produced. If the third color is introduced, the hue of the final color is altered. For example, applying a positive adjustment will cause reds to look more orange, greens more blue, and blues more purple. If you apply a negative adjustment, the hue shifts so that red is more purple, blue is more green, and green is more yellow.

HINT: Personally, I feel that unless you need to produce images direct from the camera, it is far better to leave adjustment of contrast, saturation, and hue until post-processing. Appropriate software offers a much greater degree of control over these image attributes.

[Filter Effects]: In the Monochrome Picture Control, there are options to select filter effects that emulate the results of using contrast control filters with traditional black-and-white film. The purpose of these filter effects is to modify the tonal response of the sensor to certain wavelengths (colors) of light. The options available in the D5100 are **[Off]** (default), **[Yellow]**, **[Orange]**, **[Red]**, and **[Green]**. Just like their optical filter counterparts, these filter effects reduce the amount of their complimentary color in the image. For example, the yellow, orange, and red options reduce the level of blue, making a blue sky appear darker; the yellow filter has the least effect and the red, the greatest. The result is an increase in the level of contrast between the blue sky and any white clouds, making the clouds more prominent. The green option reduces the amount of red, making red and orange colors appear darker. This option can be useful for enhancing the range of skin tones in a portrait picture and making them appear more natural, or for separating the tones of the various shades of green in landscape photography. My advice is to experiment with these options to determine if, how, and when they will best suit your needs.

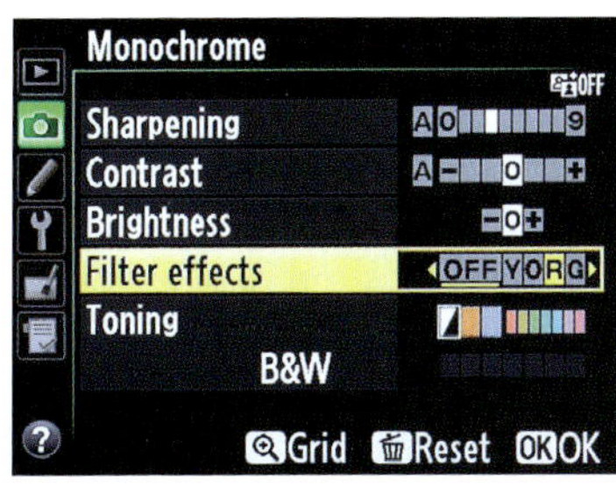

‹ The screen for the Monochrome Picture Control is different from the other Picture Control screens: It has options to apply filter effects and toning.

[Toning]: In addition to the filter effects described above, the Monochrome Picture Control also offers a range of options that emulate the effects of traditional chemical toning of black-and-white prints. The options include **[B&W]** (default), **[Sepia]** (yellowish-brown), **[Cyanotype]** (blue tint), **[Red]**, **[Yellow]**, **[Green]**, **[Blue-green]**, **[Blue]**, **[Purple-blue]**, and **[Red-purple]** (similar to selenium toning). Once you have selected the **[Toning]** option and selected the required tone, press ▼ to highlight the saturation control displayed below the tone options, and use ◀ and ▶ to adjust the saturation of the toning effect (this is not available with the **[B&W]** option).

NOTE: Regardless of the toning option selected, the D5100 always saves a black-and-white picture recorded in the NEF (RAW) format as a color RGB file. Therefore, it can always be converted back to a full-color image using the Picture Control utility in Nikon View NX2 or Nikon Capture NX2.

CREATING A CUSTOM PICTURE CONTROL

The PCS enables you to adapt any one of the six preset Nikon Picture Controls and save the new settings to create a Custom Picture Control; furthermore, once a Custom Picture Control has been saved, it can be modified at any time subsequently. While it is not possible to create an entirely new Picture Control, you may alter the settings within the parameters provided by each of the six preset Nikon Picture Controls and then save those settings.

Start by opening the Shooting menu and navigating to the **[Manage Picture Control]** item, and then press ▶ to display the next menu page. Highlight the **[Save/edit]** option and press ▶ to display the six preset Nikon Picture Controls (remember, if a preset Nikon Picture Control has been modified already, as described in the previous section above, it will be marked with an asterisk). Highlight the required Picture Control and press ▶ to display its current settings, and then use ▲ or ▼ to select the required attribute and use ◀ or ▶ to adjust its value. Once all the required adjustments have been made, press the ⓞⓚ button. Highlight a destination (C-1 to C-9) for the new Custom Picture Control and press ▶. This opens a text-entry field with a selection of characters displayed above it. By default, the new Custom Picture Control is given a two-digit suffix assigned automatically to the name of the existing preset or modified Picture Control. If you wish, you can use the controls displayed below the text-entry field to create an alternative name for the new Custom Picture Control comprising up to nineteen characters. To rename or delete a Custom Picture Control, see the "Managing Custom Picture Controls" section below.

SHARING CUSTOM PICTURE CONTROLS

Custom Picture Controls can be created in Nikon View NX2 or Nikon Capture NX2 software using the Picture Control Utility, or they can be created in another compatible camera, saved to a memory card, and then loaded into the D5100. To copy a Custom Picture Control to the D5100, highlight the **[Manage Picture Control]** item in the Shooting menu and press ▶ to display the options. Highlight **[Load/Save]** and press ▶, then highlight **[Copy to camera]**, and press ▶. Highlight the required Custom Picture Control and either press ▶ to display the current Picture Control settings, or press OK. Select the destination for the Custom Picture Control (C-1 to C-9) and press ▶ to display the text-entry dialog box. If you wish to, you can rename Custom Picture Control, as described previously under Creating Custom Picture Controls. Finally, press OK to save the new name, if applicable, and return to the Picture Control list.

To copy a Custom Picture Control to a memory card, display the **[Load/Save]** menu as described above, highlight **[Copy to card]**, and press ▶. Highlight the required Custom Picture Control located at C-1 through C-9 and press ▶ to display the **[Choose destination]** list. Select the destination for the Custom Picture Control from one of the 99 locations listed, and press OK to save the Custom Picture Control to the memory card. If you select a destination that already has a Custom Picture Control saved to it, it will be overwritten by the new save command. A maximum of 99 Custom Picture Controls can be stored on a memory card.

To delete a Custom Picture Control from a memory card, highlight the **[Load/Save]** item in the **[Manage Picture Control]** option of the Shooting menu and press ▶. Highlight the **[Delete from card]** option and press ▶ to display the list of Custom Picture Controls stored on the card. Highlight the desired Custom Picture Control and either press ▶ to display its settings, or press OK to display the **[Yes]**/**[No]** options in the **[Delete from card]** dialog box. Highlight the required option and press OK to confirm the action.

MANAGING CUSTOM PICTURE CONTROLS

To rename a Custom Picture Control, highlight the **[Rename]** item in the **[Manage Picture Control]** option of the Shooting menu and press ▶. Highlight the required Picture Control and press ▶ to display the text-entry dialog box. Create the new name for the Custom Picture Control. Finally, press ⓚ to save the name and return to the Picture Control list.

To delete a Custom Picture Control from the camera, highlight the **[Delete]** item in the **[Manage Picture Control]** option of the Shooting menu and press ▶. Highlight the required Custom Picture Control and press ▶ to display the **[Yes]**/**[No]** options. Highlight one and press ⓚ to confirm the action.

NOTE: The options available under sharing and managing Custom Picture Controls do not apply to the six preset Nikon Picture Controls; these cannot be copied, renamed, or deleted.

COLOR SPACE

A color space (sometimes called color gamut) defines the range of colors that are available for reproduction and what particular RGB values should represent those colors in the digital image file. If you know in advance that your pictures will only ever be displayed on a computer monitor or you will be using a direct printing method with no intention of carrying out any post-processing, I recommend using the sRGB color space. Otherwise, for most purposes, I recommend using the Adobe RGB color space option on the D5100. It provides the widest range of colors, permitting more subtle rendition and well-graduated tonal transitions. This increases the flexibility of an image file that will be subjected to post-processing, as well as the quality of any print made from that image file produced by an appropriate printing process. To reap these benefits, it is essential that any software used for post-processing also handles the image file in the same Adobe RGB color space.

To choose a color space, highlight the **[Color space]** item in the Shooting menu and press ▶ to display the two choices: **[sRGB]** (default) and **[Adobe RGB]**. Highlight the required option and press ⓚ to confirm the selection, returning to the Shooting menu.

NOTE: While it comes very close, the Adobe RGB color space option on the D5100 does not appear to be capable of reproducing the complete gamut of the full Adobe RGB color space, as the camera does not replicate some of the green values. The LCD screen on the camera falls short of being able to display even the sRGB color space, so it certainly does not show the full gamut of the Adobe RGB space. Therefore do not attempt to make a critical assessment of color from the camera's display.

HINT: It is essential that any software used for post-processing be set to the same color space as the image file recorded by the camera. Otherwise, it is more than likely that the application will assign its own default color space and you will lose control over the rendition of colors.

ACTIVE D-LIGHTING

Active D-Lighting (not to be confused with the **[D-Lighting]** option available in the Retouch menu) applies a localized adjustment of contrast to improve detail in areas of deep shadow and bright highlights. It can be thought of as an automated dodge-and-burn effect, as opposed to a global adjustment to contrast. It is designed for use with Matrix metering, which assesses scene contrast, and is intended for situations where the scene has a naturally high level of contrast. If necessary, it will modify the exposure level by reducing it accordingly. The amount of adjustment is quite modest, typically 0.3 EV or 0.7 EV, to preserve highlight detail. Then, after the exposure has been made and while the image data is being processed, the shadow and middle tones are adjusted to optimize the dynamic range recorded by the camera by adjusting the tone curve applied to the image data. This feature is intended for any shooting situation where the level of contrast between the deepest shadows and brightest highlights is high. However, its use should be considered with some care; unlike the normal D-Lighting feature in the Retouch menu, where a copy file is created, Active D-Lighting affects the original exposure level.

I recommend practicing restraint if you use the Active D-Lighting, because this function affects exposure. If the effect of the Active D-Lighting is too strong, it may compromise the tonal range of the entire image—especially if the contrast in the scene is very high and images are recorded in the JPEG format. Any adjustment applied by Active D-Lighting to an NEF (RAW) file can always be removed later, using Nikon View NX2 or Nikon Capture NX 2 software. To maintain optimal image quality, I suggest you avoid using Active D-Lighting at ISO settings of 800 or above.

To select Active D-Lighting from the Information Display, press the info button and then press the i button. Move the cursor to the Active D-Lighting item and press OK. Highlight either A **[Auto]**, H* **[Extra high]**, H **[High]**, N **[Normal]**, L **[Low]**, or OFF **[Off]** using the Multi Selector, and then press OK. Active D-Lighting can also be selected via the menu system. Highlight the **[Active D-Lighting]** item in the Shooting menu and press ▶ to display the options listed above. Highlight the required option and press OK to confirm the selection and return to the Shooting menu. Alternatively, selection of Active D-Lighting can be assigned to the **Fn** button via CS-f1 **[Assign /Fn Button]** item in the Custom Settings menu. Once assigned, simply press the **Fn** button to open the Information Display and highlight the ADL item; keep the button pressed and rotate the Command dial to scroll through the Active D-Lighting settings.

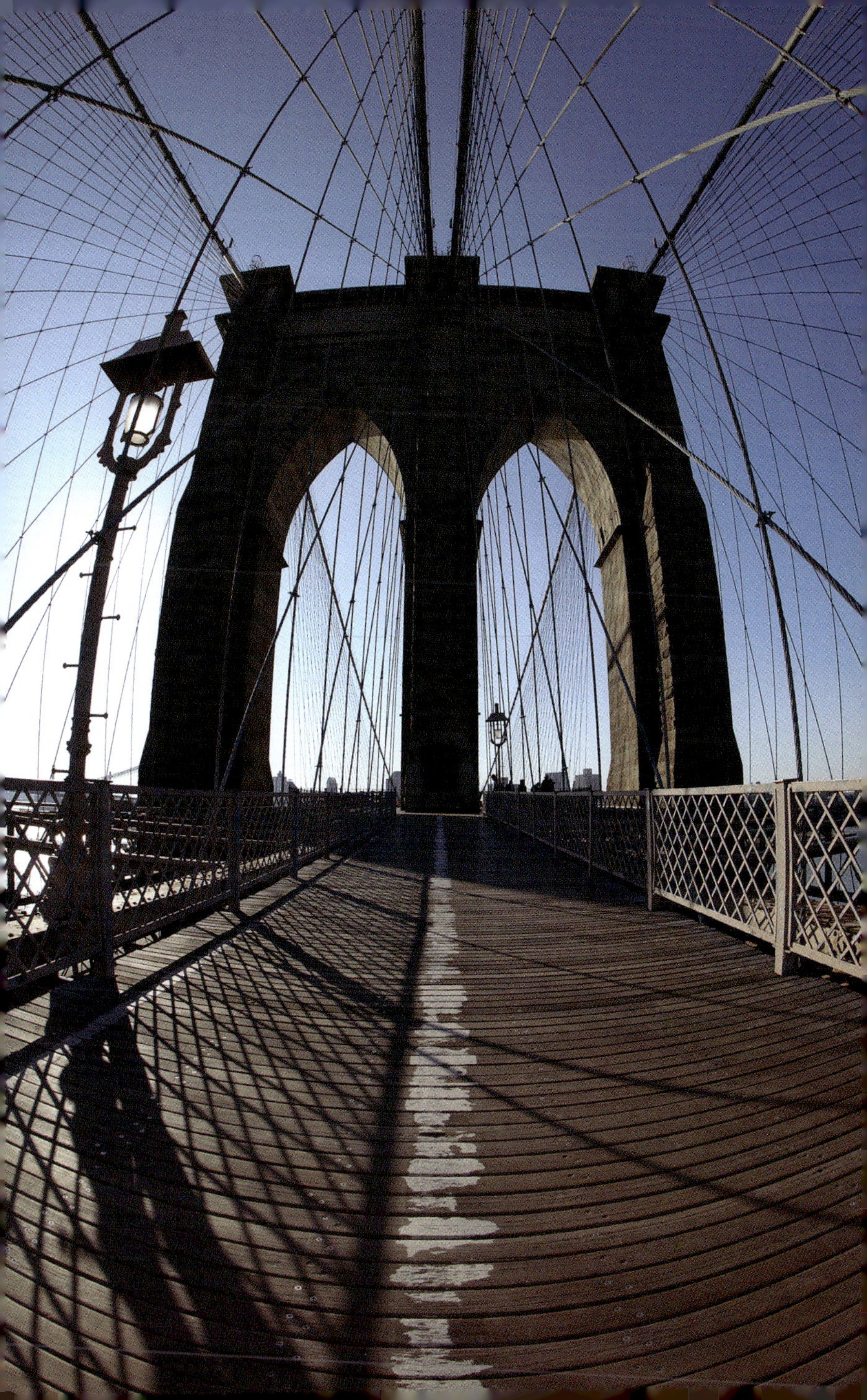

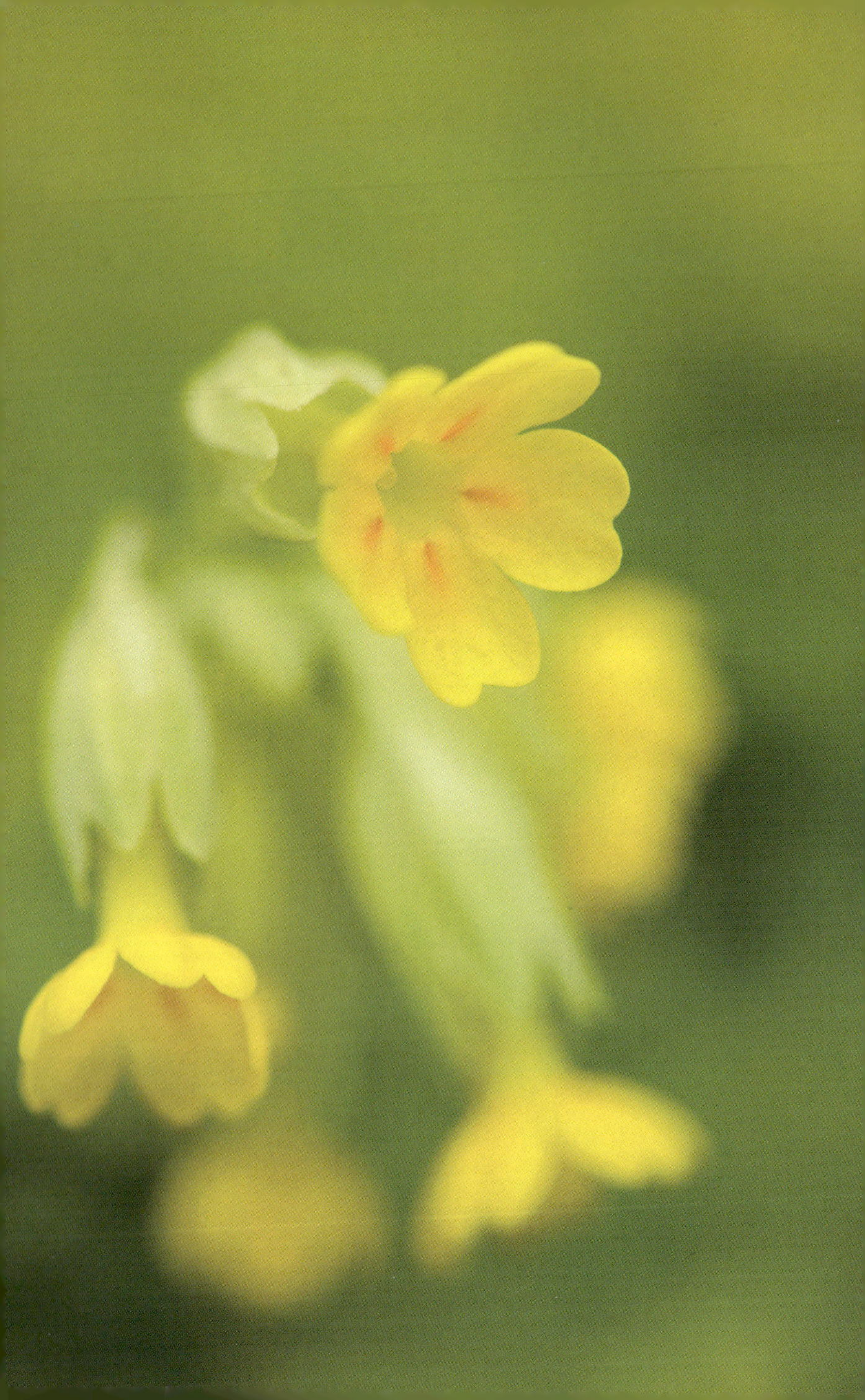

The Menu System

The control of many of the features and functions on the D5100 relies on an extensive and comprehensive menu system that is displayed on the LCD monitor. It is divided into six main sections:

- Playback menu: Used to review, edit, and manage the pictures stored on the inserted memory card.
- Shooting menu: Used to select and set a number of camera controls, such as release mode, autofocus, metering, and the built-In flash. It also allows you to influence the quality and appearance of the pictures being recorded by the camera. This menu contains several special features, such as the Picture Control, Active D-Lighting, and White Balance.
- Custom Settings menu: Allows you to select and set a wide range of controls to fine-tune camera operation to meet your specific requirements. The menu is subdivided in to six groups that each deal with a specific area of camera operation: autofocus, metering / exposure, timers / AE Lock, shooting / display, bracketing / flash, and controls.
- Setup menu: Used to establish the basic configuration of the camera. Once the settings for the items in this menu are set, they generally are not changed very frequently. It also contains the option for formatting a memory card and the self-cleaning function of the optical low-pass filter.
- Retouch menu: This menu is only available when a memory card containing picture files is inserted in the camera. It offers a range of items that enable you to crop, enhance, and add effects to a picture and save it as a separate copy without affecting the integrity of the original picture file. Plus, the D5100 has the ability to process and convert NEF (RAW) files in-camera and save the new file in the JPEG format, as well as perform very basic editing of video recordings made in the D-Movie mode.
- Recent Settings / My Menu: Recent Settings shows up to 20 menu settings used most recently. Menu items are shown in chronological order, with the most recently used item at the top of the list. My Menu allows you to create a customized list of menu options.

The D5100 's menu system comprises a total of 81 main menu items, with 20 in the Custom Settings menu alone, many of which have numerous submenus. To help overcome the challenges such an extensive and complex menu system can bring, the Recent Settings menu provides quick access to the 20 most recently used menu items. Since each page in the menu system can only display seven items, a lot of time can be spent scrolling through pages and options, using the Multi Selector to reach a desired setting. It is not possible to rearrange the order of the items in any of the five main menus, which compounds the amount of navigation required; in many cases, items that you are most likely to want to access are located beyond the first page of the menu display; however, it is possible to create a customized list of items from the five main menus within the My Menu option. Finally, as far as navigating the menu system is concerned, it is important to remember that the Information Display can be used to access a limited number of menu items directly. Where such an alternative route is available, I would recommend using it, as this will improve the efficiency of camera handling with the benefit of lower battery power consumption by reduced use of the monitor screen.

ACCESSING MENUS

To access any of the menus, push the **MENU** button and press ◀ to highlight one of the six tabs used to identify each menu (top to bottom): ▶ Playback menu, 📷 Shooting menu, ✎ Custom Settings menu, Y Setup menu, ✓ Retouch menu, and ☰ Recent Settings / My menu.

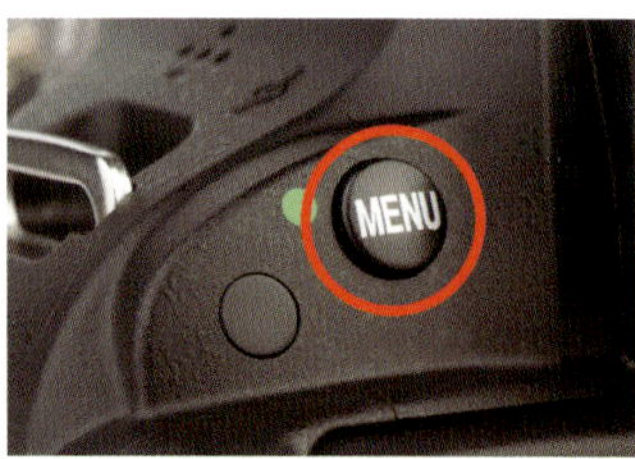

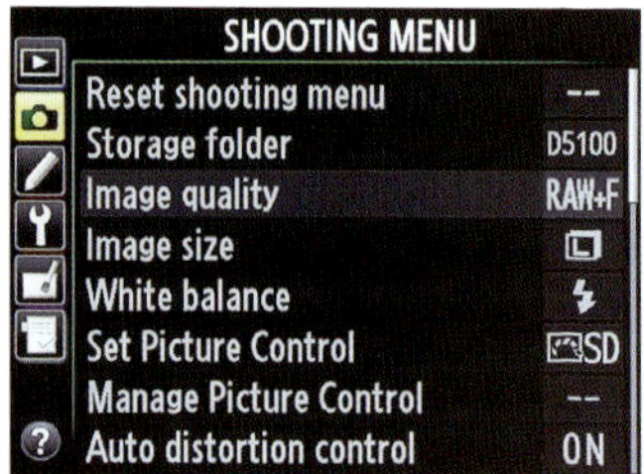

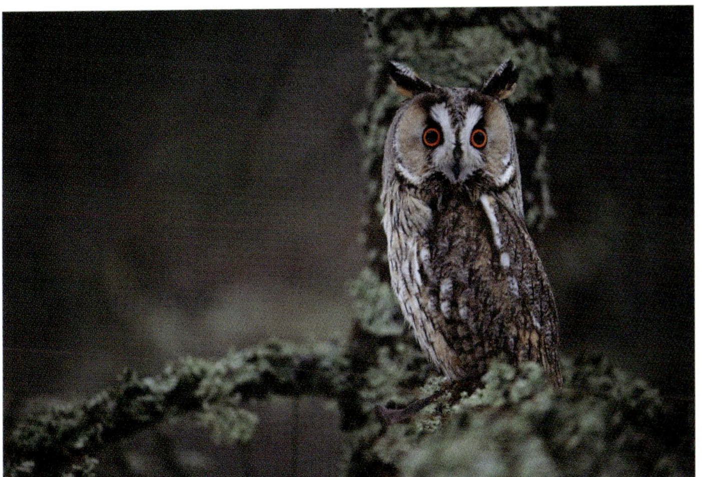

^ The menu system provides a very wide range of camera settings, enabling you to configure your D5100 for specific shooting situations.

When you have highlighted the required menu tab, the chosen menu will be displayed to the right of the six tabs. Press ▶ to enter the selected menu and highlight an option. To navigate to a specific menu item, press ▲ or ▼. To display the sub-options available for a selected menu item, press ▶. Again, use ▲ or ▼ to highlight the desired sub-option and press the OK button to confirm the selection. To exit the menu system, either press the shutter release button lightly to the halfway position or press the MENU button twice.

NOTE: Most menus have multiple pages, so keep scrolling up or down using ▲ or ▼ to access options not shown on the first page displayed

NOTE: Pressing ▶ generally has the same effect as pressing OK. However, there are some menu options that can only be selected by pressing OK.

NOTE: If a menu option is displayed in gray, it cannot be accessed. This can be for one of a number of reasons, including the current camera settings, state of the memory card, or condition of the battery.

▶ PLAYBACK MENU

The ▶ Playback Menu will only be displayed if a memory card is currently installed in the camera.

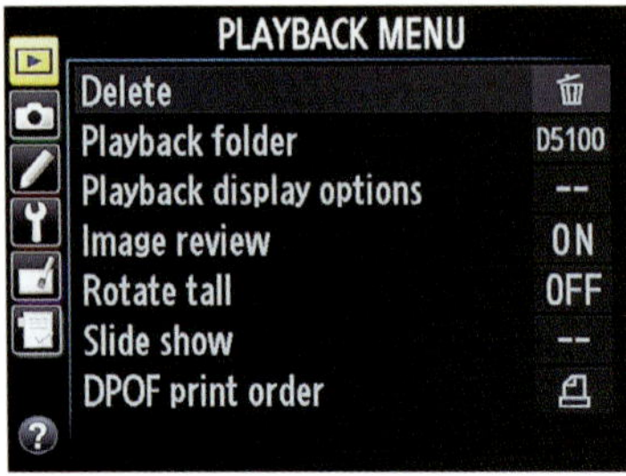

DELETE

Using the **[Delete]** option in the Playback menu, you can choose to erase individual images, a group of images, or all of the images on the card.

HINT: To delete images one by one from the D5100, it is quicker and easier to use the 🗑 button on the rear of the camera. However, using the Delete function in the Playback menu to erase a group of images will probably save a lot of time.

To delete a group of images:

1. Highlight the **[Delete]** item in the Playback menu and press ▶.
2. Highlight **[Selected]** and press ▶.
3. Thumbnails of all of the images stored on the inserted memory card will be displayed on the monitor, regardless of whether or not they are stored in different folders. Scroll through the images using the Multi Selector; a yellow frame will be displayed around the selected image. To see an enlarged view of the selected image, press and hold the 🔍 button.
4. To select the highlighted image for deletion, press the button. The 🗑 icon will appear in the upper-right corner of the thumbnail image.
5. Once all the files to be deleted have been selected, press the OK button.
6. The total number of images to be deleted will be displayed, along with two options: **[No]** or **[Yes]**. Highlight the required option and press the OK button to complete the process.

To delete a group of images taken on a selected date:

1. Highlight the **[Delete]** item in the Playback menu and press ▶.
2. Highlight DATE **[Select date]** and press ▶.
3. A list of all the dates on which images and video files have been recorded for the files stored on the installed memory card will be displayed. Highlight the required date using ▲ or ▼, and then press ▶ to place a check mark for the date. Repeat this process for each date where images are to be deleted.
4. Once the date(s) have been selected, press the OK button.
5. A warning message will be displayed, "Delete all images taken on selected date?" along with two options: **[No]** or **[Yes]**. Highlight the required option and press the OK button to complete the process.

To delete all images:

1. Highlight the **[Delete]** item in the Playback menu and press ▶.
2. Highlight **[All]** and press ▶.
3. Highlight either **[No]** or **[Yes]** as required.
4. Press the OK button to complete the process.

NOTE: Deleting all of the images on the card in this manner does not have the same effect as formatting the memory card. To prevent any problems with the memory card, it should be formatted following the correct procedure (see pages 122-123 for full details).

NOTE: It is not possible to delete pictures that have been protected.

HINT: If you select a high volume of pictures for deletion, the duration of the process can become lengthy. To avoid draining the camera battery and placing additional wear and tear on the camera, it is preferable to manage the images stored on the memory card by connecting it to a computer via a card reader.

PLAYBACK FOLDER

The **[Playback folder]** item in the Playback menu allows you to determine which images on the installed memory card will be displayed during Playback. There are two options available:

- **[Current]:** (default) Only the images in the folder currently selected for **[Storage Folder]** in the Shooting menu will be displayed during Playback.
- **[All]:** All of the images stored on the installed memory card can be displayed, regardless of the folder they are in or the camera used to record them, provided it conforms to the Design Rule for Camera File System (DCF). All Nikon digital cameras and most other current digital cameras are DCF compatible.

To select the **[Playback folder]** option:

1. Highlight the **[Playback folder]** item in the Playback menu and press ▶.
2. Highlight the desired option using ▲ or ▼.
3. Press OK to confirm the selection.

PLAYBACK DISPLAY OPTIONS

The **[Playback display options]** item on the D5100 determines which pages of image information, in addition to the File Information page, are available during single-image Playback. Choose whether or not to display **[None (image only)]**, **[Highlights]**, **[RGB histogram]**, **[Shooting Data]** (a range of pages, depending on camera settings and use of a GPS device, which show information about the image), and **[Overview]**. (See pages 101-109 for more information.)

To select an option(s) for **[Playback display options]**:

1. Highlight the **[Playback display options]** item in the Playback menu and press ▶.
2. Highlight the desired option using ▲ or ▼, and then press ▶; a check mark will appear in the box to the left of the option title.
3. Repeat step 2 for any other desired option(s).
4. Finally, highlight **[Done]** and press OK to confirm the selection and return to the Playback menu.

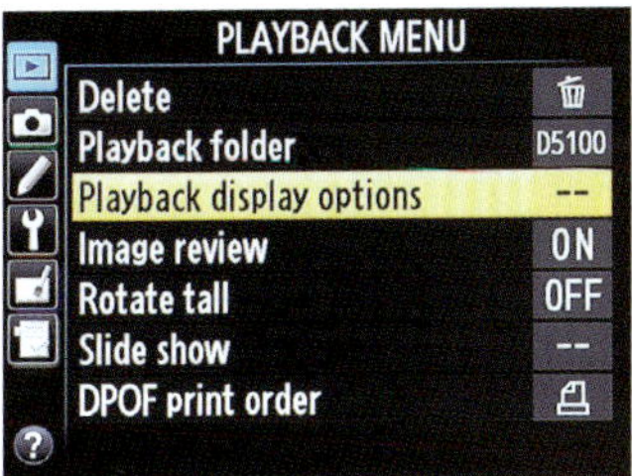

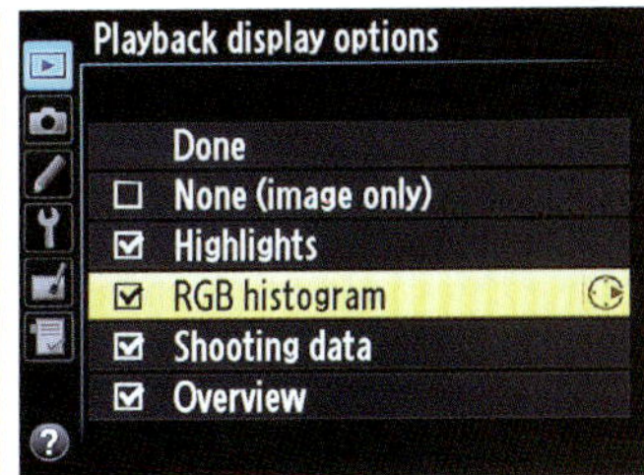

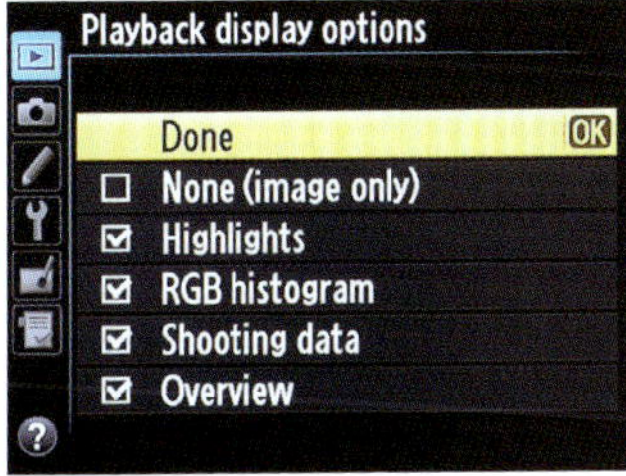

IMAGE REVIEW

The **[Image review]** option in the Playback menu determines if an image will be displayed on the monitor immediately after it is recorded. There are situations when reviewing every image recorded by the camera immediately is undesirable, such as when shooting in low-light conditions where the light from the screen is a distraction. When weighing the necessity of immediate image review, you should consider that the screen consumes a relatively large amount of power, considerably increasing the drain on the battery. My recommendation is to switch this option off and use the ▶ button whenever you wish to review an image. To select **[Image review]**:

1. Highlight the **[Image review]** item in the Playback menu and press ▶.
2. Highlight **[On]** or **[Off]** (default).
3. Press OK to confirm the selection.

ROTATE TALL

The **[Rotate Tall]** option determines whether pictures shot in the vertical (portrait) format are displayed automatically in that orientation or in the horizontal (landscape) format during Playback. Displaying an image in the vertical orientation on the monitor will decrease the overall size of the image to about 2/3 the size of an image displayed horizontally, as a horizontal image uses the full viewing area of the screen. Pictures taken with **[Off]** selected for **[Auto image rotation]** in the Setup menu will be shown in a horizontal orientation. To select **[Rotate Tall]**:

1. Highlight the **[Rotate Tall]** item in the Playback menu and press ▶.
2. Highlight **[On]** or **[Off]**.
3. Press ⓞ to confirm the selection.

NOTE: The **[Auto image rotation]** option in the Setup menu must be turned on for the Rotate Tall function to work.

SLIDE SHOW

The Slide Show option in the Playback menu allows you to view all of the images stored on the current memory card in sequential order. This can be a useful and enjoyable feature, especially if the camera is connected to view the images on a television or external monitor. To use **[Slide Show]**:

1. Highlight the **[Slide Show]** item in the Playback menu and press ▶.
2. **[Start]** will be highlighted. To commence the slide show immediately, press the ⓞ button.
3. To select the display duration for each image highlight **[Frame interval]** and press ▶ to display the four options: 2, 3, 5, or 10 seconds. Highlight the desired interval and press ⓞ to confirm the selection, and return to the **[Slide Show]** page of the Playback menu.

After applying a setting in step 3 above, repeat step 2 to start the slide show. There are a variety of controls available when the Slide Show function is active:

- To return to the previous image, press ◀.
- To skip to the next image, press ▶.
- To display and scroll the photo information pages, press ▲ or ▼.
- To pause the display, press the OK button. A submenu with three options will be displayed: **[Restart]**, **[Frame Interval]**, or **[Exit]**. Highlight as required and press OK to select the option.
- To stop the slide show and return to the Playback menu, press the MENU button.
- To stop the slide show and return to the Playback mode (full-frame or thumbnail view), press ▶.
- To stop the slide show and return to the Shooting mode, press the shutter release button down halfway.

At the end of the slide show display, a menu will be displayed with the following options: **[Restart]**, **[Frame Interval]**, or **[Exit]**. This is the same menu that is displayed when the slide show is paused by pressing the OK button. Highlight the required option and press OK.

HINT: Due to the protracted use of the monitor, the slide show function can consume a significant amount of battery power, especially if a large number of images are stored on the memory card. Ensure you use a fully charged battery or the EH-5b AC adapter with EP-5A power connector.

DPOF PRINT ORDER

The **[Print Set (DPOF)]** item in the Playback menu enables you to create and save instructions to print a set of images automatically using a DPOF-compatible printing device (see pages 303-308 for more details).

SHOOTING MENU

The following are the various items available in the D5100's Shooting menu.

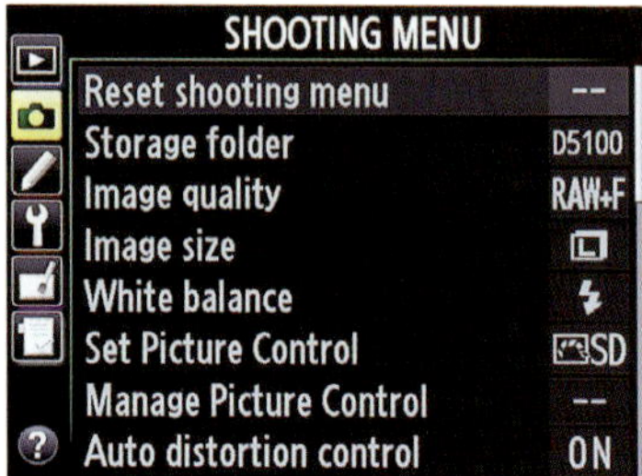

› The coverage of the Matrix metering pattern extends virtually to the edge of the full frame area (as indicated by the yellow shading, which is shown for illustrative purposes only).

RESET SHOOTING OPTIONS

To select **[Reset shooting options]**:

1. Highlight the **[Reset shooting options]** item in the Shooting menu and press ▶.
2. Highlight **[No]** or **[Yes]**.
3. Press OK to confirm the selection.

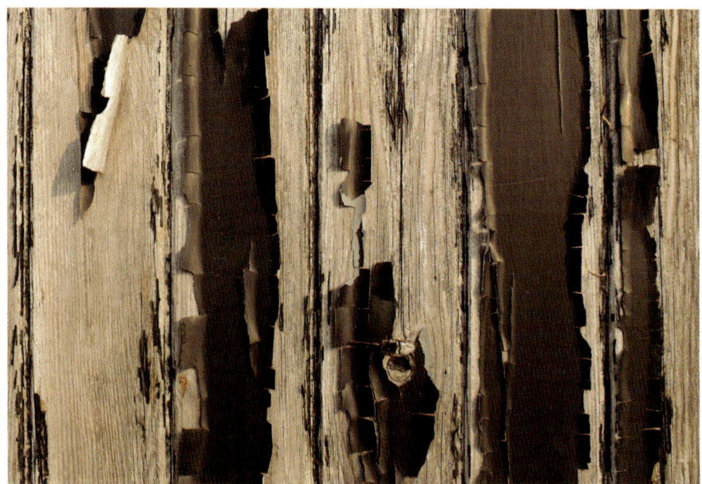

^ As you experiment with your camera, you may change settings in the Shooting menu. Rest assured that you can very easily return all of this menu's settings to their defaults using the **[Reset shooting options]** item.

If you select **[Yes]**, this item allows you to reset the items listed in the table on the following page to their default settings with a single action.

OPTION	DEFAULT SETTING
Storage folder	–
Image Quality	JPEG Normal
Image Size	Large
White Balance	Auto
Fluorescent White Balance	Cool-White
Set Picture Control	Standard
Manage Picture Control	–
Auto Distortion Control	Off
Color Space	sRGB
Active D-Lighting	Off
HDR (high dynamic range)	Off [1]
Long Exp. Noise Reduction	Off
High ISO Noise Reduction	Normal
ISO Sensitivity in P, S, A, M	100
ISO Sensitivity in other modes	Auto
ISO Sensitivity Auto Control	Off
Release mode	Single
Multiple Exposure	Off [2]
Movie Settings: Quality [3]	–
Movie Settings: Microphone	Auto Sensitivity
Interval Timer shooting	Off [4]

1 Resets **[Exposure Differential]** to **[Auto]**, smoothing to **[Normal]**.

2 Resets **[Number of shots]** to 2 and **[Gain]** to **[On]**.

3 Default value varies depending on video standard (NTSC / PAL) used in country of purchase.

4 Resets **[Choose start time]** to **[Now]**, **[Interval]** to 1 minute, **[Number of times]** to 1.

STORAGE FOLDER

The D5100 uses a folder system to organize images stored on the installed memory card. The **[Storage folder]** option in the Setup menu allows you to select which folder the images you are currently recording will be saved in and enables you to create new folders. If you do not use any of the folders options, the camera will automatically create a folder named 100D5100, in which the first 999 pictures recorded by the camera will be stored. If you exceed 999 pictures, the camera will create a new folder named 101D5100; a new folder will be created for each set of 999 pictures. The three-digit prefix is only displayed when the memory card is connected to a computer, either directly from the camera or via a card reader.

You can create your own folder(s) and name them for your reference. You can assign a five-character folder title; a three-digit number between 100 and 999 always prefixes the title. If you use multiple folders on a single memory card, you must select one "active" folder to which all images will be stored until an alternative folder is chosen.

To create a new folder:

1. Highlight the **[Storage folder]** item in the Setup menu and press ▶.
2. Highlight the **[New]** option and press ▶.
3. Designate the name / number of the new folder by using the keypad of letters and numbers that are displayed on the screen. Use the Multi Selector to select the required character and press Ⓞ to input it. To move the cursor, rotate the Command dial.
4. To delete a character at the current cursor position, press the 🗑 button.
5. Press ⊕ to confirm the action and return to the Setup menu.
6. Press **MENU** to exit without creating a new folder name.

To select an existing folder:

1. Highlight the **[Storage folder]** item in the Setup menu and press ▶.
2. Highlight the **[Select folder]** option and press ▶.
3. A list of the folders currently stored on the memory card is displayed; highlight the folder you wish to use by pressing ▲ or ▼.
4. Press Ⓞ to confirm the action and return to the Setup menu.

The **[Rename]** option allows an existing folder name to be changed. The **[Delete]** option allows all empty folders on the memory card to be deleted.

HINT: Folders may be useful if you expect to take pictures of a variety of subjects (i.e., various different locations on a vacation), but with the relatively low cost of memory cards it is probably easier and more efficient to use multiple cards.

IMAGE QUALITY

The **[Image quality]** option in the Shooting menu allows you to select the file format for images recorded by the camera. The D5100 can record images in JPEG or NEF (RAW) formats. (See pages 124-132 for more details.)

IMAGE SIZE

Image size determines the file size, or resolution, of an image. Image Size is expressed as the number of pixels used in the file. Image size adjustments will only apply to images saved using the JPEG format. NEF (RAW) files are always saved at the camera's highest resolution. (See pages 124-132 for more details.)

WHITE BALANCE

The **[White balance]** option in the Shooting menu allows you to select the color temperature at which the images you are shooting will be balanced and processed. (See pages 149-161 for more details.)

SET PICTURE CONTROL

The Picture Control System allows you to set specific controls that determine how the D5100 will perform image processing. The D5100 has six standard Nikon Picture Controls: Standard, Neutral, Vivid, Monochrome, Portrait, and Landscape (see pages 161-174 for more details).

MANAGE PICTURE CONTROL

You can create and save Custom Picture Controls, which can also be copied to a memory card and applied to another D5100 camera or used in compatible Nikon software. Picture Controls created in compatible Nikon software can be uploaded to another D5100 (see pages 171-172 for full details).

AUTO DISTORTION CONTROL

Auto Distortion Control is a proactive feature that operates while the camera is processing image data after a picture has been recorded (it is not the same as the reactive **[Distortion Control]** item in the Retouch menu that can be used to correct an image that has already been saved to the memory card installed in the camera). It is intended to reduce the effects of linear distortion that often occurs, particularly at the periphery of the frame, where straight lines are not rendered as straight. Typically, a wide-angle lens causes barrel distortion that makes lines bow outward away from the center of the picture, while long telephoto lenses cause pincushion distortion, where lines bend inward. This option is only available with D- and G-type Nikkor lenses (PC, fisheye, and certain other lenses are excluded). Select **[On]** to have the camera correct linear distortion automatically, but be aware that this may result in the edge of the image being cropped out of the final picture; image-processing time is also extended.

COLOR SPACE

The range of colors capable of being displayed in an image recorded by the D5100 is determined by the Color Space setting. The D5100 provides two options for color space: **[Adobe RGB]** and **[sRGB]**. The color space determines the range (gamut) of colors that will be available in an image file for color reproduction and should be chosen according to how the image will be processed after it has been exported from the camera. (See pages 172-173 for more details.)

ACTIVE D-LIGHTING

The Active D-Lighting feature (not to be confused with the **[D-Lighting]** item in the Retouch menu) can be used to optimize the exposure settings when using Matrix metering. Since the effects of Active D-Lighting are applied during the processing of an image file, it is not possible to reverse them when recording JPEG files. The effects of Active D-Lighting on an image recorded in the NEF (RAW) format can be altered subsequently using appropriate Nikon software. (See pages 173-174 for more details.)

HDR (HIGH DYNAMIC RANGE)

The HDR feature combines two exposures into a single image to record a broader dynamic range, so a wider range of tones from deep shadow to bright highlight can be depicted in a picture, even when shooting in high-contrast conditions. The feature works best with Matrix metering (if another metering pattern is used, an exposure differential of **[Auto]** is equivalent to approximately 2 EV). The feature is not compatible with the NEF (RAW) file format. Choose higher values under the **[Exposure Differential]** option when shooting in high-contrast conditions but do exercise some restraint as setting a value that is too high may cause inferior image quality. To select the degree to which edges in the two images are blended together, choose a value under the **[Smoothing]** option; higher values produce a smoother composite image but may reduce image sharpness in some areas. To set **[HDR]**:

1. Highlight **[HDR (high dynamic range)]** in the Shooting menu and press ▶.
2. Highlight **[HDR mode]** and press ▶.
3. Highlight **[On]** and press the OK button (Hdr will be displayed in the viewfinder).
4. Highlight **[Exposure Differential]** and press ▶.
5. Select the required option and press the OK button to confirm the selection and return to the **[HDR]** page.
6. Highlight **[Smoothing]** and press ▶.
7. Select the required option and press the OK button to confirm the selection and return to the **[HDR]** page.

Frame the picture, adjust focus and press the shutter release. The camera records two exposures and then applies its processing regime. During this period "Job Hdr" is displayed in the viewfinder; no further pictures can be taken until the in-camera processing is completed. The HDR function is turned off automatically after the camera has saved the image file; to cancel HDR shooting before making an exposure, turn the Mode dial to a setting other than P, S, A, or M.

LONG EXPOSURE NR (NOISE REDUCTION)

Images taken at long shutter speeds will often exhibit a higher level of electronic noise. Noise is the result of the amplification process that is applied to the data captured by the sensor, which is compounded by a higher internal temperature of the camera due to extended shutter speeds. It is manifest as irregularly placed, bright, colored pixels that disrupt the appearance of an image, particularly in areas of even tonality. The **[Long exposure NR]** item will help reduce the appearance of noise when shooting with a shutter speed longer than 1s. To set **[Long exposure NR]**:

1. Highlight **[Long exposure NR]** in the Shooting menu and press ▶.
2. Highlight **[On]** or **[Off]** (default) as required.
3. Press the ⓞ button to confirm the selection and return to the Shooting menu.

If **[On]** is selected for **[Long exposure NR]**, the processing time for each recorded image will increase by approximately 50 – 100%. While the image data is being processed, 'job nr' will appear blinking in the viewfinder. No other picture can be recorded while this is displayed and image processing is in progress.

NOTE: The process used by the D5100 to perform the **[Long exposure NR]** involves the camera making a second exposure known as a "dark frame exposure," during which the shutter remains closed, but the camera maps the sensor and records the values of each photodiode (pixel). Sometimes, a photodiode (pixel) can lock up and retain a value that is erroneous; this can often occur if the sensor gets hot due to use over a protracted period, as would occur in a long time exposure, or due to a high ambient temperature. After mapping the sensor for "hot" (overly bright) photodiodes, the camera subtracts the dark-frame photodiode values from the photodiode values of the main exposure in an effort to reduce the effect of noise in the final image.

HINT: Nikon states that the D5100's Long Exposure Noise Reduction feature, when switched on, will operate whenever the shutter speed exceeds approximately 8 seconds. Personally, I have found that the in-camera signal processing of the camera is so effective that there is often no necessity for this feature up to a shutter speed of 30 seconds or longer.

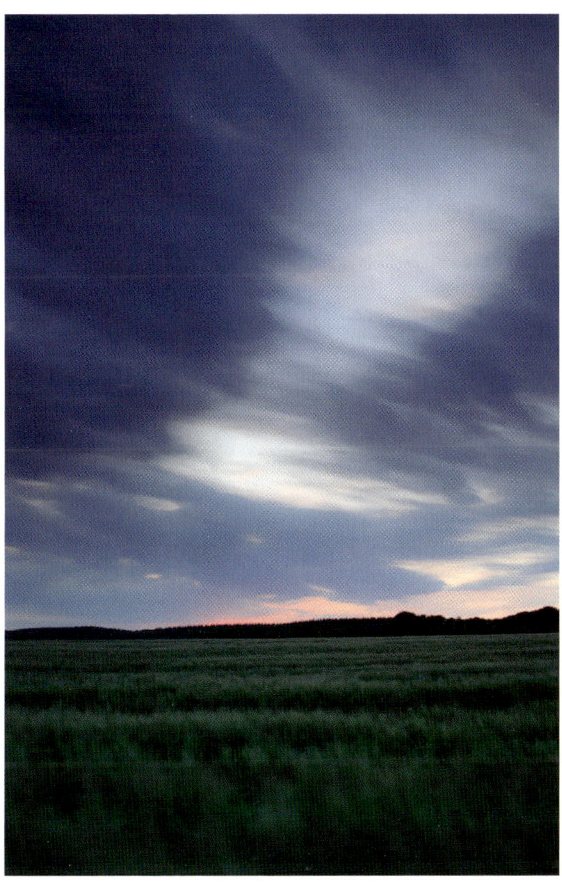

› A long, 4-minute exposure was used to capture a significant amount of blur in the crop and clouds as they where blown by a strong wind. The camera's built-in Noise Reduction helped to reduce the appearance of noise.

HIGH ISO NR (NOISE REDUCTION)

At high ISO settings, the presence of electronic noise in an image increases due to the greater degree of signal amplification that takes place during in-camera processing (it is analogous to the more visible grain structure of higher ISO film). The High ISO Noise Reduction feature, abbreviated to High ISO NR, will help to reduce the amount of noise in images taken at ISO sensitivities above ISO 800. To set High ISO NR:

1. Highlight **[High ISO NR]** in the Shooting menu and press ▶.
2. Highlight the required option from **[High]**, **[Normal]**, **[Low]**, or **[Off]** (see chart below).
3. Press the ⓚ button to confirm the selection and return to the Shooting menu.

OPTION	EFFECT
High	Noise Reduction is applied at ISO sensitivities above ISO 800. Select the level of Noise Reduction from one of the three options.
Normal	
Low	
Off	Noise Reduction is only applied at ISO sensitivities of 1600 or higher. The level applied is lower than the amount applied when **[Low]** is selected for **[High ISO NR]**.

HINT: Noise Reduction will affect the resolution of fine detail and, at high levels, the saturation of colors. The high ISO noise performance of the D5100 is extremely good, with very clean images produced at ISO settings up to and including ISO 1600. The random, almost film-like grain quality caused by noise in the D5100 images from around 1600 and above is not, for the most part, troublesome until the sensitivity goes beyond 6400.

NOTE: The in-camera Noise Reduction for higher ISO sensitivities does not offer the same level of control as a dedicated noise reduction software, so unless you really must use the camera options, I recommend applying noise reduction during post-processing.

ISO SENSITIVITY SETTINGS

ISO Sensitivity in the D5100 emulates the sensitivity to light of film bearing the same ISO number. The higher the ISO number, the greater the sensitivity to light. (See pages 45-48 for more details.)

RELEASE MODE

The options available in this item determine how the shutter operates when the shutter release button is pressed, or the camera is operated remotely using the optional ML-L3 remote control or MC-DC2 remote release cable (see pages 98-99 for more details).

MULTIPLE EXPOSURE (P, S, A AND M MODES ONLY)

The Multiple Exposure feature of the D5100 enables either 2 or 3 exposures to be shot consecutively and then combined into one image; the images are not saved individually, but as a single combined image. To use Multiple Exposure:

1. Highlight **[Multiple exposure]** in the Shooting menu, and press ▶.
2. Highlight **[Multiple exposure mode]**, and press ▶.
3. Highlight **[On]**, and press ⓚ.
2. Highlight **[Number of shots]** and press ▶, and then use ▲ or ▼ to select either 2 or 3.
3. Press ⓚ to confirm the selection and return to the **[Multiple exposure]** menu.
4. Highlight **[Auto gain]** and press ▶, then highlight either **[On]** or **[Off]** and press ⓚ to confirm the selection and return to the Multiple Exposure menu.
5. The ▣ icon will be displayed in the Information Display. Frame and shoot the images you wish to combine. In the Continuous release mode, the camera records all exposures in a single sequence and will stop once the designated number of exposures has been made. In Self-Timer mode, the D5100 will take the number of designated pictures automatically, regardless of the number of shots specified under CS-c3 **[Self-timer]** > **[Number of shots]**. In other release modes, an exposure is made each time the shutter release is pressed, so continue until the designated number has been recorded.
6. To interrupt the Multiple Exposure feature before the designated number of exposures has been recorded, highlight the **[Multiple exposure]** item in the Shooting menu, press ▶ to display the **[Multiple exposure mode]** option. Press ▶, highlight **[Off]** and press ⓚ to confirm the action.

HINT: When Auto Gain is activated, the camera will automatically make adjustments to the exposure level of each image recorded in the sequence so that the final cumulative exposure is correct. This useful feature obviates the need to make exposure calculations to compensate for the cumulative effect of combining the individual exposures.

› Here, [Multiple exposure] has been set to record two exposures, with the [Auto gain] feature applied.

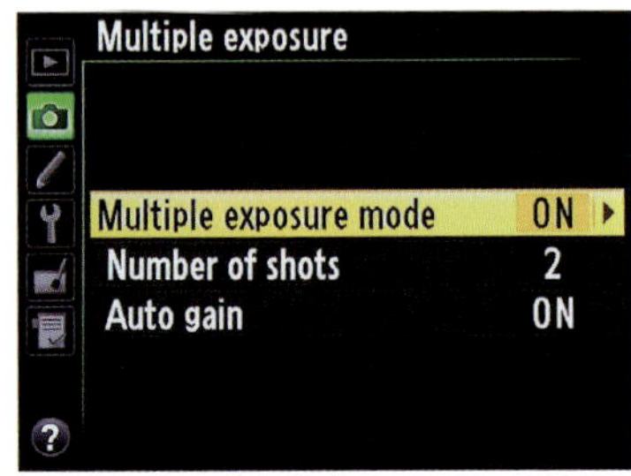

The Multiple Exposure icon (▬) will appear in the Information Display once the function has been set, and it will blink while the exposures are being made. When the selected number of exposures has been completed, ▬ will disappear from the control panel, and the Multiple Exposure feature is turned off automatically. To create another Multiple Exposure sequence at different settings, you will need to repeat steps 1-5 above. However, to shoot another sequence using the same settings for **[Number of shots]** and **[Auto gain]**, simply select the **[Multiple exposure mode]** item again, and press ▶. Highlight **[On]** and press Ⓞ. Now frame the first picture, focus and shoot.

MOVIE SETTINGS

The options available in the **[Movie settings]** item determine the quality (resolution) and frame rate of movies and operation of the built-in / external microphone while using the D5100's D-Movie mode (see pages 144-146 for more details).

INTERVAL TIMER SHOOTING

The D5100's Interval Timer shooting feature enables a set number of pictures of the same scene to be shot over a specified period of time, at predetermined intervals—a technique often called time-lapse photography, which has applications in both scientific and art photography.

Given a suitable subject or scene, this technique can produce some very interesting results, especially if you play the images sequentially in a slide show. For example, the opening and closing of a flower blossom during the course of a day or the changes that take place at a busy street corner every few minutes during rush-hour can be fascinating to observe. The D5100 provides you with the ability to capture such changing conditions using the **[Interval Timer shooting]** item in the Shooting menu.

To configure the camera for Interval Timer shooting involves several steps, but the results are definitely worth the effort. Due to the long duration required for some time-lapse sequences, it may be necessary to use the EH-5b AC adapter and EP-5A power adapter; if one is not available, make sure the EN-EL14 battery is fully charged.

NOTE: Precise and consistent framing is often an important aspect of time-lapse photography, so I recommend the use of a tripod or other form of sturdy, rigid camera support.

To configure Interval Timer shooting:

1. Highlight **[Interval Timer shooting]** in the Shooting menu and press ▶. Two options are presented in the **[Choose start time]** dialog box:
   a. **[Now]**: The camera will initiate the shooting sequence approximately three seconds after settings have been confirmed in the camera.
   b. **[Start time]**: The camera will delay the beginning of the shooting sequence until the specified time.
2. If **[Start time]** is selected, press ▶ to set the time at which you wish the first image to be taken. Press ◀ or ▶ to highlight hours or minutes and press ▲ or ▼ to adjust the numbers. The maximum delay is 23 hours, 59 minutes (if **[Now]** was selected for **[Start time]**, this step is skipped). Once settings have been made, press ▶ to highlight the interval setting options.

3. Press ◀ or ▶ to highlight hours, minutes, or seconds; and press ▲ or ▼ to adjust the time interval between each single exposure, or between each sequence of exposures. The maximum duration is 24 hours. Once settings have been made, press ▶ to highlight the options for setting the number of times (intervals) the camera will take a picture.
4. Press ◀ or ▶ to highlight the first, second and third digit for the number of intervals, and press ▲ or ▼ to adjust the setting. Press ▶ to continue.
5. Highlight **[On]** and press ⓚ to initiate the timer sequence. Highlight **[Off]** to save the settings without initiating the timer sequence and to return to the Shooting menu. The first picture will be taken at the time specified for **[Start time]**, or after approximately 3-seconds if **[Now]** was selected at Step 2. Shooting will continue until all the intervals specified at Step 5 have elapsed.

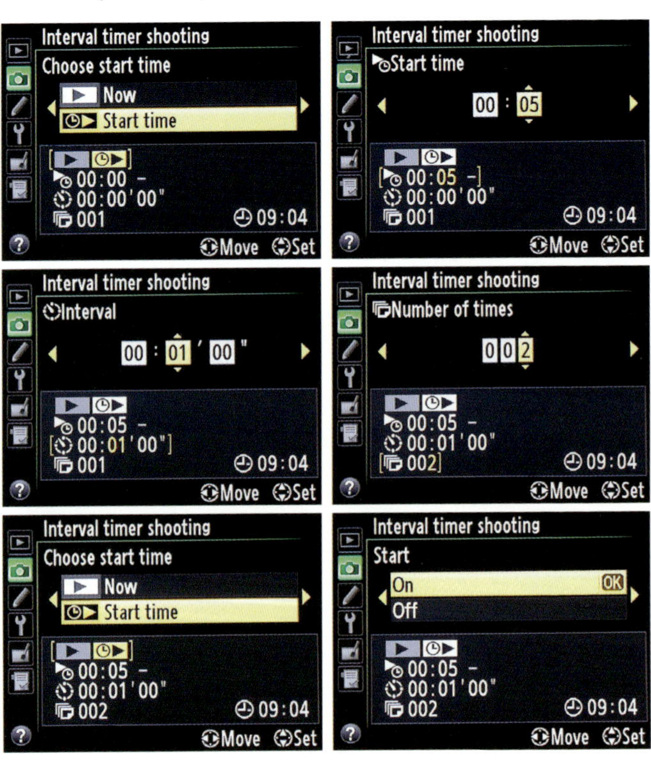

Once Interval Timer shooting has been set correctly and is activated, a message stating "Timer Active" will appear on the monitor momentarily. The release mode can be used to reduce camera noise. Exposure Bracketing, Multiple Exposure and HDR are not available during Interval Timer shooting, which can be interrupted by doing one of the following: turning the camera off and then on again, or rotating the Mode dial to another position.

NOTE: Just as with the Self-Timer release mode, if any automatic exposure mode is used in conjunction with the Interval Timer feature, it is essential to cover the viewfinder eyepiece with the supplied DK-5 eyepiece cap (See page 98 for more information.)

CUSTOM SETTINGS MENU

The Custom Settings menu allows you to fine-tune the performance of the D5100 to satisfy your particular requirements, and adapt the camera to meet the demands of specific shooting situations. It comprises a comprehensive set of no less than 20 items, each with a range of options that covers virtually every aspect of camera operation. The items are grouped logically by the nature of their function, as set out in the table below:

GROUP		CUSTOM SETTING
a	Auto focus	a1 – a3
b	Metering / Exposure	b1
c	Timers / AE & AF Lock	c1 – c4
d	Shooting / Display	d1 – d5
e	Bracketing / Flash	e1 – e2
f	Controls	f1 – f5

SELECTING CUSTOM SETTINGS OPTIONS

The Multi Selector switch is used to navigate through the Custom Settings menu. Highlight [✐] (Custom Settings menu) to display the list of five Custom Setting groups, plus **[Reset custom settings]**. Highlight the required group and press ▶ to display a full list of the items in the group. Use ▲ or ▼ to highlight the required item, and press ▶ to display the options available for the item. Use ▲ or ▼ to select the required option and use ⓚ to confirm the selection and return to the list of items in the group.

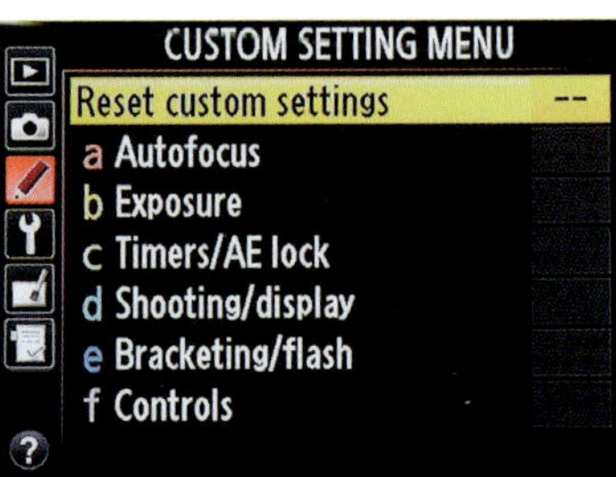

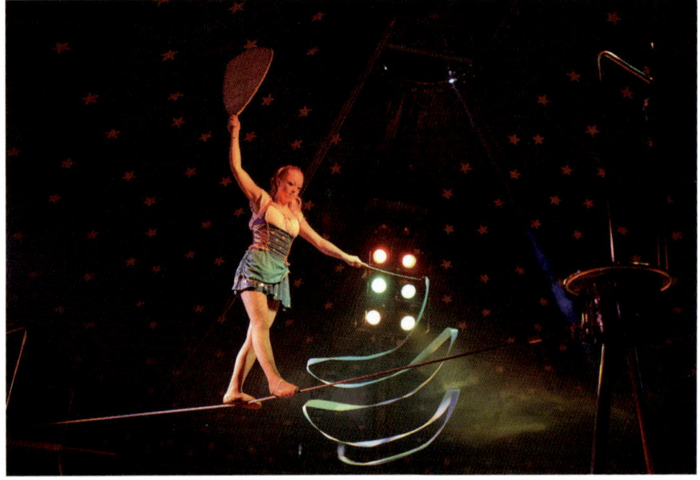

^ I selected **[AF-ON]** under CS-f2 to operate the AF system via the **AE-L/AF-L** button. This enabled me to switch between AF-C (Continuous-Servo) and locking focus, as the performer moved along the tightrope.

RESET CUSTOM SETTINGS

To reset the Custom Settings to the defaults, use the Reset option: Highlight **[Reset custom settings]** in the Custom Settings menu, and then press ▶. Highlight either **[No]** or **[Yes]** as required, and press ⓞ. See the table below for a list of the default Custom Settings.

CUSTOM SETTING		DEFAULT
Reset custom settings		
a	**Autofocus**	
a1	AF-C priority selection	Focus
a2	Built-in AF-assist illuminator	On
a3	Rangefinder	Off
b	**Exposure**	
b1	EV steps for exposure cntrl.	1/3 step
c	**Timers/AE lock**	
c1	Shutter-release button AE-L	Off
c2	Auto off timers	Normal
c3	Self-timer	Self-timer delay: 10 s; number ofshots: 1
c4	Remote on duration	1 min
d	**Shooting/display**	
d1	Beep	High
d2	ISO display	Off
d3	File number sequence	Off
d4	Exposure delay mode	Off
d5	Print date	Off
e	**Bracketing/flash**	
e1	Flash cntrl for built-in flash	TTL
e2	Auto bracketing set	AE bracketing
f	**Controls**	
f1	Assign ⏲/Fn button	Self-timer
f2	Assign AE-L/AF-L button	AE/AF lock
f3	Reverse dial rotation	No
f4	Slot empty release lock	Release locked
f5	Reverse indicators	+▪ı.ı.ı.ı.0.ı.ı.ı.ı▪−

AUTOFOCUS (a)

a1: AF-C Priority Selection: Controls whether an exposure is made whenever the shutter release is pressed (release priority) or only when focus has been attained (focus priority), in Continuous-Servo AF mode. The options are as follows:

- **[Release]** (default): When the camera is in Continuous-Servo AF mode, an exposure can be made whenever the shutter release is pressed.
- **[Focus]**: The shutter can only be released in Continuous-Servo AF mode once focus has been attained, although focus does not lock in this autofocus mode.

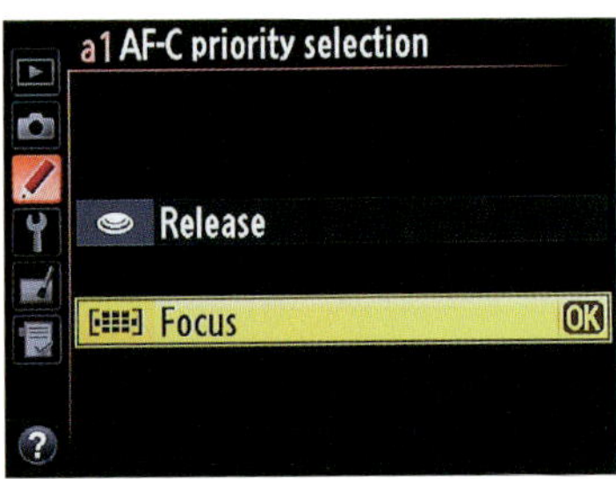

a2: Built-in AF-assist illuminator: The D5100 has a built-in lamp that activates to assist autofocus operation in low-light shooting situations. This item determines whether the lamp operates or not. The options are as follows:

- **[On]** (default): The built-in lamp that activates to assist autofocus operation in low-light shooting situations. Only available when AF-S is selected for focus mode, AF-S is selected during viewfinder shooting in AF-A mode, Auto-Area AF is selected for AF-Area mode, or an option other than Auto-Area AF is selected along with the center focus point.
- **[Off]**: The lamp does not light, regardless of the level of ambient illumination.

a3: Rangefinder: Available in all exposure modes except M (Manual), the exposure indicator scale can be used to assist manual focusing by showing whether focus has been acquired, and if not, where the focus point is located. This feature requires that a lens with a maximum aperture of f/5.6 or larger is used. The function does not operate in Live View or the D-Movie mode. The options are as follows:

- **[On]**: The exposure indicator scale shows the state of manual focus.
- **[Off]** (default): The analog exposure scale functions normally.

INDICATOR	DESCRIPTION	INDICATOR	DESCRIPTION
	Focus has been acquired		Focus point slightly behind subject
	Focus point slightly in front of subject		Focus point is significantly behind subject
	Focus point is significantly in front of subject		Camera cannot determine correct focus

METERING / EXPOSURE (b)

b1: EV Steps for Exposure Control: Use this item to select the size of the step when adjusting shutter speed, lens aperture, and exposure bracketing. The options are:

- **[1/3 step]** (default): Shutter speed and aperture change in steps of 1/3 (0.3) EV.
- **[1/2 step]**: Shutter speed and aperture change in steps of 1/2 (0.5) EV

HINT: I recommend using the **[1/3 step]** option to provide the finest degree of exposure control.

TIMERS / AE LOCK (c)

c1: Shutter Release Button AE-L: This option determines how the exposure value can be locked. Your options are:

- **[Off]** (default): Exposure is only locked by pressing the **AE-L/AF-L** button.
- **[On]**: Exposure can be locked by either pressing the **AE-L/AF-L** button or pressing the shutter release button down halfway.

c2: Auto Off Timers: This item determines how long the monitor screen stays on if no camera functions are performed during menu display and image Playback (through the **[Playback/menus]** item), how long an image is displayed after shooting (through the **[Image review]** option), and during Live View (through the **[Live view]** option), and how long exposure meters, the viewfinder, and Information Displays stay on when no camera function is performed (through the **[Auto meter-off]** selection). The options are: **[Short]**, **[Normal]** (default), **[Long]**, and **[Custom]**. The default times are show in the chart. The **[Custom]** option requires a time to be selected for each selection, and then **[Done]** must be highlighted before pressing the ㉿ button.

	PLAYBACK / MENUS	IMAGE REVIEW	LIVE VIEW	AUTO METER OFF
Short	12 seconds	4 seconds	3 minutes	4 seconds
Normal	20 seconds	4 seconds	3 minutes	8 seconds
Long	1 minute	20 seconds	10 minutes	1 minute

HINT: To prevent undue drain on the battery, I recommend using either the default setting or the 8-second option, as these provide a good compromise between having sufficient time to read and assess the meter reading, and conserving battery power.

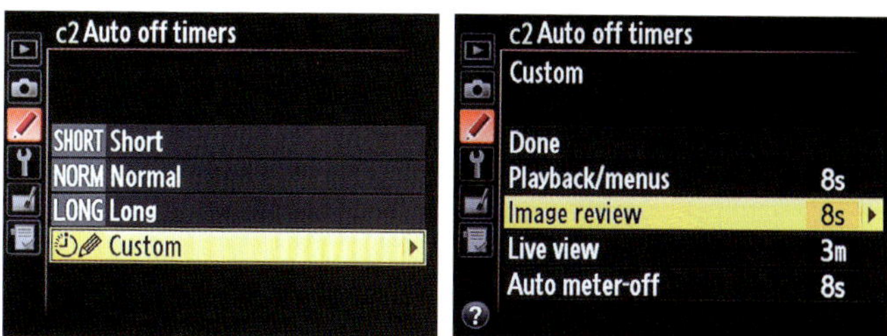

c3: Self-timer: This item controls the duration of the shutter release delay, and the number of shots taken in Self-Timer mode. The options are:

- **[Self timer delay]**: Offers durations of **[2s]**, **[5s]**, **[10s]**, or **[20s]**.
- **[Number of shots]**: Use ▲ or ▼ to select a number between 1 and 9; at a value other than 1, shots are taken at intervals of 3 seconds.

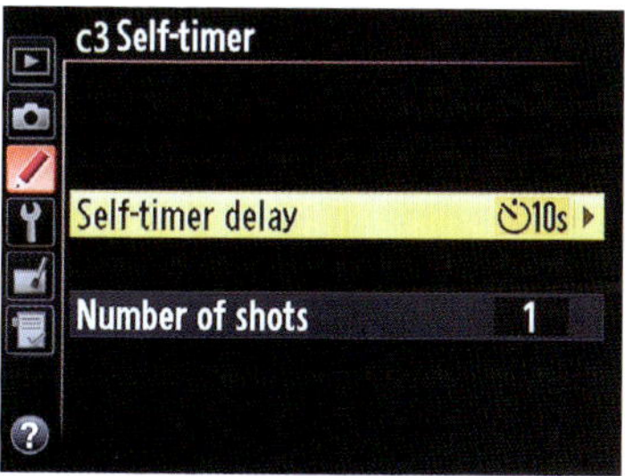

c4: Remote on Duration: This item determines how long the camera remains in stand-by in Remote release mode, when using the optional Nikon ML-L3 remote release. If no camera operation is performed within the selected period, remote shooting will end and the exposure meter turns off. To reactivate remote mode, press the shutter-release down halfway. The options are: **[1 min]**, **[5 min]**, **[10 min]**, or **[15 min]**.

SHOOTING / DISPLAY (d)

d1: Beep: Controls the pitch of the audible warning that sounds when the camera attains focus using AF-S (Single-servo AF), when focus locks in Live View, when the release timer is counting down in self-timer and delayed release modes, a photograph is taken in quick response, or when the card is locked and you attempt to take a picture. The beep will not sound during video recording, or if **Q** quiet shutter release is selected. The options are:

- **[Beep]**: **[Off]** default, **[L]** (low), or **[H]** (high)

d2: ISO Display: This item determines whether the camera will display the number of exposures remaining, or the ISO sensitivity. The options are:

- **[On]**: The ISO value is shown in place of the number of exposures remaining in the viewfinder.
- **[Off]** (default): The number of exposures remaining appears in the viewfinder and control panel.

d3: File Number Sequence: Controls whether file numbering continues in a consecutive sequence from the last number used or is reset when a memory card is formatted, a new folder is created, or a new memory card is inserted. The options are:

- **[On]** (default): Whenever a memory card is formatted or a new memory card is inserted in the camera, file numbering continues consecutively from the last number used or from the largest number in the current folder, whichever is higher. If current folder contains a photograph numbered 9999, a new folder will be created automatically, and numbering is reset to 0001.
- **[Off]**: File numbering is reset to 0001 whenever a memory card is formatted, a new folder is created, or a new memory card is inserted in the camera.
- **[Reset]**: This is the same as for **[On]**, except that the file number for the next exposure is assigned by adding one to the largest file number in the current folder, so if the folder is empty the file number is reset to 0001.

HINT: If you expect to shoot pictures using more than one memory card, I suggest, strongly, that you use the **[On]** option, otherwise potentially at the very best you will end up with duplicate file numbers, and duplicate file names is the file name is not altered using the file naming item in the shooting menu, which could become very confusing once images are saved to your computer.

d4: Exposure Delay Mode: This item enables the camera to delay the release of the shutter by approximately 1 second after the shutter release button is pressed and the reflex mirror has been raised. Its purpose is to help reduce the risk of camera vibration, which might affect the sharpness of a picture. This only has two options:

- **[On]**
- **[Off]** (default)

HINT: Since the camera has a proper mirror lock-up facility that can be used in conjunction with a remote shutter release, I see little worth in using this item for still pictures, unless you do not have the optional MC-DC2 or ML-L3 remote release accessory.

d5: Print Date: This item enables date information to be imprinted within the image area as it is recorded.

- **[Off]**: No information is recorded.
- **[Date]**: The date information is recorded within the image area.
- **[Date and time]**: The date and time information is recorded within the image area.
- **[Date counter]**: The number of days between date of shooting and a selected date is recorded. Up to three different dates can be stored in this option; after a date is selected for the first time, enter a date, and press OK to access the **[Choose date]** and **[Display options]** pages.

HINT: Since the camera records time/date information with each exposure and the information is saved in the EXIF data appended to each image file there seems to be little point in having the same information imprinted on the image itself.

e1: Flash Control for Built-In Flash: Use this item to select the flash mode for the built-in Speedlight of the D7000. The options are:

- TTL⚡ **[TTL]** (default): The camera uses its 420-segment RGB sensor (the same sensor used for Matrix metering) to control flash output automatically; it performs i-TTL balanced fill-flash (monitor pre-flashes are used), and distance information is included with a D- or G-type lenses. Standard TTL flash is used if the camera is set to Spot metering.
- M⚡ **[Manual]**: The flash can be set to deliver a specific amount of light, between its maximum output and 1/32 of its maximum output.

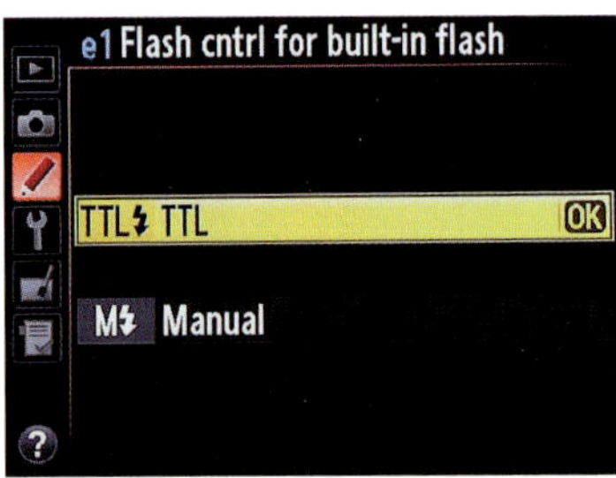

HINT: The options available within this item provide two very different ways for controlling the built-in Speedlight. See page 251-259 for a full explanation of the flash modes available here.

NOTE: If the SB-400 Speedlight is attached to the D5100 and turned on, CS-e1 changes to **[Optional flash]**, which allows the flash control mode for the SB-400 to be set to **[TTL]** or **[Manual]**.

e2: Auto Bracketing Set: This item allows you to decide which features are affected when the Automatic Bracketing feature is used. Choose from the following:

- **[AE bracketing]** (default): The camera brackets the exposure for both ambient light and flash output.

- **[WB bracketing]**: The camera brackets the White Balance value when recording pictures in the JPEG format (this feature is not available for the NEF or NEF + JPEG options).
- **[ADL bracketing]**: The camera brackets exposures using the Active D-Lighting controls.

CONTROLS (f)

f1: Assign Function Button: The **Fn** button, located on the front of the camera below the shutter release button can be assigned a variety of functions. The options available are as follows:

- **[Self-timer]**: Press the **Fn** button to switch Self-Timer mode on and off.
- **[Release mode]**: Press the **Fn** button and rotate the Command dial to select a release mode.
- **QUAL [Image quality/size]**: Press the **Fn** button and rotate the Command dial to select Image Quality and Image Size.
- **ISO [ISO sensitivity]**: Press the **Fn** button and rotate the Command dial to select ISO sensitivity.
- **WB [White balance]**: Press the **Fn** button and rotate the Command dial to select White Balance (P, S, A, and M only).
- **[Active D-Lighting]**: Press the **Fn** button and rotate the command dial to choose Active D-Lighting (P, S, A, and M only).
- **HDR [HDR Mode]**: Press the **Fn** button to switch HDR on and off (P, S, A, and M only); HDR ends when an exposure is made or the **Fn** button is pressed again.
- **+RAW [+NEF (RAW)]**: If Image Quality is set to JPEG Fine, JPEG Normal, JPEG Basic, "RAW" will be shown in the Information Display and an NEF (RAW) file will be recorded with the next exposure made after pressing the **Fn** button. To exit without recording an NEF (RAW), press the **Fn** button again. This option does not operate with Night Vision, Color Sketch, Miniature Effect, or Selective Color.
- **BKT [Auto bracketing]**: Press the **Fn** button and rotate the Command dial to select the Bracketing step (Exposure and White Balance Bracketing), or turn ADL Bracketing on and off (P, S, A, and M only).

f2: Assign AE-L/AF-L Button: The **AE-L/AF-L** button, located on the rear of the camera beside the viewfinder eyepiece, can also be assigned a variety of functions. The options are as follows:

- **[AE/AF lock]**: Press the **AE-L/AF-L** button to lock autoexposure and autofocus.
- **[AE lock only]**: Press the **AE-L/AF-L** button to lock autoexposure only.
- **[AF lock only]**: Press the **AE-L/AF-L** button to lock autofocus only.
- **[AE lock (hold)]**: Same as **[AE lock only]**, except that AE Lock is active once the button has been pressed and released, until the camera or light meter is turned off or you press the **AE-L/AF-L** button a second time.
- AF-ON **[AF-ON]**: Press the **AE-L/AF-L** button to activate autofocus; the shutter release button cannot be used to initiate autofocus.

NOTE: If **[AF-ON]** is selected, the Vibration Reduction (VR) feature, available on some Nikkor lenses, will not operate when the **AE-L/AF-L** button is pressed; VR is only activated by pressing the shutter release button. If you do use the technique of locking focus via the **AE-L/AF-L** button, when you decide to take a picture, press the shutter release button and pause briefly when it is depressed halfway to allow the VR system to activate and settle before pressing it all the way down to operate the shutter.

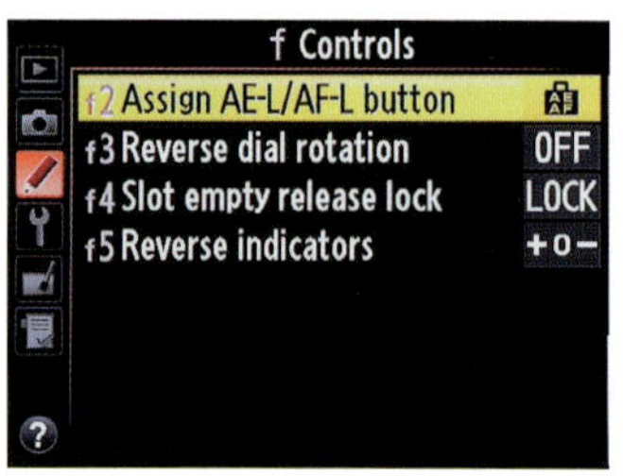

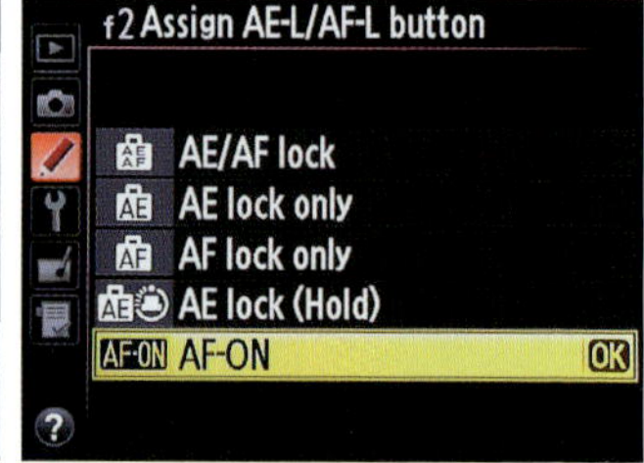

f3: Reverse Dial Rotation: This item provides additional functionality to the Command dial. The options are:

- [No] (default): The Command dial operates in the direction as described in this book.
- [Yes]: The Command dial operates in the reverse direction.

f4: Slot Empty Release Lock: This item allows the shutter to operate without a memory card being installed in the camera. The options for this item are:

- [Release locked] (default): The shutter release is disabled if no memory card is installed in the camera.
- [Enable release]: The shutter release operates if no memory card is installed in the camera. The camera stores no picture; however, the last recorded image is displayed on the monitor as a DEMO image.

HINT: Potential disaster looms with this item unless it is set to the default—you do not want the camera to operate as though it is recording pictures when in fact there is no memory card installed.

---

f5: Reverse Indicators: At the default setting, the exposure indicator display shown in the viewfinder and Information Display are shown with positive values to the left and negative values to the right. The display can be reversed using this item.

- [+ 0 -] (default): Positive values are shown to the left and negative values to the right.
- [- 0 +]: Reverses the exposure indicator display; positive values are shown to the right and negative values to the left.

SETUP MENU

The Setup menu is used to establish the basic configuration of the camera. Once the settings for most of the items in this menu are made, it is unlikely they will be changed very frequently.

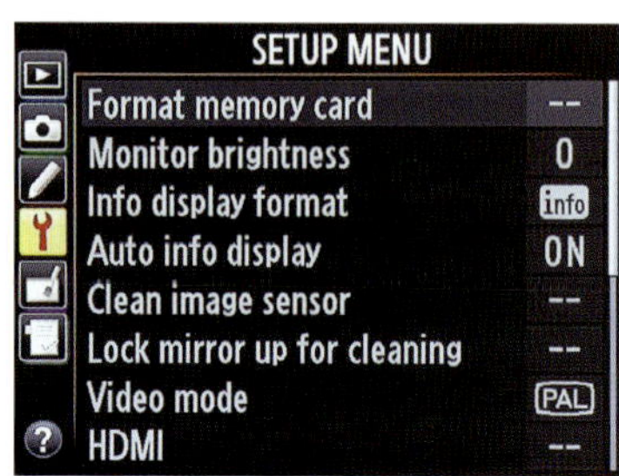

FORMAT MEMORY CARD

A new memory card should always be formatted when it is first placed into the D5100. It is also a good idea to format any memory card you insert into the camera, even if the card has been formatted using a computer. This is particularly important if you switch your memory cards between different camera bodies. Before you format a memory card, ensure that any image files stored on the card have been saved to another storage device.

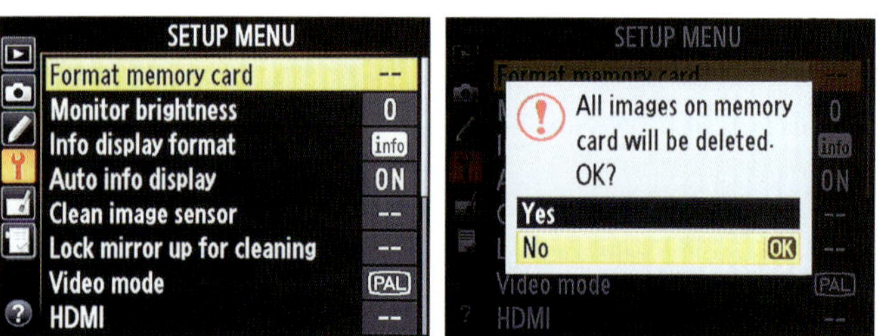

A warning message is displayed during the formatting process before the action is actually completed.

MONITOR BRIGHTNESS

The brightness of the LCD monitor on the back of the camera is set to a default value, but can be adjusted to help improve the appearance of any displayed image or page of information. To adjust LCD brightness:

1. Highlight the **[LCD Brightness]** option from the Setup menu and press ▶.
2. Adjust the brightness value up or down by pressing ▲ or ▼.
3. Press the ⓄⓀ button to confirm the screen brightness value.

A negative value reduces screen brightness, while a positive value increases screen brightness. The screen displays a grayscale to help you judge the effect of the brightness level on the full tonal range present in your images.

NOTE: I consider the default value for the screen brightness level to be too high. For a more accurate assessment of images, I suggest setting screen brightness to -1.

INFO DISPLAY FORMAT

The D5100 offers two different styles for the Information Display: **[Classic]** and **[Graphic]**. To select a style for the Information Display:

1. Select the **[Info display format]** item in the Setup menu and press ▶.
2. Highlight the desired option from **[Classic]** or **[Graphic]** and press ▶.
3. The **[Classic]** and **[Graphic]** options offer a choice of background color. Choose from **[Blue]**, **[Black]**, and **[Orange]** for **[Classic]**, and choose **[Green]**, **[Black]**, or **[Brown]** for **[Graphic]**. Press ⓄⓀ to confirm your selection.

I recommend using the **[Classic]** display because it offers the greatest clarity, although the **[Graphic]** display may be more helpful to less experienced photographers because it provides a visual representation of the lens aperture and shutter speed. When the camera is turned to shoot a picture in the vertical format, the Information Display is rotated accordingly.

AUTO INFORMATION DISPLAY

If **[On]** is selected, the Information Display will be shown on the monitor once the shutter release button is pressed down halfway. When **[Off]** is selected for under **[Image review]** in the Playback menu, the Information Display will also be shown immediately after an exposure is made. If **[Off]** is selected for **[Auto information display]**, it will be necessary to press the Info button to view the Information Display.

CLEAN IMAGE SENSOR

This option is used to automatically clean the optical low-pass filter by vibrating it (see pages 310-315 for more details).

LOCK MIRROR UP FOR CLEANING

This option is used for manual cleaning or inspection of the optical low-pass filter (see pages 314-315 for more details).

VIDEO MODE

The **[Video mode]** item allows you to select the type of signal used by any video equipment, such as a DVD player or television, to which your camera may be connected. This option should be set before connecting your camera to the device with an appropriate A/V cord (see page 300 for more details).

HDMI

The **[HDMI]** option allows you to select the output resolution to an HDMI viewing device and can be used to enable remote control of the D5100 from HDMI televisions / monitors that support the HDMI-CEC (High-Definition Multimedia Interface—Consumer Electronic Control) standard. These options should be set before connecting your camera to the HDMI device with an appropriate HDMI cord.

Use the **[Output resolution]** item to select the format for images to be output to the HDMI device. If **[Auto]** is selected, the D5100 will set the appropriate format automatically.

If **[On]** is selected for the **[Device control]** item, when the D5100 is connected to a device that supports the HDMI_CEC standard and both devices are turned on, options for Play and Slide Show will be displayed on the HDMI device screen, and its remote control can be used in place of the camera's Multi Selector and OK buttons during Playback of full-frame images or a slide show. If **[Off]** is selected for the **[Device control]** item, the remote control for the HDMI device cannot be used to control the D5100 for image display purposes.

FLICKER REDUCTION

The **[Flicker reduction]** item is intended to help reduce the effects of banding that can occur when using Live View or the D-Movie mode under fluorescent or mercury-vapor lighting. Choose the frequency that matches that of the local AC power supply. In very bright conditions, this item may not be particularly effective; in such conditions, set the camera to either M or A exposure mode and use a small aperture (large f/number).

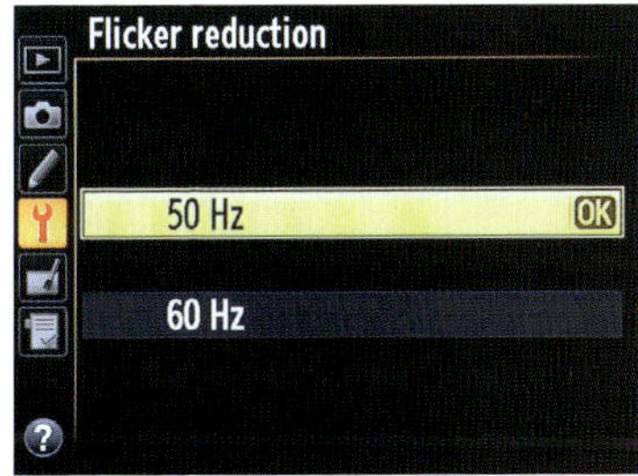

TIME ZONE / DATE

The **[Time zone and date]** item enables you to set and change the date and time recorded by the camera's internal clock and how it is displayed. To set the internal clock:

1. Highlight the **[Time zone and date]** item in the Setup menu and press ▶ to display the menu options.
2. Use ▲ and ▼ to highlight **[Time zone]** and press ▶ to display a map of world time zones.
3. Press either ◀ or ▶ to select the appropriate time zone, and press OK to confirm the selection and return to the **[Time zone and date]** menu.

4. Now, use ▲ and ▼ to highlight the [Date and time] option, and press ▶ to display the date / time clock. Use ▶ to select each item in turn and adjust as needed by using ▲ and ▼ until the full date and time have been entered.
5. Press ⓞ to confirm the settings and return to the [Time zone and date] menu.
6. Next, highlight the [Date format] option and press ▶ to display the list of choices. Use ▲ and ▼ to highlight the desired date format and press ⓞ to confirm the selection.
7. Finally, use ▲ and ▼ to highlight the [Daylight saving time] option and press ▶ to display the two choices; the default setting for [Daylight saving time] is [Off]. If daylight saving time is in effect in the current time zone, highlight [On] and press ⓞ to confirm the selection.
8. To exit the menu system and return the camera to its Shooting mode, press the shutter release button halfway down.

HINT: If you travel to a different time zone, it is only necessary to adjust the [Time zone] option; the date and time will be adjusted automatically for the selected time zone. The only other option that may need to be adjusted is the [Daylight saving time] option.

HINT: The internal clock is not as accurate as many wristwatches or domestic clocks, so it is important to check it regularly.

LANGUAGE

The [Language] option in the Setup menu allows you to select one of 24 languages for the camera to use when displaying menus and messages. To select the language, highlight the required option under the [Language] item using ▲ or ▼. Press the ⓞ button to confirm and lock your selection. If you wish to change the language at any time after the initial setup, repeat the procedure just described.

IMAGE COMMENT

The **[Image comment]** feature of the Setup menu allows you to attach a short note or reference to an image file. Comments can be up to 36 characters long and may contain letters and numbers. Since the process requires each character to be input individually, this is not a feature you will use for every picture you take. However, as a way of assigning a general comment (i.e., the name of a location / venue / event) or attaching notice of authorship / copyright, it is very useful. To attach an image comment:

1. Highlight the **[Image comment]** option in the Setup menu and press ▶.
2. Highlight **[Input comment]** from the options list and press ▶.
3. To enter your comment, highlight the character you wish to input by using the Multi Selector and press OK to select it. If you accidentally enter the wrong character, rotate the Command dial to move the cursor over the unwanted character and press the 🗑 button to erase it.
4. Press the OK button to save the comment and return to the **[Image comment]** options list.
5. To actually attach the comment to your photographs, highlight the **[Attach comment]** option, and then press ▶. A small check mark will appear in the box to the left of the option.
6. Finally, highlight **[Done]** and press the OK button to confirm the selection.

If you wish to exit this process at any time prior to step 5 without attaching the comment, simply press the MENU button. When the check mark is present in the **[Attach comment]** option of the **[Image comment]** item, the saved comment will be attached to all subsequent images shot on the D5100. To prevent the comment from being attached to an image, simply return to the **[Image comment]** menu and uncheck the **[Attach comment]** box by highlighting the option and pressing ▶. The comment will remain stored in the camera's memory and can be attached to future images simply by rechecking the **[Attach comment]** box. The comment will be displayed on the third page of the photo Information Display, available in single-image Playback. It can also be viewed in Nikon View NX2 or Capture NX2 software.

AUTO IMAGE ROTATION

The D5100 automatically recognizes the orientation of the camera as it records an image: horizontal, vertical rotated 90° clockwise, or vertical rotated 90° counter-clockwise. At its default setting, the camera stores this information, so the image will be automatically rotated during Playback. It will also be displayed in the correct orientation on a computer with compatible software. If you do not want the camera to record the shooting orientation, the **[Auto image rotation]** feature can be switched off. To set **[Auto image rotation]**:

1. Highlight the **[Auto image rotation]** item from the Setup menu and press ▶.
2. Highlight **[On]** or **[Off]** as required.
3. Press Ⓞ to confirm the selection.

NOTE: The **[Rotate tall]** item in the Playback menu must also be turned on for images to be displayed in the orientation in which they were originally taken during Playback on the camera. However, if the **[Image review]** item in the Playback menu is set to **[On]**, images taken in a vertical format will not be rotated for image review because the camera will already be in the correct orientation.

NOTE: If you shoot with the camera tilted up or down, it may not record the orientation correct. In this case, it is probably easier to select **[Off]** and rotate the pictures using an appropriate software, such as Nikon View NX2 or Nikon Capture NX2.

IMAGE DUST OFF REFERENCE PHOTO

The **[Image Dust Off ref photo]** item of the D5100 is designed specifically for use with the Image Dust Off function in Nikon Capture NX2. The image file created by this function creates a mask that is electronically "overlaid" on an NEF (RAW) file, enabling the software to reduce or remove the effects of shadows that are cast by dust particles on the surface of the optical low pass filter. To obtain a reference image for the Image Dust Off function you must use a CPU-type lens (Nikon recommends use of a lens with a focal length of 50mm or more). This function can only be used with NEF (RAW) files; it is not available for JPEG or TIFF files.

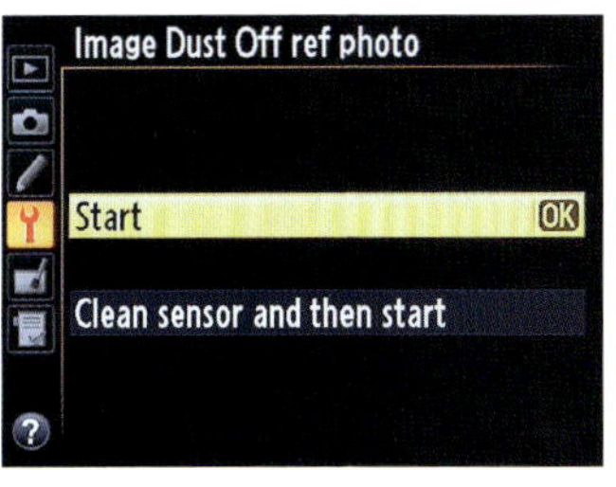

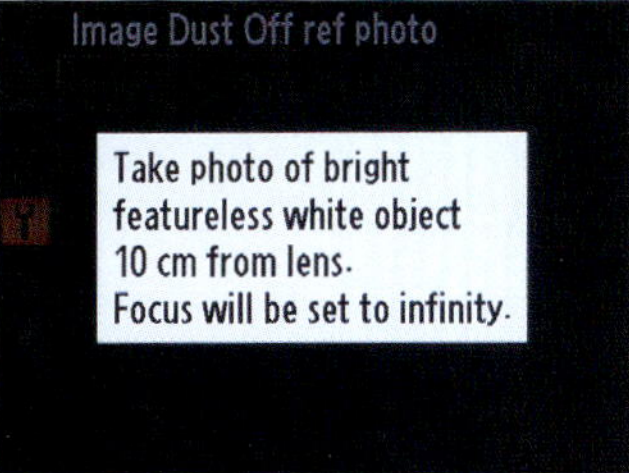

To use **[Dust Off ref photo]**:

1. Highlight the **[Image Dust Off ref photo]** option from the Setup menu and press ▶.
2. **[Start]** and **[Clean sensor, then start]** will be displayed on the screen. Highlight **[Start]** and press Ⓞ to begin the process: "rEF" will appear in the viewfinder and the following message will be displayed on the LCD screen: "Take photo of bright featureless white object 10 cm from lens. Focus will be set to infinity." If you select **[Clean sensor, then start]** and press Ⓞ, the camera will vibrate the low-pass filter before displaying the messages just described.
3. Point your camera at a featureless white subject positioned approximately 4 inches (10 cm) from the front of the lens.
4. Press the shutter release button all the way down (focus will be set automatically to infinity).

Once you have recorded the Image Dust Off reference data file, it can be displayed in the camera during Playback. It appears as a grid pattern with "Image Dust Off ref photo" displayed within the image area. A Dust Off reference data file can be identified by its file extension, which is NDF; these files cannot be viewed using a computer.

NOTE: If the reference target is too bright or too dark, the camera will probably not be able to acquire Dust Off reference data. In this case, a warning will be displayed on the monitor: "Exposure settings are not appropriate. Change exposure settings and try again." Either use a different target or change the level of illumination.

HINT: This feature is reasonably effective, but the dust particles can be dislodged and shift between shots, providing no guarantee that this technique will be completely successful if you save only one reference file. The best approach is to shoot several reference files during the course of a shoot and use the one that was closest to the time of the exposure you need to correct.

GPS

Using the dedicated Nikon GP-1 GPS unit connected to the accessory terminal of the D5100 makes it possible for the camera to record GPS information when a picture is taken.

As soon as the camera confirms communication with the connected GPS device, GPS will be displayed in the Information Display and GPS data will be recorded with each picture. If the GPS icon is shown blinking, it means the GP-1 is still searching for a GPS signal and any picture taken will not include GPS data. If the GPS icon is not displayed, it means the camera has received no new GPS data from the GP-1 for at least 2 seconds, and again, no GPS data will be recorded if a picture is taken.

The information recorded when an exposure is made with the GPS icon displayed includes current latitude, longitude, altitude, time, and heading (see note below). The time provided by the GPS device uses Universal Time Coordinated (UTC) data and is independent of the camera's internal clock. To view GPS data, open an image in single-image Playback and use the Multi Selector to scroll through the photo information pages until the GPS Data page is displayed. The **[GPS]** item in the Setup menu has three options:

- **[Auto meter off]:** Allows you to choose whether or not the exposure meters will turn off automatically when a GPS unit is attached. Highlight **[Auto meter off]** and press ▶ to display the two sub-options:
  - **[Enable] (default):** If no camera operation is performed for the period selected at **[Auto off timers]** in the Setup menu, the exposure meter will turn off automatically. While this reduces drain on the camera's battery, it may prevent GPS data from being recorded, because if the camera's meter is turned off, the GPS device may also switch off or go into a standby mode. If the shutter release is then pressed all the way down to record an exposure without pausing, there may be insufficient time for the GPS device to reactivate.

- **[Disable]:** The camera's exposure meter will not turn off automatically while the GP-1 GPS device is connected. GPS data will always be recorded, as the GP-1 device will also remain active.

- **[Position]:** Is only available if a GPS device is connected and GPS communication is confirmed; if not, the **[Position]** item is grayed out in the menu. When communication is established with the GP-1, the camera displays current latitude, longitude, altitude, and date / time (UTC data).
- **[Use GPS to set camera clock]:** Select **[Yes]** to synchronize the camera built-in camera clock with the time reported by the GPS device.

EYE-FI UPLOAD

The wireless communication-enabled Eye-Fi memory cards can only be used in their country of purchase. This item is only displayed when a dedicated Eye-Fi memory card is installed in the D5100. To upload JPEG files directly from the camera to the predetermined destination, select **[Enabled]**. If the Wi-Fi signal is not sufficiently strong, image upload will not take place. In areas where Wi-Fi is unavailable or wireless devices are prohibited, make sure that the **[Disable]** option is selected.

FIRMWARE VERSION

When **[Firmware version]** is selected from the Setup menu, the current versions of the firmware installed on the camera are displayed on the monitor screen. To check the current firmware installed on your camera, highlight the **[Firmware version]** option from the Setup menu and press ▶. The details of the firmware are displayed on the next page. Press ⓞ to return to the Setup menu. Firmware updates can be downloaded from any of the Nikon technical support websites. To check for current updates visit: www.nikon.com.

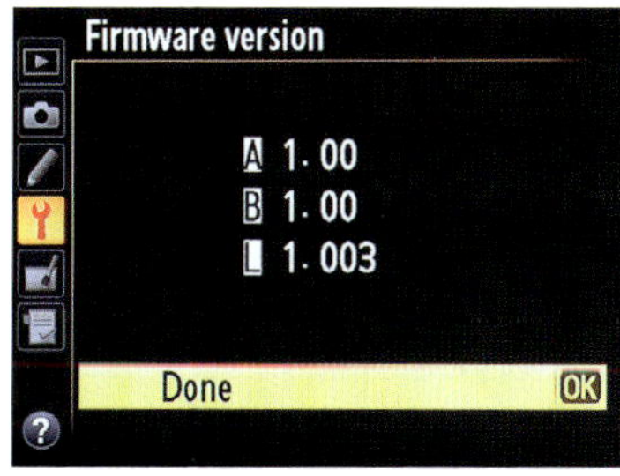

RETOUCH MENU

The Retouch menu enables you to create retouched (modified), trimmed (cropped), or resized versions of the image files saved on a memory card installed in the camera. When the features in this menu are applied to an image, a new copy of the file is created and stored on the same memory card. The original image file remains on the card in its original, unmodified form.

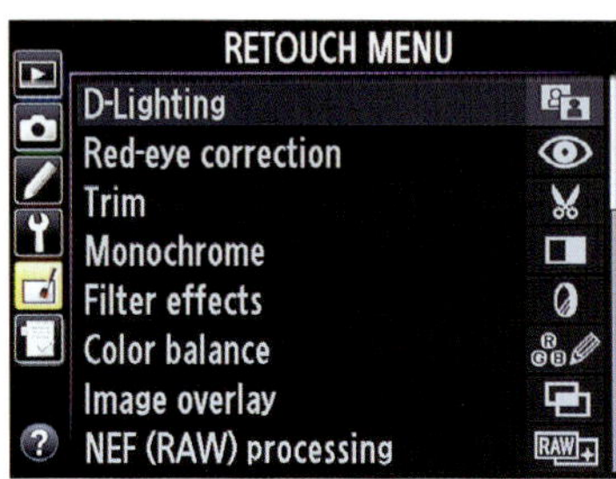

While I feel options available in the Retouch menu are a useful aspect of camera control, I believe it is important to keep them in perspective. The items available in this menu cannot be considered anywhere near as sophisticated as their equivalent adjustments in any good image-editing software. They are intended to provide a quick, convenient, and largely automated method of producing a modified version of the original image without the use of a computer. As such, they offer an unprecedented level of control when using in-camera processing to produce a finished picture directly from the camera.

SELECTING IMAGES

To select an image directly from the Retouch menu, open the Retouch menu, highlight the desired function, and press ▶ to select it and display a set of thumbnail images on the screen to choose from. For some items, a further menu of options may be displayed before the thumbnail images. In these cases, highlight the required option and press ▶ again to continue to image selection. Use the Multi Selector to scroll through the thumbnail images; a yellow border will frame the currently selected picture. To view an image full-frame, press and hold 🔍.

Once you have selected the picture to be modified and copied, press ⊛ to display the Retouch options (see details below for each Retouch menu item). To cancel the process at any time, press the **MENU** button. To apply the Retouch option and save the new copy image, press ⊛.

Alternatively, it is possible to access the Retouch menu directly from full-frame Playback. Display the picture to be modified on the monitor and press the ⊛ button. The Retouch menu will be displayed; highlight the required item by using ▲ and ▼ and press ▶ to open the options for that item. To return to the full-frame Playback, press ▶. Press ⊛ to create the retouched copy. An ☑ icon in the upper left of the image identifies the retouched copy file.

IMAGE QUALITY AND SIZE

The quality and size of the copy image created by the Retouch menu will depend on the quality and size of the original image file(s). The selected option within the Retouch menu may also affect image size and quality. Except in the case of the **[Trim]**, **[Image overlay]**, **[NEF (RAW) processing]** and **[Resize]** options, the following explains how image size and quality will be affected:

- Copies created from JPEG images are the same size and quality as the original file.
- Copies of NEF (RAW) files are saved as JPEG files with **[Large]** and **[Fine]** selected for size and quality.
- Time stamps added with CS-d5 **[Print date]** may be cropped out or rendered illegible depending on the effect(s) applied.

The copy the **[Image overlay]** option creates is always saved at the image quality and size currently set on the camera, regardless of the fact that this option is only available with NEF (RAW) images. If you wish to save the copy image as an NEF (RAW) file, ensure that Image Quality on the camera is set to NEF (RAW) before you apply the **[Image overlay]** option.

NOTE: Each effect can only be applied to a given file once, with the exception of the **[Image overlay]** and **[Edit movie]** > **[Choose start point/Choose end point]** options. If an option is displayed grayed out, it is not available.

D-LIGHTING

The D-Lighting feature of the Retouch menu brightens shadow areas to reveal more detail. It is not an overall brightness control; its application is selective. By modifying the tone curve applied to the image, it only affects the shadow areas of the recorded image and preserves the mid- and highlight tones.

Select the image (as described on pages 222-223) and press the OK button to display two thumbnail images: one unmodified (left) and the other modified (right). You can select three levels of D-Lighting: low, normal, or high by using ▲ and ▼. To view the preview image full-frame, press and hold ⊕. Once you have decided which level is most appropriate, press the OK button to apply the change and create the copy image. You can press the MENU button to cancel the function without making any changes.

RED-EYE REDUCTION

This option is only available with pictures taken using either the built-in Speedlight of the D5100 or an external Nikon Speedlight. Select the image (as described above) and press OK. If no flash was used for the chosen exposure, a small yellow box containing a cross is displayed over the thumbnail image, and the image cannot be selected. If flash was used but the camera cannot detect the presence of red-eye, a message stating "Unable to detect red eye in selected image" will be displayed.

If the D5100 detects what it considers to be a red-eye effect, the image will be displayed with a small navigation window. Press and hold the ⊕ button to zoom in on the image. You can navigate around the image to view other areas of the picture not visible by using the Multi Selector; the area currently displayed on the screen is shown with a yellow border in a navigation window. To scroll rapidly to another area of the picture, press and hold the Multi Selector down.

If you can see the effects of red-eye in the selected picture, press OK to cancel the zoom control and return to the full-frame Playback and then press OK again. The D5100 will then create a copy image automatically, using processed image data, to reduce the red-eye effect.

NOTE: Since this is a completely automated process, it is possible for the camera to inadvertently select an image not affected by red-eye but containing an area that looks like red-eye; this is why it is important to double check the preview image before confirming the operation of the process.

TRIM

The **[Trim]** option enables you to crop the original image to exclude unwanted areas. Highlight the **[Trim]** option in the Retouch menu and press ▶ to display a set of thumbnail images. Select the image and press ⓞ. The selected image is displayed on the LCD monitor, along with a yellow frame to show the crop area; you can move the crop frame around the image using the Multi Selector. Press the thumbnail/zoom out button to reduce the size of the crop. Use the zoom in button to increase the size of crop; the crop size is displayed in the top left corner of the image in pixel dimensions (width x height). It is also possible to adjust the aspect ratio of the cropped area; rotating the Command dial allows you to switch between 3:2, 4:3, 5:4, 1:1, and 16:9. Once you have decided on the location, size, and aspect ratio of the crop area, press OK to create the cropped copy. The new copy image will be displayed on the LCD monitor. Press the MENU button to return to the Retouch menu display.

NOTE: Copies created from NEF (RAW), NEF (RAW) + JPEG, or TIFF (RGB) files have an image quality of JPEG Fine. Copies created from JPEG files have the same image quality as the original. The size of the copy file varies according to the crop size and aspect ratio; it is displayed in the upper left of the monitor.

MONOCHROME

This item allows you to save the copied image in one of three monochrome effects: **[Black-and-white]** (grayscale), **[Sepia]** (brown tones), or **[Cyanotype]** (blue-and-white tones). In all three cases, the image data is converted to black-and-white using an algorithm dedicated to this feature; it is a different algorithm than the one used for the **[Monochrome]** option in the Picture Controls. The image data for the black-and-white copy is still saved as an RGB file (i.e., it retains its color information).

Select the image as described on pages 222-223. With this item, you must select the desired option before the thumbnail images are displayed. If you select either the **[Sepia]** or the **[Cyanotype]** options, the appropriate color shift is applied after the copy picture is converted to black-and-white. The degree of the color shift can be adjusted using ▲ to increase and ▼ to decrease the effect. Once you are satisfied with the preview image, press ⓞ to save the copy picture.

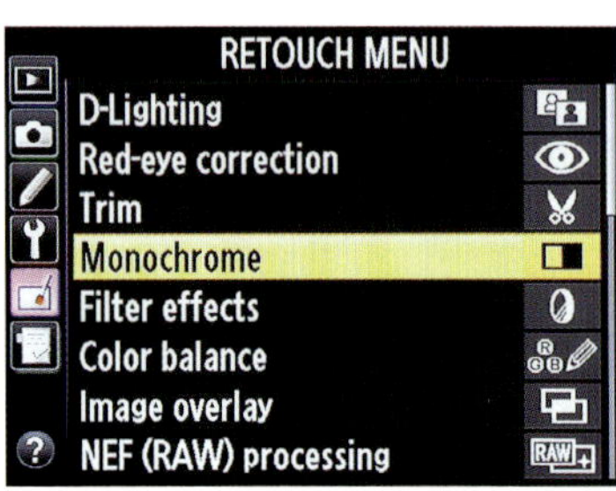

FILTER EFFECTS

The **[Filter effects]** option in the Retouch menu offers choices that simulate the results of effect filters that were more commonly used with film photography. Select the image as described above. With this item, the desired option must be selected before the thumbnail images are displayed.

- **[Skylight]**: Nikon describes this option as emulating the effect of a Skylight filter. The effect is very subtle, reducing the amount of blue in the image by a very modest amount.
- **[Warm tone]**: This effect increases the amount of red in the image and produces a result similar to the use of a Wratten 81-series color-correction filter. Again, the effect is subtle; proper White Balance control should eliminate the need to use it.
- **[Red intensifier]**: Intensifies red; use the Multi Selector to select one of three levels: ▲ to increase and ▼ to decrease the effect.
- **[Green intensifier]**: Intensifies green; use the Multi Selector to select one of three levels: ▲ to increase and ▼ to decrease the effect.
- **[Blue intensifier]**: Intensifies blue; use the Multi Selector to select one of three levels: ▲ to increase and ▼ to decrease the effect.
- **[Cross screen]**: Adds a starburst effect to point light sources in the image. This option has a number of sub-items, providing greater control over the effect, as follows:

- **[Number of points]**: Select from 4, 6, or 8.
- **[Filter amount]**: Choose the brightness of the light sources affected.
- **[Filter angle]**: Select the angle of the star points.
- **[Length of points]**: Select the length of the star points.
- **[Confirm]**: Use to preview the effects of the filter (to preview in full-frame, press the ⊕ button).
- **[Save]**: Create the Retouch copy.
- **[Soft]**: Adds a soft filter effect; use the Multi Selector button to select one of three levels: 1 (high), 2 (medium), or 3 (low).

In all **[Filter effects]** options, a preview image is displayed showing the effect of the selected item on the original image; press OK to apply it and create the copy image.

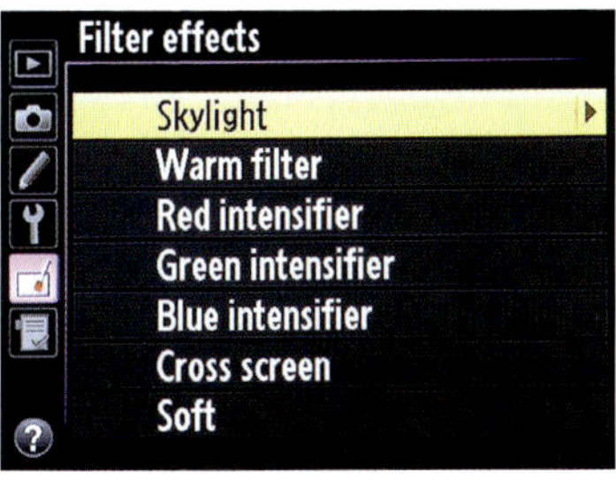

COLOR BALANCE

The **[Color balance]** item is used to produce a copy image with a modified color balance from the original file. Select the image (as described above) and press OK to display the control options.

A thumbnail image of the selected picture is displayed alongside histograms for the composite RGB, red, green, and blue channels. Below the thumbnail is a two-dimensional CIE color space map with a vertical and horizontal axis aligned on its center. The central point of the color space map represents the color balance of the original file. Press the Multi Selector up to increase the level of green and down to increase the level of magenta. Pressing the Multi Selector to the left increases the level of blue, and to the right increases the level of amber. The black square cursor will shift position accordingly. The histograms will reflect the altered color distribution, and the thumbnail image can be used to preview the effect.

IMAGE OVERLAY

[Image overlay] enables the merging of a pair of NEF (RAW) files, combining them to form a single, new image (the original image files are not affected by this process). The images to be used do not have to be taken in consecutive order, but must have been recorded by a D5100 and be stored on the same memory card. To use **[Image overlay]**:

1. Highlight the **[Image overlay]** option in the Retouch menu and press the ▶ button. The **[Image overlay]** page will open with **[Image 1]** highlighted.
2. To select the first picture, press ®; a thumbnail view of all NEF (RAW) files stored on the memory card will be displayed. Scroll through the images using the Multi Selector to highlight the image you wish to select.
3. Press ® and the selected image will appear in the **[Image 1]** box and the **[Preview]** box.
4. Adjust the gain value of **[Image 1]** by pressing ▲ and ▼. The effect of the gain control can be observed in the preview box. (The default value is x1.0, x0.5 cuts the gain in half, and selecting x2.0 doubles the gain.)
5. Highlight the **[Image 2]** box and repeat steps 2 – 4 above.
6. Once you have adjusted the gain of both images to achieve the desired effect, highlight the **[Preview]** box by pressing ◀ or ▶. Highlight **[Overlay]** using ▲ or ▼ and press ® to display a preview of the combined images. If the result is satisfactory, press the ® button to save the new image; otherwise, press ⊖ to return to the previous step.
7. To save the image without displaying a preview, highlight **[Save]** at step 6 above, instead of **[Overlay]**, and press the ® button. The new image will be displayed full-frame.

The image will be saved on the memory card using the Image Quality and Image Size settings currently selected on the camera. Image attributes such as White Balance, sharpening, color mode, saturation, and hue will be copied from the image selected as **[Image 1]**. The shooting data is also copied from **[Image 1]**. Image Overlays saved as NEF (RAW) files use the same compression and bit depth as the original files; overlays saved as JPEG files utilize size-priority compression.

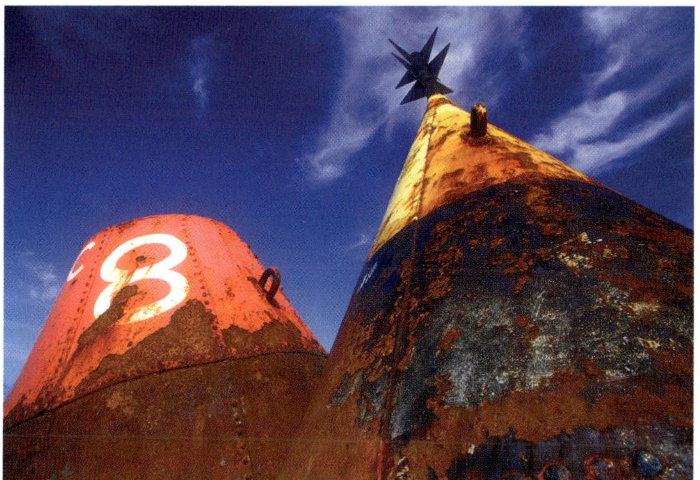

If the original image file was saved in only the NEF (RAW) format, it is still possible to output a JPEG file from the camera using the **[NEF (RAW) Processing]** item in the Retouch menu.

NEF (RAW) PROCESSING

This item can be used to create JPEG format copies of pictures saved and stored on the installed memory card at an image quality of NEF (RAW) or NEF (RAW) + JPEG. To use **[NEF (RAW) processing]**:

1. Highlight **[NEF (RAW) processing]** in the Retouch menu and press ▶.
2. Select the required NEF (RAW) picture from the displayed thumbnail pictures by pressing the Multi Selector; note, only NEF (RAW) pictures will be displayed. Press OK to select the highlighted picture.
3. A preview image is now displayed next to a menu of options:
   a. **[Image quality]**: Choose image quality from JPEG Fine, JPEG Normal, or JPEG Basic.
   b. **[Image size]**: Choose image size from Large, Medium, or Small.
   c. **[White balance]**: Choose White Balance settings, specify fluorescent lighting type, and apply White Balance Fine-Tuning. (Photographs taken at a White Balance of Preset Manual can only be subjected to Fine-Tuning from the Preset Manual White Balance option, and the **[Preset manual]** sub-option is only available for pictures taken at this White Balance setting.)

d. **[Exposure compensation]**: Adjust the exposure level ±2 EV.

e. **[Picture Control]**: Choose a Picture Control option.

f. **[High ISO NR]**: Select a level of noise reduction.

g. **[D-Lighting]**: Select a level of D-Lighting

4. Highlight the required option and press ▶. Select the required setting and press ⓞ to return to the preview image and menu display. Repeat the selection process for any other options to be used.
5. Once all settings have been adjusted, highlight EXE.
6. Press ⓞ to create and save a JPEG format copy and return to full-frame Playback.
7. Press the **MENU** button to return to full-frame Playback without creating a JPEG copy image.

NOTE: The Exposure Compensation option should be treated with some caution, as the ±2EV range is rather optimistic. The extended dynamic range of the NEF (RAW) files recorded by the D5100 does permit some adjustment to the exposure level, but only across a more limited range if image quality is to be preserved. I would suggest trying to limit adjustment to no more than ±1EV. To maximize image quality it pays to get the exposure as accurate as possible in-camera.

RESIZE

The **[Resize]** item offers options to reduce the resolution of the original image to create a copy that has a far smaller file size:

- 1920 x1280 pixels: Suitable for playback on a television set.
- 1280 x 856 pixels: Suitable for playback on a television set.
- 960 x 640 pixels: Suitable for display on web pages.
- 640 x 424 pixels: Suitable for display on web pages.
- 320 x 216 pixels: Suitable for sending as an attachment to e-mail.

To use this option via the Retouch menu, proceed as follows:

1. Open the Retouch menu, highlight **[Resize]**, and press ▶ to display two options: **[Select image]** and **[Choose size]**.
2. Highlight **[Choose size]**, and then press ▶ to display the five size options (listed above), and highlight the required size.

3. Press ⓞ to confirm your choice and return to the previous page.
4. Highlight **[Select picture]** and press ▶ to display the thumbnail images. The currently selected image is shown framed by a yellow border.
5. Use the Multi Selector to highlight a desired image (the yellow border will shift accordingly) and press 🔍 to select it (a small ▣ appears in the top right corner of the thumbnail to indicate it has been selected). Press 🔍 to view an enlarged picture.
6. Repeat as required. Once you have selected all the images you want to reduce in size, press ⓞ. A confirmation page will be displayed indicating how many images will be processed.
7. Select **[Yes]** to proceed with the process, or **[No]** to return to the previous page. If you select **[Yes]**, press ⓞ to apply the effect and save the copy picture(s).

QUICK RETOUCH

This item can be used to make a rapid enhancement to color saturation and contrast; the D5100 will apply D-Lighting accordingly to increase the brightness of strongly backlit subjects. Select an image as described above and press ⓞ to display the image, alongside a preview of the adjusted image. Use ▲ or ▼ to select one of three values: **[Low]**, **[Normal]**, or **[High]**. Press and hold 🔍 to view the preview image full-frame, and press ⓞ to make the copy image. To return to the normal full-frame Playback, press the ▶ button.

STRAIGHTEN

If you shoot a picture and then find that it is not aligned as it should be—for example, a horizon line slopes to one side—this item can be used to straighten the image. The image can be rotated by up to 5°, in steps of approximately 0.25°, by pressing ▶ to turn the image clockwise, or ◀ to turn the image counterclockwise. A pattern of gridlines is displayed on the monitor to assist in aligning the image. The edge of the image will be trimmed to produce a square copy. Press ⓞ to create the copy image. To return to full-frame Playback without copying the image, press the ▶ button.

DISTORTION CONTROL

Optical distortion from a lens can cause straight lines close to the edge of the frame to appear bowed. Typically, wide-angle lenses produce barrel distortion that causes lines to bend outward away from the center of the image, while telephoto lenses cause pincushion distortion that causes lines to bend inward toward the center of the image. This item corrects for such optical distortion. The **[Auto]** option applies correction automatically, and then you can refine the correction using the Multi Selector. Alternatively, you can select the **[Manual]** option and press ▶ to reduce barrel distortion or ◀ to reduce pincushion distortion. The greater the degree of correction, the more the peripheral area of the original frame will be cropped. Press OK to copy the picture and save the adjustments. To return to normal full-frame Playback without copying the image, press the ▶ button.

FISHEYE

This item modifies an image to emulate the appearance of a picture taken using a fisheye lens. This type of lens is not corrected to render straight lines as straight but, instead, with an increasing amount of distortion the farther the line is from the center of the frame. Select **[Fisheye]** and press ▶ to display the thumbnail images. Select the required image and press OK. Press ▶ to increase the (barrel) distortion or ◀ to reduce the effect. Be aware that greater distortion will result in more of the image being cropped at the edges. Press OK to copy the retouched picture. To return to normal full-frame Playback without copying the image, press the ▶ button.

COLOR OUTLINE

This item converts a conventional color picture into an outline image that can be used as a starting point for a drawing or a painting. Select **[Color outline]** and press ▶ to display the thumbnail images. Select the required image and press OK. The image is displayed as a monochrome line drawing. Press OK to save the effect and copy the image. To cancel the process, press the ▶ button.

COLOR SKETCH

This item converts a conventional color picture into an image that resembles a hand-draw sketch made with colored pencils. Select **[Color sketch]** and press ▶ to display the thumbnail images. Select the required image and press ㊀. The image is displayed with two controls: Highlight **[Vividness]** or **[Outlines]** by pressing ▲ or ▼, and press ◀ or ▶ to adjust the level as required. Increase vividness to boost color saturation, or reduce it to make the image appear less saturated. Outlines can be made broader or narrower; broad outlines make color more saturated. Press ㊀ to copy the retouched picture. To return to normal full-frame Playback without copying the image, press the ▶ button.

PERSPECTIVE CONTROL

This item is used to correct the perspective of an image—for example, the converging vertical lines that occur when shooting a picture of a tall building with the camera tilted upward. Select **[Perspective control]** and press ▶ to display the thumbnail images. Select the required image and press ㊀. Use the Multi Selector to adjust the image as required, using the scales displayed along the bottom and left side of the LCD monitor as a guide. Press ㊀ to save the adjusted copy image. To cancel the process, press the ▶ button.

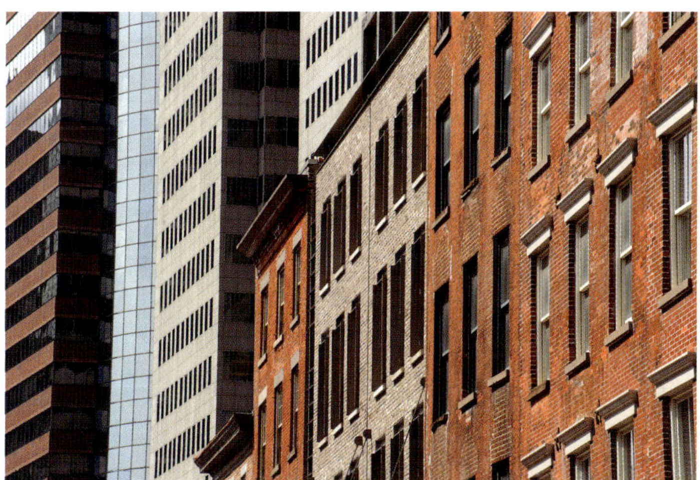

The Distortion Control and Perspective Control items in the Retouch menu offer the chance to adjust an image so that straight lines are rendered properly and parallel to each other.

MINIATURE EFFECT

This option is intended to emulate the effect of using a Nikkor PC-E Tilt / Shift lens when shooting pictures with a tilt movement applied. By reducing the depth of field to a very narrow region, it creates an effect as though the viewer is looking at a model of the scene. For the best results, shoot pictures to be converted with this item from a high vantage point.

1. Select **[Miniature effect]** and press ▶ to display the thumbnail images.
2. Select the required image and press ⓄⓀ. The image is displayed full-frame with a narrow oblong box marked with a yellow outline.
3. If the picture is in a horizontal (wide) format, press ▲ and ▼ to determine the area of focus (the area confined within the yellow box).
4. Press ◀ and ▶ to position the area of focus if the picture is in a vertical (tall) format.
5. Press and hold 🔍 to view the preview image full-frame.
6. Press ⓄⓀ to save the copy image.
7. To cancel the process, press the ▶ button.

SELECTIVE COLOR

This item converts a conventional color picture to one in which only a limited number of colors / hues are rendered in the retouched copy of the image.

1. Select **[Selective color]** and press ▶ to display the thumbnail images.
2. Select the required image and press ⓄⓀ. The image is displayed full-frame with a small square marked with a yellow outline.
3. Use the Multi Selector to position the square cursor over an object and press to select its color as one that will be retained in the Retouch copy of the picture (the camera may not detect less saturated colors). To increase the accuracy of color selection, you can enlarge the image by pressing 🔍. Press 🔍 to return to the normal view.
4. Rotate the Command dial to highlight the color range value next to the color box, and press ▲ and ▼ to increase or decrease the range of hues similar to that of the selected color that will be retained; change values from 1 to 7, where a higher number represents a wider range of hues.

5. Repeat steps 3 & 4 to select another color and repeat again for a third color.
6. Press 🗑 to deselect the highlighted color, or press and hold 🗑 to deselect all colors.
7. Press ⓞ to save the copy image.
8. To cancel the process, press the ▶ button.

SIDE-BY-SIDE COMPARISON

Use this item to compare a retouched copy with the original (source) file. It is only available if the button is pressed to display the Retouch menu when an original or copy image is shown in full-frame Playback.

1. Select either a picture that has been retouched or a retouched copy (indicated by the icon) during full-frame Playback for **[Side-by-side comparison]**.
2. Press ⓞ to display the original source image to the left and the retouched copy on the right. The options used to create the copy are displayed above the two images.
3. Use ◀ and ▶ to switch between the two images; the selected version is shown with a yellow border.
4. Press and hold 🔍 to view an enlarged view of the selected image.
5. If the image was created using the **[Image overlay]** option, use ▲ or ▼ to view the second source image.
6. Press the ▶ button to return to the Playback mode.
7. To return to Playback mode with the selected image displayed, press ⓞ.

NOTE: There must be at least one retouched image or retouched copy file stored on the selected memory card for the **[Side-by-side comparison]** item to be available in the Retouch menu, as accessed from full-frame Playback by pressing the ⓞ button.

EDIT MOVIE

This item allows you to trim video clips recorded in the D-Movie mode or to save a selected frame from a video clip as a JPEG file picture.

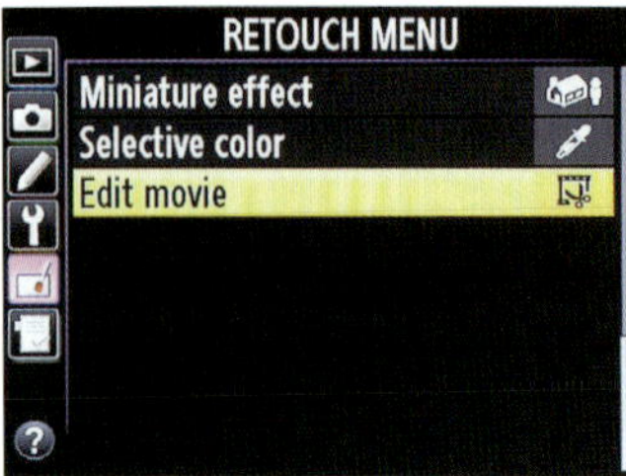

^ The **[Edit movie]** item, shown here highlighted in the Retouch menu, can only be used with files created through the D-Movie mode.

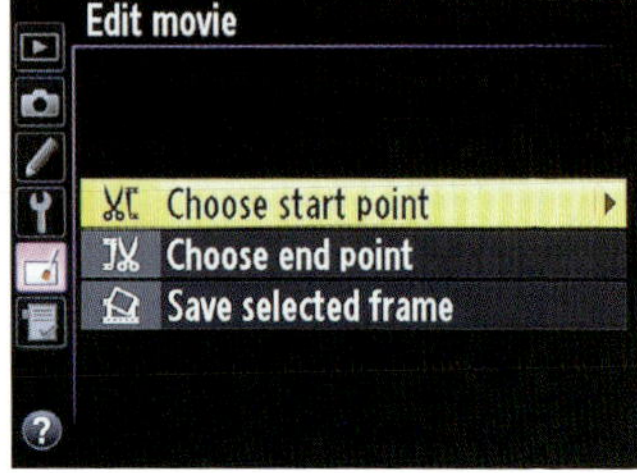

^ When you select **[Edit movie]** from the Retouch menu, you will see the options above.

To trim a movie clip from the Retouch menu, choosing where it will begin:

1. Select **[Edit movie]** and press ▶ to display the options.
2. Select **[Choose start point]** and press ▶ to display a thumbnail of the movie clips stored on the memory card.
3. Select the required movie clip and press OK. Press OK again to begin Playback of the video clip.
4. Press ▲ to pause the clip and display **[Proceed]**.
5. Select **[Yes]** to delete all frames prior to the displayed frame and save a new trimmed copy of the video clip, starting at the point selected.

To trim a movie clip from the Retouch menu, choosing where it will end:

1. Select **[Edit movie]** and press ▶ to display the options.
2. Select **[Choose end point]** and press ▶ to display a thumbnail of the movie clips stored on the memory card.
3. Select the required movie clip and press OK. Press OK again to begin Playback of the video clip.
4. Press ▲ to pause the clip and display **[Proceed].**
5. Select **[Yes]** to delete all frames after the displayed frame and save a new trimmed copy of the video clip, ending at the selected point.

To select an individual frame and save it as a JPEG picture through the Retouch menu:

1. Select **[Edit movie]** and then press ▶ to display the options.
2. Select **[Save selected frame]** and press ▶ to display a thumbnail of the movie clips stored on the memory card.
3. Select the required movie clip and press ⓞ.
4. Press ⓞ again and the clip will begin to play back. Press ▼ to pause Playback.
5. Press ◀ or ▶ to rewind or advance, respectively, frame-by-frame.
6. To save the currently displayed frame, press ▲ and display **[Proceed]**.
7. Highlight **[Yes]** and press ⓞ to create a JPEG picture.

Alternatively, it is possible to edit a movie clip directly from full-frame Playback:

1. Display the movie clip full-frame on the monitor screen by pressing the ▶ button, and by pressing ◀ or ▶.
2. Play the movie clip back by pressing ⓞ. Use the ⓞ button to start and resume Playback, and press ▼ to pause Playback. To trim the opening section of the movie clip, pause on the first frame you wish to retain. Or, to trim the end of the movie clip, pause on the last frame you wish to retain. Press ◀ or ▶ to rewind or advance video clip frame-by-frame to fine-tune the edit point.
3. Press the **AE-L/AF-L** button to display the **[Edit movie]** item from the Retouch menu.
4. To create a copy that includes the current frame and all subsequent frames, highlight **[Choose start point]** and press ⓞ. To create a copy that includes the current frame and all preceding frames, select **[Choose end point]** and press ⓞ.
5. Press ▲ to delete all frames before or after the current frame (for **[Choose start point]** or **[Choose end point]**, respectively).
6. Highlight **[Yes]** and press ⓞ to save the edited copy.

The saved copy can be trimmed further by repeating the movie-editing process through either method.

RECENT SETTINGS / MY MENU

The last tab on the left-hand side of the root menu page is for both My Menu and Recent Settings. By default, it is My Menu, but you can toggle between the two using the **[Choose tab]** item, selectable from either menu. To toggle from one to the other, highlight **[Choose tab]** and press ▶ to display the two options: **[My menu]** and **[Recent settings]**. Highlight the one you want and press the OK button.

[My menu] allows you create a customized menu from practically any combination of items in the Playback, Shooting, Custom Setting, Setup, or Retouch menus. Items can be added, deleted, and reordered at any time. Given the complexity and size of the menu system, this useful feature allows those menu items that you frequently use to be located in a single menu. Up to four items can be added to the **[My menu]** list of items before it becomes necessary to scroll to additional pages. The default My Menu control items, **[Add items]**, **[Remove items]**, and **[Rank items]**, are always displayed.

In **[Recent settings]**, up to 20 of the most recently used menu items will be displayed; as different menu items are used, they will be added automatically to the top of the Recent Settings menu list in chronological order. To scroll these items, use ▲ or ▼, and use OK to select the highlighted item.

To revert back to using **[My menu]**, open the **[Recent settings]** item, highlight **[Choose tab]**, and press ▶ to display **[My menu]** and **[Recent settings]** again. Highlight **[My menu]** and press the OK button.

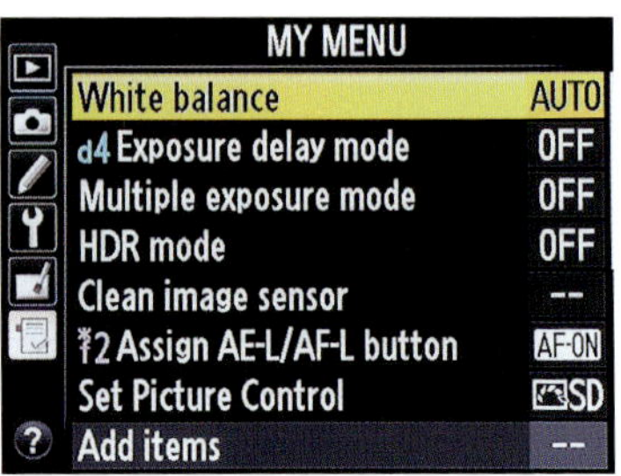

USING MY MENU

To add a menu item:

1. Open **[My menu]**, highlight **[Add items]**, and press ▶ to display a list of the five menus.
2. Highlight the desired menu and press ▶.
3. Highlight the item that you want to add to My Menu and press the (OK) button.
4. To position the selected menu item in the **[My menu]** list, use ▲ or ▼; once it's positioned, press the (OK) button to add the new item.

To delete a menu item:

1. Open **[My menu]**, highlight **[Remove items]**, and press ▶ to display the list of items in **[My menu]**.
2. Highlight the item to be removed and press ▶; a check mark will appear in the box to the right of the selected menu item.
3. To confirm the deletion of the selected item, highlight **[Done]** and press the (OK) button. A confirmation dialog box is displayed with the message "Delete selected items?" If you wish to proceed, press the (OK) button.

REORDER MENU ITEMS

To reorder the items in **[My menu]**:

1. Open **[My menu]**, highlight **[Rank items]**, and press ▶ to display the list of the menu items in My Menu.
2. Highlight the item to be relocated and press (OK).
3. To position the item in the menu list use ▲ or ▼; a solid yellow line indicates the location for the menu item.
4. Once positioned, press the (OK) button and the menu item will be moved.

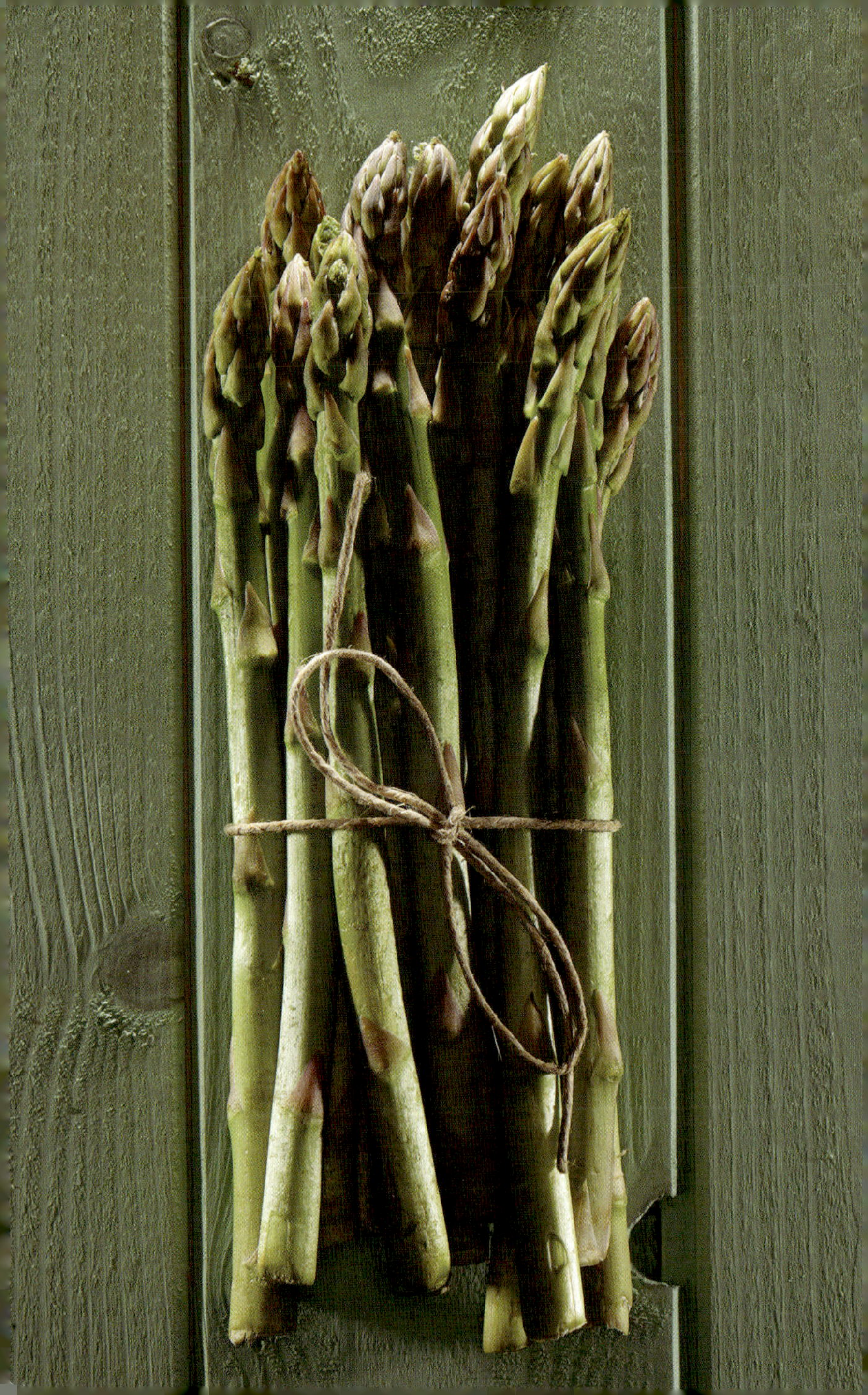

Nikon Flash Photography

Before we take a look at the flash capabilities of the D5100, it is helpful to understand some basics about the physics of light and flash exposure. One of the most important principles that influences flash exposure is the Inverse Square Law. It states that light from a point light source, such as a flash unit, falls off as it travels over a distance by the inverse of the square of that distance. Put simply, if you double the distance from a light source, its intensity drops by a factor of four because as light travels from the source, it spreads out, illuminating a wider area. So, at double the distance from the source, light covers four times the area. At four times the distance, the light covers sixteen times the area, so it is reduced to 1/16 of its intensity at the original distance.

Besides the Inverse Square Law, it is also essential to appreciate how exposure of light from a flash unit is influenced by the ISO sensitivity, lens aperture, and shutter speed settings of a camera. Just as when exposing for ambient light, the amount of light required for exposure from a flash occurs in direct proportion to the ISO setting on a camera. So, if the ISO value is doubled, the amount of light required from the flash to maintain the same flash exposure level (assuming no other factors change) is halved; conversely, if the ISO value is halved, the flash output must be doubled to maintain the same flash exposure level. Equally, altering the lens aperture, which controls how much light passes through the camera lens, has the same effect on flash exposure as altering the ISO level. So, if the aperture is changed from f/8 to f/5.6, to allow twice as much light to pass through the lens, the flash only needs to output half as much light to maintain the same flash exposure level (again, assuming no other factors are altered). If the lens aperture is changed from f/8 to f/11, to allow only half as much light to pass through the lens, the flash output must be doubled to maintain the same flash exposure level.

The intensity of the light produced by an electronic flash unit is always the same; therefore, the flash exposure is controlled by the duration of the flash output. At its maximum output of light, the duration of the flash pulse from a modern Nikon Speedlight flash unit is typically about 1/1000 second; as the amount of light output from the flash is reduced from its maximum level, the duration of the flash pulse becomes even briefer. Yet, the fastest flash synchronization (sync) speed of the D5100 is 1/200 second—the briefest shutter speed at which the opening and closing of the shutter allows the light from the flash to be recorded fully by the camera. Therefore, provided the shutter speed is set to either the flash sync speed or a slower (longer) shutter speed, it has no effect on the flash exposure. The only time the shutter speed is of any consequence when shooting with flash is if ambient light is also being recorded as part of the overall exposure. In this case, the ambient light exposure will be influenced by the shutter speed, but it still has no effect on the flash exposure.

Because a flash unit emits a precise, fixed amount of light (based principally on the flash-to-subject distance, ISO setting, and lens aperture) the light from the flash will only illuminate the subject properly at one specific distance. Therefore, any element in the scene closer to the flash than the subject will be overexposed and anything farther away will be underexposed. The degree of over- or underexposure will depend on how much closer or farther away the element is in relation to the flash unit, since the intensity of the light will be determined by the effect of the Inverse Square Law described previously.

Finally, the output of an electronic flash unit, often referred to as its power, is quantified by a value known as its guide number (GN); the higher the guide number, the more powerful the flash unit. Guide numbers are quoted as a distance (feet or meters) for a given ISO level and angle of view (usually expressed as a lens focal length). For example, the built-in Speedlight of the D5100 has a GN of 39 feet (12 m) at ISO 100, 18mm. When comparing guide numbers, make sure that the same units are used for linear measurement, ISO value, and focal length. (See the section, "Manual Flash Exposure Control" on pages 264-265 for details on how to use the GN value to calculate flash output manually.)

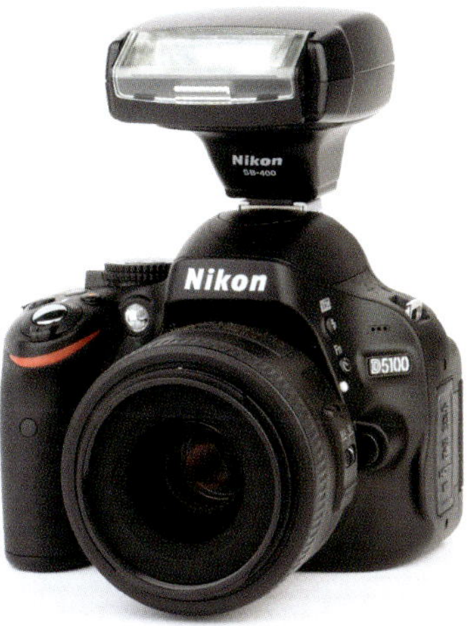

^ The D5100 with Nikon's most compact flash unit, the Nikon SB-400 Speedlight. Its flash head can be tilted for bounce flash (but not rotated), making it more versatile than the built-in flash.

THE CREATIVE LIGHTING SYSTEM

The most sophisticated flash system developed by Nikon to date is the Nikon Creative Lighting System (CLS); it is more refined and more comprehensive compared with any previous Nikon flash control system. The CLS encompasses a range of features and functions that are as much a part of compatible cameras as the Speedlight flash units themselves. Features include: intelligent through-the-lens (i-TTL) Flash Exposure Control, the Advanced Wireless Lighting (AWL) system that provides wireless control of multiple Speedlights using i-TTL, Flash Value (FV) Lock, Flash Color Information Communication, Auto FP High-Speed Sync, and Wide-Area AF-Assist to improve autofocus accuracy with cameras that have multiple AF points covering a large part of the frame area. Currently, CLS compatibility encompasses the D5100, together with the D3-series, D2-series, D700, D300-series, D200, D90, D7000, D5000, D3100, D3000, D80, D70-series, D60, D50, D40-series, and F6 cameras, including the internal Speedlight units of those models that possess them. The CLS includes the following external Nikon Speedlights: SB-900, SB-800, SB-700, SB-600, SB-400, and SB-R200. However, some of the listed camera models do not support all the features of the CLS.

The Auto FP High-Speed Sync and FV Lock features are not available with the D5100 when used with either its built-in Speedlight or an external CLS compatible Speedlight. Furthermore, its built-in Speedlight does not have a Commander mode for remote control of compatible Speedlights using the AWL system, and there is no Repeating Flash mode (although this feature is supported with compatible external Speedlights).

TTL FLASH MODES

When used in combination with a CPU-type lens, the D5100 supports two methods of TTL-controlled flash exposure with its built-in flash unit or a compatible external Speedlight. To select TTL flash control for the built-in Speedlight, when shooting in the P, S, A, or M exposure modes (TTL flash control is always used in any other exposure mode), open the Shooting menu and navigate to the **[Flash cntrl for built-in flash]** item and press ▶. Highlight **[TTL]** and press ⓞⓚ. When using an external Speedlight, the flash mode is selected via the controls of the Speedlight.

i-TTL BALANCED FILL-FLASH

This is Nikon's third generation of TTL Flash Exposure Control—the most sophisticated to date. When the D5100 is set to Matrix metering, a D- or G-type Nikkor lens is mounted on the cameras, and the built-in Speedlight (or an external Speedlight such as the SB-700, SB-800, or SB-900) is activated, i-TTL Balanced Fill-Flash will attempt to balance the ambient light, which will generally be lighting the background, to the flash output, which is usually illuminating the foreground.

It is important to note that whenever you see the term "i-TTL Balanced Fill-Flash," existing ambient light and flash are being mixed in a fully automated process to produce the final exposure. How the two light sources are mixed and in what proportion will depend on a wide variety of factors, including ISO sensitivity, lens aperture, exposure mode, Exposure Compensation value, brightness of both the ambient and flash illumination, and the nature of the scene being photographed.

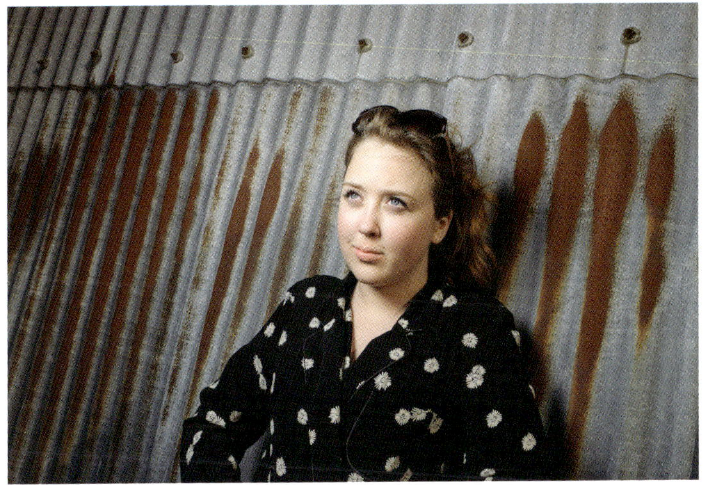

^ Flash (a Nikon SB-900 fired through a softbox) provided the main light source for this shot, despite the subject being lit by strong direct sunlight from camera right.

Fill-flash is a recognized lighting technique in which the flash is used to supplement the main ambient light source. The level of illumination provided by the flash is generally weaker than the ambient light; its purpose is to provide a small amount of additional light in the shadows and other under-lit areas of a scene to help reduce the overall level of contrast. Many photographers also use this technique when shooting portraits to put a small catch light in their subject's eyes.

When the camera is in Manual exposure mode (M), only the flash exposure is determined by the i-TTL system. However, when i-TTL is used with any of the D5100's automated exposure modes, the camera has full control of the exposure for both the ambient light and flash output. It assesses the flash output level and the ambient light in an attempt to create a balanced exposure using both light sources. To achieve this, the D5100 will often adjust the exposure for either the ambient light or the flash output, and sometimes both. Consequently, any compensation you apply to adjust either the ambient light exposure or flash output level is frequently overridden (or even ignored). This often results in a picture where the flash output is too strong, spoiling the fill-flash effect. The lack of user control also makes it difficult to achieve consistent, repeatable results.

STANDARD i-TTL FLASH

This flash mode differs from the i-TTL Balanced Fill-Flash mode in that the measurement of ambient light in the scene remains wholly independent of the flash output control, and is not integrated in any way with the flash exposure calculations.

So, if you want to achieve consistent, repeatable results when using a true Fill-flash technique—where the flash is the supplementary light—I recommend that you use standard i-TTL flash. This is because any Flash Output Compensation or Exposure Compensation you have set will be applied without influence from the camera. Likewise, in any situation where you wish to use flash as the main source of illumination and have control over the flash output level as well as the exposure of ambient light, I also suggest you select standard i-TTL flash.

The i-TTL Balanced Fill-Flash is the default flash exposure control method for the built-in flash unit of the D5100. The only way to override this is to set the camera to Spot metering, which causes the camera to use Standard i-TTL Flash control. When using the Nikon SB-400, SB-600, SB-700, SB-800, and SB-900 Speedlights, the flash exposure control method is selected directly on the flash unit; but if you set the D5100 to Spot metering, the camera will override this selection and always use standard i-TTL flash control.

i-TTL FLASH EXPOSURE CONTROL

i-TTL offers an enhanced and refined method of flash exposure control. Currently, the SB-900, SB-800, SB-700, SB-600, SB-400, and SB-R200 are the only external Speedlights that support i-TTL and the CLS, while the SU-800 Wireless Speedlight Commander can be used to control any of these units, with the exception of the SB-400. If any other external Nikon Speedlight is attached to the D5100, TTL flash exposure control is not supported; this applies to all earlier Speedlights, even DX-types, designed for earlier Nikon DSLR cameras. The i-TTL system works in the following way with the D5100:

- i-TTL uses fewer monitor pre-flashes than other systems, but they have a higher intensity. This greater intensity improves the efficiency of obtaining a measurement from the TTL flash sensor. By using fewer pulses, the amount of time taken to perform the assessment is reduced, which enables the camera to perform this process before lifting the reflex mirror.
- The D5100 uses its 420-pixel RGB metering sensor located in the prism head for TTL control of flash exposure, regardless of whether the camera is used with its built-in Speedlight, a single external Speedlight, or multiple Speedlights controlled via an SU-800 wireless Speedlight commander in the AWL system. In all cases, monitor pre-flashes are always emitted before the reflex mirror is raised.
- The i-TTL system of the D5100 is designed to work with ISO sensitivities between 100 and 6400; at an ISO setting above ISO 6400, flash exposure control may be less accurate.

The following is a summary of the sequence of events used to calculate flash exposure by the D5100 when it is used with the built-in Speedlight or external CLS Speedlights and a D- or G-type Nikkor lens:

1. Once the shutter release is pressed, the camera reads the focus distance from the D- or G-type lens.
2. The camera sends a signal to the Speedlight to initiate the pre-flash system, which then emits the monitor pre-flashes (pulses of light) from the Speedlight(s).
3. The light from these pre-flashes is bounced back from the scene, through the lens, and onto the 420-pixel RGB metering sensor (via the reflex mirror).
4. The information from the pre-flashes gathered by the 420-pixel RGB metering sensor is analyzed, along with measurements of the ambient light in the scene and information supplied by the focusing system. The camera then determines the amount of light required from the Speedlight(s) and sets the duration of the flash discharge accordingly.
5. The reflex mirror lifts up, out of the light path to the shutter, and the shutter opens.
6. The camera sends a signal to the Speedlight(s) to initiate the main flash discharge, which is quenched the instant the amount of light predetermined in Step 4 has been emitted.
7. The shutter closes at the end of the predetermined shutter speed duration, and the reflex mirror is lowered to its normal position.

NOTE: In the D5100, the emission of the monitor pre-flashes occurs before the reflex mirror is raised. Thus there is a slight chance that during the short delay between the reflex mirror being raised and the shutter opening, the light from the pre-flash may cause the subject to blink.

FLASH OUTPUT ASSESSMENT

The most crucial phase in the sequence described above is step 4, which is the point when the required output from the flash is calculated. As stated previously, this is accomplished using the 420-pixel RGB metering sensor that is positioned in the viewfinder head of the D5100. The ability of this sensor is enhanced by the Scene Recognition System (SRS), which made its debut in the original D300 camera model in mid-2007. A diffraction grating located immediately in front of the metering sensor separates the light falling on it, from both the reflected monitor pre-flash illumination and the ambient light, into its component colors. This enables the sensor to recognize shapes and objects by the distribution of color and contrast, enabling it to work more effectively and efficiently. The Scene Recognition System only operates with Matrix metering and is particularly sensitive to skin tones; however, if Center-Weighted or Spot metering is selected, the D5100 uses a simple grayscale metering system—in other words, it is not sensitive to color.

When Matrix metering is used, this evaluation of the shape and color of elements in the scene is performed together with conventional assessments of the overall levels of brightness and the level of contrast. This information is then combined with information from the autofocus (AF) system. The camera assesses the brightness of each of the 420 pixels on the RGB metering sensor, and then compares them relative to each other to establish scene contrast while it looks for patterns. For example, a distribution of bright pixels in the upper part of a frame and darker pixels in the lower part may be indicating a light sky above the subject area. The metering system assumes the subject is covered by the active AF point(s); by checking which AF point(s) report focus, it can determine the likely location of the subject within the frame. Provided a D- or G-type Nikkor lens or a third-party lens that supports communication of focus distance is mounted on the camera, the metering system will also integrate the approximate focus distance into the calculations for flash output.

Once the camera has collected all the information pertaining to the shapes, colors, brightness, and range of contrast in the scene, it compares these values against brightness pattern information from actual photographs held in a stored database of over 30,000 sample exposures, covering an enormous range of lighting conditions. If the first comparison generates an evaluation that conflicts with the stored exposure data, the pattern of pixels may be re-assessed and then a further analysis performed. For example, if any group of pixels reports an abnormally high level of brightness in comparison to the others on the sensor, the metering system will usually ignore this information in its flash exposure calculations. This can occur if there is a highly reflective surface, such as glass or water, in a part of the scene; this could result in a bright reflection of the light from the flash that would otherwise cause the metering system to underexpose the picture.

FOCUS INFORMATION

As described above, when using Matrix metering and a D- or G-type Nikkor lens, focus information is provided to the metering system in two forms: camera-to-subject distance and the level of focus / defocus at each AF point. The basic strategy of the Matrix metering system is to optimize flash output while avoiding overexposure; therefore, in most cases, the focus distance information will influence which pixels of the RGB metering sensor affect ambient exposure and flash output calculations. For example, if the subject is positioned in the center of the frame and the lens is focused at a middle-to-long distance, the camera will assess all the pixels on the sensor but place slightly more emphasis on those at the center of the frame. In this situation, if flash is the main source of illumination and the background is much farther away from the flash than the subject, it is likely to result in a typical "party picture" where the subject is well lit by the flash but set against a completely black background (due to flash fall-off). Conversely, assuming the subject is positioned in the center of the frame, the lens is focused at a short distance, and the level of illumination is fairly even across the frame area, the camera will generally place slightly more emphasis on those pixels that cover the outer part of the frame area and slightly less on the central ones as it attempts to prevent loss of highlight detail in the subject. However, an exception to this occurs if the camera detects a very high level of contrast between the central and outer areas of the frame; in this situation, the metering system commonly reverses the emphasis and weights the exposure calculations according to the information received from pixels at the center of the frame area to ensure exposure accuracy in this region.

Essentially, what the camera is trying to do in both cases just described is prevent overexposure of the subject. As each AF point is checked for its degree of focus, individual focus point information is integrated with focus distance information. This provides the camera with information about the probable location of the subject within the area of the scene. Using the examples given in the previous paragraph, the metering system knows that the central AF point has acquired focus while the other AF points each report varying levels of defocus. Therefore, exposure is calculated on the assumption that the subject is in the center of the frame, and the camera biases its computations according to the focus distance information it receives from the lens.

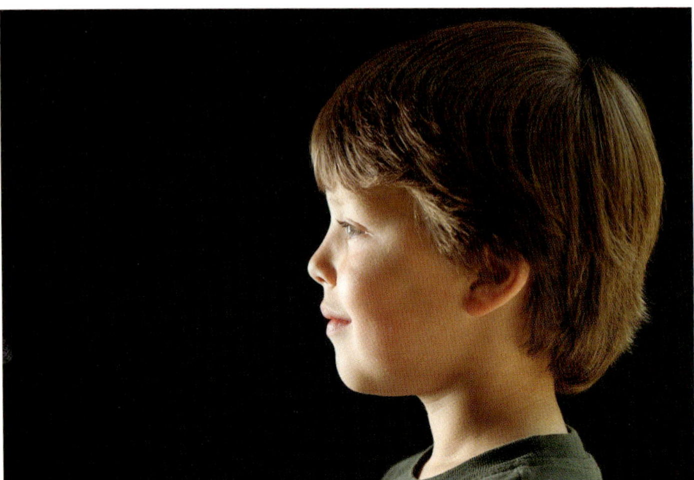

^ **Taking the flash off the camera is the quickest and most effective way to improve the quality and versatility of the lighting. Here, an SB-700 was fired through a softbox at camera left and slightly behind the subject, while a reflector to camera right filled in the shadows.**

However, it is important to understand that other twists occur in this story of interaction between exposure calculation and focus information. For example, when you acquire and lock focus on a subject using the center AF point and then recompose the shot so that the subject is located elsewhere in the frame, the camera will generally use the exposure value it calculated when it first acquired focus. However, if it assesses that the level of brightness detected by the pixels at the center of the frame has changed significantly from the level when focus was first acquired, the camera can and often does adjust its flash exposure calculations—sometimes not necessarily for the better. It may be necessary to apply Flash Output Compensation to help improve flash exposure accuracy in such situations.

NOTE: A D- or G-type Nikkor lens or a third party lens with equivalent specification must be used for the focus distance information to be available to the camera when it computes flash exposure.

THE BUILT-IN SPEEDLIGHT

The D5100's built-in Speedlight has an automatic flash Guide Number of 39 feet (12 m) at ISO 100, 68°F (20°C), and 43 feet (13 m) for manual flash. The camera's maximum flash synchronization speed in all exposure modes is 1/200 second, regardless of the type of Speedlight that is used; unlike some more sophisticated models, the D5100 does not support the Auto FP high-speed flash sync feature of the CLS. To prevent errors, the D5100 will not allow a shutter speed above 1/200 second to be set when either the built-in Speedlight or an external Speedlight is being used.

The subject must be farther from the camera than the minimum flash range of 2 feet (0.6 m); the camera may not calculate a correct flash exposure at shorter distances. If the camera is set to one of the automatic Scene modes that support use of flash, and the meter determines that flash is needed, the built-in Speedlight will pop up automatically. In P, S, A, and M exposure modes, it must be activated manually by pressing the ⚡ Flash Mode button that is located immediately below the ⚡± Flash Exposure Compensation icon on the lower left side of the viewfinder head.

The built-in Speedlight draws its power from the camera's main battery—extended use of the flash will have a direct effect on battery life. As soon as the flash unit pops up, it begins to charge. The flash-ready symbol ⚡ appears in the viewfinder to indicate charging is complete and the flash is ready to fire. If the flash fires at its maximum output, the same flash-ready symbol will blink for approximately three seconds after the exposure has been made. This indicates the flash is not yet ready for another exposure, warning of the potential for underexposure. The flash-ready symbol operates in exactly the same way when using an external Speedlight.

Press the ⚡ button to pop up the D5100's built-in flash. Once the flash is popped up, as shown below, it takes a second to charge, and you will see the ⚡ icon in the viewfinder when it is finished.

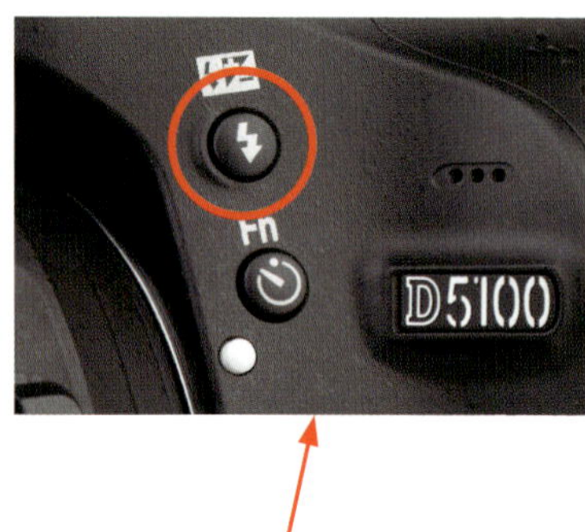

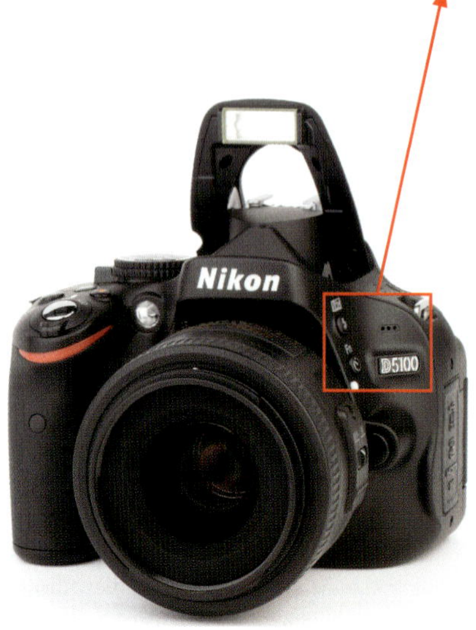

RANGE, APERTURE, AND ISO SENSITIVITY

The built-in flash unit's shooting range will vary depending on the values set for the lens aperture and ISO sensitivity:

ENS APERTURE AT ISO							RANGE	
00	200	400	800	1600	3200	6400	METERS	FEET
.4	2	2.8	4	5.6	8	11	1.0 – 8.5	3.25 – 27.92
	2.8	4	5.6	8	11	16	0.7 – 6.0	2.33 – 19 .66
.8	4	5.6	8	11	16	22	0.6 – 4.2	2 – 13.75
	5.6	8	11	16	22	22	0.6 – 3.0	2 – 9.83
.6	8	11	16	22	22	-	0.6 – 2.1	2 – 6.92
	11	16	22	32	-	-	0.6 – 1.5	2 – 4.92
1	16	22	32	-	-	-	0.6 – 1.1	2 – 3.58
6	22	32	-	-	-	-	0.6 – 0.7	2 – 2.33

LIMITATIONS

While the built-in Speedlight of the D5100 is not as powerful as an external Speedlight, it can still provide a useful level of illumination at short ranges, especially for the purpose of fill flash, since it supports Flash Output Compensation. However, if you want to use the built-in Speedlight as the main light source, you should be aware of the following:

- The Guide Number (GN) is limited, thus flash shooting ranges are relatively short (see table above).
- The proximity of the flash head is much closer to the central lens axis when compared to an external flash; hence, the likelihood of red-eye occurring is significantly increased.
- This close proximity of the built-in Speedlight to the central lens axis often means that the lens obscures the output of the flash, especially if a lens hood is in place. For example, the obstruction of the light from the flash may cause a shadow to appear on the bottom edge of the picture if the camera is held in a horizontal orientation.
- The angle of coverage achieved by the built-in Speedlight is limited and only extends to cover the field-of-view of a lens with a focal length of 18mm or more. If used with a shorter focal length lens, the flash will not be able to illuminate the periphery of the frame and these areas will appear underexposed. Even at the widest limit of coverage, it is not uncommon to see a noticeable fall-off of illumination (vignetting) in the corners of the frame.
- The built-in Speedlight draws its power from the camera's battery, so extended use will exhaust it quite quickly.

LENS COMPATIBILITY

The built-in flash can be used with CPU lenses (i.e., all AF and Ai-P types) with focal lengths between 18mm and 300mm. Regardless of the lens, the built-in flash has a minimum range of 2 feet (0.6 m) making it impossible to use with the close focus distances of macro lenses. Furthermore, it is not possible to use the built-in Speedlight with the AF-S 14–24mm f/2.8G ED—light is obscured regardless of the focal length with this lens. The built-in flash may be unable to illuminate the entire frame area evenly when using the following lenses at focus distances less than those given in the following table:

LENS	ZOOM POSITION	MINIMUM DISTANCE WITHOUT VIGNETTING
AF-S DX Nikkor 10–24mm f/3.5–4.5G ED	24 mm	2.5 m / 8.2 ft.
AF-S DX Zoom-Nikkor 12–24mm f/4G IF-ED	20 mm	3 m / 9.8 ft.
	24 mm	1 m / 3.25 ft.
AF-S 16–35mm f/4G VR	28 mm	1.5 m / 4.9 ft.
	35 mm	1 m / 3.25 ft.
AF-S DX Nikkor 16–85mm f/3.5–5.6G ED VR	24–85 mm	No vignetting
AF-S Zoom-Nikkor 17–35mm f/2.8D IF-ED	24 mm	2 m / 6.6 ft.
	28 mm	1 m / 3.25 ft.
	35 mm	No vignetting
AF-S DX Zoom-Nikkor 17–55mm f/2.8G IF-ED	28 mm	1.5 m / 4.9 ft.
	35 mm	1 m / 3.25 ft.
	45–55 mm	No vignetting
AF Zoom-Nikkor 18–35mm f/3.5–4.5D IF-ED	24 mm	1 m / 3.25 ft.
	28–35 mm	No vignetting
AF-S DX Zoom-Nikkor 18–70mm f/3.5–4.5G IF-ED	18 mm	1 m / 3.25 ft.
	24–70 mm	No vignetting
AF-S DX NIKKOR 18–105mm f/3.5–5.6G ED VR	18 mm	2.5 m / 8.2 ft.
	24 mm	1 m / 3.25 ft.
AF-S DX Zoom-Nikkor 18–135mm f/3.5–5.6G IF-ED	18 mm	1 m / 3.25 ft.
	24–135 mm	No vignetting
AF-S DX VR Zoom-Nikkor 18–200mm f/3.5–5.6G IF-ED	24 mm	1 m / 3.25 ft.
AF-S DX NIKKOR 18–200mm f/3.5–5.6G ED VR II	35–200 mm	No vignetting

LENS	ZOOM POSITION	MINIMUM DISTANCE WITHOUT VIGNETTING
AF Zoom-Nikkor 20–35mm f/2.8D IF	24 mm	2.5 m / 8.2 ft.
	28 mm	1 m / 3.25 ft.
	35 mm	No vignetting
AF-S NIKKOR 24mm f/1.4G ED	24 mm	1 m / 3.25 ft.
AF-S NIKKOR 24–70mm f/2.8G ED	35 mm	1.5 m / 4.9 ft.
	50 mm	1 m / 3.25 ft.
	70 mm	No vignetting
AF-S VR Zoom-Nikkor 24–120mm f/3.5–5.6G IF-ED	24 mm	1 m / 3.25 ft.
	28–120 mm	No vignetting
AF-S NIKKOR 24–120mm f/4G ED VR	24 mm	2.5 m / 8.2 ft.
AF-S NIKKOR 28–300mm f/3.5–5.6G ED VR	28 mm	1.5 m / 4.9 ft.
	35 mm	1 m / 3.25 ft.
AF-S Zoom-Nikkor 28–70mm f/2.8D IF-ED	35 mm	1.5 m / 4.9 ft.
	50–70 mm	No vignetting
AF-S VR Zoom-Nikkor 200–400mm f/4G IF-ED	250 mm	2.5 m / 8.2 ft.
	350 mm	2 m / 6.6 ft.
AF-S NIKKOR 200–400mm f/4G ED VR II	200 mm	5 m / 16.4 ft.
	250 mm	3 m / 9.8 ft.
	300 mm	2.5 m / 8.2 ft.
	350–400 mm	No vignetting
PC-E NIKKOR 24mm f/3.5 ED *	24 mm	3 m / 9.8 ft.

* When not shifted or tilted.

HINT: Always remember to remove the lens hood to prevent the light from the flash being obscured and causing a shadow in the image.

FLASH SYNCHRONIZATION

Flash Synchronization (sync) modes determine when the flash is fired in relation to the opening and closing of the shutter, and should not be confused with the Flash Exposure Control modes described earlier (i.e., i-TTL Balanced Fill-Flash, Standard i-TTL Flash, or Manual Flash). The availability of a particular Flash Sync mode will depend on the exposure mode selected via the Mode dial. In turn, the choice of Flash Sync mode will influence the range of available shutter speeds (see the Shutter Speed Restrictions chart on page 258).

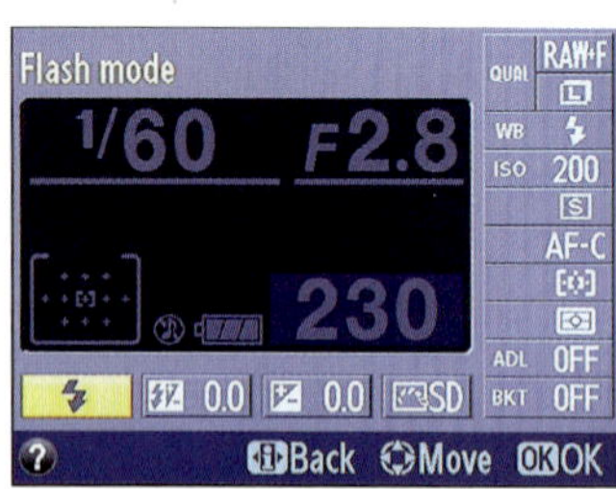

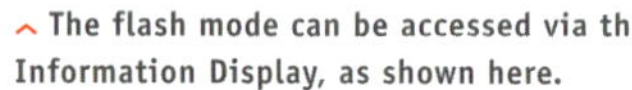

▲ The flash mode can be accessed via the Information Display, as shown here.

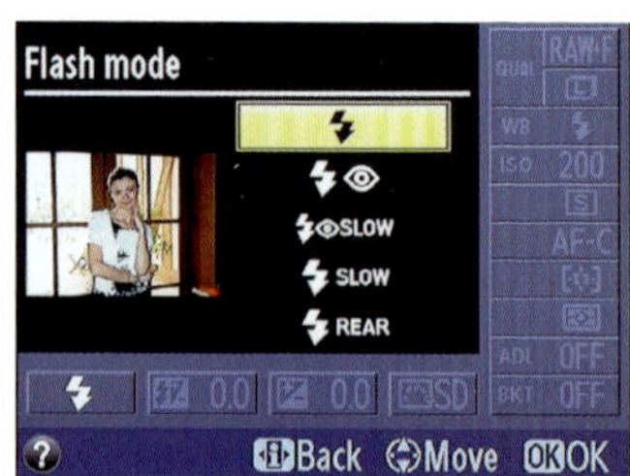

▲ The available flash modes for the selected exposure mode are listed beside example pictures.

To set a sync mode on the D5100, press the info button to activate the Information Display on the monitor, and then press the i button to place the cursor. Use the Multi Selector to highlight the flash mode in the Information display, and then press the OK button. Use ▲ and ▼ to highlight a flash mode and press OK to select it. The options available are as follows when using the AUTO, , , , , , and modes:

- Auto Flash: The built-in flash will pop up automatically if the camera determines that the ambient light level is low or the subject is strongly backlit.
- Auto Flash with Red-Eye Reduction: This operates the same way as Auto, except the Red-Eye Reduction lamp will illuminate briefly before the flash fires. When using the built-in flash, the Red-Eye Reduction lamp lights for approximately 1 second before the main flash output; with an external Speedlight, a short series of low-intensity light pulses are emitted before the main output. The purpose is to induce the pupils in the subject's eye to constrict, thus reducing the risk of red-eye.
- Flash Off: Operation of the flash unit is cancelled, regardless of the prevailing light conditions.

HINT: Red-Eye Reduction mode not only alerts your subject that you are about to take a picture, but it also causes a delay in the shutter's operation, by which time you may have missed the shot! Personally, I never bother with this feature. Red-eye can be removed in post-processing quite easily.

Using mode:

- AUTO SLOW Auto Flash with Slow Sync and Red-Eye Reduction: This operates in the same way as Auto flash with Slow Sync, except the Red-Eye Reduction lamp will illuminate briefly before the flash fires.
- AUTO SLOW Auto Flash with Slow Sync: The built-in flash pops up automatically when the camera detects low light. This option differs from flash, because it offers an extended range of shutter speeds between 1/200 and 1 second to enable the camera to record the ambient light.
- Flash Off: Operation of the flash unit is cancelled, regardless of the prevailing light conditions.

Using mode:

- Fill Flash: The built-in flash will pop up automatically if the camera determines that the ambient light level is low or the subject is strongly backlit. The flash fires as soon as the shutter has opened.

Using P and A Modes:

- Fill Flash: The built-in flash will pop up only if the button is pressed. The flash fires as soon as the shutter has opened.
- Fill Flash with Red-Eye Reduction: This operates in the same way as Fill Flash, except the Red-Eye Reduction lamp will illuminate briefly before the flash fires.
- SLOW Slow Sync with Red-Eye Reduction: This operates in the same way as Slow Sync flash, except the Red-Eye Reduction lamp will illuminate briefly before the flash fires.
- SLOW Slow Sync: This operates in the same way as Fill Flash, except all shutter speeds between 30 seconds and 1/200 second are available. It is useful for recording low-level ambient light as well as those areas of the scene or subject illuminated by the flash (see pages 265-266 for a full description).

- **REAR** Rear-Curtain Sync: The flash fires immediately before the shutter closes. As with Slow Sync flash, all shutter speeds between 30 seconds and 1/200 second are available; it is not only useful for recording low-level ambient light as well as those areas of the scene or subject illuminated by the flash, but also for creating motion blur trails that appear to follow a moving subject (see page 266 for a full description). **SLOW** is displayed in the shooting information once the setting for this mode is completed.

Using M and S modes:

- Fill Flash: The built-in flash will pop up only if the button is pressed. The flash fires as soon as the shutter has opened.
- Fill Flash with Red-Eye Reduction: This operates in the same way as Fill Flash, except the Red-Eye Reduction lamp will illuminate briefly before the flash fires.
- **REAR** Rear-Curtain with Slow Sync: The flash fires immediately before the shutter closes. All shutter speeds between 30 seconds and 1/200 second are available; it is not only useful for recording low-level ambient light and those areas of the scene or subject illuminated by the flash, but also for creating motion blur trails that appear to follow a moving subject (see the page 266 for a full description).

NOTE: If an external Speedlight is attached to the D5100, the flash will fire in every exposure mode, with the exception of , , and , even in modes that do not normally support the use of the built-in flash, such as .

SHUTTER SPEED RESTRICTIONS

When using the D5100's built-in Speedlight, the range of available shutter speeds varies according to the selected exposure mode as follows:

MODE	SHUTTER SPEED RANGE
AUTO, , , , , , P, A	1/200 – 1/60 second
	1/200 – 1/125 second
	1/200 – 1 second
S	1/200 – 30 seconds
M	1/200 – 30 seconds, bulb

The following table summarizes how the shutter speed and lens aperture values are influenced by the selected exposure mode when an external Speedlight is used:

EXPOSURE MODE	SHUTTER SPEED	LENS APERTURE
Programmed-Auto (P)	Set automatically by camera between 1/200 – 1/60 second [1]	Set automatically by the camera
Shutter-Priority (S)	Value between 1/200 – 30 seconds available for selection by the user	
Aperture-Priority (A)	Set automatically by camera between 1/200 – 1/60 second [1]	Value selected by the user
Manual (M)	Value between 1/200 – 30 seconds, plus bulb available for selection by the user	

[1] Shutter speed may be set as slow as 30 seconds in Slow Sync, Slow Rear-Curtain Sync, and Slow Sync with Red-Eye Reduction flash modes.

USING EXTERNAL SPEEDLIGHTS

The D5100 offers full i-TTL Flash Exposure Control with five external Nikon Speedlights that are compatible with the CLS:

- SB-R200 with a GN of 33 feet (10m) at ISO 100
- SB-400 with a GN of 69 feet (21 m) at ISO 100
- SB-600 with a GN of 98 feet (30 m) at ISO 100 with the flash head set to 35mm
- SB-700 with a GN of 92 feet (28 m) at ISO 100 with the flash head set to 35mm
- SB-800 with a GN of 125 feet (38 m) at ISO 100 with the flash head set to 35mm
- SB-900 with a GN of 111 feet (34 m) at ISO 100 with the flash head set to 35mm (and with Normal light distribution selected)

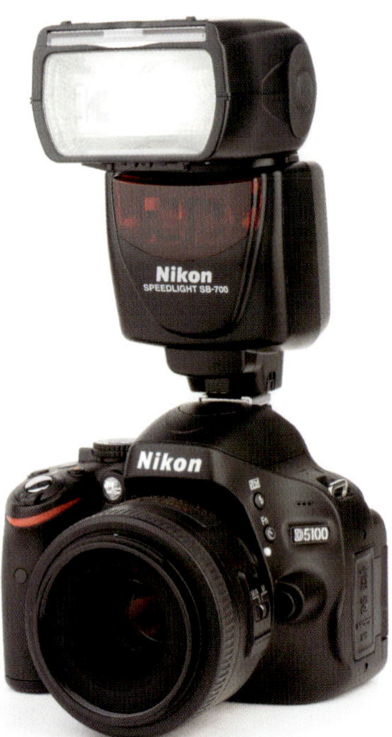

The SB-700 (shown here) and earlier SB-600 are small, compact, external flash units that considerably increase flexibility and creativity for flash photography with the D5100.

The external Speedlights can be mounted on the accessory shoe on top of the D5100, or alternatively, connected to the camera via the accessory shoe by one of the Nikon dedicated TTL flash cords, such as the SC-28.

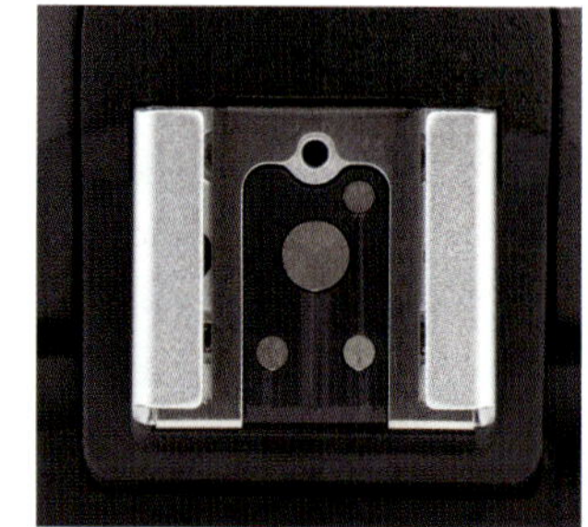

FLASH UNIT / FLASH MODE/FEATURE						ADVANCED WIRELESS LIGHTING					
						COMMANDER			REMOTE		
		SB-900 SB-800	SB-700	SB-600	SB-400	SB-900 SB-800	SB-700	SU-800[1]	SB-900 SB-800	SB-700 SB-600	SB-R200
i-TTL	i-TTL balanced fill-flash for DSLR[2]	✓[3]	✓[3]	✓[3]	✓[4]	✓	✓	✓	✓	✓	✓
AA	Auto aperture[2]	✓[5]	—	—	—	✓[6]	—	✓[6]	✓[6]	—	—
A	Non-TTL auto	✓[5]	—	—	—	✓[6]	—	—	✓[6]	—	—
GN	Distance-priority manual	✓	✓	—	—	—	—	—	—	—	—
M	Manual	✓	✓	✓	✓[7]	✓	✓	✓	✓	✓	✓
RPT	Repeating flash	✓	—	—	—	✓	—	✓	✓	✓	—
AF-assist for Multi-Area AF[2]		✓	✓	✓	—	✓	✓	✓	—	—	—
Flash Color Information Communication		✓	✓	✓	✓	✓	✓	—	—	—	—
REAR	Rear-Curtain sync	✓	✓	✓	✓	✓	✓	✓	✓	✓	✓
	Red-eye reduction	✓	✓	✓	✓	✓	✓	—	—	—	—
Power zoom		✓	✓	✓	—	✓	✓	—	—	—	—

1 Only available when SU-800 is used to control other flash units.
2 CPU lens required.
3 Standard i-TTL flash for DSLR is used with Spot metering or when selected with flash unit.
4 Standard i-TTL flash for DSLR is used with Spot metering.
5 Selected with flash unit.
6 Auto Aperture (AA) is used regardless of mode selected with flash unit.
7 Can be selected with camera.

All models except the SB-R200 can either be attached to the camera directly or via the dedicated Nikon TTL remote flash cords: SC-28, SC-29, or the now discontinued SC-17. The SB-R200 can only be controlled as part of the Nikon Advanced Wireless Control (AWL) flash system via either the SU-800 commander unit or the SB-700, SB-800, and SB-900 Speedlights when used as master flash units.

The five Speedlights that can be attached to the accessory shoe of the D5100 offer additional versatility because their flash heads can be tilted and—in the case of the SB-600, SB-700, SB-800, and SB-900—swiveled for bounce flash. Unlike earlier Nikon Speedlights, which cancelled monitor pre-flashes if the flash head was tilted or swiveled for bounce flash, the SB-400, SB-600, SB-700, SB-800, and SB-900 emit pre-flashes regardless of the flash head orientation. The four latter units also have an adjustable auto zoom-head (SB-600: 24-85mm, SB-700: 14-120mm, SB-800: 24-105mm, SB-900: 12-200mm) that controls the angle of coverage and a wide-angle diffuser to allow them to illuminate even wider fields of view. With the diffuser, the SB-600 and SB-800 can cover down to 14mm, while the SB-700 and SB-900 can cover down to 12mm.

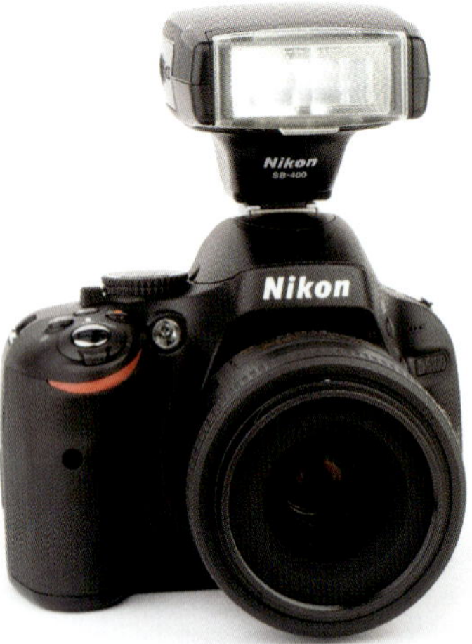

The SB-400 Speedlight is one of five external accessory flash units compatible with the D5100, all of which can be mounted on the camera via its accessory shoe.

NOTE: IF the SB-400 is attached to the D5100 and turned on, the CS-e1 **[Flash cntrl for built-in flash]** item in the Custom Settings menu changes to **[Optional flash]**, which allows **[TTL]** or **[Manual]** to be selected for the flash mode.

When used with the D5100, the SB-900 and SB-700 automatically adjust their zoom heads to match the coverage of the lens focal lengths with the camera's DX-format sensor. However, this is not the case with other Speedlights. Thus, the zoom head coverage of the SB-600 and SB-800 is set to correspond to the field of view of lens focal lengths based on the assumption that the Speedlight is attached to a camera with an

FX-format (35mm or full-frame) sensor. Because the smaller DX-format sensor of the D5100 causes an effective reduction in the angle of view of any given lens focal length, the flash will illuminate a greater area with the D5100 than is necessary. Consequently, this will restrict the potential shooting range and squander flash power. In this situation, use the following table to adjust the zoom head position and thus maximize the performance of the flash unit:

FOCAL LENGTH (MM)	ZOOM HEAD POSITION (MM)
14	20
18	24
20	28
24	35
28	50
35	50
50	70
70	85
85	105[1]

[1] Available on SB-800 only

AUTOMATIC FLASH WITH THE SB-800 AND SB-900

When using the SB-800 and SB-900 Speedlights with the D5100, there are two additional non-TTL flash modes available; these are selected on the Speedlight:

Auto Aperture (AA): In this mode, the SB-900 and SB-800 read the ISO sensitivity setting, lens aperture, and the command to fire the flash from the camera automatically. The AA flash mode can be used in Aperture-Priority or Manual exposure mode. The flash output level is determined using a sensor on the front panel of the Speedlight to monitor the flash exposure, and as soon as this sensor detects that the flash output has been sufficient, the flash pulse is quenched. If you decide to alter the focal length or change the lens aperture between exposures, the Speedlight will adjust its output accordingly to maintain a correct flash exposure. The problem with this option is that the sensor does not necessarily "see" the same scene as the lens does, which can lead to inaccuracies in flash exposure.

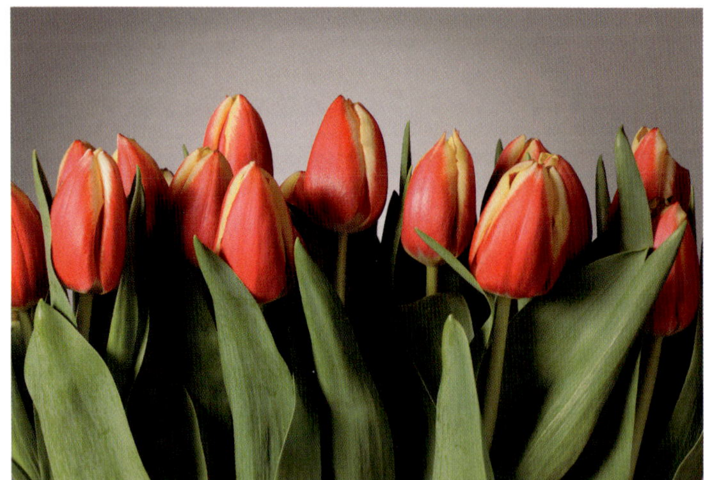

^ Under controlled conditions, such as in a studio, manual flash exposure control makes achieving accurate and repeatable results straightforward. Here, two SB-700 Speedlights were used, one at camera left fired through a diffuser, and the second positioned behind the flowers, facing the background. A reflector at camera right completed the lighting setup.

Automatic (A): This is the only automatic, non-TTL flash mode available with the SB-800 and SB-900 Speedlights. It can be used in Aperture-Priority or Manual exposure mode. Like in the AA mode, a sensor on the front of the SB-800, SB-900, or DX-type Speedlight monitors flash levels and shuts off the flash when the Speedlight calculates that sufficient light has been emitted. However, the lens aperture and ISO sensitivity values must be set manually on the Speedlight to ensure that the subject is within the flash shooting range. As with the AA mode, the sensor does not necessarily "see" the same scene as the lens does, which can lead to inaccuracies in flash exposure.

MANUAL FLASH EXPOSURE CONTROL

In Manual flash mode (available in P, S, A, and M exposure modes only), you set the output of the Speedlight (built-in or external) to a fixed level. In this situation, it is necessary to calculate the correct lens aperture as determined by the flash-to-subject distance and the Guide Number (GN) of the Speedlight. To select Manual Flash control for the built-in

Speedlight, open the Custom Settings menu and navigate to CS-e1 **[Flash cntrl for built-in flash]** and press ▶. Highlight **[Manual]** and press ⓞ. When using an external Speedlight, the flash mode is selected via the controls of the Speedlight.

For example, at its base sensitivity of ISO 100, the built-in Speedlight of the D5100 has a guide number (GN) of 43 ft (13 m). The **[Flash cntrl for built-in flash]** item determines the output level of the built-in Speedlight in Manual flash; a value between 1/1 (full output) to 1/32 can be selected. Since there is only one specific exposure value for any given level of sensitivity (ISO) at a particular flash-to-subject distance, it is necessary to calculate the lens aperture required to record a proper exposure. Use the following equation: Aperture = GN / Distance.

For example, with the built-in Speedlight of the D5100 set to 1/1 (full output) at a flash-to-subject distance of 11 feet (3.4 m), the lens aperture required to obtain a correct exposure of the subject will be f/4 (4 = 43/11 approx.). Similar calculations will have to be performed when using an external Speedlight in Manual flash mode. Check the Guide Number (GN) for the particular Speedlight model and ensure that you conduct the calculations using the same unit of distance throughout.

SLOW SYNCHRONIZATION FLASH

The camera will normally set a shutter speed that is within the restricted range of 1/60 to 1/200 second when using the built-in flash or a compatible external Speedlight, and the camera is in Program (P) or Aperture-Priority (A) exposure mode. The actual speed that is used within this narrow range depends on the level of ambient light (the brighter the conditions, the shorter the shutter speed).

This restriction can have a significant effect on the overall exposure. For example, if you photograph a subject outside at night or in a dark interior, any area of the scene illuminated by ambient light alone will be lit dimly compared with those areas that will be illuminated by the flash. It is more than likely that the level of ambient light will not be sufficient for a proper exposure within this restricted range of shutter speeds; consequently, these areas of the scene will be underexposed. A typical photograph taken under these conditions has a well-exposed subject set against a dark, featureless background.

To prevent this, select the appropriate Slow Sync mode. This enables the camera to use a wider range of slower shutter speeds, extending from 1/200 second to the longest available shutter speed of 30 seconds. Therefore, the camera will be able to select a more appropriate shutter speed for the low level of ambient light, ensuring the correct exposure can be achieved for the background (remember, the flash output will have little if any effect in this region because the intensity of light from the flash will diminish according to the Inverse Square Law). However, the flash output will be controlled for a proper exposure of the subject and its surroundings.

HINT: Since the shutter speed may be very slow when using Slow Sync flash mode, consider using a tripod or other camera support to avoid the effects of the camera shake.

REAR-CURTAIN SYNCHRONIZATION

If a subject you want to photograph is moving, it is possible to achieve some interesting effects by using Slow Sync flash mode in combination with a slow shutter speed—the flash will illuminate the subject briefly to record it as sharp while the slow shutter speed will record the ambient light, resulting in the subject's ambient motion trail being recorded as a blur. Rear-Curtain Sync fires the flash at the end of the exposure, just before the shutter closes, causing the motion trail to be recorded in a natural-looking manner—following the moving subject.

This technique can be particularly effective when Rear-Curtain Sync flash mode is used in either Shutter-Priority (S) or Manual (M) exposure mode. Alternatively, in Programmed-Auto (P) or Aperture-Priority (A) exposure modes, use Slow Rear-Curtain Sync flash mode. In each case, it will cause the blur from the subject's movement to appear as though it is following the sharp image of the subject formed by the flash illumination, producing a more natural appearance of the subject's movement.

FLASH OUTPUT COMPENSATION

Flash Compensation is used to modify the level of flash output. To set Flash Compensation on the D5100, press the Info button to display the shooting information on the monitor, and then press the i button to place the cursor in the Shooting Information Display. Use the Multi Selector to highlight the Flash Compensation option and then press the OK button. Use ▲ and ▼ to highlight the required level of compensation and press OK to confirm the setting. This method can be used with either the built-in Speedlight or a compatible external Speedlight.

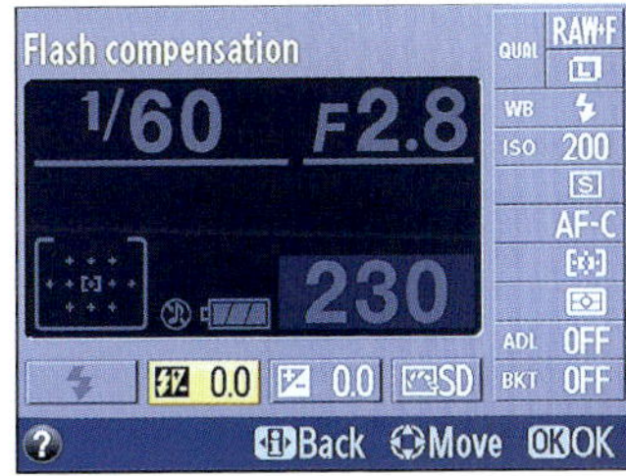

^ The Flash Compensation option, shown highlighted in the Information Display

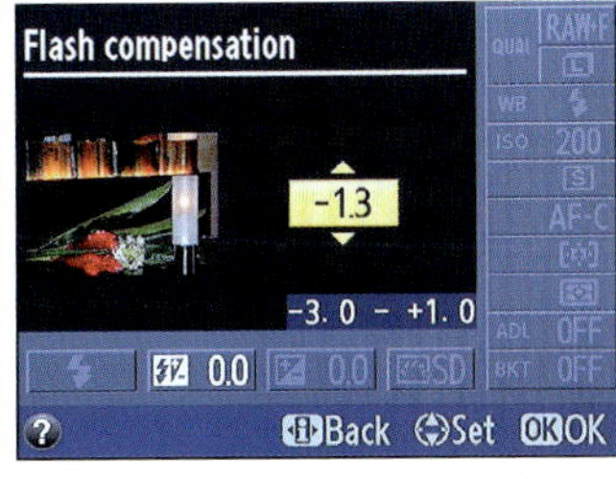

^ Flash Output Compensation can be adjusted in steps of 0.3 EV.

Alternatively, press and hold the and buttons, and then rotate the Command dial to set Flash Compensation. Whichever way you decide to apply the compensation, will be displayed in the viewfinder once a compensation value is set. Compensation can be set over a range of +1 EV to –3 EV in steps of 0.3 EV. To restore normal flash output, set the Flash Compensation back to ± 0.0.

Flash Compensation can also be applied directly on compatible external Speedlights (the SB-900, SB-800, SB-700, and SB-600). If Flash Compensation is applied on both the D5100 and an external Speedlight at the same time, the effect is cumulative. For example, applying a value of +1 EV to both the camera and external Speedlight results in Flash Compensation of +2 EV.

As discussed earlier in this chapter, the default i-TTL Balanced Fill-Flash mode will automatically apply Flash Compensation based on scene brightness, contrast, focus distance, and a variety of other factors. The level of automatic adjustment applied to flash output by the D5100 will often cancel out any compensation value entered manually. Since there is no way of telling what the camera is doing, you will never have control of the flash exposure. To regain control, set the flash mode to Standard i-TTL by either selecting Spot Metering on the camera (this is the only option for the built-in Speedlight) or by setting the Flash Control mode on an external Speedlight accordingly; in the latter case, ensure that only TTL is displayed in the control panel of the Speedlight for the flash mode, not TTL-BL.

FLASH COLOR INFORMATION

When Automatic or Flash White Balance is selected on the D5100 and you are using the SB-900, SB-800, SB-700, SB-600, or SB-400 Speedlight (directly mounted on the camera), the external flash unit automatically transmits information to the camera about the color temperature of the light it emits. The camera will then use this information to adjust its final White Balance setting in an attempt to match the color temperature of the light from the flash and the color temperature of the prevailing ambient light.

NOTE: The Flash Color Information feature will only operate with the Automatic and Flash white balance options; it is unavailable with any other white balance option.

WIDE-AREA AF-ASSIST ILLUMINATOR

The purpose of the AF-Assist Illuminator built into the SB-900, SB-800, SB-700, and SB-600 external Speedlights and the SU-800 wireless commander unit, is to facilitate autofocus in low-light situations. In order to match the broader spread of the multiple AF points in many CLS-compatible cameras, the frame area covered by the AF-Assist Illuminator in these Speedlights is much wider than with previous non-CLS types. These external lamps are also much more powerful than the built-in AF-Assist Illuminator of the D5100, which has the further disadvantage of being obstructed by many Nikkor lenses due to its proximity to the lens mount.

When a compatible external Speedlight with an AF-Assist Illuminator is used off the camera (see section below), the light emitted by the lamp may not be reflected with sufficient strength to be effective if it strikes the subject at an oblique angle. In this situation, consider using the Nikon SC-29 TTL flash cord, which has a built-in AF-Assist Illuminator in its terminal block that attaches to the camera accessory shoe. This places the AF-Assist Illuminator immediately above the central axis of the lens to help improve the accuracy of autofocus.

OFF-CAMERA FLASH

When you work with a single external Speedlight, it is often desirable to take the flash off the camera. As mentioned already, there are multiple different dedicated Nikon cords for this purpose: the SC-17 (discontinued), SC-28, and SC-29. All three cords are 4.9 feet (1.5 m) long; up to three of the SC-17 or SC-28 cords can be connected together to extend the operating range away from the camera. Whenever you take a Speedlight off the camera and use any TTL flash mode that will incorporate focus distance information in the flash output computations, take care as to where you position the flash. If the Speedlight is moved closer or farther away than the camera-to-subject distance, the accuracy of the flash output may be compromised—the TTL flash control system works on the assumption that the flash is located at the same distance from the subject as the camera. Likewise, when using Manual Flash Exposure Control, remember to calculate the lens aperture based on the flash-to-subject distance, not the camera-to-subject distance. The benefits of taking a Speedlight off the camera include:

- Increasing the angular separation between the central axis of the lens and the flash head will significantly reduce the risk of the red-eye effect with humans or eye-shine with pets and other animals.
- In situations where it is not practical to use bounce flash, moving the flash off-camera will usually improve the quality of the lighting. This is especially evident in the degree of modeling it provides when compared to the typical flat, frontal lighting produced by a flash mounted directly on the camera.

- By taking the flash off the camera and directing the light from the Speedlight accordingly, it is often possible to control the position of shadows so that they become less noticeable.
- When using Fill Flash, it is often desirable to direct light to a specific part of the scene to help reduce the level of contrast locally.
- An SB-900, SB-700, or SB-800 Speedlight connected to the camera via one of Nikon's dedicated TTL cords can be used as the master / commander flash to control multiple Speedlights off-camera using the Advanced Wireless Lighting system (see below).

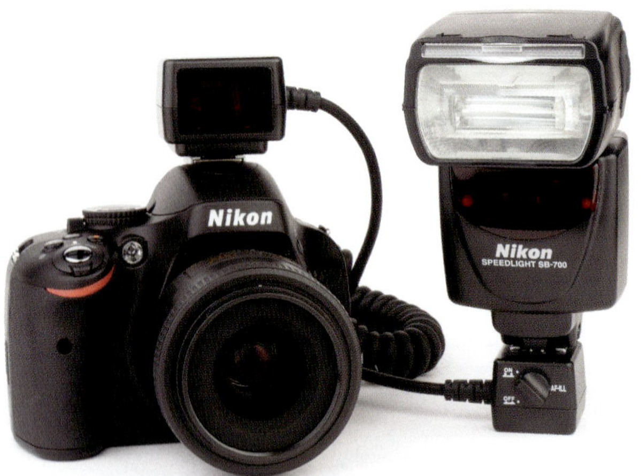

The SC-29 TTL flash cord is one of three cords that can be used to connect external Speedlights to the D5100 (the other two are the SC-28 and SC-17). It is shown here with the SB-700 Speedlight. Note the built-in AF-Assist lamp on the terminal positioned in the camera's accessory shoe.

WIRELESS FLASH CONTROL

Wireless flash control is compatible with the SB-900, SB-800, SB-700, SB-600, and SB-R200 Speedlights, together with the SU-800 Wireless Speedlight Commander unit. It allows for one or more remote Speedlight(s) to be operated and controlled wirelessly in P, A, S, and M exposure modes. The remote Speedlights can be used in a variety of flash modes: TTL, Auto Aperture (for use with remote SB-900/SB-800 Speedlights only), or Manual.

Up to three independent groups of remote Speedlights can be used via one of four dedicated communication channels. The built-in Speedlight of the D5100 does not support this feature, so it is necessary to use either an SB-900, SB-700, or SB-800 Speedlight as the master / commander flash. Alternatively, the SU-800 Wireless Speedlight Commander unit can be used instead of a Speedlight. In master flash or flash commander mode, these units communicate with the remote Speedlights via pulsed infrared light (IR).

FLASH COMMANDER UNIT EFFECTIVE RANGES

When the following units are used as the master flash or commander unit for wireless control of compatible remote Speedlights (SB-900, SB-800, SB-700 and SB-R200), the effective range of operation is:

- SB-900 / SB-800 / SB-700: When either the SB-900, SB-700, or SB-800 Speedlight is used as a master flash, the maximum effective operating range between it and the remote Speedlights is 33 feet (10 m) within 30° of the central axis of the lens, and 16 feet (5 m) within 30 to 60° of the central axis of the lens.
- SU-800: The SU-800 is a dedicated IR transmitter (i.e., unlike flash units that emit control signals as part of a full spectrum emission, the SU-800 only emits IR light). It is more powerful than Speedlights that can perform the master flash role and is capable of controlling remote SB-900, SB-800, and SB-600 Speedlights from up to 66 feet (20 m).
- SU-800 & SB-R200: Nikon states that when the SU-800 is used as the commander unit, the maximum effective operating range between it and remote SB-R200 Speedlights is 13 feet (4 m) along the central axis of the lens, and 9.8 feet (3 m) within 30° of the central axis of the lens.

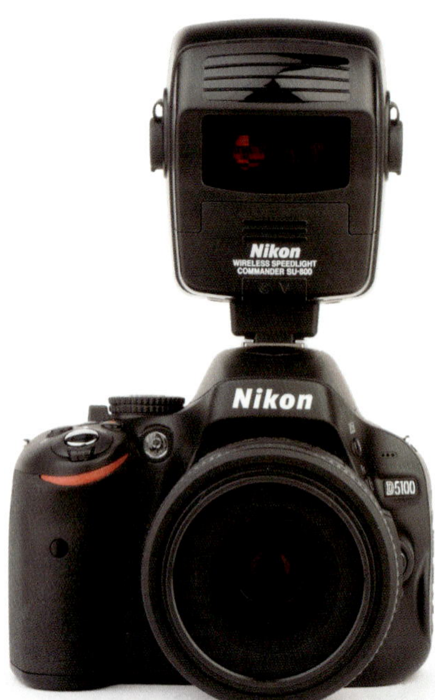

‹ The SU-800 Commander Unit enables independent control via a wireless communication of up to three separate groups of compatible Nikon Speedlights; each group can consist of one or more Speedlight(s).

I have found the quoted maximum operating ranges for the components of the Advanced Wireless Lighting system to be very conservative. For example, I have used both SB-900 and SB-800 Speedlights as master and remote units at ranges upwards of 100 feet (30 m) or more, particularly in situations where there have been reflective surfaces like walls and foliage close by to aid transmission of the IR control signals—this is three times greater than the suggested maximum range. However, in bright sunlight, which contains a high level of naturally occurring IR light, you may find the practical limit of the operating range is reduced.

HINT: I have managed to use remote flash units successfully even without direct line-of-sight between the master flash / commander unit and the sensor on the remote Speedlight(s). However, every shooting situation is different, so my advice is to set up the lighting system to your requirements and always take a test shot to ensure that it works as intended.

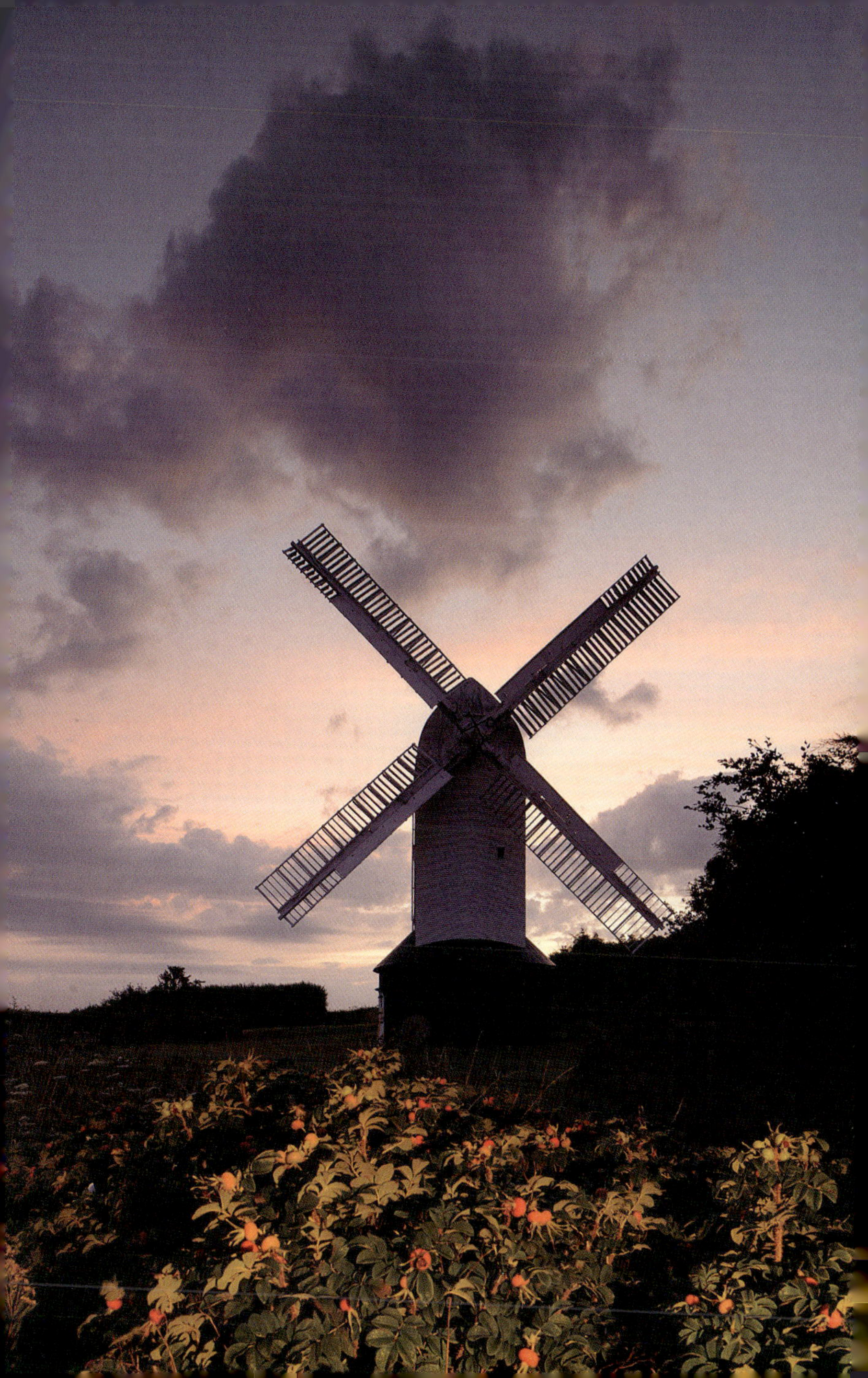

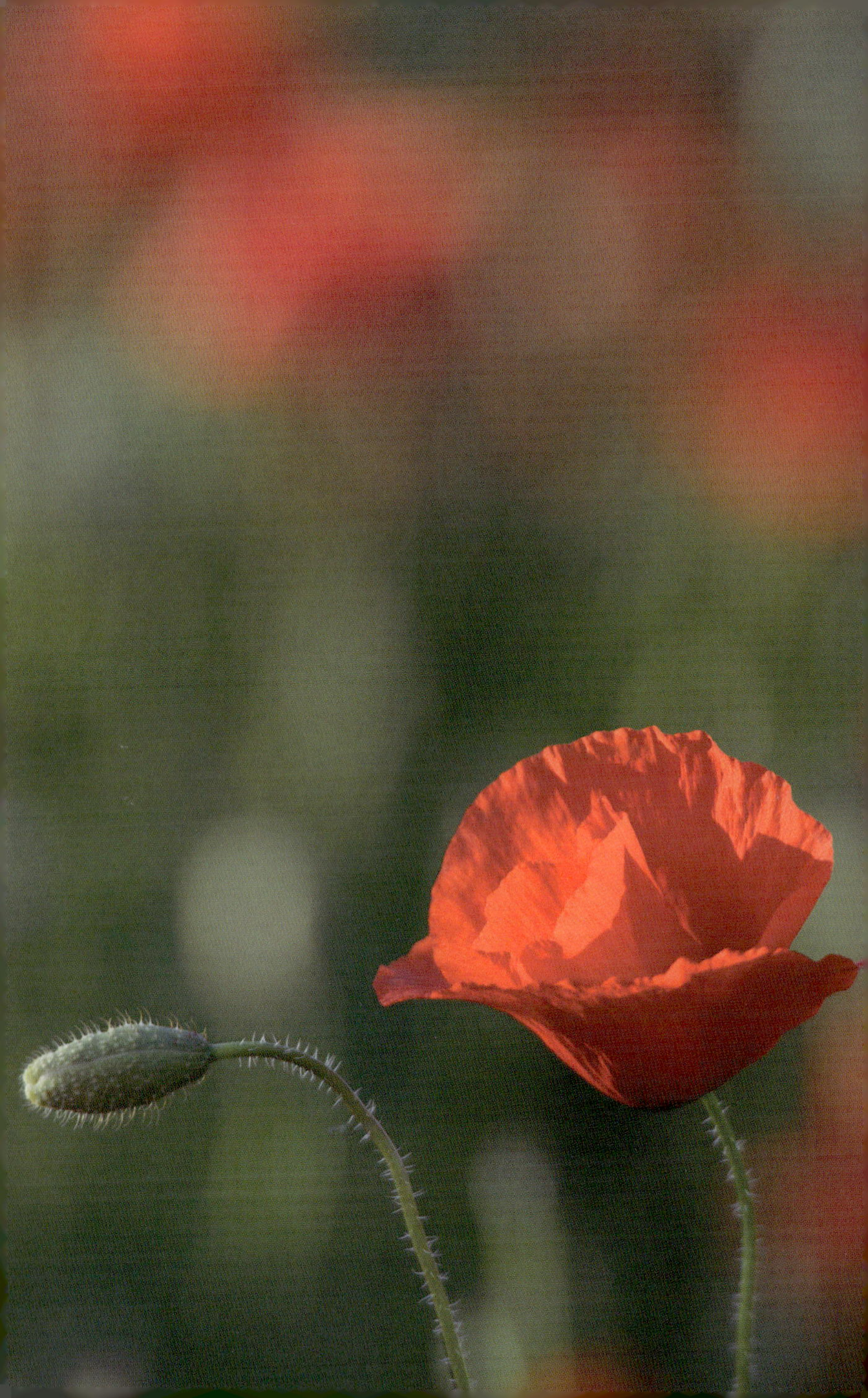

Nikon Lenses and Accessories

Nikon currently makes a range of approximately 60 lenses for their DSLR and film camera models. These lenses are known by their proprietary name, Nikkor. The "F" mount used on these Nikkor lenses is legendary; it has been used on all Nikon 35mm film and digital SLR cameras since the introduction of the original Nikon F SLR in 1959. As such, a great many of the lenses Nikon has produced in the past five decades can be mounted on the D5100, including most manual focus lenses that conform to the Ai lens mount standard that was introduced from 1977.

The fullest level of compatibility is offered by current AF-S (D-type and G-type) and the earlier AF-I autofocus Nikkor lenses, both of which have an integral motor for driving the focus. The integral motor is necessary because, like its predecessor the D5000, the D5100 does not have its own built-in focusing motor. Excluding this motor reduces the weight of the camera by about 30 grams (approximately one ounce) and enables the lens mount to be located closer to the base of the camera, helping to reduce the overall size of the camera body. This means any other type of Nikkor lens used on the D5100 must be focused manually; furthermore, the level of compatibility between the camera and lens is severely restricted if a non-CPU type lens (see pages 281-282) is attached to the camera.

Nikon also produces a range of software applications and camera accessories for the D5100. A vast amount of information and assistance with these products is available onlinc. In addition, there is a wide range of other useful off-brand accessories available from other sources, some of which are referenced in the Resources section at the end of this chapter (see pages 293-294).

MOUNTING / REMOVING A LENS

Whenever you attach or detach a lens from the D5100, make sure the camera is turned off. To attach a lens, identify the mounting index mark (white dot) on the lens and align it with the mounting index mark (white dot) next to the bayonet ring of the camera's lens mount. Enter the lens bayonet into the camera and rotate the lens counter-clockwise until it locks into place with an audible click. To remove a lens from the camera, press and hold the lens release button (located on the front of the camera to the left of the lens mount), and then rotate the lens until the two index marks are aligned before lifting the lens clear of the camera body. If you do not intend to mount another lens immediately, make sure you place the BF-1B body cap back on the camera to help prevent unwanted material from getting inside.

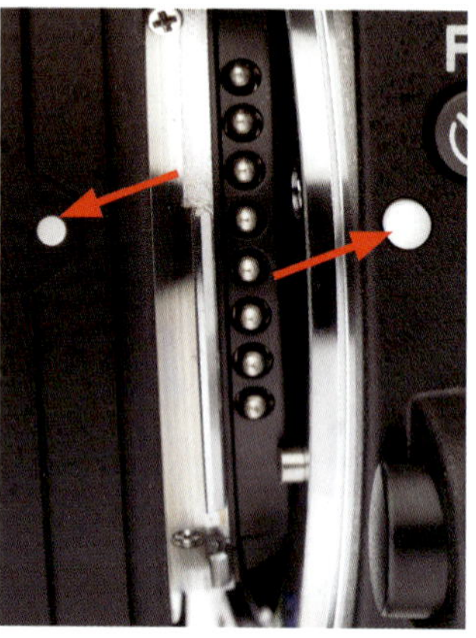

The lens can be mounted to or released from the camera when the mounting index marks on the D5100 body and a lens are aligned.

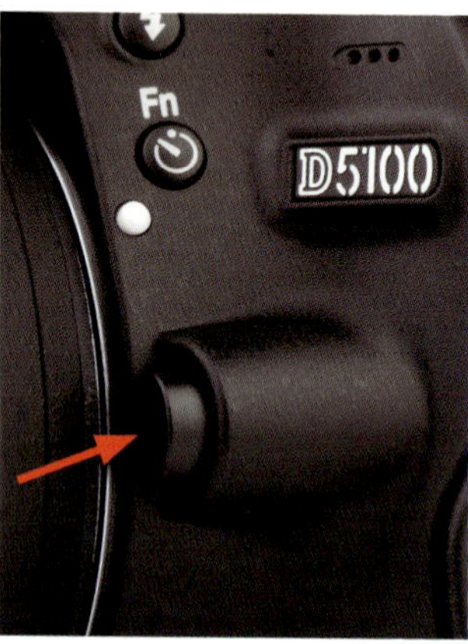

The lens release button is located on the front of the camera, adjacent to the lens mount.

When using a CPU lens with an aperture ring, make sure it is set and locked to its minimum aperture value (highest f/number). If FE E appears blinking in the information display and viewfinder, the lens has not been set to its minimum aperture value and the shutter release will be disabled.

NOTE: The latest G-type Nikkor lenses lack a conventional aperture ring.

DEMYSTIFYING NIKKOR LENSES

The designations of Nikkor lenses, particularly modern autofocus types, are peppered with initials. Here is an explanation of what some of these stand for:

- AF-type: These lenses are the predecessors to the later D- and G-type designs. They have a conventional aperture ring but do not communicate focus distance information to the camera.
- AF D-type: These lenses have a conventional aperture ring and an integral electronic chip that communicates information about lens aperture and focus distance between the lens and the camera body. Nikon refers to this chip as a central processing unit (CPU), but to be strictly accurate, it is an integrated circuit. A "D" appears on the lens barrel following the maximum aperture value.
- AF G-type: These lenses have no aperture ring and are only compatible with Nikon cameras that allow the aperture value to be set from the camera body. They contain an electronic chip that communicates information about lens aperture and focus distance between the lens and the camera body, similar to the D-type lenses. A "G" appears on the lens barrel following the maximum aperture value.
- AF-I: The predecessor to the AF-S lens type; these lenses have an integral focusing motor.
- AF-S: These lenses use a silent-wave motor (SWM) for focusing; alternating magnetic fields drive the motor, which moves the lens' elements to shift focus. This system offers the fastest autofocus of all AF Nikkor lenses. Most AF-S lenses have an additional feature that allows you to switch between autofocus and manual focus by simply taking hold of the focus ring, without needing to adjust any camera controls. "AF-S" appears on the lens barrel.
- DX: These lenses have been specially designed for use on Nikon small-format DSLR cameras. They project a smaller image circle than lenses designed for 35mm format cameras, and the light exiting their rear element is more collimated (actually parallel) to improve the efficiency of the photo diodes (pixels) on the camera's sensor. "DX" appears on the lens barrel.
- ED: To reduce the effect of chromatic aberration, Nikon developed a special type of glass known as Extra-Low Dispersion to bring various wavelengths of light to a common point of focus.
- IF: To speed up focusing, particularly with long focal length lenses, Nikon developed their internal focusing (IF) system. This system moves a group of elements within the lens so that it does not alter the length of the lens during focusing and prevents the front filter mount from rotating, facilitating the use of filters such as a polarizer.

- Nano Crystal Coat: This is a specialized lens coating that is applied to the surface of some lens elements to help reduce the level of light reflection, improving overall image quality. An "N" appears on the lens barrel.
- Non-CPU: Nikon uses the term "non-CPU" to describe any Nikkor lens lacking the components and electrical connections that enable communication of information between the lens and the camera body. With the exception of the PC-E 24mm f/3.5D, PC-E Micro 45mm f/2.8D, PC-E Micro 85mm f/2.8D, PC-Micro 85mm f/2.8D lens, and Ai-P type Nikkor lenses, all manual focus Nikkor lenses are non-CPU types.
- Micro-Nikkor: "Micro" is the name given to specialized lenses designed specifically for close-up and macro photography; the optical formula of these lenses is optimized for close focusing.
- PC-E: This is a special type of lens that offers the ability to shift and tilt the lens relative to the plane of the sensor in the camera to control perspective and depth-of-field. "PC-E" appears on the lens barrel.
- VR: Vibration Reduction (VR) is Nikon's name for a sophisticated technology that enables a lens to counter the effects of camera shake and other vibrations. A set of built-in motion sensors that cause micro-motors to shift a dedicated set of lens elements are used to improve the sharpness of pictures. "VR" appears on the lens barrel.

The AF-S DX 18-55mm f/3.5-5.6G VR II is one of a number of Nikkor lenses designed specifically for the DX format of the D5100.

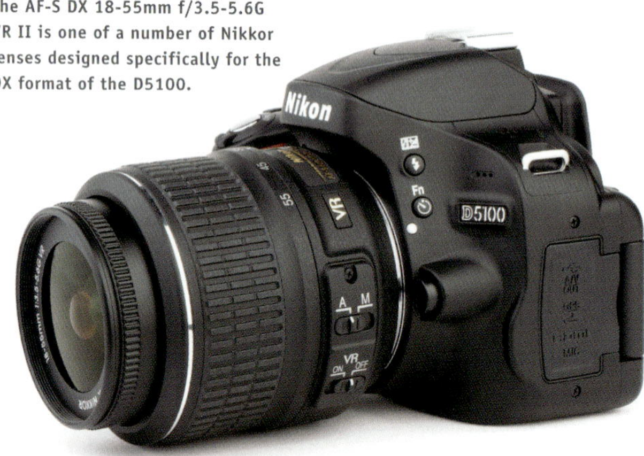

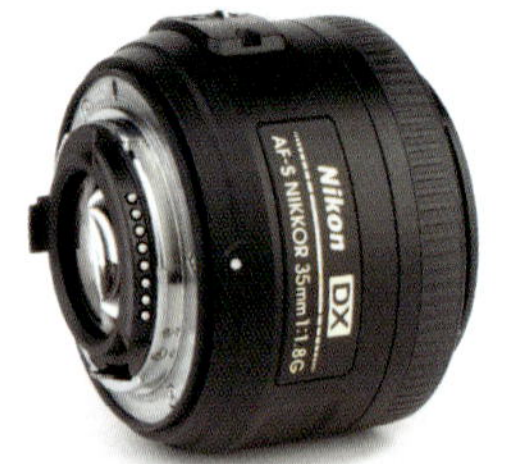

‹ A Nikkor CPU-type lens is readily identified by the electrical contact pins set around the lens mount flange; note the AF-S and G designations on the lens barrel.

LENS COMPATIBILITY

As mentioned previously in this chapter, the D5100 does not have an electric motor built into the camera to drive the focus action of those Nikkor AF lenses that lack their own integral AF motor; therefore, autofocus is ONLY supported with either the AF-S or the AF-I type Nikkor lenses. Other AF Nikkor lenses can be used with the D5100, but focusing must be performed manually.

Nikon classifies all AF-S, AF-I, and AF Nikkor lenses, plus manual focus Ai-P Nikkor lenses, as CPU-type lenses; these lenses can be readily identified by the electrical contact pins set around the edge of the lens mount bayonet flange. The following table provides details of the compatibility of CPU-type Nikkor lenses with the D5100:

CAMERA SETTING / LENS/ACCESSORY	Focus			Mode		Metering		
	AF	MF (with electronic rangefinder)	MF	M	Auto and scene modes; P, S, A	3D	Color	
AF-S, AF-I Nikkor [1]	✓	✓	✓	✓	✓	✓	–	✓[2]
Other type G or D AF Nikkor [1]	–	✓	✓	✓	✓	✓	–	✓[2]
PC-E Nikkor series	–	✓[3]	✓	✓[3]	✓[3]	✓[3]	–	✓[2, 3]
PC Micro 85mm f/2.8D [4]	–	✓[3]	✓	✓	–	✓	–	✓[2, 3]
AF-S/AF-I teleconverter [5]	✓[6]	✓[6]	✓	✓	✓	✓	–	✓[2]
Other AF Nikkor (except lenses for F3AF)	–	✓[7]	✓	✓	✓	–	✓	✓[2]
Ai-P Nikkor	–	✓[8]	✓	✓	✓	–	✓	✓[2]

1 Use AF-S or AF-I lenses to get the most from your camera. Vibration Reduction (VR) is supported with VR lenses.

2 Spot metering meters the selected focus point.

3 Cannot be used with shifting or tilting.

4 The camera's exposure metering and flash control systems may not function as expected when the lens is shifted and/or tilted or an aperture other than the maximum aperture is used.

5 AF-S or AF-I lens required.

6 With maximum effective aperture of f/5.6 or faster.

7 When the AF 80-200mm f/2.8, AF 35-70mm f/2.8, AF 28-85mm f/3.5-4.5 (New) or AF 28-85mm f/3.5-4.5 lenses are zoomed all the way in at the minimum focus distance, the In-Focus indicator may be displayed when the image on the matte screen in the viewfinder is not in focus. Focus manually until image in viewfinder is in focus.

8 With maximum aperture of f/5.6 or larger.

USING NIKON AF-S/AF-I TELECONVERTERS

The Nikon AF-S/AF-I teleconverters can be used with the following AF-S and AF-I lenses:

- AF-S VR Micro 105mm f/2.8G ED [1]
- AF-S VR 200mm f/2G ED
- AF-S VR II 200mm f/2G ED
- AF-S VR 300mm f/2.8G ED
- AF-S VR II 300mm f/2.8G ED
- AF-S 300mm f/2.8D ED II
- AF-S 300mm f/2.8D ED
- AF-I 300mm f/2.8D ED
- AF-S 300mm f/4D ED [2]
- AF-S 400mm f/2.8D ED II
- AF-S 400mm f/2.8D ED
- AF-I 400mm f/2.8D ED
- AF-S 500mm f/4D ED II [2]
- AF-S 500mm f/4D ED [2]
- AF-I 500mm f/4D ED [2]
- AF-S 600mm f/4D ED II [2]
- AF-S 600mm f/4D ED [2]
- AF-I 600mm f/4D ED [2]
- AF-S 70–200mm f/2.8G ED VR
- AF-S 70–200mm f/2.8G ED VR II
- AF-S 80–200mm f/2.8D ED
- AF-S 200–400mm f/4G ED VR [2]
- AF-S 200–400mm f/4G ED VRII [2]
- AF-S 400mm f/2.8G ED VR
- AF-S 500mm f/4G ED VR [2]
- AF-S 600mm f/4G ED VR [2]

[1] Autofocus is not recommended. At close focusing distances, the maximum effective aperture is likely to be less than f/5.6.

[2] Autofocus is not guaranteed when used with the TC-17E II or TC-20 E II teleconverter, as maximum effective aperture is less than f/5.6; although in bright conditions or with good levels of contrast in the subject, it will often work quite well, but a little slower.

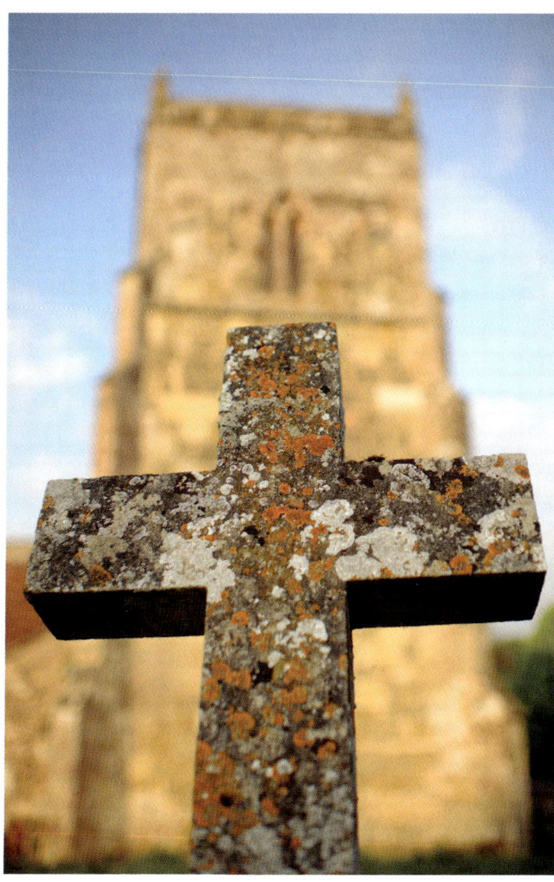

› In many shooting situations, setting the lens aperture is probably the most important consideration, as it allows you to control the depth of field. Here, shooting at f/2 to reduce depth of field has isolated the subject.

USING NON-CPU LENSES

Although the Nikon F mount has basically remained unchanged for almost fifty years, the design of modern cameras has moved on considerably. The introduction of electronic communication between the lens and camera for the purposes of exposure metering and autofocus has meant a number of changes have been introduced, such that older non-CPU type lenses offer a very restricted level of compatibility with the D5100. In this case, the camera can only be used in Manual exposure mode (if you select another exposure mode, the camera disables the shutter release automatically). The lens aperture must be set using the aperture ring on the lens, and the autofocus system, TTL metering system, electronic analog exposure display, and TTL flash control do not function. However, provided the maximum effective aperture of the connected lens is f/5.6 or larger (smaller f/number), the electronic rangefinder does operate with the following non-CPU type lenses unless otherwise stated:

- Ai-modified, Ai, Ai-S, and E-series Nikkor lenses
- Medical Nikkor 120mm f/4 (can only be used at a shutter speed of 1/100 or slower)
- Reflex Nikkor lenses (electronic rangefinder does not operate)
- PC Nikkor lenses (electronic rangefinder does not operate if the lens is shifted)
- Ai-type teleconverters (electronic rangefinder requires an effective aperture of f/5.6 or larger to operate)
- PB-6 Bellows focusing attachment (D5100 must be attached in vertical orientation but can be used subsequently in horizontal orientation)
- Extension rings PK-11A, PK-12, PK-13, and PN-11

INCOMPATIBLE LENSES AND ACCESSORIES

The following accessories and lenses are incompatible with the D5100. If you attempt to use them, it may damage the equipment.

- TC-16A AF teleconverter
- Non-Ai lenses
- Lenses that require the AU-1 focusing unit (400mm f/4.5, 600mm f/5.6, 800mm f/8, 1200mm f/11)
- Fisheye (6mm f/5.6, 7.5mm f/5.6, 8mm f/8, OP 10mm f/5.6)
- 2.1 cm f/4 (old type)
- K2 extension rings
- ED 180–600mm f/8 (serial numbers 174041–174180)
- ED 360–1200mm f/11 (serial numbers 174031–174127)
- 200–600mm f/9.5 (serial numbers 280001–300490)
- Lenses for the F3AF (AF80mm f/2.8, AF ED200mm f/3.5, TC-16 teleconverter)
- PC 28mm f/4 (serial number 180900 or earlier)
- PC 35mm f/2.8 (serial numbers 851001–906200)
- PC 35mm f/3.5 (old type)
- 1000mm f/6.3 Reflex (old type)
- 1000mm f/11 Reflex (serial numbers 142361–143000)
- 2000mm f/11 Reflex (serial numbers 200111–200310)

DEPTH-OF-FIELD CONSIDERATIONS

When a lens brings light to focus on a camera's sensor, there is only one plane of focus that is critically sharp. However, in the two-dimensional picture produced by the camera, there is a zone in front of and behind the plane of focus that is perceived to be sharp. This area of apparent sharpness is referred to as the depth of field, and its extent is influenced by the camera-to-subject distance together with the focal length, which determines the degree of subject magnification, together with the size of the lens aperture. A high level of subject magnification, which can be achieved through use of a long focal length and/or close focus distance combined with a large lens aperture (low f/number), will produce a shallow depth of field, while a low level of subject magnification and small lens aperture will render a deep depth of field.

So, if the focal length and camera-to-subject distance are constant, depth of field will be shallower with large apertures (low f/numbers) and deeper with small apertures (high f/numbers). If the aperture and camera-to-subject distance are constant, depth of field will be shallower with a long focal length (telephoto range) and deeper with a shorter focal length (wide-angle range). If the focal length and aperture are constant, depth of field will be greater at longer camera-to-subject distances and shallower with closer camera-to-subject distances. Depth of field is an important consideration when deciding on a particular composition, as it has a direct and fundamental effect on the final appearance of the picture.

A very important consideration concerning depth of field is that it is slightly less for images shot using the DX format when compared with those taken on the FX-format cameras such as the Nikon D700 and D3-series models. This is due to the smaller size of the imaging area of the DX format (23.6 x 15.6 mm) used in the D5100 as compared with the FX format (36 x 23.9 mm); the DX-format picture must be magnified by a greater amount compared with the FX-format shot to achieve any given identical print size. Therefore, at normal viewing distances, details that appear to be sharp in a print made from an FX-format shot may no longer look sharp in a print of the same dimensions made from a DX-format shot. If you use the depth-of-field values given in tables for 35mm film, you will find they do not correspond to images shot on the DX format with the same camera-to-subject distance and focal length. To guarantee that the depth of field in pictures taken on the DX format is sufficiently deep, use the values for the next larger lens aperture. For example, if your lens is set to f/11, use the depth-of-field values for f/8 in the DX format.

DIFFRACTION

Diffraction is an optical effect that, under certain circumstances, will limit the resolution you can achieve in a photograph. Assuming conditions of a uniform atmosphere (i.e., still, clear air), light waves will travel in straight lines. However, if those same light waves have to pass through a small hole, such as the aperture in the iris diaphragm of a camera lens, they become dispersed, or diffracted. At wide apertures (low f/numbers), the number of diffracted light waves is proportionally very small to the total number that pass through the aperture, hence the diffraction effect is negligible; but the proportion of diffracted waves increases as the size of the aperture is reduced, and the effect can become significant. After passing through a small aperture, the previously parallel light waves diverge, spreading out in different directions and, consequently, travel different distances between the iris diaphragm and the digital sensor, causing some light waves to shift out of phase and interfere with others. This process of interference creates a diffraction pattern that results in a general softening of detail in the image.

At a particular lens aperture (different for each lens and camera combination), the loss of resolution (softening) that occurs due to the effects of diffraction cancels out any gain in perceived sharpness due to increased depth of field. At this point, the camera lens is said to have become "diffraction limited." It is essential to know the diffraction limit for your lens(es) and different cameras, since there is no point in selecting aperture values beyond the diffraction limit, as image resolution will become increasingly degraded and exposure times extended with the risk of further loss of resolution through camera or subject movement.

I recommend you test each of your lenses with your D5100 to determine the diffraction limit for your own equipment. As a general rule, common with other Nikon DX-format camera models, I find that the D5100 diffraction limit is around f/11 to f/13; bear this in mind when you are looking to maximize depth of field by choosing smaller lens aperture values.

SHUTTER SPEED CONSIDERATIONS

If you handhold your camera, it is worth remembering a rule of thumb concerning the minimum shutter speed needed to prevent a loss of sharpness due to camera shake, assuming that the lens lacks Nikon's Vibration Reduction (VR) feature. For the DX format, multiply the focal length of the lens by 1.5x—the approximate magnification factor of the D5100 sensor compared with the FX format—then take the reciprocal of this value and use it as the slowest effective shutter speed. For example, a focal length of 300mm would require a minimum shutter speed of 1/450; the closest value available on the D5100 is 1/500.

The shutter speed can also be used for creative effect because it controls the way motion of the subject or camera is depicted in a photograph. Conventionally, a fast shutter speed is used to freeze motion in sports or action photography. However, slower shutter speeds can be used to create a degree of blur that will often evoke a greater sense of movement than a subject that is rendered pin-sharp. The panning technique is an example of a creative blur effect; using a slow shutter speed while moving the camera to track the subject results in the subject appearing relatively sharp against an increased level of blur in the background.

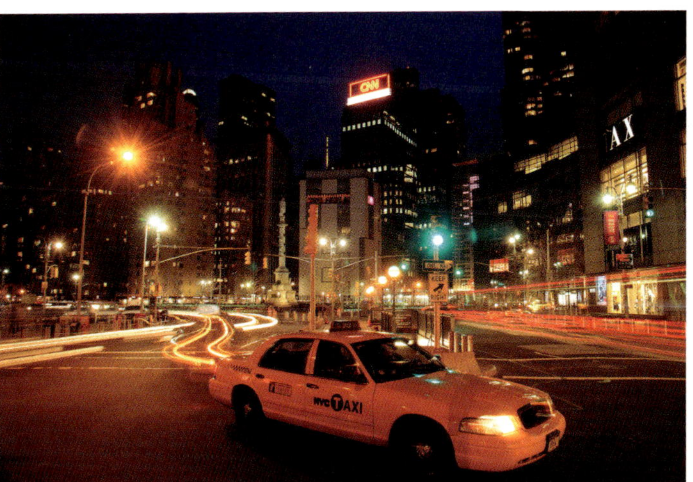

^ **Using a long shutter speed, in this instance 10 seconds, has allowed the camera to record the low level ambient light and render the lights of the traffic as light trails.**

NIKON SOFTWARE

It is beyond the scope of this book to describe fully the features and functions of Nikon's dedicated software, but details can easily be obtained from the technical support sections of the websites maintained by the Nikon Corporation. The D5100 is supplied with a copy of Nikon View NX2, which incorporates the Nikon Transfer 2 application. The following section is intended to provide a brief overview of the three principal Nikon software applications in their current versions at the time of this writing:

- Nikon View NX2 (version 2.1.2 – Windows, and version 2.1.1 – Mac)
- Nikon Capture NX2 (version 2.2.7)
- Nikon Camera Control Pro (version 2.9.0)

For Windows, the following operating systems are supported:

- Microsoft Windows XP Professional (Service Pack 3 – 32-bit versions)
- Microsoft Windows XP Home Edition (Service Pack 3 – 32-bit versions)
- Microsoft Windows Vista (Service Pack 2 – 32 & 64-bit versions)
- Microsoft Windows 7 (32 & 64-bit versions)

NOTE: Nikon software is compatible with both 32 and 64-bit versions of Windows 7 and Vista; however, under 64-bit versions, it will only operate as a 32-bit application.

For Macintosh, the following operating systems are supported:

- Mac OSX 10.4.11
- Mac OSX 10.5.8
- Mac OSX 10.6.6

NOTE: For information about Nikon software and to download updates to existing applications, I recommend you visit the various technical support web sites maintained by Nikon. These can be accessed via www.nikon.com; note that in some cases Nikon software is regionalized according to geographical location, so make sure you obtain software updates from the appropriate web site.

NIKON TRANSFER 2

Nikon Transfer 2 is Nikon's updated utility for downloading images from the camera or memory card to your computer. Nikon Transfer 2 provides a simple, intuitive workflow suitable for all users, from beginners to professionals. It is included as part of Nikon View NX2 (a copy is supplied with the D5100) and it can also be downloaded for free from any of Nikon's technical support web sites. Features include:

- Automatic recognition/auto start after connecting a camera or inserting a CF/SD card.
- Transfers images from CD, external hard drive, or other removable media.
- Transfers images to computer's hard drive.
- Easy selection and viewing of images on up to five external devices before transfer.
- Transfers image data to a primary destination and also to a backup location simultaneously.
- Adds metadata during transfer; both XMP/IPTC standards are supported.
- Selects the application the images are displayed in after transfer.

NIKON VIEW NX2

View NX2 offers photographers a fast solution to the organization and classification of their digital images. This software uses your computer's file directory to display and browse images. Nikon View NX2 is included with the latest Nikon DSLR cameras, such as the D5100, and can also be downloaded for free from Nikon's web site. Features include:

- High-speed thumbnail and preview display.
- Three customizable workspaces that are selected according to the images being worked on: Browser, GeoTag, and Edit.
- D-Movie editing tools that allow selection of start and stop points of individual movie clips, frame grab, merging of movie and JPEG files with transition effects, and the ability to add audio tracks.
- A simple way to choose images, operating similarly to Explorer/Finder.
- Fast sorting using image rating and labeling classification systems, plus integration with GPS data recorded by the camera.
- Image enhancement tools, such as Sharpness, Contrast, and Brightness controls, along with tools such as Highlight and Shadow protection, D-Lighting, and Color Booster.

- Adjustment tools such as Crop, Straighten, and Auto Red-Eye Correction.
- Includes Picture Control Utility (including Sharpening, Contrast, Saturation, Hue, Brightness, and Black-and-White Conversion).
- Batch processing to convert file format, resize, rename, change settings, and save to multiple destinations.
- Integration with Capture NX2.
- Printing functions.
- Attachment of images to email messages.
- IPTC/XMP data compatible (user settings retained when image is opened in other supported applications).
- Quick Adjustment features for NEF (RAW) images, including White Balance, exposure adjustment, correction for axial chromatic aberration, and creating custom curves.
- Full integration with Nikon Picturetown—Nikon's online image storage and sharing service. Images can be uploaded directly from Nikon View NX2 via a simple drag-and-drop action, or stored images can be browsed directly from Nikon View NX2.

NIKON CAPTURE NX2

In mid-2008, Nikon released an updated version of Capture NX, called Capture NX 2; while not an extensive reworking of the program, it does introduce some key improvements. As a general-purpose image-editing application, Nikon Capture NX 2 is really quite good; all the adjustment features work with JPEG and TIFF files as well as with NEF (RAW) files. It incorporates the same unique U Point technology that permits complex selections of an area (or areas) within an image to be made with accuracy and speed that is far greater than can be achieved using other digital imaging software currently available. The program offers an extensive toolbox to enhance and modify any image file, regardless of whether it was saved in the NEF (RAW), TIFF, or JPEG format.

Capture NX 2 applies non-destructive image processing to NEF (RAW) files, which means that the original image data is never compromised. Each enhancement made is saved in an edit list with the original data and thumbnail. However, changes made to JPEG or TIFF files will alter the data of the original image. To avoid this from occurring, the image can be saved using a different file name or converted into Nikon's NEF (RAW) format. Parameters set on any Nikon camera-produced NEF (RAW) file—such as White Balance, Sharpening, Color Mode, and Saturation—are applied to the image when it is opened in

Nikon Capture NX 2 for editing, so the camera settings are preserved. Key features in the latest iteration include:

- A new Workspaces option provides four pre-defined palette and toolbar configurations (Browser, Metadata, Multi-Purpose, and Edit) with support for two monitors, plus you can create your own custom Workspace (desktop layout), which can be supported across one or two displays. The pre-defined and custom Workspaces can be assigned a keyboard shortcut to help improve efficiency. Option/Alt keys + keys 1 through 9 are assignable for this purpose.
- An improved image browser palette with an extended feature set that should lessen the need to switch between Capture NX and View NX for thumbnail viewing. There is also a new Favorite Folders option, which makes accessing frequently used folders very fast. The time to open an image from the image browser has been improved significantly.
- New Quick Fix and Adjust sections of the Edit List improve the general layout and access to key tools such as Exposure Compensation, Levels and Curves adjustments, Contrast, Saturation, and the new Highlight Protection and Shadow Protection controls.
- The U Point technology of Capture NX, which is the key to its image-editing simplicity, has been extended to almost all photo adjustment tools, including Noise Reduction and Unsharp Mask, to enhance an already powerful feature for applying local changes to an image.
- Separate controls for the correction of both axial and lateral chromatic aberration.
- There is a new Auto Retouch Brush that provides a one-click tool to remove the effects of dust spots and other blemishes in an image.
- Enhanced batch-processing speeds.
- Advanced White Balance control with the ability to select a specific color temperature or sample from a gray point.
- An advanced NEF (RAW) file control that permits attributes such as Exposure Compensation, Sharpening, Contrast, Color Mode, Saturation, and Hue to be modified after the exposure has been made, without affecting the original image data.
- The Image Dust Off feature, which compares an NEF (RAW) file with a reference image taken with the same camera to help reduce the effects of any dust particles on the low-pass filter.
- The D-Lighting tool, which emulates the dodge and burn techniques of traditional photographic printing to control highlight and shadow areas, producing a more balanced exposure.
- A Color Noise Reduction tool, which minimizes the effect of random electronic noise that can occur, especially at high ISO settings.

- An Edge Noise Reduction tool that accentuates the boundary between areas of an image to make them more distinct.
- The Color Moiré Reduction feature helps to remove the effects of moiré, which can occur when an image contains areas with a very fine repeating pattern.
- The LCH Editor, which allows for control of luminosity (overall lightness), chroma (color saturation), and hue in separate channels.
- The Lens Vignette control to correct for uneven illumination across an image, particularly near the corners.
- The Fisheye Lens tool, which converts images taken with the AF Fisheye-Nikkor DX 10.5mm f/2.8G lens so they appear as though they were taken using a conventional rectilinear lens with a diagonal angle-of-view equivalent to approximately 120°.

NIKON CAMERA CONTROL PRO 2

Nikon Camera Control Pro 2 enables the D5100 to be controlled remotely from a computer via a wired connection to the camera's USB terminal. Virtually all camera settings can be controlled from the computer, while the images it records, both stills and video, are saved to the computer's hard drive.

- Most settings of Nikon DSLR cameras, such as exposure mode, shutter speed, aperture, and White Balance can be controlled remotely.
- Full control of the 11-point AF system of the D5100.
- Support for the Picture Control system of the D5100; Picture Control parameters can be selected and adjusted on a computer, and custom curves (to modify contrast) can be created and saved.
- Support of the Live View and D-Movie modes, including control of the contrast-detect AF system in Live View from a computer monitor.
- Recording of stills and video images directly to the computer hard drive.

NOTE: In order to view images (stills or video) captured using Camera Control Pro 2, it is necessary to have Nikon View NX2 installed on the computer, since Camera Control Pro 2, version 2.9.0, no longer has the built-in viewer feature of earlier versions of the application.

- AS-15: An accessory shoe adapter that has a standard PC sync socket for connecting the D5100 to a non-dedicated flash unit via a PC sync cable.
- BF-1B: Supplied with the D5100, a body cap that will help prevent dust from entering the camera; keep it in place at all times when a lens is not mounted on the camera.
- DK-20: The standard viewfinder eyecup for the D5100; one is supplied with the camera.
- DK-20C: Supplementary eyepiece correction lenses for use when the built-in diopter adjustment is insufficient.
- DR-6: The right-angle viewfinder attachment.
- EG-D2: The video cable to connect the D5100 to a TV set.
- EH-5b: The multi-voltage AC adapter used to power the D5100: the camera is also compatible with the EH-5 and EH-5a AC adapters.
- EN-EL14: The dedicated Lithium-ion battery for the D5100; one is supplied with the camera.
- EP-5A: The adapter required to connect the D5100 to the EH-5-series multi-voltage AC adapters.
- GP-1: The GPS unit for the D5100; it connects to the remote accessory terminal of the camera.

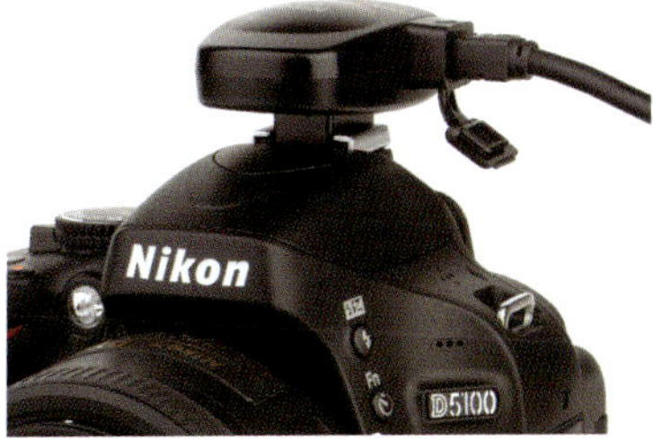

› The Nikon GP-1 GPS unit is shown here attached to the D5100; the camera will record GPS data and embed it in the EXIF data of the image file when this unit is attached. Nikon View NX2 software supports GPS data for GeoTagging of image files.

- MC-DC2: The remote shutter release cord with lockable shutter release button.
- MH-24: The multi-voltage AC charger for a single EN-EL14 battery; the MH-24 is supplied with the D5100.

- ML-L3: The infrared (IR) remote shutter release; the D5100 has IR receivers on the front and rear.

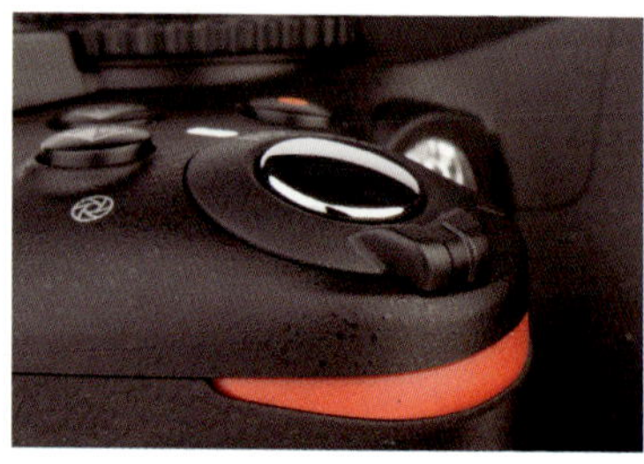

› The IR receiver for the ML-L3 IR remote shutter release is located on the front of the right-hand finger grip. The D5100 has a second IR receiver on the rear of the camera.

- SB-400: An external Speedlight (flash unit) for the D5100; it can be attached to the camera's accessory shoe or via the SC-28/SC-29 TTL flash cord.
- SB-600: An external Speedlight for the D5100; it can be attached to the camera's accessory shoe or via the SC-28/SC-29 TTL flash cord.
- SB-700: An external Speedlight for the D5100; it can be attached to the camera's accessory shoe or via the SC-28/SC-29 TTL flash cord.
- SB-800: An external Speedlight for the D5100; it can be attached to the camera's accessory shoe or via the SC-28/SC-29 TTL flash cord.
- SB-900: An external Speedlight for the D5100; it can be attached to the camera's accessory shoe or via the SC-28/SC-29 TTL flash cord.
- SB-R200: An external Speedlight for the D5100 intended for close-up and macro photography; it cannot be attached to the camera's accessory shoe but is fitted to an adapter ring that is attached to the front of the lens.

NOTE: Triggering the SB-R200 requires the use of the optional SU-800 Speedlight Commander Unit or an SB-700/SB-800/SB-900 Speedlight used in its Commander/Master flash mode.

- SC-28: A TTL flash cord that maintains full functionality between a compatible external Speedlight and a D5100.
- SC-29: A TTL flash cord that maintains full functionality between a compatible external Speedlight and a D5100; the terminal unit that attaches to the camera has a built-in AF-assist lamp.
- SD-8a: An external battery pack for SB-900 or SB-800 Speedlights.
- SD-9: An external battery pack for SB-900 Speedlights.

- SK-6/SK-6a: A power bracket for SB-900 or SB-800 Speedlights; it attaches to the base of the D5100 allowing the flash to be mounted farther from the central axis of the lens.
- UC-E6: A USB cable for connecting the D5100 to another USB-compliant device.

RESOURCES

A number of other manufacturers and suppliers provide equipment to compliment and enhance the performance of the cameras and flash accessories produced by Nikon. The following is a list of some that you may find useful:

- Adobe: Authors of the popular Photoshop, Photoshop Elements, Premiere, and Lightroom software: www.adobe.com.
- Apple: Authors of the popular Aperture, Final Cut Express, and Final Cut Pro software (Mac only): www.apple.com.
- B&W: Manufacturers of filters and accessories; www.schneideroptics.com.
- Gitzo: Manufacturers of tripods, monopods, and general camera support accessories; www.gitzo.com.
- HDRsoft: Authors of the popular Photomatix high-dynamic range (HDR) software; www.hdrsoft.com.
- Honl Photo: Manufacturers of the popular light modifying accessories for Nikon Speedlights: www.honlphoto.com.
- Kirk Enterprises: Manufacturers of camera and flash accessories, including flash brackets; www.kirkphoto.com.
- Lastolite: Manufacturers of lighting accessories for portable flash units and a wide range of reflectors, diffusers, and other light modifying devices; www.lastolite.com
- Lee Filters: Manufacturers of both lens and lighting filters, including graduated filters; www.leefilters.com.
- Lexar Media: Manufacturers of flash memory cards, including Secure Digital (SD) and high-capacity Secure Digital (SDHC) cards compatible with the D5100; www.lexar.com.
- Lightshpere: A range of flash diffusion devices designed by photographer Gary Fong; www.garyfong.com.
- Lumiquest: Manufacturers of flash modifiers and diffusers; www.lumiquest.com.

- Manfrotto: Manufacturers of tripods, lighting stands, and flash support accessories; www.manfrotto.com.
- Nik Software: Authors of the popular Color Efex Pro, Silver Efex Pro, Viveza 2, Dfine, and HDR Efex Pro software: www.niksoftware.com.
- Really Right Stuff: Manufacturers of an extensive range of camera, flash, close-up, and panoramic photography accessories; www.reallyrightstuff.com.
- Rode: Manufacturers of high-quality external microphones: www.rodemic.com.
- SanDisk: Manufacturers of flash memory cards, including Secure Digital (SD) and high-capacity Secure Digital (SDHC) cards compatible with the D5100; www.sandisk.com.
- Sennheiser: Manufacturers of high-quality headphones and external microphones: www.sennheiser.com.
- Singh-Ray: Manufacturers of camera lens filters, including graduated filter types; www.singh-ray.com.

WEB SUPPORT

Nikon maintains product support and provides further information online at the following sites:

- www.nikon.com – Global gateway to Nikon Corporation.
- www.nikonusa.com – Continental North America.
- www.europe-nikon.com – Most European countries.
- www.nikon-asia.com – Asia, Oceania, Middle East, and Africa.

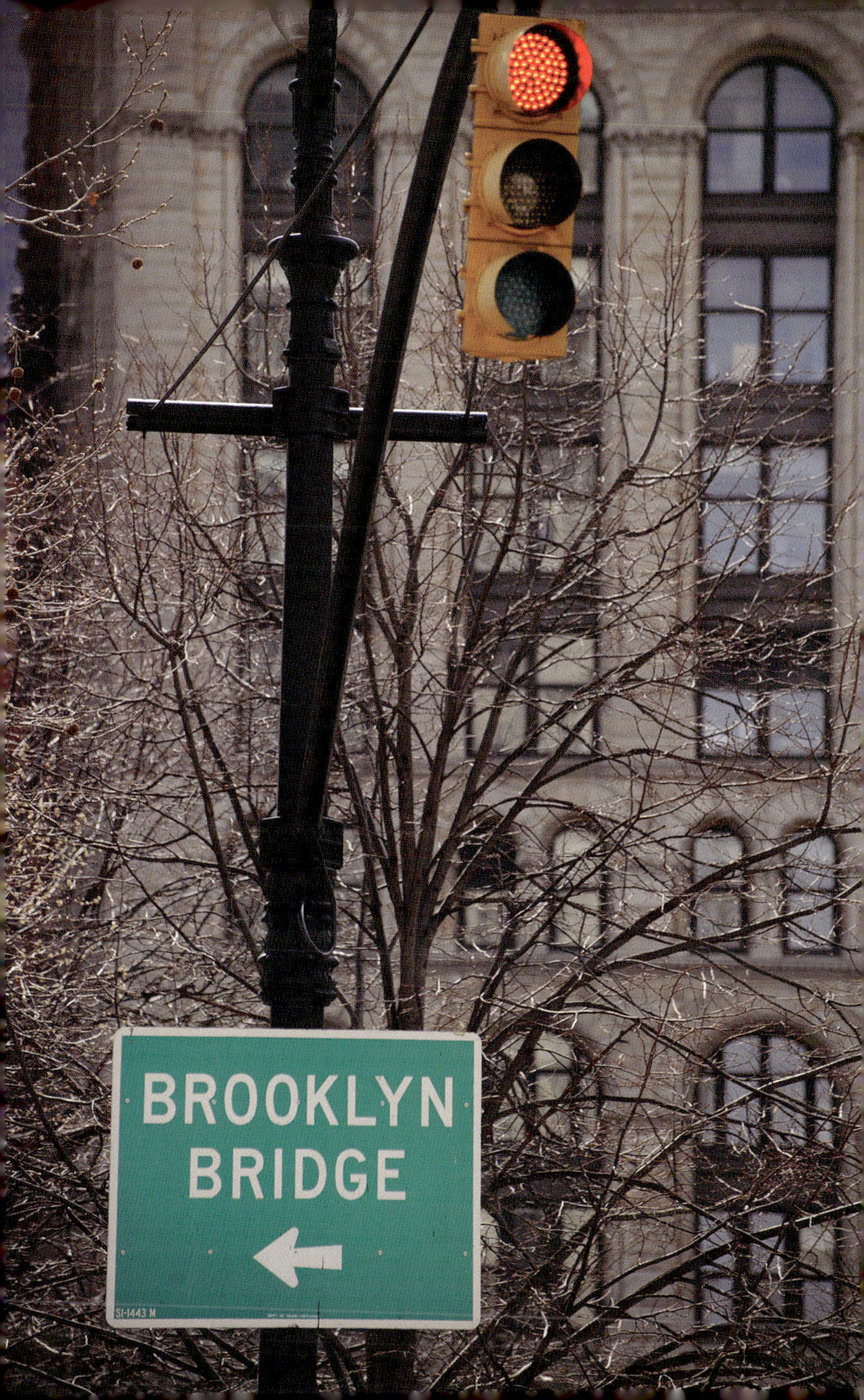
BROOKLYN
BRIDGE
SI-1443 M

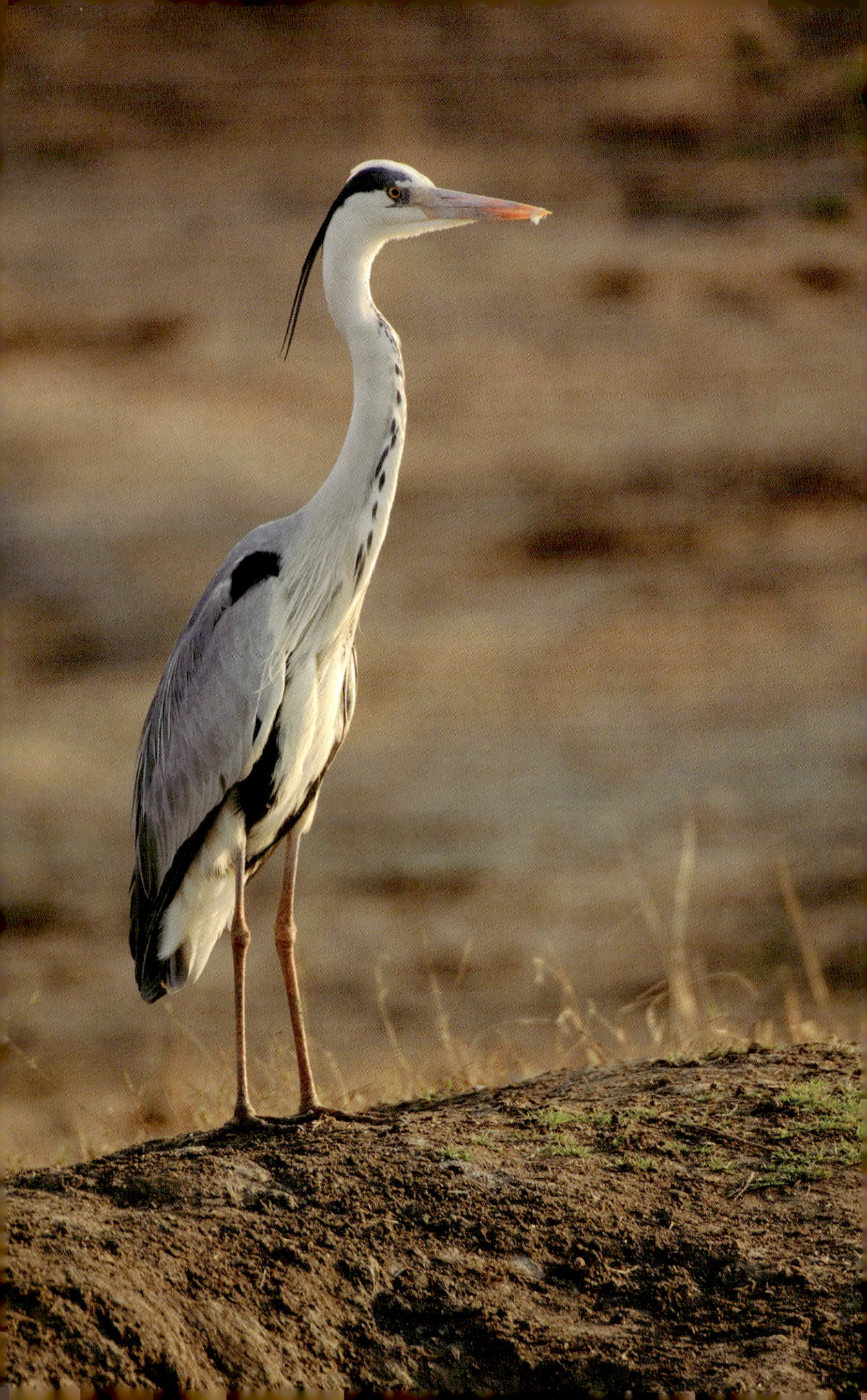

Digital Workflow

The world of digital photography requires today's photographer to be knowledgeable about what happens after the picture is taken if they are to make the most of their images. This chapter covers everything from the different types of information stored with each image, camera-to-device connections, printing, digital workflow, to cleaning and troubleshooting the D5100.

IMAGE INFORMATION

You may be surprised to learn that, apart from image data, the picture files generated by the D5100 contain a wealth of other information, including the shooting parameters and instructions about printing pictures. This information is tagged to the image file using a number of common standards, depending on the sort of information saved with the image file. The supported standards are as follows:

DCF (v 2.0): Design Rule for Camera File System (DCF) is a standard used widely in the digital imaging industry for defining the camera's file management system. It includes the directory structure, file naming format, metadata format, and more.

DPOF: Digital Print Order Format (DPOF) is a standard used widely to enable pictures to be printed from a print order created and saved on a memory card.

PictBridge: A standard that permits an image file stored on a memory card to be output directly to a printer without needing to connect the camera to a computer or download image files from the memory card to a computer.

EXIF Data (v 2.3): The D5100 uses the EXIF (Exchangeable Image File Format) standard to tag additional information to each image file it records. Most popular digital imaging software is able to read and interpret the EXIF tags so the information can be displayed onscreen. The information recorded includes:

- Nikon (the name of the camera manufacturer)
- D5100 (the model number)
- Camera firmware version number
- Exposure information, including shutter speed, aperture, exposure mode, ISO, EV value, date/time, Exposure Compensation, Flash mode, and focal length
- Thumbnail of the main image

Examining EXIF data by either viewing the image information on the LCD screen or accessing the shooting data in appropriate software is a great teaching aid, as you can see the exact camera settings for each shot. By comparing pictures and the shooting data, you can quickly learn about the technical aspects of exposure, focusing, metering, and flash exposure control.

Metadata: Metadata is any data that helps to describe the content or characteristics of a file. You may be familiar with viewing and perhaps adding some basic metadata through the File Info or Document Properties box found in many software applications and some operating systems. Most digital image management applications can search file properties and display them for you.

IPTC (DNPR)/XMP Metadata: Other metadata that can be tagged to an image file include the use of a standard developed by the International Press Telecommunications Council (IPTC). Known as Digital Newsphoto Parameter Record (DNPR), it can append image information to include details of the origin, authorship, copyright, caption details, and keywords for searching purposes. Any application that is DNPR compliant will show this information and allow you to edit it. If you are considering submitting any pictures you shoot with the D5100 for publication, you should make use of DNPR (IPTC) metadata, as most publishing organizations require this information to be present before accepting a submission.

Adobe's Extensible Metadata Platform (XMP) is an open standard digital labeling technology that allows metadata to be embedded into an image file. Any XMP-enabled software application allows descriptions and titles, searchable keywords, plus author and copyright information, to be stored in a format that is easily understood by other software applications, hardware devices, and even file formats. Since XMP is extensible, it can accommodate existing metadata schemes.

The EXIF metadata recorded by the D5100 is not saved in standard IPTC/XMP metadata fields; however, it can be embedded automatically in images recorded by the D5100 during transfer by completing the appropriate IPTC/XMP data fields under the tab in Nikon Transfer software. Nikon View NX2 (which includes Nikon Transfer 2) and Nikon Capture NX2 also support the EXIF, IPTC, and XMP standards.

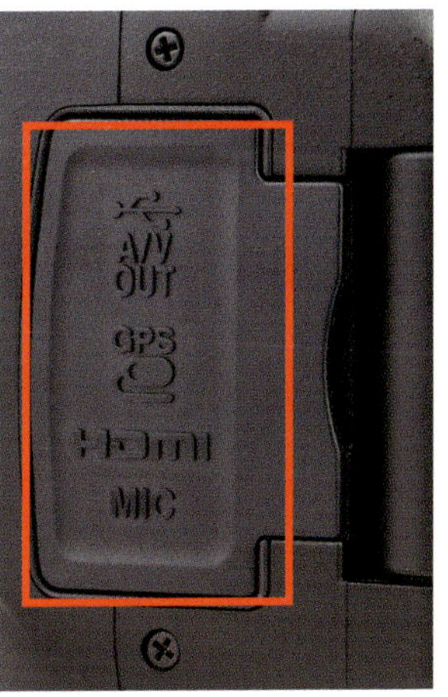

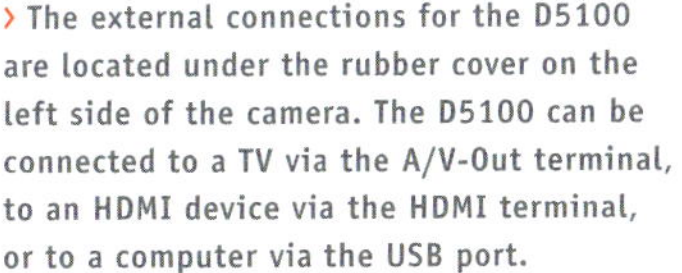
› The external connections for the D5100 are located under the rubber cover on the left side of the camera. The D5100 can be connected to a TV via the A/V-Out terminal, to an HDMI device via the HDMI terminal, or to a computer via the USB port.

AUDIO/VIDEO (A/V)

The optional Nikon EG-CP14 A/V cord enables the D5100 to be connected to a television set or LCD screen for playback, or alternatively to a VCR or DVD player for recording of saved images. First you need to select the appropriate video standard. NTSC is the video standard used in the USA, Canada, and Japan, while PAL is used in most European countries. To set the video standard, open the Setup menu, navigate to the **[Video Mode]** item, and press ▶. Highlight the required option, **[NTSC]** or **[PAL]**, and press ▶ again to confirm the selection. Note that selection of a particular video standard will also influence the options available under **[Movie quality]** in the **[Movie settings]** item of the Setup menu.

Before connecting the camera to the video cord, make sure the camera power is switched off. Open the rubber cover on the left side of the camera body to reveal the video out (A/V) port. Connect the narrow jack-pin of the EG-CP14 cable to the A/V terminal of the camera and the other end to the TV, LCD screen, VCR, or DVD player (the yellow plug goes to the video input, while the white plug goes to the audio input). Tune the TV to the video channel, then turn on the camera and press the ▶ button. The image is displayed on the television screen and can now be recorded to video or DVD. The image is also displayed on the LCD screen of the camera, and all camera operations will function normally. This means that you can take pictures while the camera is connected to a TV set and use review/playback functions simply by looking at the TV monitor screen. It is probably best to use the EH-5b AC adapter and EP-5A power connector to power the camera if you intend to use the camera for image playback via a television screen for an extended period of time.

CONNECTING VIA HDMI

The D5100 can be connected to an HDMI device using a type-C mini-pin HDMI cable. Set the HDMI format and control options in the Setup menu under the **[HDMI]** item (see pages 214-215 for more information), then switch the camera off and connect the HDMI cable to the HDMI port (it is located immediately below the A/V connector under the large rubber cover on the left side of the camera body). Tune the device to the HDMI channel, then turn the camera on and press the ▶ button. The camera monitor will remain blank, as the display of an image or menus on the LCD monitor is not supported when the camera is connected via the HDMI output; however, all other camera operations will function normally.

CONNECTING TO A COMPUTER

The D5100 can be connected directly to a computer via the Nikon UC-E6 USB cable supplied with the camera. The camera supports the high-speed USB (2.0) interface that offers a maximum transfer rate of 480 megabytes per second (Mbps). You can download images from the camera using the supplied Nikon Transfer software. Images can be viewed and organized using the supplied Nikon View NX2 software, while the optional Nikon Capture NX2 can be used to enhance images (see pages 286-290 for more information).

HINT: If you use the D5100 tethered to a computer for any function, ensure that the installed camera battery is fully charged. The preferable option is to use the EH-5b AC adapter in conjunction with the EP-5A power connector to prevent interruptions to data transfer by loss of power. The earlier EH-5 and EH-5a AC adapters are also compatible with the D5100.

Before connecting the D5100 to a computer, check that one of the following operating systems is running:

- Windows 7 (32-bit or 64-bit versions)
- Windows Vista Service Pack 2 (32-bit or 64-bit versions)
- Windows XP Service Pack 3 – 32-bit versions (Home Edition or Professional)
- Macintosh OS X (version 10.4.11, 10.5.8, or 10.6.6)

Also make sure that the appropriate versions of Nikon software—Nikon View NX2 (2.1.1) and/or Nikon Capture NX2 (2.2.7)—are installed.

Direct USB Connection: To connect the camera to a computer, start by turning the camera off, then turn the computer on and wait for it to start up. Connect the UC-E6 USB cable to the USB port of the camera (located under the rubber cover on the left side) and to the computer, and then turn the camera on. Nikon Transfer 2 should start automatically. The first time you use the application, I recommend you set the preferences by clicking on the Preferences tab before clicking on the Transfer button to initiate data transfer. The camera can be turned off as soon as the data transfer is complete. It is also possible to control the camera directly from the computer while tethered via the UC-E6 USB cable using the optional Nikon Camera Control Pro 2 software.

NOTE: Always connect the D5100 directly to the computer via the USB cable; do not connect the camera to a USB hub, or USB port on a keyboard.

Memory Card Readers: Although the D5100 can be tethered directly to a computer for transferring image data, there are several reasons why you should consider using a dedicated memory card reader as an alternative:

- If you use the tethered camera method, you will drain battery power and risk data being lost or corrupted if the power fails.
- Using a card reader allows you to run software to recover lost or corrupted image files as well as diagnose problems with the memory card.
- You can leave a card reader permanently attached to your computer, which further reduces the risk of losing or corrupting files as a result of a poor connection due to the wear and tear caused by constantly connecting a USB cable to the camera.

DIRECT PRINTING

As mentioned previously, the D5100 supports a standard that allows either individual or multiple pictures to be printed directly from the camera via a USB connection without a computer. This feature is only compatible with JPEG image files and a printer that supports the PictBridge standard.

NOTE: Nikon recommends that images selected for direct printing should be recorded in the sRGB color space. Use the **[Color space]** item in the Shooting menu to select this setting.

To print pictures directly from the camera to a PictBridge compatible printer, start by turning the camera off. Then turn the printer on before connecting the printer to the camera directly using the UC-E6 USB; do not connect the camera and printer via a USB hub. Turn the camera on and a welcome message will show on the camera LCD screen, followed by the PictBridge Playback display.

NOTE: It is essential that you make sure the camera battery is fully-charged, or use the EH-5b AC adapter and EP-5A power connector, to ensure the connection to the printer is not interrupted by a loss of camera power.

PRINTING A SINGLE PICTURE

To select a picture for printing from the PictBridge Playback display, scroll through the images saved on the memory card using ◀ and ▶; use ▲ and ▼ to display photo information. To view an enlarged section of the image, press the button; press to return to the normal full-frame view. To view up to six thumbnail images at a time, press . Use the Multi Selector to highlight an individual thumbnail picture and press to display the selected thumbnail image in full frame.

To print a single image selected in the PictBridge Playback display, press the button to show the PictBridge Print menu. Use ▲ or ▼ to select the required option and press ▶ to select it:

OPTION	DESCRIPTION
Page Size	Press ▲ and ▼ to select the appropriate paper size from the **[Page size]** item; choose **[Printer default]**, **[3.5x5 in.]**, **[5x7 in.]**, or **[A4]**. Then press ⓞ to select the option and return to the PictBridge Print menu
Number of Copies	Press ▲ and ▼ to select the number of copies of the highlighted image to be printed (maximum 99), and then press ⓞ to select the option and return to the PictBridge Print menu.
Border	Press ▲ and ▼ to select **[Printer default]** (uses default setting of current printer), **[Print with border]** (white border), or **[No border]**. Then press ⓞ to select the option and return to the PictBridge Print menu. Only options supported by the selected printer will be displayed.
Time Stamp	Press ▲ and ▼ to select **[Printer default]** (uses default setting of current printer), **[Print time Stamp]** (date and time of image exposure prints on image), or **[No time stamp]**. Use ⓞ to select the option and return to the PictBridge Print menu.
Cropping	Press ▲ and ▼ to select **[Crop]** (picture can be cropped in-camera) or **[No Cropping]** (printed full frame). Selecting **[No cropping]** and pressing ⓞ returns you to the main Print menu. Selecting **[Crop]** and then pressing ▶ displays a dialog box; press 🔍 to increase the size of the crop, and press 🔍 to reduce the crop. Use ✥ to position the crop frame. Press ⓞ to return to the main Print menu. Note that this item is only available if supported by the selected printer.
Start Printing	Select **[Start printing]** and press ⓞ to print the image highlighted in the PictBridge display. To cancel the process before all copies have been printed, press the ⓞ button.

PRINTING MULTIPLE PICTURES

Multiple pictures can be printed by connecting the camera to a compatible printer and selecting images through the PictBridge menu or by using the DPOF feature (see pages 306-307 for more on DPOF). When using the DPOF feature, either the camera or a memory card alone can be connected directly to the PictBridge printer.

To print directly from the camera, connect it to a compatible printer as described on page 303, and make sure the PictBridge Playback display is shown on the LCD screen. Press the ▶ button to display the available options (a description of these four options is below), highlight the required option, and press ▶.

OPTION	DESCRIPTION
Print Select	The selected images are printed.
Select date	Print one copy of all the pictures taken on the selected date.
Print (DPOF)	The current DPOF print order set is printed (DPOF date and information options are not supported).
Index Print	Creates an index print of all images saved in the JPEG format. (If the memory card contains more than 256 JPEG images, only the first 256 will be printed.)

Print Select: If the **[Print select]** option is chosen from the PictBridge menu and ▶ is pressed, six thumbnail images will be displayed on the LCD screen. Use the Multi Selector to scroll through the images, and press and hold 🔍 to see the highlighted image full frame. To select the image currently highlighted for printing, press ▲; the image is marked with the 🖶 icon and the number of copies to be printed is set to one [1]. To specify the number of copies of the image to be printed, use ▲ and ▼ to increase or decrease the number respectively. Repeat this process for each image to be printed. To deselect a picture for printing, press ▼ when the number of prints is set to [1]. Press OK to display the print options for multiple printing, and set **[Page size]**, **[Border type]**, and **[Time stamp]** options as required (according to the "Printing a Single Picture" instructions above).

NOTE: There is no option for cropping images when printing multiple pictures, unlike when printing a single picture.

NOTE: Images saved in the NEF (RAW) format will be displayed in the **[Print select]** menu, but it is not possible to select them for printing. However, it is possible to create a printable JPEG copy of an NEF (RAW) file by using the **[NEF (RAW) processing]** item in the Retouch menu.

Select Date: To print all the pictures taken on a specific date, highlight the **[Select date]** option from the PictBridge menu and press ▶; a list of the dates for images recorded on the installed memory card will be displayed. Press ▲ or ▼ to selected the desired date, and then press ▶ to select it. Press ▶ again to deselect the date. To view the pictures taken on a specific date, highlight the date and press ; use the Multi Selector to scroll through the pictures and press and hold the button to view the highlighted picture at full screen. Once a specific date is selected, press ⓀⓀ to display the print options for multiple printing and set the **[Page size]**, **[Border type]**, and **[Time stamp]** options (as described in the instructions above under "Printing a Single Picture").

Print (DPOF): The D5100 supports the Digital Print Order Format (DPOF) standard that embeds an instruction set in the appropriate EXIF data fields of an image file. This allows you to insert the memory card directly into any DPOF-compatible home printer or commercial mini-lab printer, and automatically get a set of prints of only those images you wish to print. This feature can be particularly useful if, for example, you are away from home on vacation; you can still produce prints from your digital files even if you do not have access to your own printer.

To select images for printing using the DPOF feature, it is necessary to create a DPOF print order. Start by highlighting **[Print set (DPOF)]** from the Playback menu of the D5100; the **[Select/set]** option will be highlighted. Press ▶ to confirm the selection and the camera will display thumbnails of all the images stored on the inserted memory card in groups of up to six. Use the same procedure as described under the "Print Select" section (page 305) to select the required pictures and the number of copies to be printed. Once all images to be printed have been selected, press the OK button to save the selected group of images, and display the options for data imprinting.

To imprint shooting data on the image, highlight **[Print shooting data]** and press ▶ to switch the option on or off. To print the date/time of the recording onto the image, highlight **[Print date]** and press ▶ to switch the option on or off. In both cases, a check mark will appear in the box to the left of the item title in the menu screen to indicate the option is turned on. To finish, save the print set order by highlighting **[Done]** and press ⓞ.

To print the current DPOF print set saved to the installed memory card when the camera is connected to a compatible PictBridge printer, highlight **[Print (DPOF)]** from the PictBridge Playback display and press ▶ to select it. The camera will display thumbnails of all the images in the current DPOF print set in groups of up to six at a time. If desired, the current print set can be modified using the same procedure as described under the "Print Multiple Pictures" section above; you can change the number of copies of each picture to be printed and set **[Page size]**, **[Border type]**, and **[Time stamp]** as desired. To print the existing print set without modification, or print it once any modifications have been completed, highlight **[Start printing]** and press ⓞ.

NOTE: If the currently saved print set is modified by deleting images using a computer or other device, the print order may not print correctly.

To deselect the entire print set, highlight **[Print set (DPOF)]** from the Playback menu and press ▶, then highlight **[Deselect all?]**. Press ▶ and highlight **[Yes]** or **[No]** and press ⓞ to confirm the selection.

NOTE: Information entered via the **[Print shooting data]** and **[Print date]** options is not printed when the DPOF print set is printed using a direct USB connection between the camera and the printer, but only when the memory card is inserted directly into a PictBridge-compatible printer.

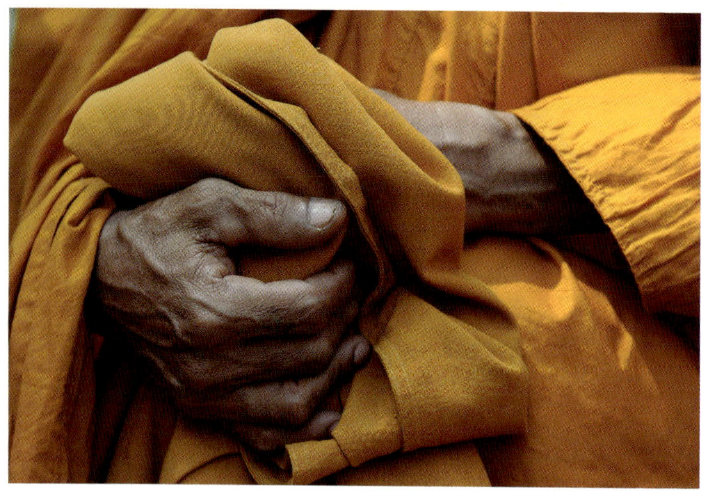

^ Creating an index print of a collection of pictures makes it very easy to identify an individual image.

Making an Index Print: To make an index print (multiple images on the same page), connect the camera to a compatible printer as described above. Once the PictBridge Playback display is open on the LCD screen, it is possible to create an index print of all the JPEG files on the memory card. Start by pressing the MENU button, select the **[Index print]** option in the PictBridge menu, and then press OK.

Next, press OK to display the PictBridge printing options and set **[Page size]**, **[Border type]**, and **[Time stamp]** options as required according to the instructions under "Printing a Single Picture" (page 303); if the selected page size is too small, a warning will be displayed. Finally, select **[Start printing]** and press OK to start printing. To cancel printing, press OK again.

NOTE: There are subtle differences in the functionality between the direct printing routes. For example, direct printing of a single image with the D5100 connected to a PictBridge-compatible printer allows you to perform cropping before printing, whereas printing multiple images from the camera or memory card using a print set created using the DPOF standard can only be printed full frame.

CARING FOR YOUR D5100

Obviously, keeping your camera and lens(es) in a clean, dry environment is very important. Regardless of how scrupulous you are about doing this, dust and dirt will eventually accumulate on or inside your equipment. Since prevention is better than a cure, always keep the body and lens caps in place when not using your equipment. Always switch the D5100 off before attaching or detaching a lens to prevent particles from being attracted inside the camera by the electrical charge in its electronic components. Remember, gravity is your friend! Whenever you change lenses, get into the habit of holding the camera body with the lens mount tilted downward.

For the same reason, do not carry or store your D5100 on its back, as particles already inside the camera will settle on the optical low-pass filter. Periodically, vacuum-clean the interior of your camera bag/case; it is amazing how much debris can collect there! Sealing your camera body in a clear plastic bag, which you then keep within your camera case, will add another valuable layer of protection in very dusty or damp conditions. In the latter situation, keep some packets of silica gel inside the bag to absorb any moisture. Putting together a basic cleaning kit is straightforward. You should consider the following:

- 1/2 inch (12 mm) artist's paintbrush made from soft sable hair for general cleaning
- Micro-fiber lens cloth for cleaning lens elements
- Micro-fiber towel (available from any good outdoors store) for absorbing moisture when working in damp conditions; I find these towels invaluable in all sorts of conditions, and they are soft enough to use for cleaning lenses and filters.
- Rubber-bulb blower made for cleaning lenses and the low-pass filter

Always brush or blow as much material off your equipment as possible before wiping it with a cloth. For lens elements and filters, use a micro-fiber cloth and wipe surfaces in short, straight strokes—not long, sweeping circular movements. Turn the cloth frequently to prevent depositing the dirt you have just removed back onto the same surface! For any residue that cannot be removed with a dry cloth, you will need a lens cleaning fluid suitable for photographic lenses. Apply a small amount of fluid to the cloth—never directly to the lens, as it may seep inside and cause damage. Wipe the residue away and then buff the glass with a dry area of the cloth. Any lens cloth should be washed on a regular basis to keep it clean.

CLEANING THE LOW-PASS FILTER

Unwanted material such as dust or particles of lint can accumulate inside the D5100 and may settle on the surface of the optical low-pass filter (OLPF). This is an unfortunate problem that can afflict any digital camera, especially those with interchangeable lenses, as foreign matter can enter the camera when a lens is removed or changed. Focusing or adjusting the zoom ring of a lens causes groups of lens elements to be

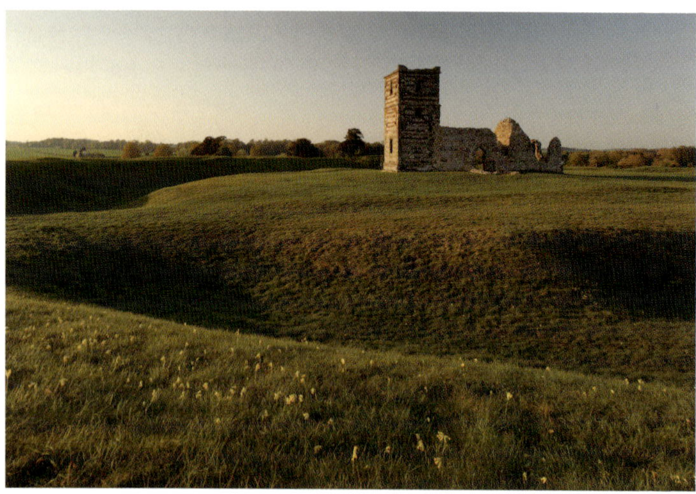

^ Keeping the optical low-pass filter (OLPF) spotlessly clean will cut down on the work required in post processing; the shadow of dust spots on the OLPF will show up clearly, especially in areas of continuous tone, such as a clear sky.

shifted inside the lens barrel, creating very slight changes in air pressure. This can cause dust in the atmosphere to be drawn through the lens into the camera. Furthermore, the operation of internal camera mechanisms such as the shutter and reflex mirror can generate minute particles due to the wear and tear of the moving parts. During the manufacture of the D5100, Nikon has attempted to reduce the incidence of such problems by cycling the shutter mechanism many hundreds of times before it is installed in the camera.

Any dust or other material that settles on the low-pass filter will often appear as dark spots in your pictures; they cast a shadow on the camera's sensor that is located behind this filter. The exact nature of the appearance of these shadows will depend on the size of the particle and the lens aperture you use. At very large apertures (f/1.4) it is likely that most very small dust specks will not be visible. However, at small apertures (f/22) they will probably show up with well-defined edges.

Self-Cleaning: The D5100 incorporates a self-cleaning function that vibrates OLPF at four different frequencies using a piezo-electric oscillator. The cleaning process can be set to activate automatically when the camera is turned on, turned off, or both. Alternatively, it can be activated at any time the user deems it necessary.

To configure the self-cleaning feature, open the Setup menu and navigate to the **[Clean image sensor]** item, and press ▶ to display two options: **[Clean now]** and **[Clean at startup/shutdown]**. **[Clean now]** is highlighted by default, and pressing the (OK) button will initiate the process, during which the message "Cleaning Image Sensor" is displayed on the LCD screen.

Whenever you use the self-cleaning feature, make sure the camera is placed base down on a solid surface. There are two good reasons for this; first, the effect of vibrating the low-pass filter will be most efficient when the camera is supported firmly, and second, there is a strip of highly adhesive material located along the bottom edge of the low-pass filter that is designed to capture and retain any dislodged material.

HINT: It is worth getting in to the habit of checking images periodically as you shoot for any particle shadows by pressing the 🔍 button to zoom into the images during playback.

To have the cleaning process commence automatically, open the Setup menu and navigate to the **[Clean image sensor]** item and press ▶, then highlight the **[Clean at startup/shutdown]** option and press ▶ to display four options:

- ON **[Clean at startup]**: Cleaning is only performed at startup.
- OFF **[Clean at shutdown]**: Cleaning is only performed at shutdown.
- ON OFF **[Clean at startup & shutdown]** (default): Cleaning is performed at startup and shutdown.
- **[Cleaning off]**: Automatic cleaning function is off.

NOTE: Using any other camera control or function will interrupt the sensor-cleaning process. If the built-in flash is being charged, the sensor-cleaning process may not operate when the camera starts up.

Airflow Control System: Nikon's innovative Airflow Control System has also been incorporated into the D5100 to supplement the self-cleaning function described in the previous section. It is designed to use changes in air pressure caused by the movement of the reflex mirror to direct air inside the mirror box toward ducts set into its base; this helps draw dust particles away from the low-pass filter located in front of the camera's CMOS sensor. Below the bottom edge of the OLPF and the ducts in the base of the mirror box are areas covered with an extremely adhesive material that is designed to capture dust and other particulate matter dislodged by the self-cleaning processes.

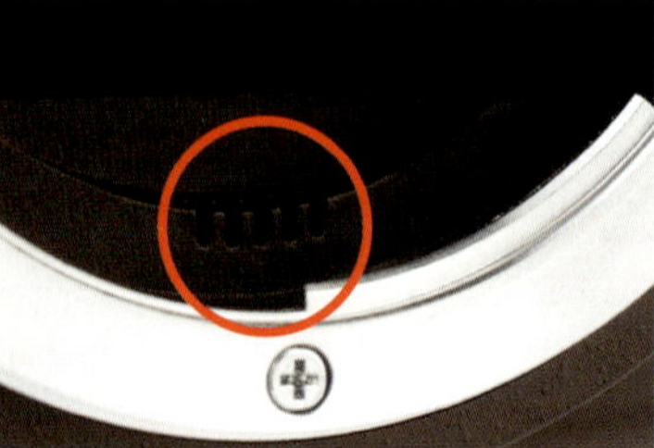

› The air ducts of the Airflow Control System can be seen just inside the lens mount at the base of the mirror box.

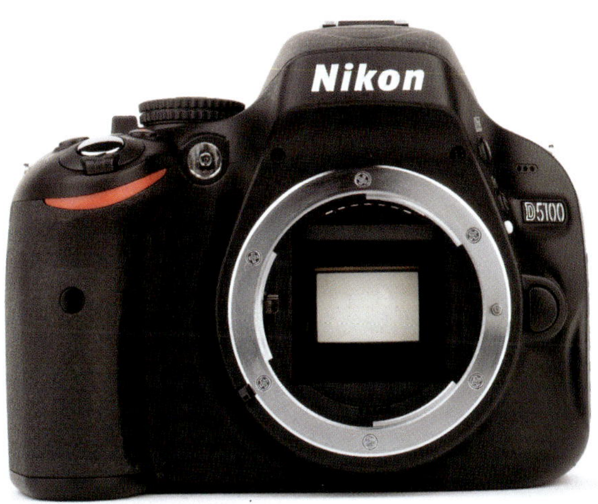

^ Access to the OLPF for cleaning is via the lens opening. The reflex mirror must be raised and the shutter opened, using the [Lock mirror up for cleaning] item in the Setup menu, to reveal the front surface of the OLPF.

Manual Cleaning: Nikon expressly recommends that you should leave manual cleaning of the optical low-pass filter to an authorized service center. However, in recognition of the fact that this is likely to be impractical for a variety of reasons, the D5100 has a feature that enables the reflex mirror to be locked up in its raised position and the shutter opened to provide access to the front surface of the OLPF.

CAUTION: Nikon states that under no circumstances should you touch or wipe the surface of the OLPF, as it is extremely delicate. Any manual cleaning process you perform is done entirely at your own risk; any damage caused to the low-pass filter or any other part of your camera as a result of manual cleaning by the user will not be covered by warranties provided by Nikon.

To inspect and/or clean the low-pass filter, you need to perform a few preparatory steps. First, ensure the camera has a fully charged battery installed or is powered by the optional EH-5b AC adapter via the optional EP-5A power connector. Second, remove the lens, or body cap, and keep the camera facing downwards. Now switch the camera on, navigate to the **[Lock mirror up for cleaning]** item in the Setup menu, and press ▶ to display **[Start]**. Press Ⓞ and a dialog box will appear with the following message: "When shutter button is pressed, the mirror lifts and shutter opens. To lower mirror, turn camera off."

When the shutter release is pressed all the way down, the mirror will lift and remain in its raised position and the shutter will open, while the LCD screen and viewfinder will go blank. Keep the camera facing down so any debris falls away from the filter; look up into the lens mount to inspect the low-pass filter surface (it is probably helpful to shine a light on it).

NOTE: The **[Lock mirror up for cleaning]** item in the Setup menu is not available if the battery level is [battery icon] or less; it will be grayed out.

NOTE: Since each photosite on the CMOS sensor of the D5100 is approximately just 4.78 microns (1 micron = 1/1000 mm) square, offending particles are often very, very small, and it is unlikely you will be able to detect them by eye.

To clean the low-pass filter, keep the camera facing down and use a rubber bulb blower to gently puff air towards the low-pass filter surface. Take care that you do not enter any part of the blower into the camera. Never use an ordinary blower brush with bristles, which can damage the surface of the low-pass filter, or an aerosol-type blower, which might emit propellant agent or condensation that can leave a residue. Once you have finished cleaning, switch the camera off to close the shutter and return the mirror to its lowered-position. If the blower bulb method fails to remove any stubborn material, I recommend you have the sensor cleaned professionally.

CAUTION: If the power supply fails during the cleaning process, the shutter will close and the mirror will return to its down position. This has potentially dire consequences if you have any cleaning utensils in the camera at that time! Therefore, always use a fully charged EN-EL14 battery or the optional EH-5b AC adapter via the optional EP-5A power connector.

NOTE: If power from the installed battery begins to run low while the mirror is locked up for cleaning, the camera will emit an audible warning and the Self-Timer lamp will begin to flash, indicating the mirror will be automatically lowered in approximately two minutes.

For a user with plenty of confidence, there is a wide range of proprietary sensor-cleaning materials that can be used to clean stubborn material from the low-pass filter. These include brushes, swabs, and fluids available from a number of manufacturers (see the list of resources on page 293-294). It must be stressed that if you use any such materials or implements, it is done entirely at your own risk!

CAUTION: If you decide to clean the low-pass filter of your D5100 with a wet process, make sure you NEVER use any alcohol-based (e.g., ethanol or methanol) cleaning fluid. The low-pass filter of the D5100 has a special anti-static coating that can be damaged by such chemical compounds.

Finally, if you have Nikon Capture NX 2 software, you can use the Dust Off Reference Photo feature with NEF (RAW) files shot using the D5100 to help remove the effects of dust particles on the low-pass filter by masking their shadows electronically (see pages 218-220 for more details).

Index

3D Color Matrix Metering 24, 50, 77
3D Tracking 22, 73, 76-78, 83, **84-85**, 86-87

A *(see Aperture-Priority mode)*
AA *(see Auto Aperture)*
AC adapter **39-40**, 291
Accessories **291-294**
Active D-Lighting 54, 60, 107, 109, 134, **173-174**, **190**, 209
AE-L *(see Autoexposure Lock)*
AE-Lock *(see Autoexposure Lock)*
AF *(see autofocus modes, autofocus system)*
AF-A *(see Auto-Select Autofocus mode)*
AF-Area modes 54, **83-87**, 134-136
AF-Assist Illuminator 55, **88-89**, **202**, 268-269
AF-C *(see Continuous-Servo autofocus mode)*
AF-L *(see Focus Lock)*
AF-S *(see Single-Servo autofocus mode)*
anti-aliasing filter *(see Optical Low-Pass Filter)*
aperture 24, 48, 53-58, 65-67, 105, 109, 139-140, 241-242, **253**, **259**, 263, 277, **283-284**
Aperture-Priority mode (A) 48-52, **66**, 156, 256
Auto Aperture (AA) **263**,
Auto-Area AF 52, 76-78, **84**, 202
Auto Distortion Control *(see Distortion Control)*
Autoexposure Lock (AE-L) **69-70**, 81-82, 87-88, 141, 145-147, 204, 210, 237
Auto flash 34, 36, 54, 251, **256-258**
Autofocus-Area modes *(see AF-Area modes)*
Autofocus Lock (AF-L) *(see focus lock)*
autofocus modes **78-80**
autofocus (AF) system 14, 73, 76, 90, 94
Auto Image Rotation 101, 184, **218**
Auto Information Display **214**
Auto ISO Sensitivity **48**
Auto (Flash Off) shooting mode 34, 53-**55**, 61, 256
Auto Meter Off
  Auto Off Timers 34, 93, **204**
  GPS 42, **220-221**
Auto-Servo AF **78-79**, 84
Auto shooting mode 34, 36, **54**, 164, 256
Auto White Balance 15, **152**
A/V cable 214, **300**

batteries 34, **36-42**, 291-292
Bayer pattern filter 25
beep 96, 99, 117, **206**
black and white 47, 58, 60, 162-163, 169-170, **225-226**, 288
buffer **94**-95, 100
built-in flash 36, 41, 61, **208**, 244-247, **251-259**, 265-268, 271
Bulb mode **68-69**

Calendar Playback **110**
camera care **309-315**
camera connections **299-302**
card reader 35, **121**
CCD sensor *(see sensor)*
Center-Weighted metering 32, 49-**51**, 69, 248
charging a battery *(see batteries)*
Child Scene mode **56**
clean image sensor *(see cleaning the optical low pass filter)*
cleaning the optical low-pass filter **310-315**
clock, internal 35, **40**, 215-216, 220-221
Close-Up Scene mode 56
Cloudy White Balance **154**
color balance 72, 160, **227**
color space 106, 109, **172**, **190**, 227
color temperature 106, 109, **150-155**, **158-161**, 189, 268, 289
commander flash 89, 109, 244, 246-247, 260, **270-271**
compression *(see also image quality)* **124-131**, 139, 228
Continuous release mode 94, **96**, 100, 195
Continuous-Servo autofocus mode (AF-C) **80-84**, **86**, 202
contrast and image processing **58-60**, 124, 126-130, **163-168**, 173-174, 191, 231, 248
  and exposure / focus 47, 50, 53, 80-81, 84, 115
contrast detection autofocus 113, 139, 149
Copying White Balance values **158**
Creative Lighting System (CLS) **243-244**, 247, 251, 259, 268
Custom Settings menu 34, 42, 69, 70, 81, 82, 87, 88, 89, 93, 93, 121, 141, 157, 174, 177, 178, **199-211**, 262, 265

Date and Time 35, 40, 207, **215-216**
Date Imprint **207**
deleting files 36, 100, 110, **112**, **122-123**
depth of field 234, 278, **283-284**
diffraction 50, 248, **284**
diopter adjustment **31**, 35, 291
direct printing 298, **303-304**
Direct Sunlight White Balance **153**
Display Mode 105-107
Distortion Control **190**, **232**
D-Lighting **173-174**, **224**, 229-231, 287, 289
D-Movie mode 41, 134, 135, **139-147**, 196, 215, 236-237, 287, 290
DPOF *(see direct printing)*
Dust Off Reference Photo **218-219**, 315
DX format 24, **28-30**, 262-263, **277**, 283-285
Dynamic-Area AF 75, 78, **84-86**

INDEX

Edit Movie 147, **236-237**
electrostatic interference **40**
EN-EL14 battery 34, **37-39**, 41-42, 291
EXIF (Exchangeable Image File Format) 125, 207, 291, **298**, 306
Expeed image processing 22-23, **124-126**
Exposure Compensation **70-71**, 114, 140, 141, 142, 230, 289, 298
exposure modes **65-67**
Eye-fi Upload **221**

Face Priority AF-Area mode **136**
file formats
(see JPEG, NEF, TIFF)
File Number Sequence **206**
Filter Effects **169**, **226-227**
firmware 128, **221**
fisheye
effect **232**, 290
lens 190, 232, 282, 290
Flash Color Information Communication **268**
Flash Compensation
(see Flash Output Compensation)
flash modes *(see also flash synchronization)*
Flash Output Compensation 246, 251, 253, **267-268**
flash photography
(see Nikon flash photography)
flash synchronization 93, 242, 251, **256-259**, 265-266, 291
Flexible Program **65**
Flicker Reduction 138, **215**
Fluorescent White Balance **152-153**
focus area modes
(see AF-Area modes)
Focus Lock **87-88**
focus modes **78-81**
focus tracking *(see Predictive Focus Tracking)*
format memory cards 35, **122-123**, **212**
f/number *(see aperture)*
f/stop *(see aperture)*
Full-Time Servo AF (AF-F) 135
Function (**Fn**) button **209**
FX format 24, 28-30, 283, 285

GPS 42, **220-221**, 287, 291

HDMI **214-215**, 299, **300-301**
High ISO NR
(see Noise Reduction)
highlights warning 104, 116
Hi (ISO) 45-47, 48
histograms 72, **113-116**, 134, 182
hue **168-169**

Image Comment **217**
Image Overlay **223**, **228**, 235
Image Review 30, 41, **100-116**, 137, 183, 204, 214, 218
Image Quality **124-132**, 189, 209, 223, 229
Image Size **131-132**, 189, 209, 223, 229
Incandescent White Balance **152**, 161
Information Display **33-34**, **319**
information pages
(see Photo Information pages)
ISO 15, **45-48**, 140, 174, 193-194, 206, 209, 230, 241, 242, 247, 253
i-TTL flash control 50, 208, 243, **244-248**, 259, 261

JPEG 104, 114, 120, 124-125, **126-128**, **130-132**, 161, 163, 189, 209, 218, 223, 225, 229-230, 236, 237, 288, 303, 308

Landscape Picture Control 162, **163**
Landscape Scene mode **55**, 57
Language 34, **216**
lenses 23-24, 29-30, 41, 76, 88-89, 190, 232, 254-255, **275-285**, 309-310
Live View 59, 60, 62, 63, 64, **133-138**, 140-142, 144, 145, 204, 290
Long Exposure NR
(see Noise Reduction)

M *(see Manual exposure mode)*
Manual exposure mode (M) 48, **67**, 156, 245, 263, 264, 281
Manual flash **264-265**, 269
Manual focus 78, **80**, 135, 203, 277

Matrix metering **49-51**, 69, 190, 191, 208, 244, 248, 249
memory card 34-36, **116-123**, 143, 156, 171, 177, 180, 181, 182, 187-188, 189, 206-207, 211, 212, 221, 293, 294, 297, 298, 302, 306, 308
memory card slot 121
menu system **176-239**
metadata 297, **298-299**
metering *(see TTL metering)*
Miniature Effect **60**, **63**, 209, **234**
Mirror Lock-Up 214, **313-315**
Monochrome Picture Control 162, **163**, 169, 170
Monochrome (Retouch menu) **225-226**
Movie mode
(see D-Movie mode)
Movie Settings **144-145**, 196, 300
Movie Quality **144-145**

NEF (RAW) 104, 114, 119, 120, 124-126, 127, **128-130**, 131-132, 167, 174, 189, 190-191, 209, 218, 223, 225, 229-230, 288, 289, 305, 315
NEF (RAW) Processing 223, **229-230**, 305
Neutral Picture Control 162, **163**, 168, 189
Night Landscape Scene mode **57**
Night Portrait Scene mode **57**
Nikkor lenses *(see lenses)*
Nikon flash photography **240-273**
Nikon software **286-290**
non-CPU lenses 278, **281-282**
Normal-Area AF **136**, 138
Noise Reduction
High ISO 47, **193-194**, 230
Long Exposure 93, **192**

optical low-pass filter 26, 27, 310-313

P *(see Programmed-Auto mode)*
Perspective Control **233**
photo information pages **101-109**
PictBridge **298**, 303, 304-305, 306-307, 308

Picture Controls 115, 124-125, 127, 140, **161-172**, 177, 189, 225, 230, 288, 290
playback *(see image playback)*
Playback Folder 112, **182**
Playback menu 41, 100, 101, 103, 107, 112, 177, 178-179, **180-185**, 214, 218, 306, 307
Playback zoom 99-100, **111**, 224, 311
Portrait Picture Control 162, **163**, 165, 189
Portrait Scene mode **55**, 57, 58
Predictive Focus Tracking 80, 81, **82**
Preset Manual White Balance **155-158**
Print Set *(see DPOF)*
Programmed-Auto (P) mode 48, **65-66**, 98, 265
protecting images **112**

Quick Adjust 106, 162, 164-165, 288
Quick Retouch **231**
Quiet Shutter release mode **99**, 206

RAW *(see NEF)*
Rear-Curtain Sync 258, **266**
Recent Settings menu 41, 177, 178, **238-239**
Red-Eye Reduction 57, 94, **224-225**, 256, 257, 258
release modes 69, **95-99**, 195, 199, 205, 209
remote
  flash 244, 261, 270-272
  Remote Release **98-99**, 195, 205, 207, 291-292
  television remote 214-215
reset
  Custom Settings **201**
  file numbering **206-207**
  Shooting menu **186-187**
Resize 223, **230-231**
resolution *(see image size)*
Retouch menu 177, 178, 190, **222-237**
Rotate Tall 101, **184**, 218

S *(see aperture-Priority mode)*
SB-400 57, 208, 243, 244, 246, 259, 262, 268, 272
SB-600 57, 89, 244, 246, 259, 261, 260, 262, 268, 270, 271, 292
SB-700 89, 244, 246, 250, 259, 260, 261-262, 263-264, 268, 270, 271, 272, 292, 293
SB-800 89, 244, 246, 259, 261-262, **263-264**, 268, 270, 271, 272, 292, 293
SB-900 89, 244-245, 246, 259, 261-262, **263-264**, 267, 268, 270, 271, 272, 292, 293
SB-R200 246, 259, 261, 270, 271, 292
Scene modes 34, 53-54, **55-61**
Scene Recognition System 22, 50, 73, **76-78**, 84, 152, 248
Self-Timer **96-98**, 195, 205, 209
sensitivity *(see ISO)*
sensor **24-30**
  cleaning *(see cleaning the optical low-pass filter)*
Setup menu 33, 34, 35, 40 ,42, 54, 101, 122, 139, 177, 178-179, 184, 187, 188, **212-221**, 300, 311, 313, 314
Shade White Balance **155**
sharpening 111, 126, 127, 128, 130, 140, 161-162, 164-166, **166-167**, 288
shooting information display *(See Information Display)*
Shooting menu 46, 47, 68, 88, 132, 144, 151, 153, 156, 158, 159, 162, 164, 170, 172, 171, 174, 177, 178, **186-199**, 244, 303
shooting modes
  (see exposure modes)
Shutter-Priority mode (S) 48, **66**
Single-Frame release mode **95**, 195, 209
Single-Point AF 51, 75, **83**, 85, 86, 88
Single-Servo autofocus mode (AF-S) **79**, **80-81**, 84, 86, 135, 202, 206
Slide Show **184-185**, 214-215
Slot Empty Release Lock 121, **211**
Slow Sync 257, 258, **265-266**
sound (movies) 143-144, **145**
Sports Scene mode **56**
Spot metering 49, **52**, 68, 246, 268
standard i-TTL flash
  (see Nikon flash photography)
Standard Picture Control **163**
Storage Folder 182, **187-189**
Straighten **231**, 288
SU-800 Wireless Speedlight Commander Unit 89, 246-247, 261, 268, 270, **271**, 272
sync (flash)
  (see flash synchronization)

teleconverters **280**, 282
TIFF 130, 225, 288
Time Zone / Date 35, 40, **215-216**
Toning 169, **170**
trap focus **82-83**
Trim
  still photos 223, **225**
  movies **236-237**
TTL flash cords (SC-28, SC-29) 89, 94, 260-261, 269, 270, **292**

USB
  cable (UC-E6) **293**
  direct connection **302**

Vibration Reduction **278**, 285
video mode
  (see D-Movie mode)
viewfinder **30-32**, 35-36, **320**
viewfinder accessories 30-31, 98, **291**
viewfinder focus 31-32, 35
Vivid Picture Control **163**

WB *(see White Balance)*
web support **294**
White Balance 140, **149-161**, 189, 209, 229
  creative use of White Balance **161**
  Fine-Tuning White Balance **158-160**
  Preset Manual White Balance **155-158**
  White Balance Flash Color Information **268**
Wide-Area AF Assist Illuminator **268-269**
wireless commander unit
  (see SU-800 Wireless Speedlight Commander Unit)
wireless flash (AWL) **270-272**

XMP data **298-299**

zoom in playback
  (see playback zoom)

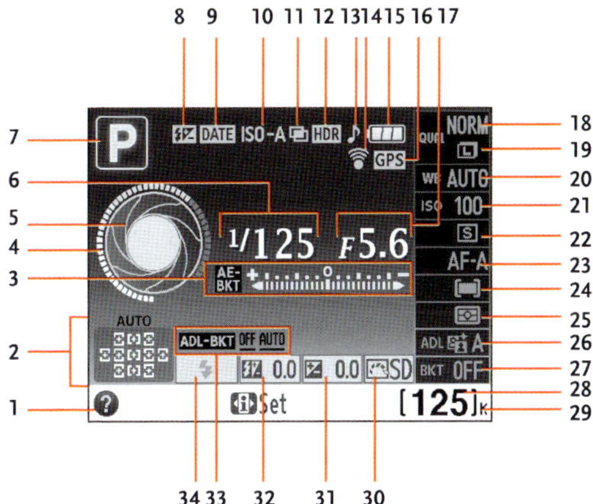

1. Help icon
2. Auto-Area AF/3D-Tracking indicators/Focus point
3. Exposure/Exposure Compensation/Bracketing progress
4. Shutter speed display
5. Aperture display
6. Shutter speed readout
7. Shooting mode
8. Manual flash/Flash Compensation (optional flash units) indicators
9. Print date
10. Auto ISO (sensitivity) indicator
11. Multiple exposure indicator
12. HDR indicator
13. Sound (beep)
14. Eye-Fi connection
15. Battery level
16. GPS connection
17. Aperture readout
18. Image Quality
19. Image Size
20. White Balance
21. ISO sensitivity
22. Release mode
23. Focus mode
24. AF-Area mode
25. Metering mode
26. Active D-Lighting
27. Bracketing increment
28. No. of remaining exposures / White Balance recording indicator
29. K appears when enough memory for >1000 exposures
30. Picture Control
31. Exposure Compensation
32. Flash Compensation
33. ADL bracketing amount
34. Flash mode

VIEWFINDER

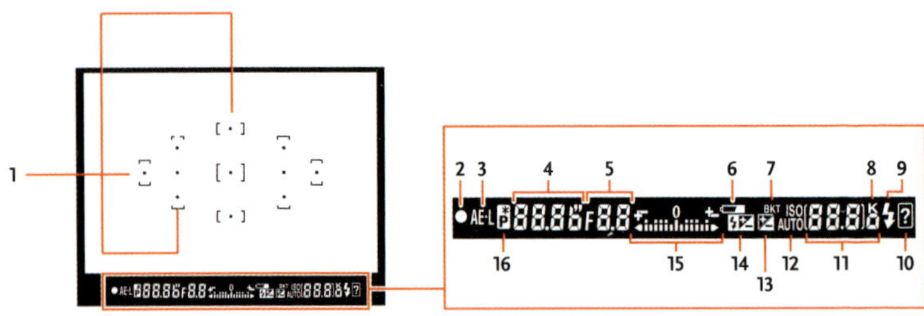

1. Focus points
2. Focus indicator
3. Autoexposure Lock (AE-L) indicator
4. Shutter speed
5. Aperture
6. Battery level
7. Exposure/WB/ADL Bracketing indicator
8. K appears when enough memory for >1000 exposures
9. Flash ready indicator
10. Warning indicator
11. No. of remaining exposures/ No. of shots before buffer fills/ Preset White Balance indicator/ Exposure Compensation value/Flash Compensation value/Capture mode/ ISO value
12. Auto ISO indicator
13. Exposure Compensation indicator
14. Flash Compensation indicator
15. Exposure/Exposure Compensation display/Electronic rangefinder
16. Flexible Program indicator